PENGUIN BOOKS

THE TROPICAL TRAVELLER

John Hatt was born in London in 1948. After leaving university he worked as a banker, bookseller, and publisher. In 1980 he took a two-year sabbatical to travel extensively in Africa, the United States and Asia, after which he wrote the first edition of *The Tropical Traveller*. In 1982 he founded Eland, a small publishing company dedicated to republishing the most readable travel literature, including the best works of Norman Lewis and Martha Gellhorn. Since 1986 John Hatt has also had a part-time job as Travel Editor for *Harpers & Queen*. He prefers, however, to take no more than five foreign trips a year, as he is determined that travel should remain a pleasure rather than a labour. He has now visited more than seventy countries.

D1635018

JOHN HATT

THE TROPICAL TRAVELLER

THIRD EDITION

PENGUIN BOOKS

PENGUIN BOOKS

Published by the Penguin Group
Penguin Books Ltd, 27 Wrights Lane, London W8 5TZ, England
Penguin Books USA Inc., 375 Hudson Street, New York, New York 10014, USA
Penguin Books Australia Ltd, Ringwood, Victoria, Australia
Penguin Books Canada Ltd, 10 Alcorn Avenue, Toronto, Ontario, Canada M4V 3B2
Penguin Books (NZ) Ltd, 182–190 Wairau Road, Auckland 10, New Zealand

Penguin Books Ltd, Registered Offices: Harmondsworth, Middlesex, England

First published by Pan 1982
Second edition 1985
Third edition published in Penguin Books 1993
1 3 5 7 9 10 8 6 4 2

Typeset by Datix International Limited, Bungay, Suffolk
Set in 10½/12½ pt Monophoto Bembo with Futura
Printed in England by Clays Ltd, St Ives plc

CONTENTS

	Acknowledgements	ix
	Introduction	xi
Chapter 1	Preparation	1
Chapter 2	Money	29
Chapter 3	Equipment	46
Chapter 4	Flying	124
Chapter 5	Health	154
Chapter 6	Animal Hazards	218
Chapter 7	Transport and Accommodation	250
Chapter 8	Some Practical Hints	270
Chapter 9	Photography	296
Chapter 10	Human Hazards	321
Chapter 11	Culture Shock	346
Chapter 12	Taking the Plunge	375
	Postscript	408
Appendix 1	Further Reading	411
Appendix 2	Equipment	418
Appendix 3	Useful Addresses	424
Appendix 4	Emergency Telephone Lists	433
Appendix 5	Language Survival List	438
Appendix 6	Conversion Tables	440
Appendix 7	A Guide to the Rainy Seasons	442

Appendix 8	Check-list	448
Appendix 9	Artificial Resuscitation	452
Appendix 10	Twelve Top Tips	453
	Index	455

DISCLAIMER

The author and publisher have tried to make the advice and information as accurate as possible, but they accept no responsibility for loss, injury, inconvenience or other liability arising from any person using this book.

England is a fine country for many things, but unless they go abroad, its inhabitants cannot know the true meaning of *la douceur de la vie*.

Gerald Brenan, *The Face of Spain*

To travel is to discover that everybody is wrong. The philosophies, the civilizations which seem at a distance so superior to those current at home, all prove on a close inspection to be in their own way just as hopelessly imperfect. That knowledge, which only travel can give, is worth, it seems to me, all the trouble, all the discomfort and expense of a circumnavigation.

Aldous Huxley, *Jesting Pilate*

Collecting experiences is just one way of filling up with unrelated pieces of junk; but a lucky encounter can change the part in us that does the experiencing.

P. J. Kavanagh, *The Perfect Stranger*

ACKNOWLEDGEMENTS

Thanks to the following, who have helped with the three editions of this book, many of them strangers who were kind enough/to send useful advice: James Barclay, Anthony Battersby, Bridget Beck, Jarig Bergsma, Jay Bernstein, Andrew Blacker, David Blacker, Professor Bradley, Hilary Bradt, Professor George Braun, Stuart Brittan, the late John Brooks, Dr Sandy Cairncross, Peter Calamai, Alex Campbell, Charlotte Causton, Michael Causton, Dr Colbourne, Roger Cooper, Jack Davey, Major A. C. Dawson, Dr Stephen Dealler, Richard Dorment, Peter Edwards, James Fenton, Richard Ford, Howard Gallagher, Dr Hemda Garelick, Carlo Gebler, Martha Gellhorn, Richard Gobel, Helen and Colin Goodwin, Paul Greening, Finn Guinness, Nicholas Guppy, Steven Hankey, Nick Hanna, Jo and Bryan Hanson, Stephen Harris, Martin and Tanis Jordan, Dr Bent Juel-Jensen, Dr Penelope Key, Gabrielle Kirby, Dr G. Lea, Marie Lippens, Rosemary Lowe-McConnell, John Macalister, Julian McKintosh, Luis Martinez, Sonny Mehta, Mark Melichar, Tony Morrison, Leif Ness, Dr Newlands, Redmond O'Hanlon, Wing Commander B. J. O'Reilly, Mark O'Shea, Bruce Palling, Emma Parsons, Dr M. Pendharkar, John and Eric Platter, Gerry Ricks, Carolyn Rockman, Patricia Rudland, John Ryle, Hilary Sanseverino, Kenneth Savidge, Mike Shawcross, Janet Silver, Philip Smiley, Xan Smiley, Frances Somers-Cocks, David Speck, P. M. Stoker-Murdy, Martin Stokes, Mrs G. R. Strachan-Gray, Mrs J. M. Street, Andrew Tank, Hetty Thistlethwaite, Ron Townend, Frank Tuohy, Sebastian Verney, Peter Washington, Andrew Watt, Dr Lewis Wild, Susan Wilkinson, Jan Wilkman,

Anne Williams, C. D. Wilson, John Wreford-Smith, Dr George Wyatt, Peter Wychodil.

Special thanks to the following, who have given a big lump of precious time to helping with this book: Adrian and Sabina Bailey, Chris Breen, Paul Goodyer, Larry Goodyer, Jack Jackson, Lesley Levene, Ravi Mirchandani, Hallam Murray, Raghubir Singh, Lt Colonel 'Tanky' Smith, Professor Warrell, Dr Jane Wilson, and Shane Winser. Also to Jason Lewis for the illustrations.

Extra special thanks to Patricia Rudland, who helped with the production of the whole book, Shervie Price for the index, and Selina Hastings, who valiantly helped improve my English (any mistakes are hers).

INTRODUCTION

There is nothing wrong with a relaxing beach holiday. Personally I am entirely happy when seated under an umbrella, sipping a rum punch, and reading my way through a pile of paperbacks. Few people want a strenuous holiday when they have slogged away in an office all year.

But occasionally the itch takes some of us to discover and savour the character of a foreign country, and this is no longer as easy as before. In a recent anthology of travel literature,[*] the first words are: 'There's no doubt about it: the easier it is to travel, the harder it is to be a traveller.' How true! Until recently you had only to catch a plane to Brazil, Kenya, or Thailand to be instantly transported to magical exotic places, quite unlike anything at home. But now you are flown from one enormous city to another. These massive conurbations increasingly resemble each other – the common features being nauseous fumes, brutal office blocks, hamburger bars, advertisement hoardings, neon lighting, and traffic jams. Most of the cities in the developing world have *quintupled* in size within the last four decades. The traffic explosion has been even worse: in 1950 there were 2,000 private cars in Istanbul; today there are more than half a million.

Having left the cities with a sigh of relief, one is also liable to be disappointed by the traditional sightseeing circuit. There has been such a spectacular growth in world tourism that the great sights of the world are usually overcrowded and overdeveloped. And because some tourists have always behaved foolishly or offensively, the relationship between local people and foreigners

[*] *A Taste for Travel*, John Julius Norwich (Macmillan, 1985)

in these areas is often an unhappy one. Instead of any interesting contacts, you are more likely to come across thieves, beggars, and money-grubbers.

It must quickly be added here that we should be careful about disdaining even the most unpromising parts of the globe. I have noticed that the most impressive travellers are able to extract interest and delight from almost any destination; the most perceptive manage to find Majorca, or even Bournemouth, as interesting as Irian Jaya.

This book, however, is aimed at those of us who aren't so admirable, or who desire an invigorating dose of the exotic; it is especially aimed at those who would like to travel more independently and a bit more adventurously, but are apprehensive about the problems. I, myself, have often been an incompetent traveller, and have made plenty of mistakes; therefore I have plenty of advice to dispense.

Two more explanations about this book's niche. Strictly speaking, the word 'tropical' refers to those regions between the tropics of Capricorn and Cancer. More often it is used in a looser sense, and I have presumed that tropical travellers might be going to any hot countries in Asia, Africa, or South America.

I should also add that the majority of my advice isn't aimed at the most intrepid travellers, such as campers, trekkers, or explorers. I would be a fraud if I gave them too much of my own advice: in recent years I have been Travel Editor of *Harpers & Queen*, and would hardly recognize a rucksack if a porter dropped it on my toes. However, where there are gaps in my knowledge I have given lists of specialist institutions and books, which should be able to provide more detailed information. And, as this book is packed with hints, I hope that every type of traveller will find some nugget of useful information: perhaps a canoeist will learn something about photography, or an explorer will discover a cure for car-sickness.

I have an important warning to give about *The Tropical Traveller*: it should not be treated as a textbook. Information goes out of date; experts change their minds; and new brands of equipment supersede old ones (I discuss this further in Chapter 3).

Furthermore, although this book may be written in a dogmatic style, almost every decision is ultimately one of judgement. Consider, for instance, the question of drinking water during a hot march. I have advised walkers to drink deeply before setting out – instead of sip-by-sip while walking. This is my firmly held view, reached both from anecdotal and written evidence, and also from my own personal experience. If I qualified this advice, I would have to qualify all my advice. But it still isn't infallible: I *have* met an experienced walker who finds it suits him better to drink sip-by-sip.

If you approach too seriously the colossal amount of information in this book, you could become overwhelmed and alarmed, thus detracting from the pleasure of your travels. It will be better if you just pick and choose a few hints. Much of the advice will anyway be glaringly obvious to most people; however, it is still worth including if it is of use even to a very few. The knowledgeable can skip.

There is another reason not to treat *The Tropical Traveller* too respectfully. On the two occasions when I've revised it, I have looked at many passages in earlier editions, and thought to myself, 'How could I have written such rubbish?' When next revising the book I shall no doubt think the same. If I am likely to reach this decision about my own advice, then the reader better beware! Treat all my judgements with scepticism. I hope the book will be valuable, not because it supplies answers, but because it raises most of the important questions, and supplies some hints and ideas to help you find your *own* solutions.

If you feel like passing on any of those solutions, or if you have any other comments, criticisms or possible ideas for future editions, then please write to me at 53 Eland Road, London SW11 5JX.

CHAPTER 1

PREPARATION

Deciding whether to travel alone

This is one of the most crucial decisions you will make. The choice of travelling alone or travelling with companions offers two entirely different experiences. Many people don't realize this and consider travelling alone simply as a lonelier version of travel with others. So I will therefore point out some of the advantages of solo travel.

When you travel with other people they almost invariably act as a barrier between yourself and the country. However great your efforts, it is hard to avoid the cosy jokes, the shared attitudes, and the familiar conversations of home life. In countless subtle ways this homespun cocoon discourages the risk-taking and spirit of adventure which are essential for interesting travel.

When travelling alone you are more open to new friendships – some of them of a type you would never make at home. This may be because of losing your self-consciousness, or because of loneliness, but whatever the reason, many adventures spring from such acquaintances, and risks like this must be taken if you want any real insight into a country.

Most people you meet are prepared to do far more for one person than they would for a couple or a group. Solitary travellers can be loaded on the backs of motorbikes, they can be squeezed into a car, and they don't take up too much room at the family table. They are altogether a more attractive proposition.

Lone travellers don't need long discussions with companions about whether they will take up the offers of strangers. They can judge for themselves the physiognomy of their new-found

1

friends, and can quickly accept or reject each offer as it comes. If you want interesting experiences, it is necessary to accept the risk of boredom. When I'm with companions I am less prepared to accept risky invitations because I get so embarrassed if, through my fault, they have to watch three excruciating hours of local dancing. When alone, I'm prepared to take the risks, and occasionally have wonderful experiences which would otherwise have been missed.

When on the move each day, there are a surprising number of arguable decisions to be made; these put a strain on relationships and a large number of friendships come to an end during long journeys. When alone, you can make up your own mind quickly, and when things go wrong, you have only yourself to blame.

When travelling with companions, each person in the group is a hostage to fortune; each additional companion is someone who might have their passport stolen, or get dysentery, heatstroke, or malaria. When you are travelling with a large group, someone has diarrhoea every day.

During my early travels I rarely felt lonely in the daytime, but occasionally felt desperately lonely in the evenings. No longer. Books are now my friends. At home I don't get nearly enough time for reading, so when I'm away I don't want to listen to the chatter of a friend (probably by now an enemy) when I could be enjoying a book. In fact nearly all the books I've most enjoyed have been read during a trip – because instead of reading them bit by bit when tired at the fag-end of a day, I can read and savour them at long stretches. With a reserve of good books, I am never bored or lonely anywhere.

Of course, there are some **advantages of travelling with companions**. An important one is the reduction in expense. In most places the charge for a double room is the same whether it is occupied by one or by two; and there are many other expenses (such as taxis, hired cars, and guides) which can be shared between two people.

I especially miss companionship during moments of excitement or beauty that demand to be shared; afterwards these moments can rarely be satisfactorily described. I also miss friends during periods of hardship. I shall never forget an unhappy and lonely night in a hotel in Juli, Peru: its cockroach-infested restaurant was so cold that the waiter wore a balaclava, and my damp bed was littered with cigarette butts. With a friend I might have laughed; instead I was miserable.

Many people disagree with my ideas about solo travel. John Brooks, the much-admired late editor of *The South American Handbook*, wrote to me:

I still think your preference for lone travel is an idiosyncratic one: I don't share it, and I think most people don't. You mention missing companionship during moments of excitement or beauty and also during periods of hardship – but one experiences plenty of both, they are by definition the highest and lowest parts of one's trip. For the high points, the evening my wife and I spent in a bar in Diamantina, Central Brazil, talking and listening to the locals singing and playing serestas, and finally serenading us, could not possibly have been as good without a companion – indeed, it wouldn't have happened on one's own.

You can gather from the above that the decision on solo travelling is a very personal one. I shall try to sum up by saying that travelling with a companion is sometimes an adventure and occasionally more enjoyable; travelling alone is sometimes less enjoyable, but it is always an adventure.

The subject of women travelling alone is covered in Chapter 8.

Two or more

If two or more travellers do journey together, there is a likelihood of friction over money, though often this is unspoken. Even the most reasonable people have misunderstandings. I have known of several holidays during which each of the two travellers suspected the other of financial unfairness. Frequently this problem doesn't ever get fully discussed, with the result that grudges aren't resolved. Although it may seem pedantic at the time, the remedy is to work out *in advance* some type of financial arrangement which covers all possibilities, including tips. A pooled kitty, with private money separate, is often the answer.

Similarly, when you are travelling with a group, consider formulating a constitution before you leave. There are a hundred small decisions to be made each day, and each one of these provides potential for friction. The journey can be chaotic if these arguments aren't quickly resolved. Agree on some type of voting procedure, with perhaps the leader of the group holding a casting vote.

Years of trial and error have proved that expeditions cannot be successful without a leader who has near-dictatorial powers. And it is not just necessary to have a leader for bossing the expedition; it is also essential to have a figurehead for formal liaising with the outside world.

Choosing the length of trip

Most of us don't have a choice, because we are constrained by the limitations of the customary holiday periods. Nevertheless, even when there is a choice, many seasoned travellers don't necessarily choose to take the longest possible trip.

Although I have occasionally travelled for months on end in order to grab opportunities which may never occur again, my ideal journeys would rarely be for longer than three months. After that, my senses tend to become dulled, my spirit of adventure dimmed, and sometimes I get homesick.

Some people last longer without losing enthusiasm, but rarely go on indefinitely. Tanis and Martin Jordan, who undertook a remarkable series of South American river trips, have written: 'For us, five or six months is a suitable period to spend travelling. Any longer and we find that we have become saturated and cease to appreciate the new things we see and experience.'★

On short trips, though, it is always worth trying to grab every bit of extra time. Just as weekenders know that a three-day

★ *South American River Trips*, Vol. 2 (Bradt, 1982)

weekend becomes twice as long as a two-day weekend, so a ten-day break becomes twice as long as one of a week, and a three-week holiday becomes twice as long as one of two weeks. This is because the beginnings and ends of holidays are often blighted by the paraphernalia of travel (or being stuck in a dull capital city), and some other days tend to be wasted by tedious transport. Just a few extra days, therefore, can double the amount of time when you can completely relax and appreciate the country.

Styles of travel

Few travellers want subjective advice on their style of travel. But I still can't resist dispensing advice, because of my distress at seeing so many travellers' enjoyment being unnecessarily diminished.

When visiting a country, most people attempt to cover the entire territory. Not surprisingly, they are keen to see all the country's sights, and therefore often plan a programme that keeps them continually on the move. As a result they are too often forced into an unsatisfactory rhythm of travel. On arriving at one of their many goals, they tend to be exhausted and dispirited from arduous travelling. If they settled for a day or two, they might begin to unwind; but their remorseless timetable keeps them on the move. Travellers like this never relax and never make friends; nor do they ever discover the nicest beaches, coral reefs, hotels, or walks. It would be far better for them to plan an uneven programme, so that at one stage at least they settle down – even at the expense of missing a few sights. You should also work on the presumption that you won't relax properly in those places where you aren't staying long enough to bother unpacking.

A result of over-ambitious programmes is frequent disappointment at long-awaited goals. Too often the weary traveller arrives at some famous monument, looks round once, and departs, while wondering what all the fuss was about. Some sights, such as the Taj Mahal, have remarkable initial impact, but this is rare. There is often a barrier against the appreciation of subtle beauty, and sometimes this barrier is broken only after a period of time. One reason is that the mind remains confused by the stresses of travelling, and needs an interval to relax and adjust.

Great music rarely reveals its beauty at a first hearing (and music which charms at first often turns out to have only superficial appeal). Similarly, when you wish to fully appreciate landscapes or buildings, it is best to revisit them several times, contemplate them under a different light, and find excuses to linger as long as possible.

Countries may also be better appreciated at second viewing. I have sometimes fallen into the trap of rushing determinedly into every corner of a country on my first visit. On the second visit, I've usually taken things more easily, not needing to look at the sights, or to seek for spectacular first impressions. As a result of my first visit, I have a good idea of what I want to do, and where I intend to visit; and I usually have the advantage of knowing a smattering of the language. And if you visit the same place repeatedly, you may develop local friendships, which will mean that you are no longer treated as a tourist. Although I'm still struck by the thrill of visiting each new country, when I'm older I plan to choose a few countries to visit again and again.

I mention later that your choice of hotels shouldn't be too influenced by guidebooks. Nor should your sightseeing. When you are about to explore a town, or look at a sight, consider setting aside the books, and seeing things for yourself – with your *own* eyes. Use your own brain, and draw your own conclusions. By all means look at the books afterwards, for they will tell you what you have missed and fill gaps in your knowledge. But excessive use of guidebooks takes away the real thrill of discovery, and diminishes the intensity of appreciation.

Itinerary

Preferably, you should never be glued to an itinerary that leaves no time for spontaneous travel or possible adventures. If you hear about an idyllic small hotel, or if a family wants to take you to a wonderful festival in the mountains, it will be a nightmare if you are tied to a rigid schedule.

However, for shorter trips an itinerary is sometimes necessary. In my opinion most travel companies' written itineraries aren't clear enough: you can't see at a glance precisely what you are going to be doing. And in particular it's rarely immediately clear how many *full* days you will be staying in a specific place.

To repeat, it is important to realize that three nights in Palmyra is by no means the same as three days in Palmyra, though it will often look the same in many itineraries. Three nights in a place means that you only get two full days. And it's important to be sure of how many *full* days you are getting, because these are likely to be the most enjoyable ones; during the days of departure and arrival there is far less chance of the relaxed enjoyment of any destination. Therefore, for any of my trips that have a programme, I draw up my own itinerary which makes it clear how many full days I have in each place (see Fig. 1).

A few more points about my own type of itinerary. In the left-hand column, I put *both* the day of the week and the date. Occasionally this helps avoid a calamitous mistake with the date; besides, it is sometimes useful to know which day is Sunday, or Friday (in Muslim countries), and so on. In the middle column I put my full days in capitals, just to make that clear, and I also put complete details about flight numbers. I then put my itinerary on top of my transparent document bag (see Table 1, Chapter 3), and it can then be frequently and easily consulted without becoming grubby.

Group tours

Although group tours are rather outside the niche of this book, I will mention a few pros and cons because readers might be considering an organized tour, especially if they want to go to one of those countries where it is difficult to travel independently.

The great advantage of escorted tours is that they save you worry. Because so many more people are now travelling, it may be necessary to book hotels months in advance. A confirmed hotel can be very important for those requiring a certain level of

ITINERARY: SYRIA

Date	Day	Night
Sun 12th April	Royal Jordanian Airlines Dep HlR (Term 3)11·45. fl no. RJ118 Arr Damascus 22·00	Damascus Cham Hotel.
Mon 13th April	Damascus	Damascus Cham Hotel.
Tues 14th April	Damascus	Damascus Cham Hotel.
Wed 15th April	Dep. Damascus. Lunch Hama. Arr. Aleppo	Aleppo Baron's Hotel.
Thurs 16th April	Aleppo	Aleppo Baron's Hotel.
GOOD FRIDAY.	Aleppo	Aleppo Baron's Hotel.
Sat 18th April	Aleppo	Aleppo Baron's Hotel.
EASTER SUNDAY	Aleppo	Aleppo Baron's Hotel
Mon 20th April	Dep. Aleppo Arr. Safita	Safita.
Tues 21st April	Safita (visit Crac des Chevaliers)	Safita.
Wed 22nd April	Dep. Safita Arr. Palmyra.	Palmyra.
Thurs 23rd April	Palmyra	Palmyra.
Fri 24th April	Dep. Palmyra Arr. Bosra	Bosra
Sat 25th April	Bosra	Bosra.
Sun 26th April	Dep. Bosra Arr. Damascus	Damascus Sultan Hotel.
Mon 27th April	Damascus	Damascus Cham Hotel.
Tues 28th April	Royal Jordanian Airlines Dep. Damascus 9·00 fl no. RJ136 Arr Heathrow 16·45.	

Fig. 1 Sample itinerary.

comfort; many people don't want to arrive in an unknown town, and then spend tiring – possibly fruitless – hours in search of an adequate hotel. And those who have slaved at a desk for most of the year may find it a relief not to have to make decisions, and to be organized from dawn to dusk.

In recent years organized travel has offered much greater variety. It is no longer necessary to choose only from the large companies that shuttle you around on unimaginative tours. If you look in magazines such as *BBC Wildlife* or *Climber and Hillwalker*, you will find advertisements from small companies offering a variety of interesting and specialist trips. These may also be suitable for those who are daunted by the responsibilities of independent travel, or who are too young for it. And many people will positively like going on holiday with others; they may relish the company or want the opportunity to make interesting and like-minded new friends.

However, organized tours aren't all bliss, and here are some of the disadvantages. The major one is that most of the tours are very badly planned. The travel companies cram their itineraries as full as possible so as to make them appear value for money. In places where a traveller should spend two full days (i.e. *three* nights), the itinerary probably allows only one night. Far too often, the people on group tours become exhausted, numbed, and unable to fully appreciate the wonderful things they have come to see.

Groups always seem to have to get up at an uncomfortably early hour, and this is rarely so that they can look at a Greek ruin during the perfect light of dawn; instead they always seem to be loaded into a charabanc for a gruelling four-hour ride before looking at the ruin under the scalding heat and flat light of the midday sun.

Even the grandest tour companies seem unable to avoid hiring guides who spend far too much time leading their groups into expensive carpet-shops, where the guide knows he will earn a commission.

One final problem. A highish proportion of people on group

tours tend to be old, because older people are more likely to be able to afford them. As a result many itineraries exclude some interesting sights and excursions, because old and less fit people are unable to cope with them.

Overlanding groups

There is another, completely different, type of group tour – the long overland trips in the same vehicle, often a specially adapted truck. These trips are far more strenuous, may last as long as twenty-eight weeks, and usually attract a younger clientele. They used to be very common on the route to India, but now mostly take place in Africa or South America. Some of the pros and cons of these trips are the same as for the more luxurious group tours. I would, however, be sure to ask to see a layout of the seating, because sometimes the seats face inwards, with the result that the passengers spend the journey gazing not at the view but at the sweaty faces of their exhausted friends.

Travelling with infants and children

A child of some friends of mine was being a pest in a Portuguese restaurant – he was playing with the kitchen swing-door and getting tangled in the legs of harassed waiters – so my friends called the child to heel and ticked him off. A furious waiter then came to their table, and said, 'That is not how we treat children in Portugal. The little boy can play with the swing-door if he likes.' Although children can be a fearful burden, travellers often remark that foreigners are much more doting than we are, and that it can be fun to travel with children because they are such wonderful ice-breakers.

The disadvantages of travelling with children are mostly obvious: the reduction in freedom, the increase in luggage (huge piles of nappies and toys) and worries about health. Babies can't tell you if they have a pain in their tummy, and they are far more prone to dangerous dehydration (see Chapter 5).

The worst age to travel with children is when they are 'toddlers'. Before then, when they are just babies, they are much less of a problem, and when they are still being breast-fed, there aren't so many worries about food and sterilized bottles. Once the child is a toddler, it has to be watched continually in case it falls into a pool, plays with a knife, or shoves its finger into an electric socket. When the children are older, they are less of a worry. This age is reached when they can understand instructions ('Sit down and watch' or 'Don't pat that lion'), when they can dress themselves, and when the world around can be explained. Then parents are often able to get vicarious pleasure from the child's sense of wonder and exploration.

Having never travelled with children, I shan't pontificate at length on the subject, but here are a few tips – mostly gleaned from friends.

Keep in mind that on the child's second birthday the cost of airfares tends to go up from 10 per cent to 50 per cent of the full price, so if the children are near their second birthday, a few days can make a great difference in cost.

Infants are usually given the most suitable seats, which are just behind the bulkhead, therefore in case there are many infants on the plane, it is best to book these seats in advance.

If you have a choice of airline, remember that some are likely to be more children-friendly than others. As a general rule the American, British, and Dutch airlines, for instance, aren't good with children, while the Mediterranean and Asian ones tend to be much friendlier. In *Travel with Children* (see Appendix 1), Maureen Wheeler strongly recommends 'trainer cups':

These were so useful I always packed two, just in case one got lost along the way. Drinking juice or anything out of plastic cups is quite a difficult feat for small children; it invariably ends up on you, them, or your seat. If you just make a blanket rule that while on the plane all drinks must be drunk from the spout cup, your trip will be much drier.

Boiling water kept for half an hour in a thermos will be ultra-safe for infants, so a thermos could be an asset.

Bin liners may be useful for disposing of dirty nappies. A couple of non-disposable nappies (and an appropriate cleaner) may be useful in case you run out of disposable ones. Don't use plastic pants, because in the tropics they are likely to cause itching and rashes.

If you do need to use a feeding bottle, a brand called Playtex, which has disposable liners, will avoid the need for complicated sterilizing.

When travelling with children, it is best to *settle* in one place more than you usually would. This will give you time to find cheap, trustworthy, and reliable child-minders, which will make your life freer and easier.

Try to buy some children's game that is easily played with children who don't speak the same language. Snakes and Ladders is brilliant for this; a small, travelling, magnetic set can be bought very cheaply.

Colourful, peelable stickers are extremely light to carry, and for a surprisingly long time can keep children harmlessly entranced.

Be aware that in less than five minutes babies can be badly burned by the sun; cover them up.

Although a Walkman is a little bulky, it may be a great asset, for tapes of books (or even *Peter and the Wolf*) will keep many children quiet for hours.

Timing your visit

Never underestimate the importance of weather. When at home it is tempting to have too much confidence in a tropical climate. In fact the weather makes a crucial difference to the enjoyment and interest of a trip. Heavy rains make bad roads impassable, and if you are going to the desert, the season of dusty winds makes life miserable. Even within a small area the climate can be sufficiently varied to affect your plans. In Sri Lanka, for instance, the monsoon blows on one side of the island for half the year, and on the other side during the other half. This fact is ignored by a large number of tourists, who find themselves on holiday in the rain.

Another reason for careful consideration of season and climate is the question of insects. There are times of year when the weather brings out enough insects to make outdoor life miserable. One expects this to be true for certain rivers in South America, but even in parts of the United States, such as Maine, there are months when plagues of gnats prevent any chance of enjoyable walking.

If you are going to do any game-watching, the weather will also make a great difference. After the rains, the high vegetation often hides the animals; by contrast, at the end of the dry season the lack of vegetation makes them more visible. The animals are also easier to find in the dry season, for they tend to congregate around the few remaining water-holes.

Most guidebooks have climate charts, and you can also consult a useful publication, *World Weather Guide* (see Appendix 1), which gives charts of rainfall, humidity, and temperature for most parts of the world.

Don't, however, rely entirely on charts. They need interpretation, and it is always best to get a common-sense opinion of the weather from someone who knows the country. The chart may make it seem as if Baganda Island gets constant rain, but in fact this rain may be concentrated in only one hour's downpour after dark – and these downpours may ensure crystal-clear days of brilliant sunshine. Other charts in the same book may show that neighbouring Maduga Island is free from rain, but in fact the island may be depressingly cloudy and hazy for days on end.

It is also worth finding out about public holidays and festivals. If you don't make inquiries, you may be irritated to find yourself arriving in Allahabad only a few days after the great (Kumbh) Mehla, which takes place once every twelve years; or you might find yourself leaving Trinidad just before its wonderful carnival.

Sometimes you want to avoid certain times. I remember problems when I flew to Kuching, where I immediately needed to obtain a visa extension: I arrived just in time for the Governor's birthday, which was followed by the weekend, which was followed by the Dayak holiday, which was followed by the King of Malaysia's birthday. I was eager to be off on a river trip, but had to waste five precious days. In strict Muslim countries the season of Ramadan may be a mild blight on travelling, and the subsequent festivities ensure that all public transport is usually booked solid.

Physical preparation

If you are going to undertake a strenuous trek, it is a good idea to limber up a bit before leaving home, A little extra fitness makes walking far more enjoyable, and could prevent some type of physical collapse.

A useful book for gently leading your sedentary body into a state where it can cope with unaccustomed exertion is *The Penguin Book of Physical Fitness*. Its exercises, which are derived from the training of the Canadian Air Force, need only be done for eleven minutes a day. They are less tedious when done to music.

Among traditional people in the Third World you may spend long periods sitting on the floor. This is surprisingly painful for those not accustomed to it, and can be even worse when local usage obliges you to cross your legs. Men usually need more practice than women. It is also useful to develop the ability of squatting comfortably in the lavatory posture. One reader has pointed out: 'Westerners find squatting very uncomfortable until they learn to balance with their feet flat. The Western method of squatting is torture to the Achilles tendon; but squatting is so useful an art that it is worth acquiring.'

Passport

Check well in advance that your passport isn't going to run out; the passport office may take a long time to renew it, especially in the summer.

If you do need an emergency passport, try ringing the Peterborough office (tel. 0733 895555) to see if they are any quicker than your local one. If you live in London, it takes only a bit more than an hour to get there on the train, and they can sometimes work much faster than the London office.

Also ensure that you have plenty of clear pages in your passport for visas and stamps. Pages can be filled surprisingly fast –

in Mali a whole page may be inscribed every time you visit a new town. If you expect to visit a large number of countries, the British passport office will issue a jumbo-sized passport. At the time of writing, this is the old style of passport, and therefore less convenient (but more handsome) than the ugly modern one, which can be squeezed into the smallest pocket.

There are some countries (at present Israel, Cuba, South Africa, and Taiwan) whose stamp on your passport may make it impossible for you to enter some other country. The British passport office can help by issuing a spare passport, but this isn't always necessary, because the authorities in most of these countries will agree, on request, not to stamp your passport. Try not to travel with both passports at the same time, for there are places where this is an imprisonable offence.

An elastic band wrapped round the spine of the traditional larger passport is most useful for holding immunization certificates, custom dockets, or any other papers you may need at airports. At present the immunization certificates are usually too large to be conveniently wrapped in the smaller passport.

If you are very punctilious, take photocopies of your passport's relevant pages, including the one with the visa and the page giving the expiry date. In the modern passport all the relevant details, except for the visa, are on one page. Keep your photocopy in a separate place, and it will be a great help in the event of losing a passport.

In many countries you are supposed to carry your passport with you at all times. Where it is highly likely to be stolen, some travellers carry only a photocopy of the relevant pages while they are wandering around a town, and they leave the actual passport somewhere more secure. This ploy may not be legal, but in Brazil, for instance, it is often accepted.

Visas

To be safe, start applying for your visas several weeks in advance. They may take longer, and be more of a problem, than you would expect. Information about visas goes out of date fast, so don't rely entirely on the advice of books. Some unexpected countries require a visa; many Britons don't realize, for example, that they need one for Australia. Until recently they didn't need one for India, but now the regulations have changed.

An annoying visa problem sometimes occurs when you are going on a long trip: you won't be arriving in, say, Zarabia, for three months, but the visa you get from the Zarabian Embassy at home expires before your intended arrival; furthermore you are told that British subjects can only obtain the visa in Britain. Luckily, other travellers usually tell you this information is wrong, and that the visa is obtainable in another country on your route.

Experienced travellers will also tell you when it is actually advantageous to obtain a visa outside Britain; you may get the visa much cheaper, and it could save you from having to buy expensive 'currency vouchers' which some countries insist on.

Embassies sometimes give another piece of misleading information: they advise you that a visa is best acquired on entering a country; but on arriving at the frontier, you discover this is a two-week visa, strictly not extendible, and a six-week visa could have been obtained at home.

Trying to get several different visas before you leave home can be irritating and time-consuming; embassies keep eccentric office hours, and there may be petty complications and long queues. Even a single visa may necessitate several visits to the same embassy; and on reaching the front of a three-hour queue, you tend to discover that you have brought only six passport photographs, instead of the obligatory eight. Those who have a full-time job may prefer to luxuriate in the advantages of a visa service. Their runners are experts who know the office hours, the charges, the best times to queue, etc. In terms of time-saving, their charges may not seem too expensive. I list some London visa services in Appendix 3.

Immunizations

I explain in Chapter 5 why you may need to start your immunizations well in advance, occasionally as long as two months before departure, and also why you should start taking your malaria tablets a week in advance.

Safety warnings

If you have doubts about an area's safety, you can get an official view on it by ringing the Travel Advice Unit of the Foreign Office (tel. 071 270 4129).

Dentist

Get your teeth checked before leaving. This is more important than ever before, because you don't want to risk getting either hepatitis B or HIV from faulty medical equipment or procedures.

TEFL courses

I will mention them in more detail in Chapter 11, but those who are hoping to work abroad might benefit greatly from doing a Teaching English as a Foreign Language course. Learning some of the local language is strongly recommended, and this is also discussed in Chapter 11.

Security chart

Making a security chart may seem laborious, and I'm sure most readers won't bother. But in the event of a disaster, even a simple one could save days of trouble and heartache.

Fig. 2 shows one that I've made for myself. It is intended only as a guide; create your own so that it includes every useful piece of information you could need. Here are some points about the chart.

I have made the first section a permanent one that is repeatable for each trip. This cuts down on a lot of the work. All that is necessary is to take photocopies of your main chart, and then on each photocopy you only need fill in the relevant details for specific countries.

Credit-card numbers I have checked with the credit-card

A. PERMANENT SECTION

Passport no. 000793386   Date and place of issue Glasgow 19/12/89.

Credit card nos. and telephone no. to ring if stolen

Access 5224 0064 2115 2262   Tel. (O) 5327 78899
NatWest card 49361800070258/8681 Tel. (o) 5327 78899.

Tel no. if Amex travellers cheques stolen (0) 273 571 600

Home Doctor's tel no. (0) 71 228 4021

Home Optician's tel no. (O) 71 486 9915

Camera description and no.

50mm F1·8   4320182
FE2 Body   2350615

B. SPECIFIC TO TRIP CHILE

British Consulate La Concepcion, 177 Santiago   Tel 223 9166

Insurance membership no. 3742 109744   Emergency no. (O)81 680 7080

Ticket booking ref no. H 1323   Ticket serial no. & date of issue 125 4413 661 850 : 1/8/91.

Departure Tax US $ 12·50

UK Direct telephone no. OO (wait) 0344

Local telephone no. if traveller's cheques stolen USA (1) 801 964 6665

C. TRAVELLER'S CHEQUES
$20 $

FC 900 007 660   D2 305 306 405
  ''   ''   661   ''   ''   406
  ''   ''   662   ''   ''   407
  ''   ''   663   ''   ''   408
  ''   ''   664   ''   ''   409
  ''   ''   665

Fig. 2 Sample security chart.

companies, who told me that it isn't a risk to include your card numbers on the chart, provided that you don't include the cards' expiry dates. They also pointed out that, if you are still worried about fraud, you could transpose some of the numbers.

Cancellation numbers If your cards are stolen it is useful to know that you can, in theory, cancel them by informing any institution (such as a bank) that displays the card company's logo. But I have included the cancellation numbers at home, because I expect they are much safer. (I have also included the main numbers in Appendix 4.)

Doctor's telephone number I have included this, because very valuable diagnosis can be effected on the telephone (see Chapter 5). If you are likely to need specific medicine, also make a note of its generic name (as opposed to its usually shorter trade name, which may not be universal).

Consulate Should you need emergency assistance, such as a replacement for your passport, you turn to the Consular Department of your embassy. It is worth finding their address, telephone and fax in advance: when you need it most, you won't have access to a telephone book. Another important reason for noting the consulate's address and numbers is that they keep a list of English-speaking doctors. This could be life-saving. If you are well away from the capital, there may also be consulates in provincial cities; in Brazil, for instance, there are twelve. To find out addresses of consulates, look in the Diplomatic Service List at your local library, or ring up the Travel Inquiries number of the Consular Department (tel. 071 270 3000).

Air ticket details As discussed in Chapter 4, it is often the booking reference number (sometimes called the locator number) which is important, not necessarily the ticket serial number. The booking reference number is usually a few digits, and may include one or more letters. The ticket serial number is usually a much longer one, often about fourteen numbers.

Departure tax This wretched tax is becoming increasingly common, and if you are caught unawares, it may be a nightmare having to rustle up as much as $25 at the airport (often local currency is not accepted). So it is worth checking in advance. *The ABC Guide to International Travel* (see below) has the latest details.

UK Direct numbers I have described these numbers in Chapter 8, and I give a list of them in Appendix 4.

Traveller's cheques numbers Although a bit of a chore, it is worth listing them singly, because it is then easy to cross them off when you cash them. This means you will know exactly which ones to claim for, if they get stolen.

Take two photocopies of your security chart. Leave the original at home, and divide the other two among your luggage, possibly keeping one in your money-belt.

I mention later in Chapter 5, that if you are very punctilious, or if you are going on an expedition, you should know your **blood group**. You can find this out free of charge if you donate your blood.

Packing

Packing used to make me anxious because I was always sure I would leave out some vital piece of equipment. So I now keep a permanent 'abroad packing list' and thereby eliminate most of my anxiety. You can use the same slightly updated list year after year.

If you are unlucky enough to have your luggage stolen, this list will greatly help the preparation of an insurance claim.

The ABC Guide to International Travel

If you are a very regular traveller, it could be worth your while ordering a copy of *The ABC Guide to International Travel* (Reed Travel Group, Church Street, Dunstable, Beds. LU5 4HB; tel. 0582 600111). This 112-page booklet is expensive, so if you don't travel frequently, try to persuade your travel agent to let you look at theirs. *The ABC Guide* covers every country in the world, listing (among other details) visa requirements, airport tax, the dreaded departure tax, the exit permit, distance of airport from capital, an elementary climate chart for the capital, public holidays, electric voltage, driving-licence requirements, and BBC World Service wavelengths.

On reading the guide more carefully, you can also discover a wealth of recondite information. The Netherland Antilles warns that the importation of souvenirs from Haiti is 'not advisable'; Australia doesn't, thank goodness, require visas from staff of the British Royal Family; Costa Rica won't allow the entry of gypsies from any country; Thailand won't allow the entry of Afghans (although they may use transit facilities if they continue their journey within three hours).

Some reference libraries stock a much larger alternative, *The World Travel Guide*, published by Columbus.

Booking your first night

I have been on several trips where I haven't booked a single room for my entire journey. But as I grow older, I do like to book the first night in a comfortable hotel. After an exhausting flight I don't want to start trailing round an unknown city. I prefer to start my journey on a relaxed note, and sometimes it is useful at this stage to have access to a working telephone.

INSURANCE

Why you must insure

All travellers should take out an insurance policy which covers both their possessions and their health. There is an epidemic of crime throughout the world; this alone is a good enough reason for insuring your possessions. Besides, when airlines lose your luggage, the Warsaw Convention obliges them to pay only pitifully small amounts of compensation. Approximately one in fifteen holders of travel insurance claim on their policies; therefore it is clear that you are taking a big risk if you don't insure.

Illness may cause expenses beyond your wildest dreams. British families have been bankrupted by one of the family needing emergency treatment in the United States. In other countries you may need to be evacuated by helicopter or to be flown home. This might cost thousands of pounds, as you could have to pay for several seats (at full price) to accommodate your stretcher; and airlines can force you to pay for an accompanying nurse. In an emergency you might need an air ambulance. All this can cost a fortune. Aids has also made it more likely that in the event of certain illnesses you will want to be repatriated because of worries about faulty medical treatment.

Loss of luggage and illness are the most important reasons for insurance, but a good policy will also bring the benefits of cover for unforeseen cancellation, baggage delay, bankruptcy of airline or operator, and third-party liability.

It is worth getting your travel insurance well in advance, so that you can claim if your journey is unavoidably cancelled (see Point 11, below).

Within many European Community countries you should be able to get emergency treatment free of charge. For this you will need the form E111. An application form for this is included in the booklet T4 ('Health Advice for Travellers Anywhere in the World') which is available from post offices. You can also try ordering a free copy by ringing 0800 555 777. The booklet tells you how to claim the free treatment in each country, and also lists other countries where Britain has reciprocal arrangements. Don't, however, let the possibility of free treatment deter you from taking out a proper insurance policy, especially as free treatment will not include emergency repatriation.

Choosing a policy

The details of insurance are boring, but it really is worth taking trouble over choosing your policy. Don't necessarily go for the cheapest one, as there is often a reason for the cheapness. (If you are buying a packaged holiday, you may be offered free insurance. These policies should be viewed with the greatest suspicion.) Ask to see a copy of the 'Policy Wordings', which is not the same as a brochure. The small print is often tantamount to dishonesty. A friend who was setting out on a trekking holiday in Nepal discovered that his policy – from a well-known company – contained small print excluding 'overland travel in Africa and Asia'. Another traveller, who had taken care that his insurance policy covered motorcycling, discovered after an accident that this policy didn't cover him because his motorcycle was above 125 cc.

In order to research the difficult problem of choosing a good insurance policy I wrote (under a false name) to ten insurance companies specializing in travel, asking them searching questions about their policies. Many of them turned out to have small-print clauses that would be a shock for a claimant. I have therefore devised a list of questions, from which you can choose those that are relevant to you. If the irritated insurance companies don't throw you out of the door, these questions will identify some of the small-print problems, and confirm that you have the right type of policy.

1. Does the policy have an 'excess' clause? A typical excess clause deducts a certain sum, say £25, from the repayment they make to you. This is quite normal, but comes as a surprise to some claimants. One of the companies I contacted (Briggs & Hill, see Appendix 3) will waive the excess clause for an additional fee of £1.
2. What hazardous activities does the policy exclude? Insurance companies can put a very wide interpretation on hazardous activities, and frequently use this trick to refuse claims. 'Hazardous' activities may include water-skiing, windsurfing, or even riding. Some of the better policies will allow these if your holiday hasn't been essentially *dedicated* to that activity. Some policies will allow them if you pay a double premium. Scuba-diving would be considered a hazardous or dangerous activity in most policies (but some good companies will cover it for an additional premium). If you are doing anything that could be remotely considered as hazardous (including trekking in the Himalayas), then tell the company in writing. Check the policy especially carefully if you are going to be riding a motorcycle or moped.

23

3. If you are planning to do any type of job, or acting in any type of professional capacity, check that the policy covers you during that job. This is a frequent reason for a refusal of claims.

4. Check that you are covered for being a passenger in a car accident. Some companies have a small-print clause disallowing claims for accidents while you are in a 'mechanically propelled vehicle'.

5. Does the policy have an 'average' clause? This obnoxious clause means that if your stolen item is worth £400, but you have mistakenly insured it for £200, the insurance company will scale down, and pay you only a proportion of the value for which you have insured it. Thus they won't even pay you £200. I have also known cases where insurance companies have refused to pay anything in the case of under-insurance. Several companies claimed to me that all insurers have an 'average' clause, but this isn't true.

6. It is important to know that few, if any, travel policies will cover you for the replacement value of your stolen goods. They will pay the *actual* (sometimes called the *indemnity*) value – which may be the subject of much argument between you and the insurer. The *actual* value is the cost of the object, minus wear, tear, and depreciation.

7. Ask what is the policy's limit for insurance of cash. It is convenient to carry quite a lot of cash instead of relying almost entirely on traveller's cheques, and therefore this point can be quite important. Many companies will insure at least £300 worth of cash.

8. Does the company have a twenty-four-hour line for medical emergencies? And is it linked to a major emergency service, with multilingual operators, in-house doctors, etc. Does the policy cover you for an Air Ambulance flight home? Now that there is a widespread danger of Aids from contaminated blood, re-used syringes, and faulty medical practices, repatriation is advisable more often than it used to be.

24

9. In the event of a dispute, does the insurer belong to any system that provides for independent arbitration?

10. If you are more than sixty-five, check whether the company requires a certificate of health.

11. Does the company offer you any compensation in the event of enforced cancellation, such as that caused by the death of a relative, fire in your house, jury service, and so on? Some policies do include compensation for cancellation, so this security is well worth having.

12. If you are travelling far in a car, you should know that many policies exclude items stolen from an unattended car, unless they are in a locked boot. And many policies will not pay up for any items stolen from any part of an unattended car after 9 p.m.

13. Look at the financial limits to your claims. A good policy would offer a limit of at least £2 million for medical expenses in the United States. Even a routine operation there could cost you £40,000. Check also what is the limit *per item* of stolen property.

14. Ask if the policy obliges you to show purchase receipts for items you are claiming.

This covers most of the important points; but if you want a very thorough policy (and they do exist) you could also ask the following questions.

15. Is there any compensation for baggage delay? (You may have to buy clean clothes, etc. If you can't claim, you can always try the airline; see Chapter 4.)

16. If a close relative is seriously ill, can you claim for an emergency ticket to get home?

17. In the event of being injured by someone else, will the policy cover you for legal advice and costs?

If you are taking expensive items, such as cameras, it is often more practical to insure them under the 'all risks' part of your home contents insurance. There are three reasons for this: first, you *may* be able to arrange for insurance at replacement value (see Point 6, above); second, without including cameras, you will find it easier to find a cheap, standard travel policy; third, many travel policies won't insure single items for more than £250. Beware, also, that you might not be covered if you are using your camera for professional purposes.

If you travel frequently, it is a good idea to buy an annual travel insurance; otherwise, you tend to get lazy, and not take out a policy for short journeys, in which case sod's law will inevitably operate. These policies are quite rare, and the standard ones won't usually insure you for trips that last more than ninety days each. One of the few annual travel insurance policies is Centurion Assistance, which can be taken out by holders of American Express cards. It is good value, and at the time of writing covers personal money up to £500. Not everyone is happy with it, though. After a friend's radio and camera were stolen from a locked metal suitcase, which he had checked onto an Alitalia flight, Centurion rejected his claim. They wrote to tell him:

We must advise that the policy requires the insured person to exercise reasonable care for the supervision and safety of their property. Regretfully, we would advise that placing electrical equipment and valuable items in a suitcase cannot be classed as taking all reasonable precautions for the safety and supervision of your property.

When I wrote to the ten insurance companies, the first and most efficient reply came from Briggs & Hill. They also appeared to offer the most satisfactory standard travel policy, and they also offer an annual one that is cheaper than Centurion's.

Always take your original insurance policy with you, and leave a photocopy at home.

Fighting the insurance company

Many insurance companies automatically contest claims, however reasonable, and they often hire loss adjusters, who are skilled at beating you down. Most victims lose heart and give up. But as long as your claim is fair, you should win through by fighting hard.

Many of the tactics used by insurance companies are close to unethical. Once, after my Nikon was stolen, a man from the insurance company rang to settle details. During our conversation he casually remarked that many professionals use Nikons, and they were such good cameras. I agreed. The next day I received a letter saying that because I had used the camera for professional purposes, the company would be unable to compensate me. At that stage I didn't use my cameras professionally; I fought the case, and won.

A friend took out a policy with a famous company specializing in cheap travel. The small print restricted claims to £200 per 'set' of items. When he claimed, the company lumped together almost all his baggage as one single 'set', including two cameras and a tape recorder. In reply to his protest, they sent a dictionary definition of 'set' as 'a number of things being used together'. He fought this, and won.

Unbelievably, some insurance companies will try not to pay out for possessions unless you have the original receipts of purchase. Fight this, as it is unreasonable that you should keep receipts for everything you buy (but if you do have receipts, they will be a great help).

Having made insurance companies sound unreasonable, I should add that they are constantly having to cope with a deluge of fraudulent claims, which is one reason why they try to find any excuse not to pay up.

To ensure confidence in dealing with insurance companies, always make sure that you have reported any loss or theft within twenty-four hours to the police. Always get some chit from the police to prove that you have reported the incident. A photocopy is not enough, as the insurance companies consider them to be too easily falsified. Always keep all medical and doctors' receipts. And if your luggage doesn't appear after a flight, don't accept assurances that it has only been temporarily mislaid. Always fill out a Property Irregularity Report.

Always ensure that your stay is within the time limit of the policy. Even if you have overstayed only by a day, this may invalidate the entire policy.

If you fail to get payment from the insurance company, here are three institutions that may be able to help or advise:

The Insurance Ombudsman Bureau, City Gate One, 135 Park Street, London SE1 9EA (tel. 071 928 4488) – they won't be able to help unless your policy is with a company that is a member of the scheme

Lloyd's of London Advisory Department, 1 Lime Street, London EC3M 7DQ (tel. 071 623 7100)

Association of British Insurers, 51 Gresham Street, London EC2V 7HQ (tel. 071 600 3333)

Even if you have failed with all of the above, then try the very useful Small Claims Court. I have used it several times for other disputes, and have found it an effective remedy for dealing with dishonest people. It is inexpensive, and the threat of litigation usually works before the case has even come to court. You can find the court's address in the local telephone directory under 'Courts, county'.

Photocopies

At various stages in this chapter, I've recommended taking photocopies of a document. Here, to remind you, is a combined list of documents worth photocopying:

Relevant passport pages
Insurance document
Airline ticket
Security chart

CHAPTER 2

MONEY

Budgeting

No general book can give useful estimates of expenditure, which are best left to destination guidebooks. Nevertheless, a few small points are worth making.

It is often said that travellers should take half as much luggage as planned, and twice as much money. This may be an exaggeration, but you should certainly add an extra sum of money to your usual budget. Many people don't do this because they are frightened of over-spending; as a result, they are all too often forced to cable home for more money – with all the miserable complications involved. There are plenty of reasons why you might need more money, including the possibility of ending up in hospital, where you will need cash even when insured.

I frequently meet travellers whose holidays are marred by being too careful with money. If they had managed to save a bit more before leaving, they would have had a better opportunity to relax and enjoy themselves, instead of continually worrying about petty finances. I have often listened to interminable discussions about the cost of hotels, transport, and food, while the countries visited are never mentioned.

The Third World has the strange effect of making even the richest people obsessed with saving minute sums. I'm not suggesting you should be taken for a sucker, but it is easy to forget that, coming from a rich country, a measure of generosity is expected from you. In the mosques of Cairo I have seen tourists refuse the offer of shoe covers so that they can save themselves the pennies that are so desperately needed by a pauper. Besides, the spending of small sums of extra money can be highly cost-effective: when I was in Goa, for instance, the cost of a car and driver for a whole day was less than the cost of one London taxi ride.

When travellers have spent, say, £700 during a long trip, they often think that the trip has actually cost £700. But of course it hasn't. If they had stayed at home they would have had to eat, use transport, keep on the heating, and so on. Several of these day-to-day expenses are cheaper abroad, and it is possible that on their journeys travellers are spending little more than they would at home. They should consider their air ticket as the only major expense incurred, and make this an excuse for being more generous with their budgets.

And try not to underestimate your budget. If you are forced to have money wired out, there are likely to be problems with banks, who are often incompetent, and often deny receiving money which has definitely arrived. One couple were on the road for so long that on several occasions they had to have money cabled out, and as a result suffered serious delays – seven days in Rwanda, six days in Chile, fourteen days in Panama, seven days in Iran, and ten days in Turkey.*

Travellers tend to spend much more money when they are on a holiday involving continual travel. Not only does travelling tend to be an expensive process, but if you are constantly on the move, you don't have the opportunity to discover the cheap hotels and eating places. Because travelling is usually tiring, you tend to gravitate to the more expensive hotels, as you are desperate for running water, soft beds, and other luxuries. But when settled in one place, you have time to discover the best resting and eating places; and you may even find a house or rooms to rent – often the cheapest and nicest way to live. Once settled in pleasant surroundings, your tastes may become simpler; in a hot climate you often need little more than a bed and a supply of water.

* *Overland and Beyond*, Theresa and Jonathan Hewat (Roger Lascelles, 1981)

Traveller's cheques

The great advantage of traveller's cheques is that they are safe. If they are stolen, you can get a refund, often very quickly.

The disadvantages are as follows. You are giving the issuers your money in advance; the issuers charge a commission for taking your money in advance; and when your cheques are issued in a foreign currency, you may be charged twice over – when you buy the cheques, and when you cash any on your return. Traveller's cheques may be bothersome when you need a passport for cashing them, and sometimes they aren't acceptable in out-of-the-way places; they are often difficult to change on a black market; and a final disadvantage is that they often get a worse rate of exchange than cash (though, just to confuse the issue, there are a few places where you will get a better rate for your cheques).

Although there is no doubt that traveller's cheques are the safest way to carry money, the inflexibility and bother of them has encouraged me to travel – perhaps unwisely – with fewer traveller's cheques than I used to. Instead I take at least as much cash as my insurance policy will allow and a credit card; I also take one smallish batch of traveller's cheques (which will get me through an emergency) and keep this same batch for trip after trip. Although this is a bit extravagant – tying up money that could be reducing an overdraft – it does save the bother of buying the cheques each time, and of making a new list of their numbers.

Many travellers are under the impression that when their traveller's cheques are stolen, they will inevitably get an immediate refund. This is not the case. *A great many travellers find they can't get refunds within a reasonable time, and some issuers don't offer any refunding facilities abroad.* Some issuers do claim to offer immediate refunds, but on reading the small print you find that they set a limit, perhaps £250. So be cautious with your choice of cheques, and don't necessarily buy the ones pushed by your own bank. Be sure to use an institution that has a wide network of refunding agents throughout the world.

Always get the issuer to tell you, preferably in writing, the addresses and telephone numbers of the refunding agents in the country you are visiting. This may seem a chore, but when you've had your money stolen, the information will be a godsend.

My impression from both anecdotal and written evidence is that American Express cheques are still the safest if you want a quick refund: 95 per cent of their claims are settled within twenty-four hours. When you purchase your cheques, American Express will give you a telephone number (often a freephone); when you ring this number you will be told their nearest representative, who will arrange for the most convenient refund. They claim that they are prepared to send a courier to anywhere in the world except a war zone. *Condé Nast Traveler* recently experimented by 'losing' the traveller's cheques of major companies, and American Express proved to be the best for quick refunds. They are also the most widely recognized cheques, and in parts of South America are the only ones to be recognized. Their cheques can be cashed in American Express offices without a commission being charged, and if you are going on a long trip, this could bring a substantial saving. Another bonus of having their cheques is that it entitles you to use the forwarding-mail facilities in American Express offices (see Receiving mail, Chapter 8).

In what currency should your cheques be issued? In some ways it is comforting to get sterling cheques because this gives you a precise feel of what you are spending. However, I now buy dollar cheques, as the dollar has become the universal currency of the world (see Cash, below), and dollar cheques are accepted almost anywhere that traveller's cheques are accepted, even in a traditional sterling area. There are many places, such as South America, where sterling cheques are almost useless. This can be true even in North America: I was unable to cash my sterling traveller's cheques in a huge Texan bank whose central hall had six escalators and a 50-foot-high arrangement of poinsettias.

The commission charged for most traveller's cheques is 1 per cent. But some banks charge 2 per cent for dollar cheques, and some banks charge an administration fee on top of this. As American Express themselves charge only 1 per cent on their dollar cheques (with no administration fee), it may be cheaper to use them. Their cheques can also be ordered through several building societies, travel agents, and some high-street banks, including National Westminster and Lloyds; but check the commission rate.

Immediately on receipt of traveller's cheques, sign in the allotted space. If you want your potential claim for a refund to be simple and speedy, be sure to make at least two separate lists of cheque numbers (see Fig. 2, Chapter 1); keep at least one with you, and leave one at home.

Eurocheques

Despite their name, Eurocheques are used outside Europe, but they are rarely useful for tropical travellers. All the same, I mention them because they do have some advantages. First, unlike traveller's cheques, you haven't paid any money in advance. Second, you can be specific about the amount of money you want to spend. Third, you can denominate them in quite a variety of currencies.

But the cheques aren't as practical as first appears. You have to carry an accompanying Eurocheque card, and at present this card won't guarantee a cheque for more than £100. Conversion fees, too, can be high: at the time of writing, Lloyds Bank charges £5 a cheque; National Westminster Bank charges a whopping conversion fee of £24 if you write a cheque for more than £200.

Considering all the other options for raising or carrying money – traveller's cheques, charge cards, cash cards, credit cards, and cash – it seems hardly worth bothering with Eurocheques, or paying an annual fee for the accompanying card. And the cheques are useless in the remoter parts of the world, where they are often unknown.

Cash

It is often a good idea to obtain some currency of your destined country before you arrive. This can save an hour-long queue at the airport's only bank counter. And sometimes there is nowhere to change money at the airport, or the banks are closed because of a holiday, which obliges you to take an expensive taxi to a hotel where you have to change money at an exorbitant rate. Bear in mind, though, that many developing countries ban the import of their own currency.

Always carry a separate and well-hidden provision of money for emergencies. This should be *cash*. There may well be occasions when you need to pay urgently for something and a traveller's cheque won't be accepted. In the event of being caught up in a revolution or war, cash will be a lifeline. This emergency reserve of money is best kept permanently hidden, perhaps in the secret compartment of a trouser-belt.

The obvious advantage of taking sterling as cash is that it costs nothing in commissions to acquire, and there are no reconversion charges when you return home.

Dollars, though, will often be preferable. In the same way that the English language has become the lingua franca of the world, the dollar is becoming the universal currency. Even in such unlikely countries as Burma or Syria, it is best to have dollars. And the more left-wing the regime, the more likely they are to smile upon the dollar. When I was in Castro's Cuba, the hotels and government shops would accept payment only in dollars.

Dollar notes are also very practical. They come in a wide variety of denominations (including the invaluable $1 note). All the notes – whether $1 or $100 – are exactly the same size, which makes them easy to stack. And the notes are conveniently small, which also has the advantage of making it easy to fold them into hiding places.

It is most irritating to be obliged to cash a large note or cheque just before crossing a frontier; and when you do, you are usually landed with a currency that has no value outside the issuing country. So always keep plenty of small-denomination notes. A supply of $1, $5 and $10 notes is useful, and the $1 note will always come in handy for tips.

Be cautious of large-denomination notes, as people may not be accustomed to them. £50 notes are sometimes viewed with suspicion, and $100 notes are mistrusted because they have often been forged. If you must take $100 notes, Jack Jackson tells us in *The Traveller's Handbook* (see Appendix 1) that we should avoid the older $100 bills which don't have 'In God We Trust' written on them. He says that although they may not be forgeries, many dealers won't touch them.

As mentioned in Chapter 1, your insurance policy will probably cover you for a certain amount of cash – often £300, but sometimes as much as £500 – therefore bear this in mind, for cash is the most versatile way of carrying money.

Credit cards

In recent years there has been a wonderful increase in the outlets accepting credit cards. If you have any of the cards that are linked either to Visa or Mastercard, you will be able to use it at millions of garages, shops, restaurants, and hotels. Even just one card can be invaluable; Access, for instance, have more than 9 million outlets in 170 countries.

The cards can also be used for getting quite large sums of cash per day from a huge number of participating banks. At the time of writing National Westminster Access allows you to draw local currency up to the equivalent of £350 a day and can be drawn from banks in 150 countries. Barclaycard Visa allows £500 a day in 160 countries. For these transactions you won't need a chequebook. The banks will usually display the appropriate logo in their windows. Sometimes it may be worth your while to get in advance a list of participating banks; Mastercard issue a useful booklet, 'International Travel Guide', which lists cash-issuing banks in every country (if this might be of use, order it well in advance). As I write, Visa don't publish a comparable booklet.

You may have to pay interest (at a usurious rate) from the moment you get this cash; or you may have to pay just a handling charge, say $1\frac{1}{2}$ per cent, depending on the issuing bank. However, at present card companies don't make a charge if your account is in credit. Therefore, if you know you are going to be drawing cash, or if you are going on a long trip, it is an excellent ruse to pay a lump sum in advance into your account. This enables you to transfer money both efficiently and cheaply.

In the more developed areas credit cards are increasingly useful for drawing cash from street cash-dispensers, which can be very handy for emergency cash. (Ask your bank if you will have to pay interest from the day of the transaction.) Recently I was surprised to get some much-needed weekend money from a cash-dispenser in a tiny Italian hill-town.

Are you receiving a fair rate of exchange? These rates are determined not by the cards, but by the banks that plug into their system. Thus you will get a different rate of exchange by using a National Westminster Access card rather than a Lloyds Bank Access card. It has always seemed to me that the transactions on my own Natwest Access card have been done at a fair rate; the company buys and sells currencies in such huge quantities that they get a good deal, which is far better than the tourist rate. The card's rate is of course fixed not on the day of your transaction, but at the time that the voucher gets back home. This could work to your benefit or to your disadvantage. However, even when it works against you, the disadvantage may be outweighed by your getting several weeks' free credit. At the time of writing National Westminster don't make any extra charge for foreign currency transactions on their own cards. Some other banks charge as much as an additional 2 per cent, though they point out that this should still compare favourably with the tourist 'buying' rate.

If you need to hire a car, a credit (or charge) card is almost essential, because it releases you from having to pay a large deposit.

Considering that one single card will do so much for you, it seems unnecessary to have many of them. However, one extra card could be a safety net, and it will also be useful if you have exceeded your spending limit on the other one. If you do travel with several cards, consider joining one of the protection plans mentioned under Theft in Chapter 10. Otherwise you will find in Appendix 4 a list of numbers for cancelling credit and charge cards. I have also listed many Direct numbers for the UK. These will enable you to dial free of charge to an English-speaking operator, who can then make a reverse-charge call to any of the card companies.

Credit-card fraud

An increasing number of people are getting worried about the fraudulent misuse of credit cards, and I have been sent a number of alarming stories. Several guidebooks are now advising that, when paying a restaurant bill with plastic, it is important to get up from the table and actually watch the waiter processing your card. After investigating most of the worries, I have concluded that, although we should be careful, there is no need to be too panicky.

A recent letter, for instance, told me of someone who found on her statement a charge for £900 worth of jewellery which had been bought in Penang while the card was theoretically in her hotel's safe. On the whole you needn't worry about this type of fraud: provided that you have behaved legally and responsibly, you are not liable for fraudulent misuse.

Furthermore, considering the huge amount that cards are used, this type of fraud tends to be rarer than people think. All transactions have to go through an outlet, and unless that outlet is conducting a large well-planned sting, they will want to keep their relationship with the card-issuing companies.

On the other hand, you must always keep all your counterfoils. There are two reasons for this. First, there is a real chance of *minor* fraud. A friend of mine, for instance, had a crucial numeral inserted on her Visa card after buying a piece of jewellery in China. Second, most card companies allow their accounts to add 'reasonable' later charges (called a 'final audit facility'). These charges may include such items as an unpaid-for breakfast or a tankful of petrol. When you get home, always check your statement against the counterfoils.

To be absolutely safe, you should perhaps get up from your table to watch the waiter process your card; but I would never be able to face the embarrassment. And although fraud can be perpetrated at this stage – running your card twice through the machine, for instance – I have already explained that this is unlikely. And whether you follow the waiter or not, you won't keep secret the details of your card, including its number; the waiter, and any amount of other people, will have access to that. To repeat, though: make sure that you keep the counterfoil.

Set against the small chance of fraud, the benefits of a credit card are enormous. Because banks now charge nearly £1 for every entry on their statements, I particularly appreciate the card companies' free detailed statements. I keep them for years, because apart from their more obvious benefits, they occasionally serve as a primitive diary.

Charge cards

The principal difference between charge and credit cards is that the charge cards oblige you to pay your monthly account straightaway. The most famous charge cards are American Express and Diners Club. Of these two, the most useful for travellers is the American Express card, as it has more outlets. I find, though, that my Access card is accepted so widely that I very rarely use anything else. So far, I am still travelling with my American Express card, though mainly as a safety net.

Like the credit cards, the American Express card is useful for raising money in emergencies. At American Express travel offices you can use a personal cheque to obtain cash or traveller's cheques. With the ordinary green card you can raise £500 every twenty-one days; with the grander cards you can raise much more. Get a list of their offices before you leave; as I've said, they don't have their *own* offices everywhere.

Chequebook

Ordinary British cheques aren't really designed for international systems of finance, and therefore won't usually be of much use; if they are, then the transactions will probably be very expensive. But, if you have an American Express card, it might be useful for cashing cheques in their offices. If you aren't planning specifically to use British cheques, it hardly seems worth taking a chequebook, though it is occasionally useful for raising money when you have returned penniless to your home airport. You will then need your **cheque guarantee card**, which sometimes usefully doubles as a cash-card for dispensers.

Even if you don't take a chequebook, it is often a good idea to put a couple of cheques in your document bag; they may be useful in emergencies. A friend who was almost out of money at the final stage of a long trip was able to use a cheque to buy some much-needed film from another traveller.

Receiving money

I've already explained that wiring money may be tiresome and erratic. If you must have money wired out, arrange for the issuing bank to send separate confirmation with full details; you can then go into the receiving bank with the much-needed proof that your money has been sent. If you can't brandish this proof in front of cashiers, they frequently deny receiving the money, and you will be stuck.

For some trips it is practical to ask your bank to arrange one or more 'credit open' with corresponding banks. This enables you to cash personal cheques wherever you have made the arrangement. (Again insist on a written confirmation.) This is a pleasantly simple system, but check with your bank about their charges, as these tend to be high.

If you need money to be sent urgently, there is a useful new service called MoneyGram, offered by American Express. Within minutes they can send money to any one of 12,000 locations in more than fifty-five countries. The service is expensive, but it could be invaluable in emergencies. Neither party has to hold an American Express card.

Obviously it is a bad idea to send or receive cash through the post. Whenever it has been necessary I have used the traditional system of sending the cash between carbon paper; I presume that carbon paper is used because it is opaque, while being thin. So far, it hasn't failed me, but I would never send a large sum.

Changing money

Banks nearly always offer a far better rate of exchange than hotels, and therefore it's usually worth the effort of avoiding hotel cashiers. As usual, though, there are exceptions to the general rule: for instance, some hotels in Latin America offer a better rate than the national banks, which may charge a stiff rate of commission.

Don't think that just because you are in a bank, the rate offered must be fair. You may be surprised to find a difference of as much as 10 per cent between them.

Changing money may cost a lot. It is important to inquire not only about the rate but also about the commission. Charges (often discreetly hidden) can be extremely high, including in Britain. The *Evening Standard* reported the case of a tourist who changed $400 at a Chequepoint in Oxford Street. Outside on a blackboard Chequepoint said that it had the lowest rates in London; what they conveniently forgot to mention was that they had the highest commission (9 per cent). For the same amount of dollars she would have got £18 more at the Royal Bank of Scotland.

As a general rule it is best to avoid changing money at airports. The money-changers have had to bid a high price for their concession at the airport, and they get this back from the customer. You usually get a fairly reasonable deal when the money-changer is a major bank, but even they often charge a slightly higher rate of commission at airports.

If you are getting your foreign currency before you leave, shop around the various banks, as the costs can vary widely.

Some of them make a small fixed charge, which can be expensive if you are changing a small amount, but good value if you are changing a lot of money. Other banks charge a percentage commission, which may be better value for the small amounts, but more expensive for larger ones.

A currency's exchange rates may vary between different countries. In the first edition I wrote that it is sometimes very advantageous to buy a currency well away from its own country (while being aware of restrictions on currency imports). But I have since discovered that the reverse can also be true: when I last went to Turkey, the rate for the Turkish lira was 6,300 for the pound at Heathrow airport, but 6,880 in Istanbul.

Sometimes you find an excellent rate just outside the frontier, as there may be a currency glut caused by large numbers of people leaving the country and changing their money immediately. Be careful, though, when you undertake informal transactions; you could be fobbed off with worthless notes. Some countries attempt to reduce inflation by withdrawing all their old currency notes, and replacing them by a smaller number of new ones. Gullible tourists often get lumbered with old ones.

Currency movements

It is worth keeping an eye on currency movements, and getting anecdotal evidence from friends, because sometimes countries can become stunningly cheap. This is often due to a mere technical change in the currency rate, but the results can be heartwarming for the traveller. At the time of writing India is nearly 40 per cent cheaper than it was only two years ago. Sometimes a country's currency becomes so cheap that it costs only a pittance to stay in the most expensive hotels.

Exchange rates may also make a country absurdly expensive. Some of the West African countries, whose currencies are linked to the French franc, are nightmarishly expensive for the overlanding traveller. Get as much anecdotal evidence as you can, as this is more reliable than statistics. Changes in exchange rates may by themselves be misleading: although you may be getting 40 per cent more Zarabian lire for your pound, you won't be any better off if Zarabian inflation has been 40 per cent worse than ours in Britain.

Bargaining

Unless you know to the contrary, assume that the prices of all goods and services are negotiable. For instance, the following are not necessarily offered at a fixed price: a ferry-ride across a river, a car repair, an appointment with a doctor. Novice travellers often fail to check in advance the price of services, and then the person giving the service assumes that they have a free hand to ask for any sum they like. The ensuing argument is usually very unpleasant.

Most guidebooks give misleading advice about bargaining, often along the following lines: 'When a shopkeeper quotes a price, offer him half, and if you end up paying 70 per cent of the quoted figure, you have probably got a fair deal.' Unfortunately it is not as simple as that. Foreigners are often quoted five or ten times too much and, in areas regularly visited by rich tourists, they may face astonishing demands. I once heard a cycle-rickshaw driver ask a tourist for twenty times the normal fare; the tourist negotiated and, delighted by a 30 per cent reduction, climbed into the rickshaw. The next rickshaw driver in the queue also asked me for the same high fare; when I offered him a twentieth of the figure quoted, he smiled and accepted without any further negotiation.

One method of dealing with the problem is to get into the rickshaw (or taxi) while quoting a price in a tone which indicates, 'I already know the fair price so let's not bother to argue.'

There is, however, only one way to avoid the pitfalls of bargaining: know the price already. And the best way to know the price is to ask the locals. There is rarely any need to feel shy about this, because discussion of prices plays a notable part in friendly conversation. You will already have been asked to reveal the size of your wage packet, the value of the watch, or the selling price of your jacket.

The usual advice about offering half of the quoted price can also be misleading, because in some areas it isn't the custom to attempt to overcharge. In these circumstances vigorous bargaining would be inappropriate and ungracious.

Knowledge of the real price is one of the two major pillars for successful negotiation; the other is a willingness to use the walking-away technique. When you offer 100 centavos for a rug, the vendor may consider this a fair price; but there is no reason why he should accept it. If he refuses the offer, there is always the chance you may offer more, and if you walk away, he can always shout after you, 'OK, OK, I can do'. Remember that you have nothing to lose by walking away: if the vendor doesn't capitulate, you are still free to return at any stage to accept his last offer.

The sight of the actual cash offered, attractively piled in front of the vendor, may occasionally tip the balance.

I should mention that several friends of mine consider that the bargaining conducted by Westerners is often too exploitative. I think this fear is exaggerated when it concerns goods – shopkeepers are usually quite able to look after themselves – but Westerners are sometimes too ruthless when bargaining for services.

Vendors in shops will often ask you for the name of your hotel, and use this information to gauge your spending power. So always know the name of a cheap hotel.

In Chapter 7 I have written about the specialized business of bargaining for hotel rooms.

In most parts of the Third World you will be bargaining every day, so you might as well consider it as an art and enjoy yourself. Too many travellers conduct their bargaining gracelessly; just because they are arguing, they feel they should be fierce – almost to the point of rudeness. Bargaining is enjoyable and effective when conducted with smiles and laughter. If a hotel manager offers a flea-bitten room for an absurd price, many travellers are apt to snarl, 'I'm not paying that absurd price for this filthy little room.' They would do better to say, 'I would very much like to stay in your magnificent and charming hotel, but most unfortunately I can only afford the price of your inferior competitor down the road.'

Even when you know the fair price for something, it is often a good ploy to begin by offering a lower one. This enables you at a later stage to make an appropriate concession, thus saving the vendor's face. In any negotiation, whether financial or not, *you are more likely to get your way if your opponents don't lose face* when they accept your final offer. An understanding of this will help you in all of life's negotiations, whether at home or abroad.

Black markets

Since the decline of Communism there are fewer black markets, but some still exist. Although you may want to avoid them for fear of arrest, there is rarely any reason why you should have scruples about changing money on an unofficial market. The black market's existence is nearly always the result of the government having fixed the rate of exchange at a ludicrous level bearing no relation to the real value of its currency. If you change all your money at the artificially low level, you pay unjustifiably high prices for everything you buy. When I visited Zaire, I was at first paying more than £2 for a slice of bread and butter; I later changed my money at a rate five times better.

The black-market rate of exchange is variable, and most touts will want to give the worst rate of exchange they can get away with. So it is best to find out the rate from a friend living in the country. If you can't, use a double-check method by asking the touts for both the buying and the selling rates. Should you wish to buy centavos with pounds, you will get a closer idea of the correct rate if you first find out how much it would cost to buy pounds with centavos.

Instead of changing money on the street, try to find a friendly shop, as apart from the danger of someone running off with your cash, there are endless tricks by which a tout can con you out of your money. The most common is sleight of hand; the dealer appears to give you the pile of currency that you have checked, but he has deftly swapped it for another. Shopkeepers are less inclined to cheat; they know they can always be found again, and they are less likely to be police stooges attempting to trap you.

In my opinion no black market is worth the trouble or risk unless there is at least a 20 per cent difference between the free market and the government rates.

CHAPTER 3

EQUIPMENT

When you start shopping for the journey, friends will say, 'Don't bother with shopping at home, you can buy everything when you get there.' Ignore this advice. It is usually better to do all your chores before you leave, and then relax once you have begun the journey. And although you are always told that every-thing is available at your destination, even the most ordinary items tend to be uncannily absent. South America is one of the better regions for buying consumer goods, yet in Cuzco, a major tourist centre, I couldn't find a hat that was large enough for my head. Tanis and Martin Jordan reported that they couldn't find a hammock in Peru,* nor for that matter a tent in Surinam. The unavailability of goods can cause irritation and time-wasting during the start of your trip.

As I have explained in the Introduction, this book isn't aimed primarily at campers. If you are considering a camping trip, you must decide on this at the outset so that you get the right equipment (which will at least double your load). The following will become essentials: a good tent, mosquito netting, a good sleeping bag, a cooker, cooking equipment, a torch, a water bottle, and a sleeping mat.

Although in the earlier editions of this book I made it clear that I recommended people to travel as light as possible (and certainly not to take most of the items in this chapter), I still get criticized for compiling such a huge list. So let me try repeating my advice in capitals: THIS IS NOT A LIST OF RECOM-MENDATIONS – IT IS A LIST OF POSSIBILITIES.

* *South American River Trips*, Vol. 2 (Bradt, 1982)

There are two reasons why I have made it so long. First, even when you travel with very little, careful selection of your equipment can make an immense difference to your enjoyment. Any fool can be uncomfortable. Second, certain unlikely items may be useful for some trips; for instance, although not one in a hundred travellers will want to take fishing equipment, it may be a godsend for the hundredth, and therefore I have considered it worth including.

If you will be staying in just one place, then a lot of luggage might not be too much of a burden: you only have to unpack once. But if you will be constantly on the move, you won't want to be burdened with heavy baggage and the tedious chore of unpacking. Despite the immense length of this chapter, I still agree with the oft-quoted rule that it is best to take *less* luggage than you think you will need, but *more* money; and it can't be sufficiently emphasized that those who learn to travel light are always freer.

In a further attempt to forestall criticism of this huge list of kit, I'm putting the more useful items at the beginning of the chapter, and then moving on gradually to less necessary ones, concluding with a frisbee. This is then followed by separate sections for luggage and clothes. In the check-list at the end of the book (Appendix 8) I have put asterisks against those items which are most likely to be useful.

I have already mentioned in the Introduction that much of my information will go out of date. In the last edition of *The Tropical Traveller*, for instance, I recommended Teknalite torches, but by the time most people were reading the book, I preferred ones made by Maglite. Therefore the most useful parts of this chapter are the *questions* you should be asking about the various items; any brand names that I've risked recommending should be treated with caution.

Nomad (see Appendix 2) in north London have agreed that they will try to stock as many as possible of the items recommended below. Some of these items (such as gaffer tape, strong rubber sandals, and transparent kitbags) have often been tricky to find. Nomad can also dispense travellers' medical requirements, and on certain days can give you immunizations. Therefore if you check in advance that Nomad has everything you want, it could be a useful one-stop destination for all your requirements.

Torch

Never travel anywhere without at least one small torch. In underdeveloped areas it becomes an everyday tool, and in emergencies it is essential. After the IRA explosion at the Grand Hotel in Brighton, Mrs Thatcher started a habit of keeping a torch by her bed. She had discovered that you are trapped in the dark without one.

If you have lived only in developed countries, it is hard to imagine the multitude of uses for which you might need a torch, including the frequent one of going to the lavatory in the middle of the night. Even in quite developed areas, power cuts are a likely problem. In Chapter 6 I will explain how a torch could even save your life.

Because a torch is such an important item, I used to travel with a biggish one which took the Duracell size C batteries. It was large enough to throw a good beam, and yet just small enough to hold in the mouth, when I needed to use both hands. It could give continual light for about nine hours. (Batteries, though, will last longer with intermittent use.)

However, I now travel with a much smaller torch, which takes size AA batteries. My reasons for reducing the size are as follows:

1. The AA batteries have become very much a universal size of battery (often called penlite); therefore they are available almost everywhere. I try to arrange that any of my gadgets takes the same size of battery, so that spares are interchangeable. Most short-wave radios now take the AA size, and so do most camera flash attachments.

2. If you do leave the torch on, or it switches itself on (which

easily happens in luggage) this wastes only the small batteries.

3. This small size of torch is comfortable to hold in your mouth when you need both hands.

4. With a torch this size, you have plenty of room to carry a spare one. If you carry two Maglites (see below), then between the two torches you will have no less than three spare bulbs.

5. Any reduction in space and weight is, of course, welcome.

A small torch of this size gives a continual light of more than four hours. This is adequate for most travellers' needs.

At present I use Maglite torches, which I find excellent. Several times I have tested their claim to be strong by hurling them in the air and letting them fall on stone or wood floors. So far nothing has smashed, not even the bulb (in America called 'lamp'). A spare bulb is carried within the body, which is very useful. They have another advantage which isn't mentioned in the instruction manuals. The casing around the head of the torch can be completely unscrewed and then used as a base for the torch. This leaves the bulb unshaded and, as a result, it doesn't just give a directional light, but instead an all-round light, like a candle. This can be very useful – for instance, when packing.

Be careful about buying Maglite lookalikes from mail-order firms. I tried this, hoping to save money, and ended up with inferior imitations.

On certain trips I take a torch that can be attached to the forehead. An excellent and comfortable one is made by Petzl, and is now quite widely available. I find this extremely useful, for it provides a good beam while leaving both hands free to do chores. The lamp pivots up and down, and is wonderful for reading in bed. Petzl torches are also very resistant to water and humidity.

I have always used the standard variety, which takes a flat 4.5 volt battery. This lasts an extraordinarily long time (at least ten hours, and according to the manufacturers as long as seventeen) and throws a beam of about 100 feet. The British distributors of the Petzl torches have written to me to say that 'the standard bulb life is approximately 500 hours, although this does rather depend on the correct battery usage'. A spare one is fitted into the body. The disadvantage of this model is that in various parts of the world the big flat battery is quite rare; but the torch is sold with a converter that takes three AA batteries, which apparently last for eight hours. Petzl have now developed a smaller head-lamp which takes two AA batteries (the ones I have described as being almost universal). It throws quite a good beam (about 30 feet) and the batteries can last five hours or more.

Because I've become so aware of the usefulness of torches in emergencies, I also go to the extreme of carrying yet another (but very small) Maglite in my shoulder bag (see page 54). I leave the little torch there permanently. Only rarely have I had to use it, but occasionally it's been invaluable. Once I was in a car which had a puncture at night in the freezing mountains of Peru. It was my little Maglite that enabled us to change the tyre. Another time, I was deep in an ancient Egyptian tomb when the electric light failed. Without the tiny torch that is always in my shoulder bag I would have been terrified.

Because most people rarely use torches at home, they seldom realize that the life of a bulb is quite short. Quite frequently on my travels, my torch bulb has stopped working. When I inquired about the length of a bulb's life, EverReady replied that the average life is between fifteen and thirty hours. This may be shorter with rough treatment. Therefore, if you are using your torch frequently, you may need to pack a well-wrapped **spare bulb**, especially as the ones you find abroad are often of inferior quality. Your torch should be designed so that the bulb can be changed easily.

Most torches are designed with a maddening and unnecessary flaw: the switch gets turned on in your luggage. As a result, when you most need your torch, you find the batteries are flat. To avoid this, I used to reverse one of the batteries. After describing this habit in a previous edition, I received letters telling me that this was a bad practice, as it could short the batteries. Nor apparently is it a good idea to reverse both batteries, as this can drain out their energy. So perhaps it is best to just put a piece of gaffer tape (see page 63) over the top battery when the torch isn't going to be used; or to put some gaffer tape over the switch. Happily, the Maglites don't switch on too easily when in luggage.

Batteries

In the last edition I wrote a long screed on whether it was best to take ordinary (zinc carbon) or long-life (alkaline) batteries. By now the battle has been almost completely won by the alkaline ones. Although heavier, they have a far better shelf life (they lose less than 15 per cent of their capacity after being stored for two years), and their extra lasting-power more than compensates for the weight. They are also less likely to leak, which is important in the tropics. The expiry date is given at the base of most modern batteries. Duracell batteries can stay fresh for up to four years in storage.

As I've mentioned before, if you are taking a transistor, flash gun, alarm clock, torch, and anything else requiring batteries, attempt to coordinate them so they take the same battery size.

It is well worth shopping about for batteries. In the previous edition I mentioned how in John Lewis stores ('never knowingly undersold') batteries were usually far cheaper than elsewhere. The same still appears to be true. At the time of writing, a set of four AA batteries costs £2.99 in Dixons, but only £1.85 in John Lewis.

Insect repellents

A good insect repellent is essential: when insects are biting they can make your life a misery. They also carry many of the diseases you are likely to catch. (In fact the overwhelming majority of diseases that travellers are likely to catch are spread either by insects or by the faecal contamination of food and water.)

Should your repellent be in the form of an ointment, a stick, or an aerosol? Aerosols are the most convenient – one quick spray and all the work is done. They are also the best for treating clothing with repellent (see below). But most aerosols are now considered to be damaging to the ozone layer, and, besides, they aren't space-effective because they are so bulky. Inspect repellent is so important that it is usually best to take more of it, and sacrifice convenience.

In theory, ointment is the most space-effective, but I often prefer a stick, as being easier to apply and less likely to leak. For ordinary use I have found the Autan stick, which is now widely available, very effective. Ointment is slightly more practical for putting on material, and the stick is more practical for skin.

As I write, the crucial ingredient in inspect repellents is nearly always diethyl toluamide (often known as Deet). Before buying any preparation, see how much it contains. Many of them contain only small amounts: anything less than 25 per cent is usually a waste of time. Where infestations of biting insects are likely to be severe, you may need preparations with a proportion of Deet as high as 75 per cent. However, when jaguar-watching in the jungles of Guatemala, I found even this level of Deet was useless. And it is also ineffective against leeches, not to mention the dreadful midges of Scotland. For such situations you may need a preparation of 100 per cent diethyl toluamide, which can be got from specialist shops, mail-order companies or MASTA (see Appendix 2).

I have recently read in *The Backpacker's Handbook* (see Appendix 1) that the author found a Scottish product, Bugoff, extremely effective against Scottish midges and also against black flies in the Yukon. As Bugoff contains only l2 per cent Deet, this seems very remarkable. Perhaps there will soon be breakthroughs in the preparation of repellents.

You should know, however, that to some extent Deet can be toxic. A report in the *Lancet* (10 September 1988) claimed that it is absorbed through the skin, and advised that use of repellents containing more than 50 per cent Deet could be dangerous for infants and young children because of their thinner skin and greater surface–mass ratio. In some instances absorption of Deet has proved to be dangerous even for adults. Therefore frequent total-body applications of Deet for days or weeks should be avoided, especially of a strength of more than 75 per cent. This is yet another reason to put Deet on your clothes rather than your skin (this subject is covered in some detail under Mosquitoes, Chapter 6).

All Deet should be kept well away from plastics, including cameras, as it will dissolve them.

Several American hunters have told me that Skin-so-Soft, a bath oil made by Avon, is an astonishingly good insect repellent. Unfortunately I haven't yet had the opportunity to try it, but it's worth mentioning because the hunters claim that it repels the bugs in the Florida Everglades, which are the most zealous biters I have ever encountered. Avon don't know why it works so well. (Skin-so-Soft is available direct from Avon through the post; tel. 0604 232425.)

A letter to *The Times* claimed that a solution of Epsom salts had the same miraculous effects on the midges of Scotland.

If travellers are going to areas with access to electricity, they should know that there are useful gadgets on sale which take fume-dispensing pills that kill insects. These pills last an excellent length of time (ten hours), and I've now heard plenty of good reports of them. Depending on how close the plug is to your bed, though, they may not be as good as mosquito coils (see Chapter 6) for very large or airy rooms. The fume-dispensing gadgets, with names like No-bite, are fairly widely available (including in the electrical departments of John Lewis stores), and are also sold by MASTA (see Appendix 2).

The devices which allegedly deter mosquitoes by emitting high-pitched squeaks have always been bogus. Numerous experiments have proved them so. However, as recently as 1989 *Newsweek* carried a report about them, which succeeded in selling them by the thousand.

In the Mosquito section in Chapter 6 I describe permethrin, a most valuable insecticide which could be useful in many situations where insects are a problem. I also mention a few desperate remedies for those who are stuck without a repellent, and I also discuss the question of knock-down sprays and insect coils, both of which are usually best bought at your destination.

Shoulder bag

I never go on a journey without one. They are invaluable for carrying maps, spare film, a pocket dictionary, a book, snacks, and so on. I also use my shoulder bag to protect my camera equipment against dust (which is lethal for cameras) and rain.

In my own bag I also keep a few items of permanent kit. These are as follows:

1. A minute torch (already mentioned).
2. Lavatory paper (very rarely needed, but a godsend when it is). You can buy useful small packs of pocket-tissues, which will do the job, and are generally more practical.
3. A small compass (again, I rarely need it, but just occasionally it is very useful).
4. A spare biro (get a reasonably good one, or it might leak, especially during the flight).
5. Antiseptic wipes. These are marvellous for immediately dealing with minor accidents – quite often not your own. They tend to be more securely wrapped than other wipes, and therefore retain their moisture for longer. And, although an absurd extravagance, they double up as a wet tissue after, say, eating a mango in a bus.
6. A few well-wrapped sticking plasters.
7. Postcards, for presents.
8. A wafer-thin calculator, which is occasionally useful for calculations, but is also there in case I suddenly need a goodish present. (One friend reports that these thin calculators break too easily in a bag, but this hasn't yet happened to me.)
9. Spare camera battery, a lens-cleaning cloth, and a spare neutral filter.

EQUIPMENT

A good shoulder bag is so useful that it is worth choosing carefully. It should have plenty of compartments, so that different items of kit can be found quickly, and it should be large enough to prevent your kit being jammed or tangled together. I also like the bag to be large enough to take a spare jersey on occasions. In the tropics you often encounter dramatic temperature changes within a few hours, especially when ascending mountains. If you are going to be carrying camera kit in your bag, it should be fastened by a zip so that you can keep out the dust.

Books

Most travellers get through an unexpectedly large number of books. They are an indispensable aid for passing time when there is little else to do, including the inevitable long waits at bus-stops, railway stations or airports. In fact these long waits can be turned into a positive pleasure, as long as you have a good book.

To safeguard against emergencies, I never move an inch without a book in my shoulder bag or pocket; if, say, I need to visit a government office for a visa extension, I wouldn't consider going without the safety net of 300 unread pages. If something unexpected happens, such as a long detainment in a police station (perhaps after witnessing a motor accident), boredom can be avoided if you have a book. In the evenings, when language problems have finally dried up conversational resources, books may be your only entertainment.

During my travels I get special pleasure from reading for long uninterrupted periods. At home I read only during the dozy half-hour before falling asleep, and many good books have been spoilt in this way. When sleepy, I can't concentrate on anything remotely demanding, and rarely get sufficiently absorbed to appreciate a really good book. The lengthy stretches of reading when abroad are perfect for savouring books. However, these long stretches tend to develop your reading muscles, and it is possible to find yourself finishing books at an unexpectedly rapid pace. During one long boat-ride I found that I was reading three books a day unless I controlled myself. Your stock of books should therefore take into account a potential increase in reading speed.

As travellers can seldom take as many books as they would like, and as even a few are heavy, the initial choice is an important exercise. I once heard a traveller say that she never packed a book which she hadn't read before, as she wasn't prepared to risk taking one she might not enjoy. Although this is perhaps a little extreme, it is a good idea to pack one or two well-loved books that are guaranteed to give you pleasure.

It is also a good idea to build up a waiting-to-be-read shelf throughout the year. If you leave the selection of books till the last minute, you enter a bookshop only to find that you can't think of a single one you want to read – the same type of mental blackout that happens when you are asked what you want for Christmas. And if you are lucky enough to suddenly think of a title, it is certain that the shop will be out of stock. Better to have the fun of building up a selection over several months. My own unread holiday shelf (more than 100 volumes, arranged in alphabetical order of author) gives me great pleasure every time I survey it. Also, this size of choice enables me to make a careful selection sympathetic to the mood and character of each journey.

When making this selection, I choose a few demanding volumes, which I would never struggle with at home, and mix them with lighter ones for the many periods when it is hard to concentrate on anything serious. People often find that they have been too ambitious in their choice of reading matter, especially for long flights, when for some reason (lack of oxygen?) it is difficult to concentrate. I have heard of one traveller who claims to have one arm longer than another – a result of lugging Proust all over the world.

Another aspect of book selection is worth considering. Some people like to immerse themselves in reading about the country they are visiting. Others deliberately resist this temptation, as they don't want their initial impressions and perceptions to be influenced.

If you are a fast reader you will probably run out of books, however many you take. In remote places they can be more precious than gold, and it is a good idea to be alert for swapping opportunities from the moment you have finished your first volume. I canvass every English-speaking person I meet, and thereby try to keep up the quality of my stock. Be careful not to be a perpetual loser in the swapping deals; I always start the journey with a splendid selection of books, but on a long trip I usually end up with books by Karl Marx or Shirley Conran.

When your pile of books is running low, and you aren't alone, try reading to each other. Most people haven't experienced this at home and will be surprised by their great pleasure at hearing a book being read aloud.

Water-flasks

If you are travelling off the beaten track, a water-flask is an essential piece of equipment. Novice travellers, coming from countries where water is available from taps, consistently under-estimate the importance of water. Under certain hot conditions many people like to drink as much as 16 pints a day. (For the extreme importance of water in maintaining health, see Water, Chapter 12.)

The other, equally important, function of a flask is to guarantee a supply of sterilized water out of a clean container. When travellers are exhausted by difficult journeys and intense heat, they are often tempted to drink doubtful water.

Should you ever need water urgently, and haven't had a chance to get boiled water, at least with a flask you can use sterilizing tablets, which will be a lot better than nothing. The flask also ensures a supply of uncontaminated water for brushing your teeth.

Experienced doctors insist that a contaminated container is as likely a source of infection as the water itself; so when you fill up a container, scald it and its lip with boiling water.

Metal flasks are best. A plastic one can be damaged by boiling water, and, if dropped, it can crack (especially when hot).

Normal transparent plastic containers will eventually grow algae. Ideally your flask should be able to hold hot water, because (as explained in Chapter 5) boiling is the simplest and safest way of purifying water; and boiling water should be easy to find anywhere where people live.

For years I travelled with a l-litre flask, but reluctantly have reached the conclusion that when doing any strenuous walking, a 2-litre one is necessary. I try to avoid packing one, though, because it takes up a dreadful amount of room in luggage, which is especially annoying when the flask isn't being used. The 2-litre US Army collapsible bottles (sold by Nomad) are convenient because they fold up when not being used; but unfortunately they probably won't tolerate boiling water. The most convenient flasks have a belt attachment, shoulder straps, or both. The flask should have its screw-top attached by a chain so that you don't have to clutch the top while drinking. If it's not attached, you are guaranteed to drop it in a mountain stream when filling up with water. Some people like the body to be covered by a cloth, which when damp will cool the water by evaporation; others complain that this cloth becomes smelly unless frequently washed.

Many experienced travellers have strongly recommended the Sigg water-bottles, as they are extremely tough and don't leak. One very experienced expeditioner tells me that they are the only safe bottles to carry in a pack, and he points out that they are excellent for safely carrying your duty-free liquor. If you have to sleep in the cold, they can also be filled with hot water to make a comforting hot-water bottle. Their disadvantage is that they are sold without any type of handle or carrying device, though an insulating cover with a loop is available. (Some backpackers don't mind this lack of belt attachment, because they prefer to stick their water-bottle into their rucksack. They say that this prevents any chafing by the bottle, and that it stops them being tempted by the enticing gurgling of water.) Personally, I always want my bottle to have a belt attachment, as I might easily make a day trip without a backpack.

Watch out: some Sigg bottles are sold only for carrying fuel, and are unsuitable for drinking-water. Sigg also make an indestructible (and expensive) Thermos, which might be useful if you are travelling with an infant.

One correspondent, who lived for several months with his wife and child in Cuba, found a children's **collapsible bucket** totally invaluable. In many of their cheap hotels the only tap was several storeys up, so they used this bucket to collect their day's supplies.

Those who are camping may also want some type of collapsible container for gathering water, and **water-bags** are available from camping shops and mail-order companies. Get up-to-date advice from someone who has used them, however, because most are nothing like as strong as claimed.

Pocket dictionary

In Chapter 11 I shall pontificate at some length on the advantages of learning at least a smattering of your destination's language. For this, you will certainly need a dictionary to expand your vocabulary, and it can also be important for ordinary everyday use. If you are more ambitious about using a language, a **phrasebook** may be helpful as well.

Pocket dictionaries may be very inadequate, and it's worth giving them a brief check. When doubtful, I always test them with nouns from the following easily remembered mnemonic: 'The *hamster* got *syphilis* and *hepatitis* from the *tampons* in the *brothel*.' You will be surprised how many small dictionaries don't have some of these words. The Collins Gem Italian dictionary, which boasts of having more than 70,000 references, has all five of these. The Collins Gem French dictionary, with more than 50,000 references, has three. The Harraps Mini French dictionary, which is much the same size, includes only one. The American Express/Mitchell Beazley Spanish dictionary, which I once bought in a hurry, doesn't include any of them.

You might think that a word such as 'hamster' would be

unnecessary; but it is for just this type of esoteric work that a dictionary should be useful. I included 'hamster' in my mnemonic because I once did need the word – in Syria. (All the millions of pet golden hamsters descend from one pregnant animal caught near Aleppo in 1930.) I have also included two easily memorable diseases in the mnemonic, because talking to a doctor is a typical example of an occasion when a dictionary would be useful.

Maps

Above all disregard the 'you can buy them there' brigade when it comes to buying maps. You frequently can't. They are often out of stock, or sometimes even politically unacceptable. For years the best one-page map of India was unavailable in that country because of its interpretation of the Kashmir cease-fire line. And even if you want large-scale maps they are very rarely available in the country you are visiting, although they may still be stocked by the map-sellers of erstwhile colonial powers.

Be as fastidious about choosing your maps as about choosing any other piece of equipment. Surprisingly often, maps produced by reputable publishers are unsatisfactory. I once drove to India with a series of maps which proved difficult to use and inaccurate; even road junctions were marked in the wrong places – with devastating results. My irritation was compounded when I met another traveller who was driving with an excellent series. It is as great a pleasure to use good maps as it is an annoyance to use bad ones. Michelin maps of Africa, for instance, are beautifully clear, attractively coloured, and cunningly designed so that you don't have to fold out the whole map every time you wish to look at a detail. The Falk series of city maps have a special patented design, so that you can fold out one very small part at a time. Until you get used to them, this can be bewildering; but their map of Istanbul was so convenient to use that it greatly enhanced my visit to that city.

Don't count on it, but in some countries major petrol companies issue good road maps; and quite often they are free. Esso are well known for their road maps, and in Haiti the best map I found was available at Texaco service stations.

If you are likely to be using your map frequently during a long trip, you could consider covering it with a film of transparent plastic (available in most map shops and many bookshops). This brings several advantages: it prevents the creases fraying, stops the map tearing in the wind, and protects it against stains and rain. The disadvantages are that the lamination is fiddly and difficult to stick down, and that it makes the map heavy and bulky. The Map Shop (see Appendix 3) is the only shop I have found that will laminate a map for you; they do warn, though, about the bulkiness.

Specialist camping shops and mail-order companies sell special sprays for coating maps. I have never found them any good, nor have I ever heard good reports about them.

Guidebooks

Like maps, guidebooks often can't be bought after your journey has begun. Even where there are bookshops, the best guidebooks always seem to be out of stock; and there is also the possibility that they may be banned, like Bill Dalton's invaluable guide to Indonesia. Although many travellers are far too reliant on their guidebooks, there is no doubt that in many countries a good guidebook is invaluable. If someone reliable has researched a country for months on end, their wisdom will be a great asset. You may be just a mile from some really stunning sight, and without a guidebook you won't know about it. I can't imagine, for instance, going to South America without the celebrated *South American Handbook*.

Although many people do travel without guidebooks, I have noticed that they always pester me for information if I settle anywhere near them.

Towel

All travellers who don't confine themselves to expensive hotels will need a towel. For the male traveller the best size of towel is just large enough to make him decent for public trips to wash-places. Anything larger is a waste of room. A towel made of cheap thin cotton takes up less space than a more luxurious one, and it dries quicker.

If you have ever been on a long bus or train journey in intense heat, you may well have suffered from a burning bottom. This excruciating pain usually starts after about four hours, and rubbing with cream gives no relief. After several experiments I have discovered that if you start the journey sitting on a folded towel the pain is prevented – possibly because the towel sucks up moisture from the plastic seat. Sitting on a pillow is not so effective.

A friend, the photographer Raghubir Singh, accustomed himself to using a folded towel as a pillow. He now even uses one at home. If you can do this, you will sleep comfortably anywhere.

Most Third World pillows are lumpy and uncomfortable. I have discovered that their comfort is increased to an inexplicable degree by just putting a fresh towel over them. And a towel can also be quite cooling over a pillow when your face is sweating from intense heat.

I read somewhere that a dark towel dries quicker than a light-coloured one. Even though I was aware that dark-coloured clothes are more absorbent of heat, I considered this to be unlikely. All the same, I tried putting a wet green and wet white towel out to dry in my Battersea garden. The green one dried first, by a long way. Because the two towels weren't identical, I then bought three identical towels – a dark-green one, a dark-blue one, and a white one. On all of the four occasions I tried the experiment, the green one dried first, then the blue, and finally the white. Considering that backpackers often have only a short time to dry their towels before packing up, it is clear they should buy a dark one – especially as it will tend to look less grubby. Many camping shops and mail-order companies sell a special 'traveller's towel' made from an artificial fabric called Pertex. They have sold in their thousands. Because they absorb hardly any moisture, I find them useless; indeed a pocket handkerchief absorbs more. When I tackled the main retailer, a spokesman defended these towels by saying, 'They dry quicker than an ordinary towel.' He didn't point out that if they haven't absorbed any moisture, they will inevitably dry quicker.

Some people, especially if they are going to be living rough, sew a flat tape on their towel so that it can be hung on any available hook or nail.

Gaffer tape

Gaffer tape once earned me applause from an entire railway carriage in Peru. A metal cupboard-door had been relentlessly banging and, despite everyone's efforts, had proved unfixable until I secured it with two strips of gaffer tape.

Gaffer tape is a waterproof, cloth-backed adhesive tape that is extremely resilient, and yet can easily be torn crossways (I use my teeth, and don't need scissors). Its limitless functions may include mending clothes or holding a camera together. It is more or less reusable, and the tape I used on the Peruvian train was later pulled off to secure a torn camera case. Its uses are so varied that I would never travel without a reasonable length of it.

It is hard to find and in some places only available in 100-foot rolls, which is more than enough for a lifetime, and expensive. Apart from Nomad (see Appendix 2), which does stock it in practical small lengths, it can usually be bought at the largest photographic shops, musical shops (such as those in Charing Cross Road, London), where it is normally cheap, and also at theatrical suppliers such as Donmar (54 Cavell Street, London E1 2HP; tel. 071 790 1166).

Following my strong recommendation of gaffer tape in earlier editions, correspondents have related the most extraordinary uses. One has used it to tape towels in front of air-conditioning units which had caused her acute sinusitis; in dust storms it can be useful for covering up the cracks in a camera; on a bicycle it can be used for tying spare spokes to the frame. I also find it helpful at home, and have recently used it for repairing the torn spines of reference books.

Tubigrip

Tubigrip is an elasticated tube of bandage. When doubled up on the calf of your leg, it makes an excellent hiding-place for passport and money (see Chapter 10). It can also be used as an emergency bandage, and can be adapted for a wide variety of other uses. For instance, one correspondent wrote to say that, when worn under trousers, Tubigrip was effective at preventing chafing during long horse-rides. In Chapter 6, I mention its potential as a leech guard.

Bum-bag/waist pouch/belt pouch

In recent years there has been an explosion in the sale of bum-bags, a type of wallet attached to its own belt. They are useful on a plane, for instance, because you can keep your money and passport with you, rather than in your jacket on an overhead rack. In areas with thieves, however, a bum-bag is vulnerable and will attract thieves like a magnet.

Pocket-knives and clasp-knives

A good pocket-knife is almost essential for every traveller.

For some years I avoided using the famous Swiss Army knives: the 'Swiss Army' didn't impress me much, as they hadn't fought a war for 460 years, and I didn't like their red plastic handles. Nevertheless, after being persuaded to try them, I must agree with the many people who regard them as invaluable.

As there is a wide range of Swiss Army knives, it is difficult to decide which model combines the smallest size with the maximum usefulness. The largest, the 'Champion', which includes a magnifying glass, a ballpoint pen, and a fish-scaler, is far too bulky for most travellers, especially if they want to carry a knife in their pocket. I usually take the 'Traveller', a reasonably light, slim knife, incorporating a large blade, small blade, corkscrew, bottle-opener, tin-opener combined with large screwdriver and wire stripper, reamer, scissors, tweezers, and toothpick. It doesn't have a saw, which might be useful for some – for instance, campers who want to cut tent poles.

Scissors are one of the most important parts of a pocket-knife. Apart from their everyday uses, such as cutting string or toenails, they are an essential part of a medical kit, especially for cutting Elastoplast or dressings. The tweezers are more helpful than you might think: they have a keen biting edge, which is excellent for pulling out splinters or thorns. I once had the task of extracting maggots buried deep in the flesh of a dog; they were surprisingly difficult to extract, until I thought of using these tweezers. (In case anyone faces a similar problem, salt water would apparently have loosened the maggots and made them easier to grab.) The corkscrew and bottle-opener are invariably useful for picnics, when the organizers have left theirs behind.

If you want to hang your knife from a belt, make sure you buy a knife fitted with a key-ring.

Some people have told me that they don't find the Swiss Army knife's tin-opener much good, but I have always found it to be fine. It may be that they have tried to use the opener in the wrong direction. In the superior models of the knife (which include the 'Traveller' and the 'Climber'), you shift the blade forwards – the opposite direction to that used with a tin-opener at home. If you still don't find it satisfactory, camping shops sell small **tin-openers**, which are the size of two postage stamps. Personally, I can't work out how to use them.

Should you decide to buy a Swiss Army knife, beware of the many imitations: they tend to be greatly inferior, and the blades often jam or break. The only genuine models are those made by Wenger and Victorinox. Victorinox knives are by far the most widely sold, and there is an easy way to check for one of their genuine models: all their knives have the word 'Victorinox' engraved on the base of the largest cutting blade.

Victorinox make a similar-looking economy range of pocket-knives which also have 'Victorinox' engraved at the base of the largest cutting blade. It is probably best for travellers to avoid these, as they are not quite so well made, and some of the body may eventually rust. Knives in the economy range can be distinguished from superior ones: they don't include tweezers, and the emblem (a shield) is hot-stamped on the handle, instead of being inlaid.

If your knife gets clogged up after a rough journey, do the following: open up all the blades and shake the knife about in some hot soapy water; thoroughly dry it with a hair-dryer; brush all the cracks and crevices with an old toothbrush; then spray it with WD40.

For most travellers a pocket-knife is sufficient; indeed it is often a disadvantage to carry a larger knife, as it might be viewed with great suspicion by the police. However, those on more intrepid camping expeditions may need larger **clasp-knives**. Victorinox make a series of slightly larger knives which have lockable blades (an important safety point, when you are using your knife for difficult tasks). Friends who use clasp-knives tell me that their favourite models are made by Buck. These are expensive, but when you really need a good knife, it is best not to economize.

Remember that large knives aren't popular with the authorities, including customs officers.

Loose-leaf notebook

Even if you don't wish to keep a diary (discussed in Chapter 8), a spiral loose-leaf notebook is useful. You may need to make occasional notes, and you may also want to pull out sheets for laundry lists, or to leave messages, give addresses, draw diagrams, etc. If you happen to be a spy, you will be able to leave messages, without anyone noticing you have torn out a sheet of paper.

If you need to use paper in wet conditions (say, plant-collecting in a rain forest), you should know that you can buy waterproof notebooks, which can be used with an ordinary pencil in all conditions, even under water. These are available from Hawkins and Manwaring, Westborough, Newark, Notts. (tel. 0400 81492). Waterproof notebooks are also sometimes sold by mail-order companies.

Presents

Enterprising travellers are the recipients of frequent hospitality. And they may also receive a number of gifts, especially as the exchange of gifts is sometimes part of a country's culture. There-fore it is often advisable for travellers to carry a stock of presents, either for giving in return, or for the many occasions when they may wish to leave behind a token of friendship. Some people think that travellers give too many presents, and I have discussed this in Chapter 12. However, I still think there are occasions when you would regret not having a present at hand.

For reasons of luggage space, several presents may have to be bought locally, but it is still a good idea to buy a selection before you leave home. Anything from your own country will have additional novelty value and give a more personal touch. One excellent small present is a paperback English phrasebook or dictionary. A friend travelling in Burma found that Burmese–English dictionaries were received with ecstasy.

A quantity of small, cheap presents is invaluable. Among the permanent kit in my shoulder bag, I always keep at least twenty postcards. A small girl once presented me with a bunch of wild flowers while I was walking in Peru; I was delighted, but cer-tainly wouldn't have wanted to insult her by giving money in return. So I gave her a postcard, and she was thrilled. Any nice postcard of Britain will do, but there is no doubt that something with human interest gives more to talk about, and therefore the best postcard is usually one of the Queen bedecked with jewel-lery. An added advantage of a postcard is that you can write a personal message on the back.

Other welcome cheap gifts include folding scissors, unusual ballpoint pens, badges, and decorated combs. A popular, slightly more expensive present is a glossy booklet of the type showing photographs of the Houses of Parliament or the Crown Jewels. Colour printing in many Third World countries remains poor, so these booklets are a novelty. Tourist shops at home are a good source of useful presents.

Remember that your silver change (50p or 10p bits) may be prized by children or coin collectors.

On certain trips you may need more expensive presents. Small electronic items or gadgets are often the most space- and weight-effective. I once gave some watches to camp staff in Tanzania. These very light Casio watches cost £6 each from Dixons, and were excellent: they were waterproof, and showed the date, time, and year. One important feature of these watches was that their batteries lasted for seven years, for in some countries, such as Tanzania, batteries are hardly available. If there are any Communist countries left by the time you read this, you will find that their citizens yearn for gadgets, because they are so expensive and rare. At the end of a Cuban trip I gave my driver a calculator (a solar-powered one because batteries were unobtainable). The calculator had cost me £5 in England; in Cuba it was worth £120. It is becoming increasingly rare that an item such as a calculator is worth much more in one country than another, but I still carry a few wafer-thin calculators because they take up so little room. And I always keep one in my shoulder bag because, apart from being a useful emergency present, it is occasionally handy for doing some sums.

In certain circumstances duty-free drink makes an especially welcome present.

Compass

Although I almost never use one, I always keep a compass tucked in my shoulder bag. A good compass can weigh as little as an ounce, and occasionally is very useful. In emergencies it could be crucial, and serious hikers of course must take one.

Although many people think of compasses only in connection with hiking, they are very useful in cities, and in Venice essential.

If you use a compass near items made of iron or steel, such as belt buckles, light meters, and so on, it will give you a false reading, and this is also true in some regions which are rich in iron ore.

Lavatory paper/pocket tissues

As I've written in the section on shoulder bags, you don't often need lavatory paper, but when you do, you need it urgently. A whole roll takes up too much space: think of that hole inside the roll. A part-used roll could be convenient (take out the cardboard middle and squash it), or unwind some paper and wrap it in clingfilm. Even more convenient are the small packets of pocket tissues: Handy Andies, for instances, are wrapped in useful resealable packs of ten.

Laundry soap

Until recently there were few towns in the Third World where you couldn't get your clothes laundered within twenty-four hours. But many hotels now require several days to do your laundry, and they charge absurdly high prices. So most people will want to take at least some soap for washing their clothes.

If you use baby shampoo for your hair, it will double up for washing clothes, and it lathers well even in cold water. If you will be doing a lot of your own washing, you might prefer some proper washing-liquid or soap. A tube of soap, such as Travel Wash, will do fine. One friend, who laundered clothes for several months in Cuba, has told me that he found Vanish the best at getting rid of stains. The smallest size of Vanish is a convenient little stick, only 2 inches high (but its top is prone to come off). A recent report by *Which?* found that Superdrug's own brand of stain-remover was even better and cheaper.

I have been told that Fairy Liquid is excellent as a soap and shampoo when you have to use sea water.

It is usually easier to buy detergents or laundry soap locally. Washing powder or liquid can be decanted into **bottles made by Nalgene**, which are strong, don't leak, have wide mouths, and come in a wide variety of different sizes.

Personally, I can't be bothered to take any laundry soap; if I can't manage to hire someone else to do my washing, I get by with ordinary soap, and keep a small stick of stain-remover to get rid of the most stubborn stains.

Nail/scrubbing brush

A largish nailbrush is very useful for washing dirty clothes, and for cleaning dried mud off shoes.

TABLE 1   THE MERITS OF TRANSPARENCY

Years of travelling have taught me the joy of any type of transparent container. They greatly reduce the amount of worried rummaging. Instead you can see at one glance what you are carrying. I use four types of transparent containers.

1. Document holder

On almost any trip one needs to take several documents, such as spare passport photographs, or camera instructions. And one usually collects more bits of paper: maps, addresses hastily written on envelopes, hotel brochures, and so on. For these a document holder is invaluable. And when you constantly need to read something, such as an itinerary, you can put it on the inside-top of your holder, and thus read it without having to get it out, and without it getting grubby. Transparent holders, complete with zip, are available at stationery shops, including W. H. Smith. The zips are not very strong and usually last for only one trip.

The likely contents of a document holder are as follows:

Passport photographs For lengthy trips through several countries it is best to carry plenty of spare passport photographs. Many types of visa, forms, and permits use up surprisingly large numbers of them. If you don't need them, they will take up minimal room, but it is sometimes a great inconvenience not to have a ready supply.

Driving licence This is a very easy item to leave behind. For this reason, I almost always keep it in my wallet in England, so that I don't forget it when I go abroad. Some countries are satisfied with your ordinary licence; others require an International Driving Licence, so you may need both. Just to confuse things, there are two different types of International Driving Licence; find out which one is appropriate, because otherwise you tend to get offered the standard one, which may be unacceptable.

Student card If you are a student, take a student card, because it often entitles you to very large discounts on plane and train tickets, museum charges, etc. An International Student Identity Card (ISIC) is available from student unions and the many offices of the Students Travel Association (Campus Travel; tel. 071 730 3402), or from NUS Services Ltd, Bleaklow House, Howard Town Mills, Mill Street, Glossop SK13 8PT (tel. 0457 868003). If you are under twenty-six but not a student, you can buy a YIEE (Youth International Educational Exchange) card. This also carries a passport-size photograph, and brings some of the same travel discounts as an ISIC. This can be obtained from Campus Travel.

Testimonial If even the smallest part of your trip has any type of official flavour, get a testimonial on the grandest-possible headed writing paper. Ideally, the document should show some impressive insignia. Time and again these testimonials have got travellers out of trouble with minor officials in remote places. Sometimes they can save you immense problems – perhaps having to make a 400-mile round trip in order to get another signature on a permit for a national park. On three occasions I have successfully used a testimonial to bluster myself on to internal flights that had previously been considered 'full'. One friend reckons that his testimonial might have saved his life when he was arrested in a wild area by some dangerous and frightening South American police.

Airmail envelopes From my own unscientific evidence I have concluded that postcards stand less chance than letters of reaching home. It may be a good idea to slip them into an airmail envelope. There is another reason for bringing these envelopes: they display the word 'Airmail' clearly printed and in an easily recognizable way. The blue airmail stickers given out in remote post offices rarely stick without glue.

Visiting cards Should you already have visiting cards, slip a few into your document holder. They are surprisingly useful and many people appreciate receiving them. I quite often find them helpful for leaving messages. If you don't have any visiting cards, and are going on the type of trip on which you need to impress people, consider getting some printed. It's no longer very expensive. If you don't want requests for help with visas, begging letters, or even surprise visits, it may be best not to print your home address on the visiting card.

In the richer parts of the Far East most social occasions are accompanied by an exchange of cards. Even in the 1930s when exploring remote parts of China, Ella Maillart found she needed visiting cards. 'A Chinese custom dating back to pre-Christian times ordains that one must present one's name-card immediately on being introduced to a person; and when setting out on a journey one has to provide oneself with hundreds of cards.'★

2. Kit/Medical/Cosmetic bag

If you can find the right type of kitbag with rows of transparent compartments, then it will be a godsend. So far they have usually been made for women's cosmetics, and therefore can sometimes be found (with some difficulty) in the appropriate departments of stores. The joy of these bags is that they keep your small items (such as medicines, penknife, safety pins, insect repellent, universal plug, tea-spoon, etc.) all firmly in place, not jangling about in the

★ *Forbidden Journey* (Heinemann, 1937)

Fig. 3 Kitbag.

bottom of a bag. And they can all be spotted at a glance. The bags are equipped with a hanger, which can be used on any available hook or nail. A good example of this type of bag can be ordered from Home Way, The White House, Littleton, Winchester, Hants. SO22 6QS (tel. 0962 881051), and I hope that Nomad will be stocking some as well.

3. Sponge-bag

Transparent ones are at present available from the Body Shop, and are very cheap. I also use one of these transparent wash-bags to hold all my spare camera kit (lens hoods, batteries, lens cloths, etc.). A sponge-bag should, of course, have some type of strap, so that it can be hung from hooks or nails when there is no available surface.

Sponge-bag contents Most sponge-bags will include **toothbrush**, **toothpaste**, **soap**, and **shampoo.** Plastic toothpaste tubes are less likely to leak than metal ones. Shampoo shouldn't, of course, be in glass bottles, which are too heavy and breakable. The most practical type of shampoo is the thick variety that comes in tubes.

From a column of tips by Moyra Bremner I learnt an excellent way of preventing plastic bottles from leaking: take the top off, squeeze the bottle, and then, while it is still squeezed, replace the top. It is also important to exclude air before ascending to high altitudes.

Some varieties of soap are much more likely to become mushy than others. The transparent ones, such as Pears, tend to be longer-lasting. Cheap (often locally bought) soaps tend to be softer than expensive ones. A **soap holder** should have drainage holes to lessen the chances of the soap becoming mushy.

4. Film canisters

I mention in the later section on matches that film canisters are tough, waterproof, and even resist humidity. A few varieties of film canisters are transparent, and I treasure these for keeping various odds and ends, such as pills which have been decanted from larger glass bottles.

Clothes-line

For those who frequently do their own washing, a reader has sent in the following hint. You can make up a clothes-line from two long lengths of hat-elastic twisted together with hooks at each end. This takes up minimal space, and you won't need pegs because the clothes are held fast in the twisted elastic.

Another reader wrote to say that she had used dental floss (see Chapter 5) for this purpose.

Another reader wrote to say that all this was quite unnecessary, because commercial traveller's clothes-lines, which also don't need pegs, are now widely available at camping and airport shops.

These same shops often sell hooks which are supposed to attach to walls by suction. I have found them entirely unreliable.

Alarm clock

Occasionally it is vital to wake up early for a bus, train, or plane. Hotel staff are not to be relied on, and as modern alarm clocks can be extremely slim and light, it is well worth packing one. Some people can rely on being woken by the alarm of a watch, but this is rarely loud enough for me.

Shaving equipment

Intrepid travellers don't rely on electric shavers, because they often travel in areas without electricity. It is best either to grow a beard or to get used to wet shaving.

Some people who are travelling continually in humid rain forests have to grow a beard, because their shaving-cuts infect immediately.

I take a **hand razor,** a high-quality **shaving brush** and enough blades to last for the length of the trip. Canisters of shaving foam, though convenient, don't justify the space they take up. Few people realize that you don't even need special shaving soap. An ordinary cake of soap will last for a very long time; choose a good soap that won't dry your skin. I find that

Roger & Gallet soap is non-drying and lasts for months. Sometimes it is sold in convenient little plastic holders.

Even fewer people realize that you can shave adequately without any type of foam, cream, or soap. For a whole year I shaved with only water, even though my beard grows very strongly. The secret is to soak your stubble for as long as possible before shaving. I first wet the stubble, and then conduct some other task, such as cleaning my teeth. When you have to shave in cold water, you must soak your beard for longer than you would with hot water.

A mirror is quite unnecessary for shaving. You soon get used to checking for blemishes with your hands.

Foil-wrapped wet tissues

If you are stuck in a bus and have just eaten a mango, or if the child next to you has been sick on your leg, you will be grateful for a foil-wrapped tissue. A few of these are a worthwhile luxury. The best I've used were the larger ones dispensed free by Air France. It is best to find a brand which isn't stickily impregnated with scent. You can buy Baby Wipes (for baby's bottoms), which are wrapped in foil, and even in the tropics will remain wet for months. As I've mentioned, in Chapter 5, I use antiseptic wipes instead, which is extravagant but saves space. In dire emergency they are also helpful as lavatory paper.

Universal wash-plug

In the developing world plugs are rarely found except in the most expensive hotels. And in the Muslim world they are often not used at all because Muslims are obliged to wash in running water. A universal wash-plug, which is a rubber plug fitting any plug hole by suction, is indispensable. It takes up very little room in your kitbag, and this is more than justified when you want to wash clothes in a basin, or want to take a bath, or when there is a water shortage. If you are a contact-lens wearer, it prevents lenses being washed down the plug hole. The universal wash-plug is also useful in European hotels where plugs frequently don't fit properly, and I have found it useful even in New York's celebrated Sherry Netherlands Hotel.

Tampons and sanitary towels

I have mentioned in Chapter 5 that in the developing world tampons are frequently not available, and often are of inferior quality. So take as many as you can. Sanitary towels are more likely to be available, but even they may be of poor quality. Remember that, as described later, your periods may be more erratic and severe than at home. If you stop getting regular periods (see Chapter 5), then your tampons will make welcome presents.

Some people carry their tampons in tins, as once the packet is opened, they get bashed about.

Look after your tampons: a friend of mine lost hers when rats tore them open during the night – apparently they make a good lining for nests. Those left by the rats may be ripped open by customs officials, who believe they are a favourite hiding-place for drugs.

Nappy pins

Safety pins are useful; but nappy pins are even better. They are larger and stronger, and they are made with a safety clasp which stops them springing open.

Sewing kit

A sewing kit takes up minimal room. The needles are also useful for digging out thorns, etc. Consider taking a needle with a large enough eye to take dental floss, which is useful for emergency repairs.

Earplugs

Although they are an entirely unnecessary piece of equipment, I always travel with earplugs. I then know that in the noisiest room I stand a chance of getting some sleep. In much of the world, noise is considered a boon and you may be obliged to sleep against the background of a television, juke box and tape recorder all turned up to full volume.

The most effective earplugs are the malleable wax ones (quite widely available, including at Boots); but some people prefer the washable sponge ones.

All earplugs take some getting used to, but it is worth persevering if noise stops you sleeping.

Teaspoon

A teaspoon takes up minimal room and is useful for snacks either during journeys or in a hotel room. Melons, yoghurt, mangoes, etc. are all easier to eat with a spoon. If you are equipped with a penknife as well as a spoon, you can eat almost anything.

Tea-infuser

If you are going to be making your own tea, and only leaf-tea is available, a tea-infuser would be useful.

Snacks

It is well worth carrying some snacks for emergencies, even if you are not going off into the wilds. There are many occasions when they are useful: you may arrive in a town too late to buy food; you may be stuck in a place where the only restaurant is absurdly expensive; you may be stranded at an airport without facilities; or your bus may break down miles from the nearest food-store.

On the whole I think it best to avoid many of the expensive concoctions sold in camping shops. I know that Kendal mint-cake is famous as an emergency food, but I find it thirst-making and heavy, and it doesn't contain useful nutrients. It is usually better to buy snack bars from healthstores; I usually find that about two of these keep hunger at bay. Look for those which are filled with dates (which have plenty of sugar for energy), raisins, sultanas, and especially nuts, which are rich in energy-producing fats.

One or two people have written to me recommending vacuum-packed cheese, which they claim doesn't go off in tropical heat. I tested some packets by leaving them in the boiling heat of my little car during an English summer; they were still edible by autumn. A friend has recommended the small round cheeses with thick rinds. I haven't yet been able to test these.

Some dried fruits are particularly helpful, and I find dried figs and stoned dates especially filling. In some parts of the world people practically survive off dates. Sainsbury's sell good-value packets of these, as well as dried peaches, apricots, and pears; the Sainsbury packets retain moisture until opened, so the fruits remain delicious. But on the whole it would be best to concentrate on fruits that have traditionally dried well, such as figs and apricots. I sometimes also take a few thin, foil-wrapped sticks of salami-style preparations.

Candles

Should you end up in a hut where there is no kerosene lamp, you won't want to waste precious batteries, so a candle will be helpful.

An ordinary candle is useless: it breaks too easily inside your luggage, and it won't stand unsupported. You must buy the flat, squat, 'everlasting' candles, which are available in most camping shops. They are almost unbreakable. A $4\frac{1}{2}$-inch-high 'everlasting' candle burns for about nine hours.

Some mail-order firms sell an even fatter $3\frac{1}{2}$-inch-high candle, which they claim burns for about twenty-four hours. In my experience they last only about fourteen hours; but this is still quite a long time. In a good camping shop you should be able to find short tub candles which sit in their own metal cup (and thus use up all their wax).

Matches

An ordinary box of matches is of little use to travellers. When subjected to rough treatment, it falls to pieces; and should the matches become wet they are ruined. If you are going into the wilds, a guaranteed flame is essential.

Waterproof boxes of matches are sold by some camping shops and mail-order companies, but as they can also fall to pieces, I prefer to use an idea learnt from Robin Hunter's *Outdoor Companion*.* You put matches inside one of the film canisters manufactured by Kodak, and glue striking material on the inside of the lid.

* (Constable, 1979)

Even though the waterproof/lifeboat matches sold by camping shops are in more sturdy containers, they are often useless in humid conditions. I have had several bad reports. One correspondent wrote to me: 'We used those waterproof matches in caves in Madagascar, where there is 100 per cent humidity much of the time; we failed to get a single one lit, which almost caused a serious accident.' Disposable cigarette lighters will often be more reliable, and they double up as handy presents.

Heliograph and whistle

If you ever have to walk alone through difficult or dangerous territory, consider taking a heliograph and a whistle. A heliograph is a thin, small, two-sided mirror with a small hole, which can accurately flash signals over many miles, and even up to aircraft. (Recently a stranded hiker in the Himalayas was missed by a searching helicopter which was very close. He was lucky that this wasn't a final search, in which case he would have died. I suspect that with a tiny heliograph he might have had a chance of alerting the helicopter.)

Survival manuals always advise their readers to take a whistle. The internationally recognized distress signal on a whistle is six blasts in a minute, then another six blasts; but I'm not sure that an Afridi highlander will recognize this as an international distress signal.

One of the dangers of walking alone is that the slightest accident (for instance, a broken ankle) could immobilize you, and ultimately cause your death. A heliograph or a whistle could conceivably be life-saving.

Rubber door-wedge

I wouldn't take a wedge myself, but I mention it because a few travellers do take them. They are useful in cheap hotels, when you can't lock the door from the inside (the hotel may use a padlock system); sleeping friends have been robbed by thieves brazenly entering through the bedroom door. Women at risk from harassment may also find the wedge useful.

Padlock or combination lock

I have never taken a padlock, but include it in this list because so many people claim they are useful – especially for travellers who don't trust the management of their cheap hotels.

Some people like to take a **combination lock.** It can, among other purposes, be used for tying your suitcase to your bed, or to the legs of a bus or train seat. If you use your birthday or address as the number on your combination lock, it is easily worked out by officials or hotel staff, who have access to your passport or other documents. What about your best friend's telephone number? Delsey make a very small, trim, light combination lock, and I do take one of these as it is occasionally useful. No combination lock is, of course, going to stop the determined thief, but there are times when you want to deter a petty pilferer.

Address book

You may wish to take your address book, but you are foolish if you don't leave a duplicate at home. You can now get mini-computers (sometimes called 'organizers'), hardly larger than a calculator, which can carry all your addresses, and function both as a diary and a calculator. As this would be a good trophy for thieves, you would be mad not to have all the information also stored at home.

Pocket games and a pack of cards

Some people, especially when travelling with companions, like to take pocket games or a pack of cards. There may be long evenings under dim lamps, when reading can be a strain; and sometimes during long boat or train journeys it is difficult to concentrate on a book. Pocket Scrabble, backgammon and chess are all good for these moments, and there are few parts of the world where you can't find somebody to play cards with.

Watch

One of the great joys of the modern era is that watches are no longer a hostage to fortune. For just a few pounds one can buy a watch that is cheap, tough, and waterproof.

Leather straps are no use because they will rot. The popular self-fastening metal strap isn't good either: it tends to be uncomfortable in the heat, and when you are walking through undergrowth, the clasp can be flicked open. I prefer the resin straps, which feel a bit like rubber; they are both soft and tough (though by no means everlasting). These straps are equipped with the traditional and secure buckling system. For use in gruelling conditions, your watch should probably be described as water-resistant to a depth of 100 metres.

My very cheap Casio watch gives the date of the month and day of the week. I find both of these functions useful. When travelling, it is easy to lose track of the day of the week, and it is sometimes important to know when it is Saturday or Sunday. This is also useful when you are taking weekly malaria pills.

Sun-cream

You shouldn't rely on sun-cream as your only protection, but it may be necessary for fair-skinned travellers, and is almost essential if you are spending much time by or in the sea. Most creams are now graded by different 'protection factors'; thus if the cream is advertised as having protection factor '8', it theoretically enables you to stay in the sun eight times as long as you would without it. However, these measurements are very imprecise, and should only be treated as an approximate guide.

The protection factor you choose should obviously be judged by the fairness of your skin; I prefer to buy a cream with only a moderate protection factor so that my skin gets brown relatively early, and I can then forget about using creams.

The 'protection factor' only covers UVB rays, the ones that cause burning and skin cancer. A recent *Which?* report suggests that you should read the label to see if the protection also covers UVA rays, which may also be a cause of skin cancer and premature ageing. Skin cancer is rapidly on the increase, and this is another reason to take a sun-cream (see Chapter 5).

If you are swimming, windsurfing, or snorkelling, take a sun-cream that is water-resistant. The water will wash some of the cream off, but at least you will be left with a measure of protection.

Sunglasses

I sometimes wonder whether we are too quick to use sunglasses. For several thousand years our ancestors managed quite well without them, and they have come into use only within the last few decades. Some people think they need sunglasses because they wince when they first go into the sun. But in fact our eyes take about two minutes to adapt to bright light, so it may be best to wait a little. The eyes take much longer to adapt to the dark – about forty-five minutes.

On the other hand, our ancestors didn't travel within twenty-four hours from a British winter to the Kenyan sunlight; and it now seems very likely that UV light may be damaging for the eyes. It also appears to be true that the ozone layer has been depleted, and is therefore letting through more UV rays. (The EC Environment Minister has estimated that a 10 per cent reduction in the ozone layer would cause more than $1\frac{1}{2}$ million extra eye cataracts a year.) So, although it is important not to exaggerate the dangers, anyone who will be spending long periods of time in strong sunlight should certainly consider wearing sunglasses – especially as the damaging effect of UV rays is believed to be cumulative. It also seems to me there is quite a lot of anecdotal evidence that Westerners who have spent many years in bright sunlight appear to suffer more from eye problems in old age. To sum up: don't think that sunglasses are obligatory just because you are going to the tropics, but if you will be spending a lot of time actually outside in the sun (or if you like reading out of doors), then strongly consider buying a good pair. Sunglasses may also be medically important at high altitudes, above approximately 10,000 feet, where there are more UV rays. Sunglasses may also be essential when you are trekking through snow, as the reflected glare and UV rays may cause great pain and incapacitating blindness.

In parts of the world where women are likely to be harassed, dark glasses are invaluable, as they prevent eye contact. They can also enable men to glance at women without being considered obnoxious.

Buying sunglasses isn't straightforward, especially as attractive design is no guarantee of protection against harmful rays. Unfortunately most articles about sunglasses are so filled with conflicting advice or incomprehensible jargon that my file of cuttings made me no wiser. So I contacted Jack Davey of City University and Janet Silver, principal optometrist at Moorfield Eye Hospital, both of whom have been very generous with advice. Here are some of the useful points that they explained to me.

The darkness of lenses gives no indication of their effectiveness in reducing harmful UV rays. A clear lens might eliminate them all; a dark lens might not do so well.

Janet Silver recommends that the glasses should have brownish rather than bluish lenses, as these may be more effective against near-UV rays.

It is probably best to buy your sunglasses in Britain, because there is now a very useful British Standard (BS 2724/1987). Any sunglasses labelled with the British Standard label will give you sufficient protection against damaging UV rays. There is no need to spend a lot of money on sunglasses: when I last looked at the wide range in Boots, the average price was approximately £11, and yet all their sunglasses are tested for compliance with the British Standard.

The description 'safety lenses' may not be a guarantee of protection against UV rays, and may not even mean that the glasses are unshatterable. All glasses with the British Standard label give some measure of mechanical protection. If you want the strongest, look for the words 'impact resistant'.

Polarizing lenses are the only ones to cut down on *reflected* glare from such surfaces as car bonnets, roads, sand, and water. 'Polaroid' is a trade name, but all lenses made by polaroid aren't necessarily polarizing.

Some people like photochromatic lenses, which have greatly

improved in recent years. In bright sun they become dark, and indoors they become clear. Some models work faster than others. If they carry the British Standard tag, you can be sure that they also protect against UV light.

Spare pair of glasses

If you do wear glasses, you should take a spare pair. It is also a good idea to jot down on your security chart (Fig. 2, Chapter l) their prescription and the address of your optician. Before long trips I warn my optician that I may send a telegram asking him to send me a pair.

Some insurance companies report that loss of spectacles is the commonest claim on travel insurance policies. The spectacles have usually been left on a plane; often they fall off a dozing passenger, and then slip between the chairs.

Contact lenses

Remember that if you wear hard contact lenses, dust can make your life miserable. It could be best to leave them behind. And remember also that there is often a lot of dust even in unexpected places such as Burma. When watching wildlife, though, I prefer to risk the dust because binoculars are no pleasure to use when you are wearing glasses.

For some years I have been wearing the new disposable type of soft lens, which gets thrown away once a week. With these I assume there must be less chance of infection, and I find them suitable for travel for another reason; I now swim, snorkel, and windsurf in them, confident in the knowledge that if I lose them, there is always another pair waiting.

Wedding ring

Some women like to travel with a wedding ring, even if they are not married. However, in most of the developing world it isn't necessarily recognized as a sign of marriage, and in some thief-ridden places you may not want to wear even a simple ring. Your hands are prone to swell in the tropics, therefore consider abandoning the ring if it is tight.

Short-wave radio

A radio is a luxury, but for some people it is more important than any of the others. A television crew who were stuck for several weeks in southern Sudan told me they considered it a lifeline to sanity. Sports addicts can't do without one.

I never used to travel with a radio, considering it another bit of Western clutter, another gadget to get lost or stolen. And I travelled to get away from home, not to hear news of it. However, I now do sometimes take one. In the first place, they have become much lighter, smaller, and cheaper. Second, I had an experience on one trip when I bitterly regretted not having one. I was in the southern part of China during the disturbed period before the Tiananmen Square massacre. Of course, no news was available through the state channels, and my translator was furious that I didn't have a short-wave radio for finding out what was happening. Everywhere the Chinese were desperate to listen to the BBC External Services. That trip made me realize that if one is ever in a trouble spot, a few square inches of radio could be a lifeline to crucial information.

If you do take a radio, it must be a short-wave model. However, listening to one of these is quite different from listening to a radio at home: with a short-wave radio, you are obliged to change frequencies according to the time of day. Reception tends to be best after sunset, and can often be improved by moving the radio closer to a window (though even this may not be effective in any large building with a steel structure, where reception is likely to be poor). Great improvements can often be made by attaching a length of wire (somewhere between 3 and 6 feet should be sufficient) to the end of the antenna, and hanging it out of a window. Any thin, insulated copper wire should do the trick. You can also buy a gadget which holds a coil for attaching to the antenna.

To find out which are the correct frequencies at the different times of day, you can get free regional pamphlets (which include programme guides) from the World Service Shop (Bush House,

Strand, London, WC2B 4PH; tel. 071 257 2576/mail-order tel. 071 257 2575), or you can buy the BBC World Service 'Key Frequencies' sliding chart (99p at present). *London Calling* lists programmes and frequencies, and is now included within a widely available new BBC magazine, *Worldwide*.

All the best short-wave radios that I recommended in previous editions were made by Sony. Their radios have been getting much cheaper, and the latest model is wonderfully small, hardly larger than a cigarette packet. The main choice now is between a digital and a manual model. The great advantage of digital ones is that you can pre-set all the many different frequencies that you may need, but they are far more expensive and use up more batteries. In very humid conditions the display may not work, though the radio will keep functioning.

Although the Sony radios are sold without strong cases, I have never heard of one being smashed, even during rough trips. Some models have a dreadful flaw, though – they are made without a safety lock, and are therefore likely to get switched on while packed in your bag.

The World Service Shop sell a small but excellent selection of short-wave radios, and their staff can give you knowledgeable advice.

Be sure to buy a headphone or earpiece if you are going to be listening to the radio in public places or thin-walled hotel rooms.

The BBC External Services (which include the World Service) are among the few British institutions that continue to be re-spected throughout the world. At the slightest hint of a cutback, write a letter of protest to the Foreign Secretary – the External Services are funded by the Foreign Office.

Light bulb

On my first evening in Cuba I had dinner with a friend who had just spent three weeks there. She handed me a light bulb, claiming that it was one of the best presents I would ever get. She was correct. Every evening I unscrewed the miserable, dim light bulb in my hotel room, and replaced it with the 150 watt one. This cheered up the rooms no end, and, more important, enabled me to read.

Before then I had never thought of carrying a light bulb with me, partly because they seemed so breakable. But since then I've taken one on several trips, and always found it a joy. And so far none of them has smashed.

Obviously you don't buy the light bulb in England; you get a local one which you know will fit.

Money-belt

As nylon is too hot, money-belts should be made of cotton. Their use is discussed in Chapter 10, and I explain in that chapter how I prefer to keep emergency money supplies hidden either in a special trouser-belt or in a Tubigrip.

Insect powder

Those staying in simple conditions may find a small quantity of insect powder useful in case of problems with bedbugs, body lice, or head lice. When aware that infestation would be likely, I have taken one of the powders sold for use on pets, such as Bob Martin's Pestroy. I decant them into a smaller container. All insect powders are to some extent toxic, so you should avoid inhaling them.

When you use a powder for any type of body louse, reapply after a few days – the original application won't have killed any eggs.

As so many tropical households are plagued with cockroaches that are apparently indestructible, here is a tip from a book of hints published in New York (where they really know about cockroaches):

A one-pound can of Boric acid (also known as Boracic Acid) can effectively keep a house cockroach-free for a year. It will not kill roaches as rapidly as some pesticides, but it has by far the longest-lasting effect. (If they don't pick up a toxic dose of other pesticides in their first contact, they learn to steer clear. Boric acid will not repel roaches, so they keep going back into it over and over until they die.) Simply sprinkle it in cracks, crevices, under sinks and in other dark places. To rid them immediately, spray with a pesticide, and after a few days use the Boric acid method.*

In the last edition I asked readers to report on the efficacy of this advice, and one wrote to say that it had worked.

By the time you are reading this, the traditional insect powders may have been replaced by a permethrin formula (see Mosquitoes, Chapter 6). Permethrin is believed to be very safe, and my latest reports (unconfirmed) indicate that it may work even against cockroaches. It sounds too good to be true.

Fishing tackle

It may amuse you to take the bare essentials of fishing tackle – some nylon lines, a few hooks, weights, and perhaps a couple of floats. In many places you can't buy fishing equipment, but if you have this bare minimum of tackle, you will at least have a chance if there are fish to be caught. The tackle makes a marvellous present when you have finished with it.

If you are going on intrepid walking trips, these few essentials could bring you nutritious and fresh food. If you are short of bait, don't be frightened of experimenting: I have known tropical catfish to be caught with pieces of soap.

Keener fishermen may be interested to know that they can now buy collapsible and very light fibreglass rods; if you are a fly-fisherman, Hardy's of London make an excellent rod (the 'Smuggler') that divides into seven or eight sections of 15 inches, and fits in a suitcase.

Snorkel

Snorkelling is one of the greatest pleasures of the tropics (more details in Chapter 8) and, although a snorkel is quite bulky, you should strongly consider taking one when you are going anywhere near tropical reefs.

Often snorkels can't be found on the spot; and if you do find one it is usually uncomfortable, prone to leaking (which takes all the pleasure away), and expensive to hire. Properly speaking, the

* *Best of Helpful Hints,* Mary Ellen (Warner, 1979)

word 'snorkel' is just the breathing tube. You will need to take a face-mask as well. In recent years face-masks have been manufactured in silicone, which has greatly improved them. My most recent mask is exactly half the weight of my old rubber one. There are other advantages to silicone: it lasts longer than rubber and, because it can be made transparent, more light enters the face-mask.

When buying the mask, push it on your face without using the strap, and breathe in through the nose. If it is going to be a good fit, it should stay there unsupported.

Make sure that the straps can be very easily adjusted. Masks usually become looser in the water, and easy adjusting is essential.

Flippers

Flippers are cumbersome and, unless you are very keen, they are unlikely to justify their space or weight.

Space blankets

All camping shops seem to stock a variety of space blankets; some are thin metal 'survival' blankets, others are thicker. When I first travelled I used to take them, but never found them much good. The thin ones often tore before I needed them, and I found that even the thicker ones weren't indestructible. I have also heard of several instances when travellers have unwrapped their emergency blankets only to find that they had disintegrated after long periods of storage.

Survival blankets do have a few fans, though. One lady wrote to say that she had found hers useful when hiking in Lapland, as it had kept her and her rucksack dry during showers. And they are certainly useful for one purpose: reflecting the sun's heat. As the shiny side is an efficient reflector of UV, a survival blanket is indispensable as a sunshade in desert conditions. It could, for instance, be useful for reflecting the sun on top of a tent, provided that there is no wind. One correspondent reported that his blanket has been useful for covering ice boxes at picnics.

Labels on the packaging of space blankets sometimes tell you that they reflect over 90 per cent of body heat lost by radiation. This sounds good, but body heat is lost by many methods, and radiation loss amounts to only 10 per cent of the total. The Royal Aircraft establishment in Farnborough once made a study of 'space blankets' and concluded that a metallized plastic film didn't do anything more in terms of performance than a plain plastic sheeting or coated nylon fabric. They also pointed out that in a survival situation it wouldn't be much use: being a blanket, it needs tucking in all round to stop the thing from blowing away, and thus invites you to lie down at full length, causing body heat to be speedily leached into the ground. If you are likely to be stranded in extreme cold, take a **survival bag.**

Nor are space blankets good for covering your sleeping bag at night. Your body sweat condenses under them, and then drips down on to your bag. You would probably be better off with a Gore-Tex **bivouac bag.**

Neck-pillow

If you don't get the window seat on a train, bus, or plane, falling asleep can be uncomfortable: when nodding off, your head suddenly lolls uncomfortably to one side. In recent years blow-up neck-pillows have been widely marketed, and can be found in big stores or airport shops. With one of these you can sleep comfortably on any transport. They take up very little room and are a great boon. A common trade name for one is the 'Sleepover'.

Pillows

There is hardly a comfortable down or down-and-feather pillow in the whole of the tropical world. Until I got used to using a towel (see page 62), my main luxury was a small (10 × 15 inches) down-and-feather pillow. It was an extravagant use of space, but with it I knew I could sleep comfortably anywhere.

If you do take a small pillow, ensure that it's a suitable mixture of feather-and-down. Pure down compacts too well for the purposes of a small pillow, and is much more expensive. Pure feather is too bulky and less comfortable. Buy two pillowcases.

You can keep them both on the pillow, and when one is being washed the other keeps the pillow clean. An alternative is to stuff your spare clothes into a clean pillowcase.

Nylon pack-away bag

These can be invaluable for day-trips: for instance, going to the beach. The small package unzips to make a fairly capacious bag with a shoulder strap. Another variety (weighing only 3 ounces) is marketed in airport and luggage shops, and it unfolds to make a small day-rucksack. These pack-away bags are also invaluable when you have to carry wet, smelly, muddy, or sandy clothes (which in my case is quite often). And when you don't have a shoulder bag, they will suffice as a substitute.

Plastic bags

If you don't have a pack-away bag (see above), a plastic bag or two may be useful when travelling with wet clothes. They also serve a variety of other purposes, including protecting a camera against dust. In Chapter 12 I describe how useful they are for packing the items in a backpack. Many modern plastic bags (often made of the same material as bin liners) are strong, thin, and take up little room. Bring a few wire twists for sealing them. If you want something stronger and thicker, heavy-duty garden sacks are now widely available.

Condoms

Because of the risk of HIV, these are best bought at home, as foreign ones may not be tough enough. And in parts of the world they may not be large enough; in Japan, for instance, the standard size of condoms is 2 cm shorter than ours.

Binoculars

If you are planning on looking at wildlife, you must take binoculars. Don't count on sharing. The moments of drama tend to be very brief, and it is agony when someone else is holding the binoculars.

All binoculars carry two numbers – for instance, 7×50 or 8×30. The first number describes how many times the image is magnified, the second is the diameter of the front lens in millimetres. Higher magnification gives you a larger image, but brings certain disadvantages: there will be more wobble; it will be harder to pick up an object, harder to focus on it, and harder to keep it in view. A large front lens carries more light than a small one, but it increases the weight of the binoculars. Friends who are serious bird-watchers assure me that the current prince of binoculars is the Leitz 10×40. They are also very expensive. There are plenty of perfectly good binoculars at far cheaper prices. Apparently several makes are developing a synchronizing system to eliminate problems caused by the inevitable drops and bangs.

If you are not going serious game- or bird-watching, be aware that there are now some marvellous miniature binoculars. Zeiss and Leitz both make excellent models. I have often used these, but always revert to larger ones for safaris.

Travel adaptor

Travellers who insist on travelling with electrical kit should take an international travel adaptor. They are now sold in the luggage departments of most stores, as well as in camping shops and at airports. Different voltages around the world can be looked up in manuals such as *The ABC Guide to International Travel* (see Appendix 1). Be aware, though, that not all countries are standardized; and in Indonesia two different voltages are found even within one island (Sulawesi).

String or parachute cord

If you are trekking or camping, parachute cord (which is available in any good camping or mountaineering shop) will be more practical than string. It is very strong, and it will take a long time to rot. Expeditions should definitely take some.

Elastic bands

Elastic bands may remain unused for several trips in a row, but they take up minimal room, and can be helpful. I have used them to hold plastic bags together, and to grip a roll of Elastoplast which had lost its packet. They are useful for unjamming photographic filters (see Chapter 9). On a Bolivian trip elastic bands were useful for sorting into equal bundles the vast piles of banknotes needed for any transaction in that inflation-ridden country.

Spare shoe laces

Modern laces are stronger than they used to be. But if your laces are crucial, bring a spare pair, because Third World ones still tend to be unreliable.

Portable coil-immersion heaters

I have never carried one myself, and never would. But as so many readers have written to recommend them, and as they are often sold in camping shops, I am giving them a mention. The idea is that you can make yourself hot drinks in your hotel room. Be cautious, though, and buy only the most reputable make. A recent *Which?* report considered some of them to be potentially dangerous. The report says that all these heaters should have an automatic thermal cutout. Some of the heaters reviewed by *Which?* took more than fifteen minutes to bring just one cupful of water to the boil.

The heaters can, however, be invaluable when travelling with children.

Mosquito nets

For certain types of trip you will need a mosquito net, and now that malaria is getting so dangerous, a net might be very important if you are going off the beaten track. If you are camping in a dry zone, a net may also help keep out scorpions. It is sometimes a difficult decision whether to buy your net before you leave, or wait till you are nearer your destination. Because nets are bulky, it is often easier to buy them after you have arrived; but try to ascertain if you will find exactly what you want at your destination.

As with so much equipment, attention to detail is important. Some nets are bulkier than others; some are so fine they don't let through a breath of air; and many of them aren't large enough. Why is it that manufacturers make almost everything too small? If the net isn't large enough, then it may be difficult to tuck it in; and if it touches your body anywhere, that is the place insects will bite. Cotton nets tend to be more breathable than the synthetic ones, but they are bulkier and may rot if packed wet.

Some people prefer a type of net that needs support from only one end; you can usually find a tree, or a hook, or something, whereas support from two ends can be much rarer. (The problem with support from one end is that the net is more likely to touch your body, and where it touches your body you will be bitten.) Some experienced travellers prefer to buy a length of mosquito netting rather than a specially shaped net. They find that a length of netting rolls down to a smaller size, and that they can usually improvise some way of suspending it. It is sometimes sufficient to hang the net over a chair placed at the head of the bed. Some people like a type of mosquito net that includes a base sheet, but these are hard to find. One friend recommends a 'Mosquito Dome', which he reckons is invaluable in certain situations, as it is entirely self-supporting; but these are tricky to erect and hard to find.

Remember that you will greatly benefit from impregnating your net with long-lasting insecticide (see Chapter 6). A friend has advised me that permethrin is so effective that it enables one to use a net with a larger mesh, which is, of course, cooler. Get the latest advice about this.

In Appendix 2 I have listed some specialist suppliers of mosquito nets.

Sleeping bags

As all sleeping bags are quite bulky, it is an important decision whether or not to take one. During my own travels I have usually found a sleeping-bag liner (see below) sufficient in the tropics; but if you are sleeping outside, or hiking in cold hills or mountains, you will probably need a bag.

If you do take one, the first major question is whether it should be filled with down or an artificial filling. For many years people have been saying that synthetic fillings are about to eliminate down, and one reliable camping shop assured me that Quallofil-7 had finally overtaken it. But many others disagree. The advantages of down are as follows: it retains more warmth in proportion to its weight; it retains more warmth in proportion to its bulk; it breathes better; it is more comfortable to sleep in; and – most important for anyone hiking – it compresses into far less space, as little as half the space of an artificial bag which is equally heat-retaining. For this last reason alone, down would still be favoured by many hikers and mountaineers. One manufacturer who makes both down and synthetic bags estimates that with average use a down bag will last twelve years, but a synthetic one only four.

Does down have any disadvantages? Yes. It is far more expensive; it compresses more under the body; and, most important, it is hopeless when wet. Wet down is a useless insulator, and will take a long time to dry. For this reason, down is also no good where there is very high humidity.

Therefore, although serious hikers will probably still want to take a down bag, anyone who wants a bag just for the occasional night (perhaps sleeping on beaches or at campsites) might find that a down bag is not only a waste of money, but also less practical. A synthetic bag is easier to look after, and can easily be washed and left to dry quickly in the sun.

In *The Backpacker's Handbook* (see Appendix 1) Chris Townsend says that, despite their disadvantages, he still prefers down bags. He keeps them dry by using either a small tent or a bivouac bag (see page 100).

In the last edition I wrote that most people will want their bag lined in cotton, even though it is much heavier than nylon. In the past few years I have rarely used a sleeping bag, and I will risk deferring to Chris Townsend, who says that modern nylons feel far less cold and clammy than they did in the past; and he points out that they are quicker to dry, don't absorb sweat, and are far easier to keep clean. He says that Pertex nylon makes a particularly good shell material as it has all the properties of other nylons plus a very pleasant feel. It also spreads moisture out rapidly over its surface, thus speeding up evaporation. I still know people who prefer a cotton inner-lining, and, being comfort-loving, I suspect I would agree with them.

Some bags are sold with a breathable, waterproof outer shell, such as Gore-Tex; but as this adds to the weight and cost, Chris Townsend prefers to take a separate bivouac bag. Bags that are waterproof are also windproof.

If you do buy a down bag, make sure it is made of pure down and not 'down-and-feather'. By British law a 'down-and-feather' bag has to contain only 5l per cent down in weight, and a 'feather-and-down' bag has to contain only 15 per cent down. Neither of them is worth buying. When there are too many feathers, the sharp points cause damage to the bag and discomfort to the occupier. A 'pure' down bag must contain 85 per cent down. The very best down is goose, the next best is duck.

Although sleeping bags are expensive, you should be careful about economizing. If you buy a well-known brand you usually get what you pay for; and amateurs are unable to judge for themselves the vital characteristics of a good bag – even with pure down there are different grades of quality. The stitching and 'baffling' of a bag are also most important. If they aren't of a high standard, the down will be erratically dispersed, with result-ing loss of heat. The technology of sleeping bags is so complicated that it is best to find an intelligent shop assistant and discuss the problems you will be facing, especially as manufacturers' temperature-ratings are usually unreliable.

If the bag has a zip, which it probably will, check that it doesn't snag too easily with its 'baffles' (necessary to stop heat leaking out). Check also that the zip is of the length you require; in the tropics a long zip is essential. Many people like it to cover the full length and base of the bag, which can then be conveniently turned into a warm blanket.

If you are going into a cold area, make sure the bag has a hood (and that it is easily adjustable). Remember what I have said about manufacturers making everything too small: if possible, get into the bag while still dressed, and see if it is comfortable, as in cold conditions you may want to sleep in your clothes.

Travellers in the tropics probably err on the side of buying a bag that is unnecessarily hot; if you are prepared to sleep occasionally in a track suit or other clothes, you may be able to take a sleeping bag that is lighter, cheaper, and less bulky.

Down bags shouldn't be folded into their carrying sacks, but stuffed randomly. One usually rolls or folds up a bag in the same way each time; this continually stretches the same parts of the bag, which will eventually leak or even tear.

Even when choosing a **stuff-bag**, it is worth paying attention to detail. Make sure it is waterproof. Many aren't. And try to buy one with a lacing system, as it is remarkable how the lacing can squeeze the bag into a smaller bundle.

When you are storing any bag, whether down or synthetic, it is important you don't leave it tightly compressed in the sack; hang it out and let it swell to its full dimensions.

Getting a down bag cleaned is a fearful problem, and you may do best by approaching a specialist, such as W. E. Franklin (see Appendix 2). One friend disagrees about the problem: 'I don't think this is so. A cool wash in a launderette-size washing machine has always been fine for me, and tumble dry – but not with every type of lining. It is OK with cotton.'

If you want to know more about sleeping bags, I recommend Chris Townsend's *The Backpacker's Handbook,* which has ten large, detailed pages on that subject.

Insulation mat

Novices never realize the extent to which the ground can leach heat away from the body. No sleeping bags, least of all down, give sufficient protection, and you will nearly always benefit by the use of an insulation mat.

Seven years ago I recommended a Therm-a-Rest, and have heard nothing to make me change my mind. It is a self-inflating, foam-filled, nylon-covered mattress (less bulky but heavier than the familiar Karrimat). Therm-a-Rest mats are expensive, but probably not in proportion to the time they last. They are extremely tough, comfortable, and convenient. Even when you are not using sleeping bags, a sleeping mat may be useful – for instance, if you have to spend night after night on the floor of simple houses. Until you become used to sleeping without a bed, your hips can get very sore.

Both Therm-a-Rest and other mats can be bought three-quarter length or full length. If you buy a Therm-a-Rest, store it unrolled, with the valve open so that the humidity from your breath can be dissipated.

Sleeping-bag liners

Many people, like myself, find bag liners uncomfortable because they get tangled up inside the sleeping bag. And maybe with new generations of lining material for sleeping bags, they are less necessary. Some people avoid the problem of tangling by sewing tabs into their sleeping bags; bag liners can then be attached to these tags.

Although I don't use liners inside sleeping bags, I often take a sleeping-bag liner on certain types of trip: they are practical in hot weather, when you just want something light to cover your body, or when you need some protection from insects. They are also a boon when hotel sheets are dirty.

Novice travellers may think that a bag liner is just a bag liner, and buy the first one they see; however, as with most items of equipment, it is well worth choosing carefully. The most important difference in bag liners lies in the material. Some people economize by making them out of old bed-sheets; but be careful, because a liner thus made tends to be bulkier and heavier than one made with the finest cotton. Even in a camping shop I've noticed a 30 per cent weight difference between an 'Egyptian cotton' and a 'calico cotton' bag liner.

Most liners sold in camping shops are about 6 feet long. This may seem enough, but personally I find that it is not enough to leave room for tucking the sheet round one's neck against insects or cold. I usually add about another 16 inches.

Bivouac bags and micro-weight tents

A bivouac bag can be useful for emergencies when you need to sleep out of doors. It will be your saving if you have to use a down sleeping bag in the rain. It may also be useful even in a tent, because it can add an extra layer of warmth to your sleeping bag. Unless your bivvy bag is made of a breathable material such as Gore-Tex or Sympatex, it will cause uncomfortable condensation on the inside. As bivouac bags aren't much use for sleeping out night after night, expensive ones tend to be a waste of money. One experienced reader wrote to me: 'Sophisticated bivouac bags are a waste of time. For a little more money, no extra space, and almost the same weight, you can buy micro-weight tents, which are a lot more comfortable and practical. Bivvy bags are for emergency only and should be light and simple.'

But another experienced reader writes:

Micro-weight tents are an even bigger waste of money. If it doesn't rain you will not require a tent, though you may require a mosquito net. If it does rain then a bivy tent is no better or more comfortable than a bivy bag with a short tentpole at the head end. If you expect wet conditions a larger tent is necessary, so that you don't touch its sides. In a regularly damp climate Gore-Tex bivy bags are useful, but for emergency use. All the mountain rescue teams now just use a 6-foot plastic bag.

Some ponchos (see below) double-up as emergency bivouac bags.

Hammocks

The overwhelming majority of travellers never use hammocks. However, they can be very practical in jungles and forests, and in parts of tropical South America they are almost universally used – in every campsite, dosshouse, home, and guesthouse.

Sleeping in a hammock is cool – a great advantage in the tropics, whether in the jungle or in a guesthouse. And in grubby huts, a hammock may enable you to escape bedbugs and smelly blankets. For a river trip, too, a hammock is almost essential. It is easy to carry, being smaller than a sleeping bag, and weighing just a few ounces.

The disadvantages of a hammock are that it very rarely has a built-in mosquito net, so you need a large net that has to be tied underneath; if there is danger of rain, you will need some type of shelter, which also has to be very large.

If you are going to South America it is probably more practical to buy your hammock there, but be aware that many of them are too flimsy. The part of the hammock that usually fails is at the end, where the ropes are looped through the hammock material. Check that this is well stitched and reinforced, and that the rope looks strong.

Mail-order companies in Europe sometimes sell hammocks that squeeze down to the size of a fist. Friends tell me that they are too small to be comfortable.

Sleeping in a hammock can be very comfortable, but you first need instruction on how to sling it properly, and how to lie diagonally across it. Don't assume that the sleeper needs to hang like a banana in a sack. Once correctly positioned in the hammock, all parts of the body are well supported.

The SAS showed a friend of mine how to make a pole-bed. With a series of collapsible rods you can erect this bed above the ground. My friend claims that it is just as convenient and far more comfortable than a hammock, so perhaps they will eventually be manufactured for general sale.

———————

If you are camping, then you will need the following:

A cooker Make sure that it can take paraffin or low-grade petrol. It won't be practical or legal to bring fuel from home.

Cooking utensils It is often practical to take mess-tins, which are very adaptable for cooking, and can also be used as boxes for food or cooking equipment.

A tent A dome tent is now nearly always preferred to a ridge one. Domes are free-standing, can be erected without a fly sheet, often come equipped with invaluable built-in mosquito netting, and tend to be roomier and cooler. If the poles are made of fibre-glass, it may be best to convert to aluminium, or take some spares.

A few items hardly need describing, but may be worth listing in case they jog your memory.

Handkerchiefs
Credit cards (see Chapter 2)
Chequebook (see Chapter 2)
Frisbee – I have heard of campers who take a frisbie, which doubles up as a plate

Various items for the medical kit are discussed in Chapter 5.

LUGGAGE

Suitcases

The first question is whether or not to take one. Some people manage to travel with only the luggage they can carry on board a plane. What a joy for them! They suffer no lengthy queues at the luggage carousel (and therefore no long queues at immigration control); and they suffer no risk of luggage loss or theft. I have often intended to travel only with hand luggage. But I very rarely succeed because, apart from other non-essentials, I usually travel with at least a dozen books.

Many people prefer the greater mobility of backpacks: these are discussed on page 104.

If you do decide to take a suitcase, your immediate decision is whether to choose a hard-sided or soft-sided one. I prefer hard-sided, mainly because they are stronger and more secure (they can't be razor-slit). The added advantage of a hard-sided suitcase is that it can be quite a useful minor safe in your room. Most thieves from hotel rooms are sneak thieves, and they are not going to bother lugging a cumbersome suitcase out of the hotel. A very minor advantage of a hard suitcase over a soft one is that it can occasionally act as a seat on railway platforms, etc. A disadvantage of hard suitcases is that they are very inflexible – difficult to jam into the packed boots of cars or the holds of small planes.

Suitcases on wheels are a great luxury. Previously, the wheels always got damaged, but now they are better made. Recessed wheels are usually the safest. Wheelable suitcases put an end to the tiresome problem of finding baggage trolleys, and I now glide through airports and railway stations, wondering how I ever put up with the pain of carrying a suitcase loaded with a dozen books.

I always buy suitcases with built-in combination locks. Although these locks may not be as secure as ordinary ones, I prefer them because of being very prone to losing keys.

I try to arrange some journeys so that my cumbersome suitcase can be dumped in a place to which I will later return. I then set off with my nightbag, or day-rucksack, which contains all I need for side trips. On my return to the suitcase I can stock up with books, repack with clean clothes, and leave behind any items I may have bought.

Travel-packs, which are a hybrid between a backpack and a suitcase, are becoming increasingly popular. They can be used like rucksacks, which are often more convenient for public transport or walking, and yet can be converted into a more respectable-looking case. They aren't suitable for proper trekking, and personally, I wouldn't use one, for they do suffer from being a hybrid: I would rather travel with either a first-rate suitcase or a first-rate rucksack.

Nightbags

Even if you are taking a suitcase, you will almost certainly need a nightbag. On a plane it's invaluable for easy access to newspapers, duty-free drink, a spare sweater, and books.

As I have mentioned in Chapter 4, there is quite a high likelihood that an airline will mislay your luggage, so always pack your nightbag with a clean change of clothes, a book, and your wash-kit.

If you expect to be charged for overweight luggage, fill your nightbag with your heaviest possessions (often books), as you can usually avoid having it weighed.

For these reasons it is often best to choose the largest size of nightbag allowable as cabin luggage. The maximum permissible usually varies between 38 inches and 45 inches calculated by adding height plus width plus length. But in practice flight attendants judge it more by their eyes, and on some flights the most important factor is whether the bag can fit easily under your seat.

It is crucial that the nightbag should have a shoulder strap as well as the conventional handles: this makes it more comfortable to carry, and frees an often-needed hand. The shoulder strap should be adjustable. If the strap is not well anchored into the strongest material, the bag will tear on the first occasion that you carry a heavy load.

Choose the design of your bag carefully, for it will make a great difference to your day-to-day travelling. I like one with plenty of compartments.

Backpacks

The great advantage of backpacks is the mobility they give you. And if you are going on any type of hike without porters, you will certainly need one.

They aren't secure against thieves, and are easy to razor-slit. A minor disadvantage is their image: in the past backpackers have often had a tough time with immigration officers and other officials. But this prejudice has generally diminished, unless the backpacker looks like a hippie.

Because backpack straps can get caught in conveyer belts, the packs are transferred manually at some airports. This sometimes means they miss flights, and makes them more prone to theft.

Therefore old hands sometimes stuff them in a grotty army-type kitbag.

In recent times there has been a wonderful improvement in the manufacture of backpacks. Perhaps the greatest breakthrough came in the 1950s, when it was realized that the load could be transferred from the spine (which is ill-adapted to carry weight) to the hips. Since then hip belts have improved even more, and now as much as 75 per cent of the pack's weight can be carried on your hips. To get a memorable idea of this improvement, try carrying a heavy pack just with shoulder straps, and then tie up the hip belt. There have also been many other improvements in design, which mean that modern packs are tougher, lighter and more comfortable.

During all my recent hikes someone else has carried my luggage, therefore my first-hand knowledge of backpacks is out of date. If you wish to know more, I again recommend Chris Townsend's *Backpacker's Handbook* (see Appendix 1), which has sixteen detailed pages on the subject; there has also been a great improvement in literature put out by the manufacturers, and you should be able to get leaflets and good advice in the best camping shops. Here, though, are some of the basic questions for you to consider.

A major decision is whether to buy a pack with an internal or an external frame. The main advantages of the traditional external-frame pack were that it could carry a far heavier load, and as this load was held a little way away from your back, your sweat could evaporate. An internal frame is far less awkward for fitting into trains, planes, buses, and so on. It is also more stable when walking on rough ground. However, all these advantages and disadvantages are open to debate, and backpack technology changes so fast that any firm opinion is soon out of date.

Whichever you choose, be sure to experiment with several models in a shop, and to load any prospective purchase with at least 30 pounds of goods. Whatever you do, don't be tempted by a pack that is too large for your frame; even half full it will be a nightmare on your trek. We all have different-shaped bodies, and a pack that will suit one person may be torture for another. Women have narrower shoulders, therefore several major companies make packs specially for them. According to Chris Townsend:

The key measurement for fitting a pack is the distance between the top of your shoulders and your upper hipbone. This is because the hip belt should ride with its upper edge 2 or 3 centimetres above the hipbone so that the weight is borne by the broadest, strongest part of the hips when the shoulder straps are in their correct position. The most common and most precise way of achieving a good fit is with an adjustable harness, whereby the shoulder straps can be moved up and down the back of the pack to vary the distance between them and the hip belt.

He also recommends that the packs designed for moderate to heavy loads should have top-tension straps, which pull the load in over your shoulders to increase stability, and also lift the shoulder straps off the sensitive nerve around the collarbone to the much tougher shoulderblades.

No backpacks are fully waterproof, so take **waterproof pack liners**, or something like dustbin liners. Use more than one, as they can be useful to separate damp, smelly clothes. If it is likely that you will be walking in heavy rain, get an elasticated **waterproof pack cover**.

In areas where knife-wielding thieves are common, some backpackers line their pack with chicken-wire mesh, although others complain it is liable to tear their clothes.

Backpacks are a complicated piece of equipment, and no amateur can fully judge them. Therefore buy a well-known make. I have had several letters recommending particular manufacturers, the most frequently mentioned being Berghaus, Lowe, and Karrimor. At the time he wrote *The Backpacker's Handbook,* Chris Townsend's favourite two models were manufactured by Gregory and Lowe. A knowledgeable assistant in the Snow and Rock shop (see Appendix 2) was insistent that the Rolls-Royce of backpacks is made by a British company called Pod.

If you are going only for mini-hikes you could consider taking just a **day-pack** which will fit into your luggage.

CLOTHES

Hat

A hat is so important in the tropics that it is safest to buy one before you leave. A floppy, wide-brimmed cotton hat is usually best. Other hats may look more fancy, but they are of less use if they can't be squeezed down into a pocket or shoulder bag.

The traditional cotton hat can be used for umpteen other functions, including substituting as an oven cloth for campers. In my case it once stopped me from being stung by bees (see Chapter 6).

Novice travellers may not realize that the primary function of a hat is to protect you from glare. If you are walking in the sun for any length of time, glare can be nightmarish, causing dizziness and headaches. When the sun is high, dark glasses don't give full protection to the eyes. Another function of a hat is to protect the skin of your face and neck from burning; worries about skin cancer are making this especially important. For all these reasons, try to get a hat with a reasonable brim.

If you are going to encounter cold weather, a hat is also important, but the usual cotton one won't do (see Table 2, page 114).

There are a few occasions, such as river canoeing, when your hat may need a strap, or you will lose it.

When you are in the shade, it will often be more comfortable not to wear a hat: a high proportion of body sweat is exuded from the head, and a hat will slow down the cooling process of evaporation.

Shirts

Because of their drip-dry qualities shirts made with artificial fabrics, rather than cotton, are preferred by many travelling businessmen. But I'm convinced that if you want to feel cool, then the principal ingredient of your shirts and T-shirts must be cotton. Even a shirt with only 30 per cent polyester can feel disgustingly clammy. Cotton is an excellent absorber of moisture, and dries quickly enough to cause cooling through evaporation. Artificial fabrics cannot absorb the same quantity of sweat, and therefore make you feel clammy and hot.

T-shirts

T-shirts are cool and practical. As they take up little room in your luggage, you can afford to take plenty of them; this is useful in very hot conditions, when you may want to change your T-shirt several times a day.

I like to take plenty of T-shirts or collared T-shirts. A clean top is more important than clean trousers. One can somehow muddle through with trousers that are mildly grubby; but a grubby T-shirt looks terrible. And a clean top raises your morale.

If you suddenly move into cold weather, a T-shirt will double up as a vest. They can also be used to envelop a pillow of doubtful cleanliness; and when there is no pillow the T-shirt can be stuffed to make a reasonable replacement.

However, T-shirts have some disadvantages. They don't cover the nape of the neck, which is inconvenient when you are spending a long time in burning sun, and is uncomfortable if you are wearing a camera strap. T-shirts are sometimes considered disreputable by locals: in some parts of the world, for instance, it would be unsuitable to wear one for an evening call upon a schoolmaster, and it is often considered disrespectful to wear a T-shirt when calling at a government office.

A minor disadvantage of T-shirts is that they are made without those pockets (useful for lens caps, etc.) which are fitted on the front of many shirts.

A good compromise is often the collared type of T-shirt, some of which are now known as polo shirts. They do take up a bit more room, but they are more comfortable with camera straps, they usually have pockets, and they are nearly always considered more respectable.

Underwear

I will risk being dogmatic by saying that underpants must be of pure cotton. (It is just worth mentioning here two less obvious virtues of cotton clothes: if you develop a fungal infection they can be boiled; and if you are caught in a fire, they won't be as inflammable as nylon, and won't melt into your skin.)

Many men at home wear the 'jockey' style of underpants. For travelling purposes they should change over to one of the looser 'boxer' types. Anything that helps the circulation of air round the crotch will reduce the likelihood of irritation, or of infections such as dhobi itch. Women, too, should wear cotton underwear, as they will be less likely to get thrush, which is more common in a hot climate.

One reader wrote to recommend disposable paper underpants. I therefore experimented with them, but they were made of an artificial material and were horribly uncomfortable.

Respectable clothes

For some trips, it may be a good idea to take one set of respectable clothes. If, for instance, you need to negotiate permission for something from a government office, your chances will always be better if you are conservatively dressed. Upgrades on planes are given only to men wearing a jacket and tie. I have often found that a lightweight blazer sees me through most formal occasions (I swap the brass buttons for black ones). Men should forget their swanky silk **ties**; instead keep a crumple-free polyester one tucked permanently into your luggage. A bow-tie always seems rather exhibitionist to me, but they take up wonderfully little room, and they don't get covered in food stains. A woman can usually get by with one smart dress and a decent pair of shoes; suitable dresses are not difficult to find now in easy-to-pack, crumple-free material. If she wants to take some item of cheap jewellery – perhaps necklace or earrings – this might also end up as a good present.

Don't underestimate the possibility of needing some

respectable clothes; even in the backwoods you can get caught unawares – asked to a chief's wedding, invited to a church service, requested to give a speech. You will cause disappointment if you look like a scruff.

Trousers

Trousers should be loose-fitting to allow air to circulate. For this reason jeans are usually unsuitable; they are also unsatisfactory in cold wet weather (see Table 2), and take too long to dry.

After discussing trousers with Nomad, the shop sent me the following useful comment:

Cotton poplin ripstop trousers in a sand colour are probably the best all-round travel trousers. They are light in weight, very tough, windproof, and baggy enough in cold conditions to wear thermals or track suit underneath. They dry quickly and have a double seat and knees to reduce wear. They also have a waist adjuster to allow for changes in body weight.

Good and cheap tropical trousers and shorts are now more frequently found in Marks and Spencers – though the company has the unfortunate habit of immediately discontinuing any range that one finds particularly useful.

Rohan trousers, often known as Rohan bags, have become a bit of a joke – they are covered in zips, and are worn almost as a uniform by elements of the hiking brigade. They are also very expensive. However, I will list all their virtues, as these are also the qualities you might consider in any trousers you buy. They are very light and very comfortable. Although not made of pure cotton (they are 50 per cent polyester and 50 per cent cotton), they aren't at all clammy. They dry extremely fast when washed. They are marvellously tough for their weight, though they will get torn in thorny country. For me, the most convenient feature is that they pack down to a tiny size. They have plenty of pockets, some of them fitted with zips.

The dust-coloured Rohan bags absorb less heat than the blue ones. And although the blue ones are darker, they are more likely to show the dirt.

Rohan bags stain quite easily. There are three cleaning liquids which will help you to deal with this. The first choice is Shout, but being an aerosol it is only practical to use it at home. The next is Vanish (or possibly Superdrug's own stain-remover). If neither of these works, use a Stain Devil, but be sparing, as it can be corrosive.

Rohan products are sold only in their shops. To find the nearest, ring 0908 618888.

A pocket sewn on the inside waist of your trousers or skirt can be an effective and practical anti-pickpocket device.

Skirt

Pleated or gathered mid-calf skirts are useful. They are cool and comfortable, and sometimes considered more respectable than trousers in conservative areas. Skirts may bring an element of privacy when you need to take an emergency pee, and they are comfortable when you have to sit cross-legged. (If they prevent you pointing at people the often-offensive soles of your feet, so much the better.) Your size will change, therefore an elasticated waist is best; and the skirt should have pockets.

Belt

Unless your trousers are elasticated, you would be advised to bring a belt. Your waist size can vary dramatically in the tropics. In Chapter 10, I've recommended a belt with a compartment that can hide money.

Shorts

Walking in shorts is infinitely more enjoyable than walking in trousers. And they are often more practical, not becoming so muddy in dirty conditions, and being washable in a hand-basin. In some parts of the world expatriates wear them all the time. Shorts, however, aren't always preferable. Although they are cooler in hot and *humid* areas, this isn't necessarily the case when the weather is hot and *dry*. Arab or Tuareg dress, which is worn in the desert, consists of long robes covering the entire body, even the head. This slows down rapid evaporation of much-needed moisture, and protects the body against radiated heat. By contrast, the inhabitants of hot and humid climates often wear as few clothes as possible.

You should also be aware that shorts incur disapproval in many parts of the Third World, where they may be considered either low-class, indecent, or redolent of the colonial era; and they can get you excluded from interesting sites. Women should certainly think twice (or even three times) before wearing them in many parts of the world, especially Asia and the Middle East.

When buying shorts, look for the following characteristics. They should be long enough to be decent when you have to sit cross-legged on the floor. The material should be strong enough to withstand repeated sitting on rocks and logs; but the material should be light enough to be cool. The pockets should be deep, and there should be loops for a belt. And finally, they should be loose, if they are too tight (as they tend to be), they will be uncomfortable in the heat, and too indecent (both on men and women) for local tastes. For men, shorts should also be quite long in the leg, otherwise they will expose themselves when sitting cross-legged – especially as in a hot climate they may prefer not to wear underwear (instead washing their shorts more frequently). It is surprisingly hard to find shorts with all these characteristics, so stock up when you find them.

Track suit/jogging suit/zoot suit/shell suit

One of these will serve many purposes. They can be useful as pyjamas in a sleeping bag, or for pottering round camp. And if the material is thin enough, the suit can be used as thermal underwear when the weather is cold. One correspondent especially recommended a 'zoot suit' made from very thin parachute material. This type of suit can also be useful for keeping off biting insects. Survival Aids (see Appendix 2) sell a zoot suit of parachute silk with a hood. I haven't yet tried it.

TABLE 2
COLD-WEATHER CLOTHES

Don't assume that just because you are visiting hot countries, you won't need clothes for cold weather. There are fifteen glaciers on Mount Kenya, which is actually on the Equator. You will probably need warm clothes if you are travelling to higher altitudes – perhaps climbing a volcano, trekking in hills, or visiting a hill-station; and the cold in deserts at night can never be fully appreciated until experienced. Recently I visited the forests of India in April, a month which I expected to be boiling. In the early mornings I used to freeze, even though wearing three jerseys and a borrowed leather jacket.

As you won't want to take bulky clothing, and as it is conceivable that you might be stuck in the cold as the result of an emergency, it is useful to know the elementary principles of keeping warm. I shall first discuss these, and then discuss specific items of clothing with reference to them.

1. Still air will trap your body heat, because it is a very inefficient conductor of heat (unlike metal, which conducts heat very efficiently) When you have fed well, the body generates plenty of heat. It is estimated that the body's muscles, working under average conditions, generate enough heat in one hour to boil a quart of freezing water. The best way of trapping this heat is by using still air. Some materials such as wool are extremely efficient at this; animal fur is even more efficient.

The use of still air is one of the reasons why in cold weather it is useful to dress in many **layers** of clothing.

2. Moisture is a very efficient conductor of heat Therefore two important enemies of warmth are rain and trapped sweat. When exerting yourself, your body will sweat, and if this sweat can't escape you will become very cold. If you want a vivid example of how much more efficient water is than still air as a conductor of heat, then put one bottle of wine in a bucket of iced water and at the same time put another in a deep freeze. The bottle in the bucket will become cold within minutes; the bottle in the deep freeze will take far longer.

3. Wind is a very efficient convector of heat We have all heard of the wind-chill factor, and it means that in an emergency situation your priority is to get out of the wind. It also means that your choice of outer/shell garment is important.

4. Different parts of the body lose heat at a different rate Different books give different statistics about how much of our body heat escapes from the head, but it is certainly a disproportionate amount – probably at least a quarter (and it appears that when the temperature is as low as freezing, or if there is a wind, then the percentage becomes even higher). This is because the blood circulation round the rest of our body retreats from the body surface in cold weather, while the blood supply around our brain has to remain constant. Whatever the statistics, a brief experiment of your own will convince you that a hat makes a tremendous difference in cold weather.

5. In order to keep warm without feeling uncomfortable, your clothes need to be versatile The body can tolerate very little variation from its normal temperature of 98.4°F, and therefore your clothing should enable you to make frequent adjustments of temperature control.

Now we shall look at specific items of cold-weather clothing, referring to the above principles of keeping warm.

Underwear Don't wear cotton next to the skin. It will

114

soak up your sweat, and wet cotton is very chilling (for this reason jeans are deadly in cold and wet conditions). By contrast, wool, when wet, feels comparatively warm. The fibres of wool retain some air even when wet, and as wool releases moisture more slowly into the atmosphere, it doesn't cool you so fast by evaporation. Wool also has the advantage that, if one part of the material becomes wet, it doesn't immediately conduct the moisture to another.

A traveller once asked Wilfred Thesiger what equipment she should take for a journey through Ethiopia (where she expected to meet extremes of temperature) and was told to take string vests. They may not be very beautiful, but they are effective for trapping pockets of warm air in the cold, while being cool in the heat.

I have often found **thermal underwear** to be a snare and delusion. It becomes smelly extremely fast (a fact rarely mentioned), which often makes it impractical when there aren't frequent facilities for washing. Another serious disadvantage is that many makes of thermal underwear shrink disastrously when washed in hot water. For many years the manufacturers have assured us that they have overcome or are just about to overcome these problems; but there have been several false dawns, and I would inquire closely before committing yourself to thermal underwear.

Recently, specialist outdoor and camping shops have been selling sets of **silk underwear** (vests and longjohns). They are expensive but do have some advantages: they occupy a tiny space, are very light and very comfortable, and weight-for-weight are very warm. I have used them and liked them a lot. They can also usefully double up as pyjamas. Unlike underwear made from artificial fabric, silk ones don't become smelly for a long time.

Some people complain that silk underwear doesn't keep

its shape (thus losing insulating power); and the manufacturers do warn that it mustn't be washed in very hot water. I have sent mine to various laundries, and there hasn't yet been a problem. So far I have found silk underwear to be very satisfactory, but I haven't used it for very long, nor in the coldest conditions.

The well-regarded American firm Patagonia are now marketing a range of thermal underwear in an artificial material, Capilene. One of the four weights of this is remarkably similar to silk underwear; I have heard some good reports of Capilene, and wearers have sworn to me that it doesn't become fetid.

Some sportspeople and mountaineers apparently use women's tights (in the United States called pantyhose), which fulfil much the same function as longjohns, and take up very little room. Most tights are made of artificial fabrics, but it is claimed that the better ones *do* breathe. I tried them once, and found them very uncomfortable.

If sets of thermal underwear really do improve, they will be useful as pyjamas in cold conditions.

Sweaters I would never go on even the most tropical trip without at least one thin wool sweater. Even if on no other occasion, you might need it when flying: aeroplanes can be draughty and chilling, especially during long flights, when you can hardly move your muscles. And if a plane is grounded you may have to wait for hours in an excessively air-conditioned airport lounge.

I find that a thin wool sweater with long sleeves is practical, because I can take it off and wrap the sleeves round my waist. It can also be squeezed into a shoulder bag. For this reason, when the weather is colder, I would rather take two thin sweaters than one thick one.

In recent years there has been a marked improvement in

clothes made from **fleece**, an artificial fabric which is really a development from pile. In certain conditions a fleece jacket may be better than a jersey, or at least a useful adjunct to one. Fleece washes well, dries far quicker than wool, keeps moisture away from the body, and is comparatively warm even when wet. Weight for weight, fleece is warmer than wool.

Here are some of the possible disadvantages of fleece garments: they tend to be bulkier than a jersey; they have to be washed more often (but remember that they dry quicker), and in the past they have had a tendency to 'pill' (develop little balls of fluff on their surface). To avoid the pilling problem, don't buy fleece at an ordinary shop, where it might be considered a fashion accessory; instead buy a well-known make (with a reputation to defend) from a specialist shop. Unfortunately, you will probably have to put up with an ugly and prominent manufacturer's logo.

You can buy a fleece jacket with either a high neck or a hood. It is probably more practical to buy one with a high neck and to rely on a separate hat, and (in rainy or colder conditions) your shell garment's hood.

Shell garment No amount of jerseys will keep you warm in wind, which cuts through them. Nor will they keep you warm if it rains. And fleece isn't windproof. So some type of shell garment is necessary in wintry conditions. Many people buy a hip-length garment (often called an anorak), but I prefer a longer garment with a full-length zip. (The lightweight ones are often called cagoules, and the thicker ones are often called parkas. But descriptions aren't always precise.) Ideally, I like my shell garment to be long enough so that when I sit on something damp I won't get a wet bum.

A full-length two-way zip is important: the top end

is crucial for adjusting ventilation, and the bottom end is helpful for ventilation and freedom of leg movement. Ideally, the wrist fastenings should be adjustable (not just elasticated), so that your arms can be ventilated if they get too hot and sweaty. A cagoule should have a hood large enough to cover a hat.

Any garment that is waterproof is windproof as well. I quite often take a cagoule on my travels because, considering how thin and light they are and how little space they use up, the windproof element can be surprisingly effective for maintaining some warmth.

Formerly, the great problem with waterproofs was that, as well as keeping the wet out, they also kept it in. As a result, after any exertion, the wearers got soaked in their own sweat. In recent years, there have been great developments in 'breathable' fabrics, which remain waterproof while allowing sweat to evaporate.

A great many columns are written about the wonders of breathable materials, and many expensive coats are sold. But although there have been great advances in the development of these fabrics, they aren't always all they are cracked up to be. Despite recent improvements, the breathable qualities of the various garments often degrade faster than expected. Even ordinary waterproofing doesn't last for as long as many people imagine. Furthermore, breathable fabrics can't function when it is raining heavily, and, however good they are, they can't cope with all the moisture when you are sweating a lot. It is often more effective to ventilate your jacket by simply adjusting the zip.

Even if I don't take a cagoule, I often take some type of **pocket waterproof clothing** for emergencies – if only for its windproof qualities. They take up a tiny amount of space, and occasionally are a godsend when you least expect rain or cold. At present a variety of pac-a-macs is sold;

they aren't always very well designed, but they are a useful safety-net.

Poncho Most travellers won't want to take a poncho, but they can be very useful for backpackers, as they will cover both you and the pack. A good military-style poncho is versatile because it can fold out as a shelter, and it can also be buttoned up to act as a bivouac bag.

Down jacket For certain very cold conditions some people like a down jacket (or sometimes a waistcoat). Several of these are now sold with their own stuff-sack so that they fold down small. An advantage of down garments is that they can double up as a pillow. As discussed under Sleeping bags (page 95), down is useless when wet, so a down jacket will be a disaster in the rain unless you have a waterproof outer lining.

Hat As I've already pointed out, a hat is essential in cold weather. In very cold conditions, don't ignore the benefits of wearing a hat in bed – think of the nightcaps that were used in the days before central heating. In colder conditions, consider a **balaclava.**

Scarf Although the head is touted as the worst area for heat loss, I wouldn't be surprised if the neck comes a close second. Whenever it's cold a scarf makes an immense difference. If you can afford a cashmere scarf, buy one. This may seem an extravagance, but real cashmere combines almost miraculous heat-retaining qualities with the advantage of being squeezable down to a small bundle.

For less severe conditions, an Indian-type silk (not nylon) scarf makes an excellent replacement, and is very space-effective, as it squeezes into a minute bundle. In hot, dry conditions, it can be wetted, and used to cool your neck by evaporation (see Chapter 8).

119

Swimming costume

A swimming costume is the one item of clothing that I prefer to be made of artificial fabric. This is because it will dry quicker. Boxer-style swimming trunks (as opposed to briefs) may be occasionally useful as an emergency pair of shorts. I have mentioned in Chapter 11 that bikinis for women, and tight swimming-briefs for men, are often considered objectionable, especially in Muslim areas. In Indonesia a woman friend felt obliged to swim in 'Bermuda shorts and a shirt selected for not becoming see-through when wet'.

Socks

Most travellers in the tropics prefer to wear socks as rarely as possible. Should you need to take them, the material must consist of as little nylon as is compatible with durability. If the socks are made principally of nylon, your feet will get hot and sweaty, and this may also cause fungal infections.

Sometimes when you have new sandals or shoes, it's worth wearing socks for the first couple of days while your feet are getting used to them. Otherwise you'll get blisters.

As I write, Marks and Spencer sell excellent short socks made of 72 per cent cotton, which take up no room and cost only £2.10 a pair.

The colour of clothes

Don't take the camouflage-coloured clothes which are so often sold by camping shops – or any military-style clothes, including shirts with epaulettes, and trousers with patch pockets. If you are in a country when trouble flares up, you may be suspected of being a mercenary or a spy. I'm not being alarmist – this situation happens quite often.

Don't wear clothes that shriek. If you wear sober-coloured clothes like the locals, you will be less harassed and sometimes less overcharged.

It really is true that pale clothes reduce the effects of the sun's rays. I've already mentioned that people feel a difference when wearing dark Rohan bags as opposed to the lighter ones. White clothes are most effective, but soon become grubby.

I have also noticed, when walking in very hot conditions, that a fawn shirt is cooler than a green one.

Sarongs

During hot tropical evenings many people like to wear a sarong (in different places known as kikoy, lungi, sulu, etc.), as they are unbeatably cool and comfortable. I have even met expatriate managing directors who every evening change into a sarong. Unlike shorts or trousers, it allows plenty of air to circulate around the crotch.

The best sarongs are made from Javanese batik; if you are lucky enough to go to Java, buy plenty of sarongs there. A full-size one is usually about 8 feet 6 inches long and 3 feet 5 inches wide. If you buy one of a fine material, it will pack very small, as well as being light and cool.

Sarongs are handy for using as sheets when hotel sheets are dirty or clammy. They also enable you to conduct a respectable strip-wash in public. If you think you might use your sarongs as sheets, obviously don't buy the ones that have been sewn into barrel-shapes – as is often done in Malaysia and East Africa.

If you ever go to Bali, learn to tie your sarong in the formal Balinese style, rather than the Javanese, Malay, or East African styles. It is practical, and cleverly combines complete decency with total freedom of leg movement.

Shoes, sandals, boots, and flip-flops

Hot feet are a misery, so the great problem is to find shoes that are both durable and cool.

This used to be difficult, but in recent years the arrival of 'trainers' has improved the choice immeasurably. Even if you will be walking long distances, it is possible to choose shoes that are light (most important) and durable. Nor is it necessary to choose trainers that are expensive; many of the priciest are a rip-off. During a 200-mile walk in Tanzania (often crossing rivers and walking over hot, sharp stones) I wore an £18 pair of trainers from Marks and Spencer. To my astonishment they remained in excellent condition, and they never became smelly. After putting them in the washing machine on my return, they looked almost as good as new.

When buying trainers, choose those with the most breathable uppers. I hold mine up to the light, which usually gives an indication of porousness.

Not everyone agrees with my views on trainers, and many sensible people prefer 'desert boots'. Personally I find them too cumbersome and hot, but their fans claim that they are more breathable and look more respectable than trainers, and they point out that they are very tough and that their suede finish doesn't scuff.

When you don't have to do any serious walking in a hot climate, it is better to wear sandals, as this leaves much more of the foot exposed. Coolness is everything. Strong leather sandals are fine, but recently I've always taken **rubber/plastic sandals.** Here are their advantages. They are invaluable for mucking about in the sea, protecting against coral cuts and the wounds from several ground-hugging marine animals. They are useful when windsurfing, both for keeping a grip, and for protecting your feet when you fall off. Unlike leather sandals, they won't rot, and are therefore also good for walking in wet or muddy conditions, and for all types of river journeys. They are a tremendous asset when you are staying in simple hotels, because they protect your feet against slimy showers and overflowing lavatories. When rubber sandals get dirty, they are very easy to wash.

I often use my sandals day after day, so it is crucial that they are strong and comfortable. But finding a strong, comfortable pair is surprisingly difficult, especially as ones made with cheaper plastic are too clammy and brittle. For a while an excellent French make, Sarazienne, was available in Britain, but at the time of writing they have disappeared. I hope Nomad will stock something suitable. On the Continent they are more common, and are popular at seaside resorts. Some people call them 'Jellies'.

If you buy plastic sandals, remember that they work loose in water, so buy ones that you can tighten.

If you can't get sandals, then **flip-flops** (or thongs, as they are known in some parts of the world) are useful. They are light, easy to pack, cheap, and hygienic. It takes time to get used to them, but this can be worth it. Bear in mind that, like T-shirts, they are sometimes considered unrespectable. Some hotels and restaurants ban them, and it is unwise to wear them for visiting government offices. As with sandals, it is best to buy ones made of rubber, or plastic that feels like rubber. They will be more comfortable and last longer. Try to avoid white ones, as they quickly become grubby.

If you are going on a serious hike, you may sometimes need **boots** (though in my opinion not as often as people think). And hikers who are carrying a heavy load often want ankle support. Remember, though, the saying that 1 pound on your feet is equivalent to 5 pounds on your back. Many hikers have been conned into buying boots that are far too heavy, thus reducing the pleasure of their walking. Now the technology of boot-making has so much improved that even the strongest boots are far lighter that they were.

When walking through wet forest or jungle, it is essential to have boots that aren't slippery, so get ones with the best possible tread. 'Green' walking boots, with reduced tread and cut-away heels (which are supposed to be less harmful to vulnerable trails), have been implicated in serious falls on slippery hillsides.

A reader has sent advice about extremely wet conditions:

To convert the boot to jungle conditions, use a Marlin spike to make a hole in the arch close to the sole, pushing the spike from inside of the boot. The valve effect created will allow the action of the foot to squirt water out after wading, but prevent other things coming in.

Two more general points about all types of shoes. In many countries you are frequently taking your shoes on and off – for instance, when visiting temples and private houses. In these circumstances avoid shoes with laces or difficult buckles.

When walking long distances, or in the heat, your feet swell, so buy shoes that are half a size too large.

CHAPTER 4

FLYING

Arriving early

Most travellers plan to arrive at an airport only an hour before departure; others pride themselves on cutting it even finer. But when you undertake a major trip abroad it is far better to allow at least two hours before flight departure, preferably two and a half hours. Here are the reasons.

If you allow only one hour, sod's law may make you miss the plane. It is surprising what can go wrong. I chose to fly to Italy on a day when the IRA closed down the entire underground network. Taxis have a habit of not turning up. Car crashes obstruct the motorway on the way to the airport. And whenever one cuts a departure particularly fine, unexpected queues occur in the security channels. Even at Heathrow, I have had to wait as long as fifty minutes.

Even if sod's law operates only once in fifty times, the misery caused by missing a plane is so great that it is worth the effort of arriving early on the other forty-nine occasions. And remember that when you have booked a discount or charter ticket, missing a plane is a financial disaster.

There are other reasons for arriving early.

Queues for international flights start forming almost exactly two hours in advance. If you arrive even quarter of an hour before this, it is likely that there will be almost no queue at all. What joy!

When you arrive early, your luggage is less likely to be mislaid.

When you arrive early, you are less likely to be 'bumped' off the plane. This is an important point, because a confirmed ticket does not protect you, and bumping is quite frequent. A friend of mine booked a Bombay to London flight six months in advance with British Airways. She reconfirmed it three days in advance, and again on the day. She arrived at the airport two hours in advance, and she was still bumped.

You stand a better chance of being allocated a good seat (though you can often book one in advance on the telephone).

So, taking into account all these reasons, it seems mad to grudge an extra hour, when you are investing so much time and money on a trip. If the holiday is going to last 500 hours, what is the great problem in taking another hour? It is better to get to the airport early, avoid the queues, and then catch up on your reading (or telephoning) in the departure lounge. It won't be such a wasted hour after all.

Getting to the airport

It is best to check, and double check, which airport you are leaving from. This may seem absurdly obvious, but many cities now have several airports, and I have known a surprising number of people go to the wrong one.

In a few countries it is now becoming increasingly important to check your terminal. For instance, Terminal 4 at Heathrow is a great distance from the others, and if you go to the wrong terminal, you may miss your plane.

When telephoning to check this, it is also a good idea to ascertain how full your flight is. If it is very full, this will be a warning to arrive extra early.

In Britain, telephone numbers for checking all the facts about your departure can be found in the telephone directory under 'Airports'. This very useful page lists terminals, flight prefixes, airline telephone numbers, and general inquiry numbers.

If you take a taxi to the airport, be very careful not to leave the impression your house will be empty. If possible, avoid minicab firms, as they are often a magnet for villains, and frequent places for the exchange of criminal information.

Luggage

I've already mentioned in the previous chapter that if you can manage with only carry-on luggage, you won't have tedious waits at carousels or run the risk of your luggage being lost. To repeat, the limit for carry-on luggage varies from airline to airline, usually between 38 inches and 45 inches, calculated by adding height plus width plus length. But usually it is judged more by the whims of the cabin staff. When a plane is full they will be stricter.

The maximum luggage allowance is nearly always calculated by weight, but on a number of routes, especially transatlantic ones, it is calculated by the number of pieces. You are allowed one or two suitcases (though each of these may be limited to the considerable weight of 70 pounds).

If for some reason you need to take a lot of luggage, you should know about the system of **unaccompanied baggage**. The cost is usually about a third of that for excess luggage. Although this is a useful system, friends have warned me that it can be problematic when flying to Third World countries, where it can be difficult locating the luggage if it hasn't arrived with you. Sometimes airlines can make sure that the case arrives on the same plane. If for some reason you can't send your excess luggage as unaccompanied baggage, it might be worth contacting a company which acts as an 'excess-baggage bucket shop'. Two of these are the London Baggage Company (tel. 0293 543 853) and the Excess Baggage Company (tel. 081 759 3344); they claim to be able to save as much as 70 per cent off regular airline fees.

If you can't use any of these systems, you can often arrange to deliver any excess luggage to the cargo hall before you go to your check-in desk. The luggage will arrive on the same plane. This method is cheaper than paying the full price for excess luggage, but not as cheap as sending it unaccompanied.

Before checking in your luggage, remove any old baggage tags, as they may cause confusion. The staff will put on new three-letter-code baggage tabs, and the corresponding chits will be attached to your ticket. Make sure of this, for it is your only proof that the airline has taken your luggage. A good travel agent will have informed you of the correct three-letter codes for all your destinations, and it is worth checking that your chits are correct. Many of the codes are fairly obvious: London Heathrow is LHR and London Gatwick is LGW.

Your ticket may contain several coupons, each one representing a different flight. Watch out that only one coupon is removed at the check-in counter; this may appear to be fussy advice, but mistakes are frequently made.

Suitcases containing anything of value should always be locked, because baggage handlers throughout the world are notorious for dishonesty. However, the situation at Heathrow has probably got better since 1976, when Judge Edis said, 'The place has literally become a cesspool', or 1978, when Judge Gibbens observed that an honest man at Heathrow must 'stand out like a sore thumb', or 1986, when Lord Justice Watkins said that the pilfering of luggage at Heathrow was 'a national disgrace'. If you are as frightened as I am about losing keys, then use a combination lock (see Chapter 3), which will be better than nothing.

Because of widespread theft at many airports, it is best to use a hard-sided suitcase, rather than a soft one, which can be slashed. Some travellers lock their cases and fasten straps round them, in the hope that the extra time necessary for undoing straps will deter pilferers.

Since the increased control of Heathrow baggage handlers, there has been an increase of stealing on the concourse. Be particularly careful when you put your case down near banks, lavatories, and telephones; thieves know that your attention is diverted at these places. Nearly ten crimes a day are reported at Heathrow.

Films in both your hand and checked luggage are in danger from some X-ray machines. This problem is fully discussed in Chapter 9.

Labelling and mislaid luggage

Large numbers of suitcases get mislaid. The gloomiest surveys claim that as many as two passengers on each Jumbo flight are likely to be standing forlorn at the luggage carousel; from my own purely empirical observations I reckon this is an exaggeration.

Although the absence of your luggage is extremely inconvenient, you should be comforted by the knowledge that the overwhelming majority of lost luggage turns up in four days. Some statistics say 85 per cent, others say 98 per cent. Whichever it is, you stand a good chance of getting your case back.

Even though you will most likely see your case again, ensure that you fill out a Property Irregularity Report. If it turns out that your luggage is permanently lost, some airlines won't pay you compensation unless you can prove that you have reported the loss within a few hours. So don't just fill in the form, make sure you've got a copy, and cling grimly on to those baggage tags on your ticket.

You should also claim compensation for emergency relief. *Holiday Which?* reckons that if the delay in the return of your luggage is between twelve and twenty-four hours, then compensation of approximately £75 is appropriate. If you are not given compensation immediately, keep all receipts for emergency supplies, such as wash things, clean shirt, new underwear, etc. Keep your airline ticket after you have returned home because – astonishingly – the airlines sometimes ask to see your ticket before paying up. If you have trouble with the airline, look at your insurance policy, as *some* of them cover you for expenses caused by delayed luggage.

Because luggage is mislaid so often, it really is important that you should label your luggage well. Write your surname in capital letters (in the hope that it will be correctly logged on a computer) and also write down your destined airport. Many guidebooks suggest that you label your suitcase on the inside, so that baggage handlers can't read the label, and because an inside label can't be knocked off by rough treatment. By all means stick an extra label on the inside, but don't on any account rely on it. Having seen the chaos at lost luggage departments, I know that a suitcase without an easily read label will be ignored for a very long time.

You should label the outside of the suitcase both with your destination address and an address from home. It is preferable that the latter shouldn't be your house address, because there is a danger of baggage handlers selling the information. It is better to put your workplace (and its telephone number). Another advantage of this is that at most workplaces there will always be someone to answer the telephone during working hours.

If you are really thorough, you could stick a label with your home address on the inside of your case (at least you will only have to do this once) and then this just might help in the event of the outside label being destroyed.

Most cardboard luggage labels are equipped with flimsy, short pieces of string, and are likely to be torn off. As a safety precaution it is a good idea to have a permanent luggage label (protected by leather or plastic) with a home address, and then use the disposable cardboard ones for destination addresses.

A few luggage manufacturers now have a near monopoly of the market, and suitcases are becoming more standardized. If yours is one of the standard models, mark it (perhaps with coloured carpet-tape) so that you can recognize it quickly at the luggage carousel. People really do walk off accidentally with other travellers' suitcases.

Being bumped

Because so many passengers don't turn up despite their bookings, airlines routinely resort to the practice of over-booking. This means that sooner or later they will 'bump' you, and it won't make any difference that you have a confirmed ticket. Recent agreements ensure that you should be compensated by most

European and American airlines. Don't wait to be offered compensation, because they don't always volunteer to pay up. The rules lay down that passengers with a confirmed reservation should receive (at the time of writing) approximately £200 for being bumped off a short-haul flight, and approximately £400 for a flight of more than 2,170 miles. These amounts are halved if passengers can get on an alternative flight within two or four hours respectively. You can also claim reasonable expenses.

Choice of airline

For most travellers, except those on business, choice of airline is dictated by price rather than quality; but as the major airlines have become more competitive in their ticket pricing, travellers can afford to be more selective. In the event of Air India offering a London-to-Delhi ticket for only £30 more than Aeroflot, the traveller would be well advised to spend a bit more on flying Air India. Airlines aren't all much of a muchness: some airlines are unreliable, unpunctual, and even dangerous. Remember that an unreliable airline, such as Aeroflot, may delay you, not just for hours, but for days.

Duty free

Because alcohol and cigarettes make useful presents, you may want to buy duty-free goods even on departure. The shops at Heathrow impose a high mark-up, but their alcohol and cigarettes still cost less than in the high street.

Duty-free shops are often a snare and delusion: in many of them ordinary goods and gadgets are more expensive than in local shops. I've seen Sony Walkmans sold far cheaper in Tottenham Court Road than at Heathrow. Cameras are often cheaper on the streets of New York than at Kennedy Airport. Alcohol is often far cheaper in the supermarkets of continental Europe than it is in the duty-free shops. I once bought a bottle of Cointreau in Pisa; half an hour later I saw the same bottle being sold for half as much again in the airport's duty-free shop.

When travelling within the European Community there is

another reason for buying drinks in ordinary (i.e. not duty-free) shops: there is now an almost unlimited allowance for goods on which duty and tax has already been paid.

If you buy an electrical item or gadget abroad, make sure that it is far cheaper than at home; otherwise it's not worth the bother. When you legally import it, you have to pay duty; and you also pay VAT, which is calculated on the combined sum of the duty and value. If you illegally import an item and will be taking it again on your travels (for instance, a camera), your little crime will worry you every time you return home. The customs can check the origin of equipment by feeding registration numbers into a computer.

It is risky to recommend specific duty-free shops, because the situation will change by the time you read this. As a general rule, the Middle East and Far Eastern ones are the best, but this is more likely to be true for alcohol or cigarettes; know your home prices before buying any sort of gadgetry such as a radio. Within Europe, Schiphol (Amsterdam) is usually the best for alcohol, tobacco, and even gadgetry. You can check Schiphol's prices in advance, because KLM's offices issue a free booklet listing goods on sale.

One of the few benefits of the European Community might have been the abolition of the duty-free system. Passengers shouldn't be carrying all those bottles on planes: it adds to the cost of flying (liquid is heavy), and adds to the danger in the event of a crash – because of the broken glass and the flammability of alcohol. In the long term, duty free doesn't, of course, save us any money, because the government's loss of revenue has to be taken from us in some other way. Unfortunately the European Community has now delayed the abolition of duty free until at least the end of this century.

Choosing your seat

There are no sure-fire rules for choosing the best seat on an aeroplane. I have read handbooks, made friends with airhostesses, and studied the problem when I have flown; but I've yet to come up with the ultimate reliable advice. Here, though, are a few hints.

The most crucial element of aeroplane comfort is leg room. If you get to the airport early, ask at the check-in desk which rows have most leg room. It is sometimes, but not always, true that there is more leg room in the row immediately by the emergency exits. There is usually more leg room, too, right at the front of the cabin, but this row does have a snag: mothers with babies are likely to be placed there.

If you like to lean right back, be aware that seats in the row just in front of the emergency exit, and in the very back row, don't always fully recline.

Occasionally the back rows may be relatively empty, because stewardesses tend to keep them free for themselves. But these seats can be the noisiest if the plane has rear engines, and may be the bumpiest if the plane meets turbulence. I don't like them, because they are near the lavatories; therefore the area is sometimes smelly, and often crowded by people queuing.

If you want a seat which enables you to leave the plane early, then be aware that passengers usually exit from the front. The next decision is whether to choose an aisle or window seat. There are three advantages of a window seat: no one will want to clamber over you; you can see any spectacular views; and you can prop your head against the wall when sleeping. The main drawback is that you have the embarrassment of clambering over two other people (who may be sleeping) every time you want to go to the lavatory or get to the overhead locker.

The advantages of an aisle seat are that you avoid this embarrassment, and that you can take exercise whenever you like. The disadvantages are that you suffer other people clambering over you, and that your elbows get knocked by the stewards. An American writer, George Albert Brown,* has a neat suggestion.

*The Airline Passenger's Guerrilla Handbook (Blakes Publishing Group, USA, 1989)

If you are right-handed, choose the aisle seats on the right-hand aisle. This is because if you sit on the left aisle, your right elbow will stick out when you are eating and drinking, and it gets irritatingly knocked by passing stewards. On the seat by the right aisle, the problem isn't nearly so bad, as your left, non-dominant, elbow won't stick out so much. If you try to book this seat, the unambiguous expression 'With my left leg in the aisle' is sometimes used.

The seat to avoid is the middle seat, as you get all the disadvantages and none of the advantages of the other seats.

Many people don't realize that several major airlines will let you book in advance specific seats on their long-haul flights. This is an excellent way to get a comfortable seat. If you haven't done this, an early visit to the check-in counter gives you time to book a good place.

Air pressure and ear problems

During the flight, the air inside the plane is pressurized to an outside equivalent of about 6,000 feet. Passengers who don't live in Bogota aren't used to this, and because cigarettes and alcohol have an increased effect at this height, experts recommend reducing them to the minimum. The reduced air pressure may cause your body to swell a little, therefore it is sensible to wear loose-fitting clothes and shoes. Some people, including myself, often get very cold during flights; be wary of dressing too early for the tropics.

Many people are prone to ear pain when flying; this problem usually happens during descent. Try to avoid the pain by yawning, swallowing, moving your chin from side to side, and – often the best method – pinching your nose, combined with gentle blowing. Start doing this at least half an hour before landing, for descent begins early. The ear pain is likely to be excruciating when you have hay-fever or a cold. Because it is often said that flying with a cold can be dangerous, causing a ruptured eardrum, I asked for advice from several institutions, such as the Civil Aviation Authority; but though the matter is important, they were able to give me only the woolliest answers. Finally I wrote to Wing Commander B. J. O'Reilly, the Consultant Adviser for Ear, Nose and Throat Surgery in the Royal Air Force, who was kind enough to send a most useful letter. As the subject is very relevant for frequent fliers, I will quote at length:

The problems associated with flying with a cold, or any other cause of a blocked nose (such as hay-fever or polyps), are that the sinuses and the tubes that ventilate the ears (the eustachian tubes) both open into the nose. During ascent the relative air pressure within the sinuses and ears rises, and air is forced into the nose despite the obstruction there. During descent, however, the pressure outside the sinuses and ears rises, and air may not be able to enter from a blocked nose. When this occurs in the ears, the eardrums are stretched inwards, causing pain. Further pressure change may cause fluid to be sucked out of the blood vessels within the ear, and the traveller may then find their hearing is reduced (but the pain usually eases). In a more severe case, the eardrum may rupture, in which case the pain immediately settles as the pressure equalizes. Most ruptured eardrums will close spontaneously in time, but the traveller should not allow water in the ears (in other words they will not be able to swim) . . . Pressure changes across the sinuses may cause very severe pain, usually in the forehead. These pains may take some time to settle after landing and are sometimes associated with nose-bleeds.

Modern commercial aircraft passenger cabins are pressurized in contrast to the cabins of military aircraft . . . Also the rate of descent of civil aircraft is a great deal slower than that of military aircraft . . . We do not allow military pilots to fly with colds because of the risks to their ears and sinuses; however, commercial travellers fly without such restriction and, despite the fact that many must fly with colds, very few develop significant symptoms. I would say, therefore, that although there is a risk of flying with a cold, the risk is slight. Defining a severe cold is difficult. If an air traveller cannot inflate his ears (i.e. make them pop) by any of the manoeuvres that you have described in your letter, or if he already has discomfort in his sinuses, then he is at greater risk. Even in this case I do not think it is realistic to advise people not to fly when arrangements of long-standing hinge upon travelling.

I think you are quite correct to advise the use of a nasal decongestant such as Otrivine or Fenox. These should be used half an hour before descent to allow for maximum effect. I would also recommend the use of an antihistamine for travellers with hayfever.

A friendly doctor, who deals with a number of travelling hay-fever sufferers, recommends that if they are to avoid agony, an antihistamine tablet should be taken the day before the flight, and every six to eight hours on the day of the flight. The nasal spray, such as Otrivine, should be first used one hour before the estimated time of arrival, and then again a few minutes later, and then every twenty minutes. The first spray will probably not allow the drops sufficient access, but should pave the way for the second spray to be more effective.

Sick-bags

Airline sick-bags are tough and waterproof, and are therefore kept by a few seasoned travellers. Journalists have been known to keep their precious expenses receipts in them. A photographer friend found a use for one when camping in the Himalayas: when it was too cold to leave his tent, he used it as a urinal. (Sick-bags are self-standing, unlike ordinary plastic bags.) I tested their waterproofness at home by filling one of the British Airways bags with water: after a fortnight it hadn't leaked.

Forms

During the flight you may be given a form to complete. If you have already memorized the number of your passport and its date of issue, you will be doing better than the many passengers who have to get up twice — first to extract a pen, and later a passport, from their jackets in the overhead rack. Remembering your passport particulars will also be a great help in the event of its being stolen, and for all the other paperwork you may eventually face.

Some of the forms are incredibly long and tedious, so it's worth reducing your answers to the minimum acceptable. In the sections which ask for your nationality, place of issue of passport, address, place of birth, country of embarkation, I always write 'UK' instead of Britain or British. Although it is tempting to be frivolous with these boring forms, frivolity can cause dreary delays at immigration counters. So don't write 'Yes' in the section marked 'Sex'. And in the section asking if you have any intention of aiding and abetting the overthrow of the United States government, don't be like Gilbert Harding, who wrote, 'Sole purpose of visit'.

Arrival

In some countries there is no bus service from the airport to the city. As a result, taxi drivers try to bully passengers into paying extortionate fares. Arriving passengers are often exhausted and bewildered, and therefore an easy prey for rogues. Always check the price in advance, and, if it is unacceptably high, try to share a taxi with a local.

Even though I am worried about inducing unnecessary para-noia in readers (the horrors get much worse in Chapter 10), it just could prevent trouble if I warn that there have been a few cases of single girls being raped by taxi drivers they have hired at airports. I was surprised to read in the *Lonely Planet Update* (sadly now defunct) that this has happened even in Bangkok. And I have also heard of people being robbed by taxi drivers who had picked them up at Manila and Seoul. As far as I can find out, these robberies and rapes are nearly all by *unlicensed* drivers, so always take an official licensed cab, especially after dark.

I also have first-hand evidence of an unpleasant trick that has been used at Delhi airport. An immigration officer chooses attrac-tive female tourists for severe harassment. Another man then arrives and, like a guardian angel, appears to sort everything out. The bewildered and exhausted woman is then driven away by her 'protector', as well as the (now friendly) immigration officer, to a house where she is plied with drink, and then expected to provide grateful sexual favours.

Although I rarely book hotels, I like to do so for my first night or two. After an exhausting flight there is nothing worse than worrying about accommodation. It is good to start the holiday on a cheerful footing; and at the start of trips which need some organization it is often practical to stay in a hotel with a telephone.

On first arriving in a city, many travellers use taxis because they think it's difficult to learn the public transport system. But even for brief stays it is usually worth buying a transport map, as most systems can be mastered very quickly. New York has the most complicated subway system in the world, but with the invaluable 'Flashmap' anyone can use it immediately. Public transport is nearly always subsidized and therefore wonderfully cheap – and often more fun than taxis.

Jet lag

Every single written description of jet lag tells us that it is caused by the disturbance of our circadian rhythms, which are upset when we fly across time zones. But if this were true, how come that we are still shattered after a long flight from north to south? After years of deduction and experimentation I have discovered that the published explanations of jet lag are wrong. The writers have gone up the wrong cul-de-sac because it *is* true that the upsetting of our circadian rhythms is a *contributory* cause of jet lag. However, the chronic lassitude which some people suffer after a long flight is caused mostly by dehydration and salt depletion.

The air in an aeroplane goes through a process which makes it extremely dry. As a result your body is invisibly sweating, losing large amounts of water and salt, although the air is so dry that you aren't aware of the loss. Salt and water are important for all the body's main functions (this is discussed in more detail in Chapter 5), and therefore, when severely dehydrated after a long flight, you feel awful. The problem of dehydration is well known by air crews, who are instructed to drink quantities of water. I suspect that passengers aren't given the same warnings because of the logistical problems of carrying so much liquid.

While gradually realizing that dehydration was probably the main cause of jet lag, I also became aware of the associated problem of salt loss through sweating. Many years ago I suffered my worst ever jet lag after an extra-long flight to the Solomon Islands. At the same time I got acute cramps in the calves of my legs. I didn't then know that this was a classic symptom of salt depletion, nor did I connect it with my jet lag. Many fliers suffer from swollen ankles, and, although some of this may be a result of change of altitude, swollen ankles can also be a symptom of salt depletion. I have also been interested to learn that Tibetans, who live at very high altitudes, dose their tea with prodigious amounts of salt, and salt tea (this time without the butter) is also very common in north-west Pakistan. A few years ago I started experimenting by putting varying amounts of salt in my tea and drinks. When I had been flying for several hours, I was astonished to discover the amount of salt my taste-buds would tolerate. An amount that would normally have made me sick had become almost tasteless: my body obviously needed the extra salt.

All this is very unscientific, but if you suffer from chronic jet lag it could do you no harm to experiment by rehydrating the body with rehydration salts (about which much more in Chapter 5). I persuaded several friends who fly to Australia (one of the worst destinations for jet lag) to experiment with the salts, and most of them found an immense improvement. And since I've used them myself, I've never once suffered severely. This remedy is so unscientific that I can't give precise measurements: just drink plenty of liquid during the flight; use rehydrating salts once or twice during the flight and again after you have arrived. It's very simple and it works. I have mentioned in Chapter 5 that I find the tablets more convenient than the sachets.

I'm sorry to say that your extra liquid intake can't include alcohol, because it is dehydrating. Coffee and tea, to a lesser extent, are also dehydrating, because they are diuretics, so you should also abandon them (as well as for the additional reasons given below).

I will now explain more about circadian rhythms. The body functions according to a twenty-four-hour time-clock: you usually empty your bowels at the same time of the day; your pulse is lower at night; you urinate more frequently during the day; you feel sleepy in the late evening. If you fly from east to west or vice versa, these basic body rhythms continue as before, but your activities are dictated by a new schedule. Thus if you have just flown from London to Delhi, you may be getting up at eight in the morning, but your body is still functioning as if it were three in the morning. Gradually your body adapts, but meanwhile your circadian rhythms are upset; this can cause unsettled sleep, constipation, and lassitude. Extensive physiological and psychological tests have been conducted on long-flight passengers, and these tests have proved that when passengers cross several time zones, their efficiency is distinctly affected during the first two or three days. In fact their body rhythms may not fully return to normal for as long as eight or nine days.

More people (but not all) suffer worse problems when flying from west to east than vice versa. This is not surprising: if I have to get up at three a.m. in England I feel pretty rough for the rest of the day, and in effect this is what I'm having to do when I get up at eight a.m. in India. Those people who find no trouble at getting up early in the morning, but tend to feel sleepy in early evening, usually suffer worse jet lag when they are flying east to west.

I have read umpteen articles (and even one whole book) on remedies for the upset of circadian rhythms, but none of them convinces me. On the whole I think you should just conform as soon as possible to the new timetable, and rely on the effect of daylight, which will help readjust your bodily clock.

I will, however, risk giving a cranky remedy of my own. You can take it or leave it, but at least it won't do you any harm. If, as I have suggested, you don't drink coffee or tea during the flight, your body will probably suffer from mild withdrawal symptoms – most people are more addicted to caffeine than they realize. Don't drink any coffee or tea until your first-morning breakfast, and then this first hot drink will give a kick-start to your caffeine-starved body, thus helping to readjust the timing of your bowel movements and your body's clock.

Although rehydration therapy is the best remedy for reducing jet lag, I will mention two small points about reducing the stress of long flights.

Walk up and down the aisle at frequent intervals, and use any refuelling stops to take longer walks. Immobility is exhausting. In one experiment six 'passengers' simply sat in a chair all the time they weren't in bed. Within four days they were showing signs of dizziness, fainting, circulatory collapse, and nausea.

Some passengers find it helpful to wear earplugs during flights. The inside of a plane is noisier than you think – the engine noise is enough to deaden the sound of 300 chattering passengers – and some people find prolonged noise exhausting.

Whatever you do, and whether your flight is north–south or east–west, you are likely to be tired by flying. Being hurtled through the air in a noisy metal box with less oxygen than you are used to, and at an unaccustomed altitude, is an unnatural activity which is always likely to be stressful.

Fear of flying

An *Observer* journalist once joked that the Pope kisses the ground on arrival, not out of reverence, but because he can't believe that he's arrived safely. An extraordinary number of people are terrified of flying, and most of these aren't neurotics. There is nothing to be ashamed of. According to a survey by *Holiday Which?*, 53 per cent of their readers were frightened of flying. As a Travel Editor I'm constantly surprised at the number of writers who refuse commissions because they won't get on a plane.

Although the fear of flying isn't logical, passengers should still try to comfort themselves with the following information. Travelling by air is certainly more than ten times safer than travelling by car, and, depending on which statistics you read, may be twenty-five times safer. The statistics probably vary according to whether or not they include small aeroplanes. The large jets have a much better safety record. Statistics show that you are more likely to drown in your bathtub than be killed in an aircrash; in fact when you get on a large plane, your chances of being killed are less than one in a million. With Swissair, one of the safest airlines, your odds of dying have been calculated as one in 22 million.

You can also reassure yourself with the knowledge that in recent years flying has become safer, especially with the most reputable airlines. The development of jet and turbo-prop engines has brought a great improvement in technology: they are far more reliable than the earlier piston engines, enabling planes to fly way above dangerous weather. Maintenance techniques and crew training have also vastly improved.

I can offer another bit of comfort to the panic-stricken. Your fear could disappear spontaneously. For some reason I became terrified of flying during my early thirties. Every time the plane shuddered, I thought it was going to crash, and my active imagination made take-off and landing an utter misery. This period of terror lasted about three years, and then it suddenly and inexplicably disappeared.

A few more tips about safety. It is obvious that some airlines are going to be less thorough with safety and maintenance regulations; there is no doubt that the airlines of the developed world tend to be safer. African airlines are twice as likely to crash, and South American ones are four times as likely (no doubt exacerbated by dangerous flying conditions).

Choice of airline isn't the only factor in passenger safety. Following a few simple rules will reduce the risks of injury. Airlines recommend that safety belts should be kept loosely fastened throughout the flight. Passengers often think this is just a formality, but friends have given me horrific descriptions of unexpected turbulence. If your seat belt isn't already fastened, you get hurled about, and can suffer unpleasant injuries if you crash down on an armrest.

Despite strict instructions from the crew, over-eager passengers insist on standing up before the plane has come to a complete halt. Apart from being irritating, this is foolish – the pilot sometimes has to brake sharply, and it is estimated that 12 per cent of all passenger injuries happen at this time.

Although generally prejudiced against tranquillizers (huge

numbers of people have become unnecessarily addicted) I see little danger in taking them only when you fly. Maurice Yaffé, in his excellent *Taking the Fear out of Flying*,★ recommends diazepam (Valium) and lorazepam (Ativan). He suggests taking the dose thirty minutes before entering the anxiety-provoking period; but even if a panic attack has started, the medicine will still help. Another reliable doctor has sent me the following comment:

I'm not so keen on lorazepam. It is too long-acting. Diazepam comes in nice small 2 mg doses, so you can take one, and if that's not enough, take more. It is a brilliant muscle relaxant too, which helps . . . The short-acting sleeping pill, temazepam, helps you to sleep on very long flights, yet you remain rousable enough to grab the orange juice when it passes.

One friend swears by bromazepam (Lexotan); another finds beta-blockers to be more effective. None of these pills should be taken at the same time as alcohol.

There are two courses that claim to help people who are frightened of flying: Aviatours (061 832 7972) and Relax Air (081 554 8000). Unfortunately I can't yet confirm the effectiveness of these courses.

Even when there is a crash with fatalities, you have a good chance of surviving. On average more than half of the passengers now survive those crashes which have fatalities. Many more would survive if they weren't unnecessarily killed by the poisonous fumes, flames, and suffocation that follow a crash.

As you probably won't be reading this book when your plane is about to crash-land, I've tried in the next few paragraphs to concentrate on easily memorable advice.

Even if you refuse to read the flight safety card, you would do well to know the nearest emergency exits (not just one: it may be blocked); there is no universal opening mechanism for the door, so you should know how to open it, which you might

★(David & Charles, 1988)

have to do in the dark. If you have a small torch, get it ready. On my key ring, I have a tiny Maglite torch, which would be useful.

Before the crash Remove any sharp or metal objects from your pockets. A pen or comb can cause severe injury. Take off your glasses. Fasten your seat belt as tight as possible.

Immediately before impact Cover the top of your head with a pillow or blanket, because seats fold forward on impact. Cradle your head in your knees, and grasp your ankles. The aircraft will probably hit the ground more than once, so don't move from this position until it has stopped.

Immediately after impact If there are no instructions, get out fast. Fuel probably won't burn for about ninety seconds, and the dangerous gases are more survivable within the first sixty seconds. If there is thick and heavy smoke in the cabin, get down to armrest height, take a deep breath, and crawl. Don't try to rescue any possessions. Delay kills.

If there is bad smoke, try crawling (which is usually the best way to escape from smoke or a bad fire), but take care not to be trampled. There should be a series of floor lights to mark the way, and these will also indicate where there is an emergency exit.

Don't inflate your lifejacket before leaving, as it will block the emergency exit. Once you are down the chute, move well away from the plane as fast as possible.

To repeat the most important advice, *you stand an excellent chance of surviving a crash landing if you can get out of the plane within about ninety seconds.*

PLANE TICKETS

If your seat on a flight has been confirmed, the letters 'OK' should be written (under the column 'status' for each section of your flight). Any other letters indicate that your seat is not confirmed : RQ, for instance, indicates only that space has been requested, and WL means that you are wait-listed. If anything else is written there, ask for an explanation. Often the booking agents have written OK under the first section of your flight but sneakily don't tell you what they have put under the rest.

Handbooks always tell you to keep a separate record of the ticket's serial number. However, this is only a sequential number (usually of about fourteen or fifteen), most of which has already been printed on the ticket. It is sometimes far more important to keep a record of the **locator/booking reference number**, which is a shortish code usually found at the top of your ticket. This can be fed into any airline computer, and will immediately reveal all details about your booking, which the serial number won't. The booking reference number will, though, come off the computer, once the last flight on your ticket has taken place. Therefore if some drama has caused you to miss your flight, then the serial number (and place and date of issue) could be important.

It is now so easy to find a photocopier that I strongly recommend photocopying your airline ticket, and then keeping a copy in your document bag. This will provide details and convincing evidence about every aspect of your ticket, and it will also be useful if you have to claim for lost or delayed luggage (see Insurance, Chapter 1).

CHEAP PLANE TICKETS

In 1950 the average person had to work for twenty weeks before earning enough money to pay the lowest fare to New York; now they have to work for less than a week. The improvement in aeroplane construction, the increase in competition, and a more efficient use of fuel has brought us some wonderful bargains. Investigate the categories below, before deciding which ticket suits you best.

Ordinary promotions

Charter tickets aren't always the most convenient or cheapest. First, contact the most obvious airlines to find out about their own promotions, such as APEX (Advance Purchase Excursion) and PEX (Public Excursion). Nearly all these concessions involve a firm booking in advance, but if you take out a good insurance policy (see Chapter 1), you will be covered for cancelling in the event of many emergencies. These promotions may not be as cheap as discount tickets, but at least the price will give you a benchmark against which to judge others.

Discount tickets

It is useful to realize that there is a difference between ordinary discount tickets and charter tickets. Discount tickets are usually ones which have been dispersed by airlines to avoid IATA regulations. When the airlines judge they can't sell all their tickets, they sell some of them off on the cheap. Many of the cheap tickets advertised in newspapers come into this category. A recent monthly guide, *Dann's Digest* (Dann's House, New Pond Hill, Heathfield, East Sussex TN21 0NB; tel. 0435 867107), is invaluable for studying ticket prices, and identifying sources of cheap tickets. It lists a large number of companies through whom the airlines disperse their discounted tickets, and quotes prices from London, Manchester, and Glasgow. Unless you are a very regular traveller, you won't want an annual subscription (at present £35), but a single copy can be ordered at a relatively high price (at present £7.50). If your local reference library doesn't stock it (some do), you might be able to persuade them to subscribe. The guide is also a useful source on the latest round-the-world tickets (see below).

You won't actually come to any harm if you consult an ordinary travel agent, but they tend to be ignorant and unhelpful about cheap long-haul fares. In a recent survey of 253 travel agents by the Consumers' Association, four out of five couldn't find the cheapest flight to Nice, even though it was easily available from British Airways. The chains of travel agents tend to have a low calibre of staff, and it is best to find a specialist independent one. I am reluctant to recommend any companies because recommendations become out of date so fast, but here are the telephone numbers of a few companies specializing in long-haul flights. By ringing them you should get at the least a good guideline for judging cheap tickets:

Quest Worldwide (081 547 3322)
Trailfinders (071 938 3366)
STA (071 937 9962)
Bridge the World (071 911 0900)
Travel Bug (Manchester; 061 721 4000)

The Air Travel Advisory Bureau (071 636 5000) gets its revenue from the companies it advertises, but all the same I have sometimes found it a useful source of information on other companies offering cheap tickets. If you look at *Dann's Digest*, get some numbers out of the Air Travel Advisory Bureau, and ring some of the above companies, you will have completed an effective search for a cheap ticket.

Student and youth fares

It isn't only students who can get reductions; anyone under twenty-six can also get them and, depending on the airline, they are also given to anyone employed by a teaching organization, or even a student's private tutor.

Now that there are so many discounted tickets available, student ones aren't necessarily the cheapest. But it is still always worth investigating them because sometimes you will be able to get a more *flexible* ticket on a *better* airline. It is usually the major carriers that offer the best discounts. STA and Campus Travel (see Appendix 3) specialize in student fares, can issue International Student Cards, and have offices throughout the country.

Charter tickets

Charter flights rarely still oblige you to stay in their booked accommodation, but they tend not to be as convenient and comfortable as scheduled airlines. The lack of leg room can be harrowing. When a charter flight is only slightly cheaper than a scheduled one, I would take the latter.

146

If anything goes wrong, it is always the charter flights that suffer most. I remember once saving £15 by taking a charter flight from Italy. Fog in Britain was upsetting airline schedules. As a result my plane left three hours late, and finally landed at Lydd Airport instead of Gatwick. We were stranded there for hours until rescued by a freezing bus. I didn't get home until 4 a.m. The alternative British Airways flight arrived at Heathrow only an hour late.

If you buy charter tickets just before the departure date, they can sometimes be stunningly cheap, especially those to popular holiday destinations. I have seen advertisements (in the *Evening Standard*) for return tickets to Morocco for as little as £48. And I once bought a return ticket to Pisa for only £36. Because the plane has to fly anyway, and the costs are therefore fixed, it is worth the airline's while to get any money it can for a seat that would otherwise be empty.

Responding to newspaper advertisements for cheap tickets can sometimes be tiresome, as advertisers often display bogus low prices in order to encourage you to telephone. This is known as 'Bait and Switch'.

Round-the-world tickets

There has been a great boom in round-the-world (RTW) tickets, and they offer great value for those who can go round the world in one direction. They can even be a bonus to those whose primary intention isn't going round the world, and the tickets often represent mile for mile the best value in air travel. For a long time, for instance, a RTW ticket was the best way to get somewhere expensive like Fiji. The tickets will usually last for up to a year. Watch out for various exclusions, and be aware that some RTW tickets insist on minimum stays which can be as long as fourteen days. You can't usually backtrack, but you can often buy additional excursion fares at a reasonable rate.

Most of the major airlines (often combining with other airlines) offer RTW fares. You can buy an 'off-the-peg' RTW ticket, which may be cheaper, but offers you less choice, or you can buy a tailor-made one. Try ringing the following companies which specialize in RTW tickets:

Trailfinders (071 938 3366)
STA (071 937 9962)
Reho (071 242 5555)
Austravel (071 734 7755)
Quest Worldwide (081 547 3322)

Air passes

Several airlines have air passes which allow very cheap travel for foreign visitors within a specific country. You can get bargains, some of them much better than others, in a number of countries, including Brazil, Colombia, Argentina, India, Malaysia, South Africa, the United States, and Australia (Australian Airlines offers discounts of as much as 55 per cent for foreign visitors). It is sometimes necessary to fly with the appropriate *international* carrier (for example, South African Airways and several US airlines) in order to be eligible for discounts on internal flights. It is also important to know that some of these air passes can be purchased only *before* you arrive in the country. Just to complicate things, some internal flights (such as in Pakistan) are more expensive when bought abroad.

Couriers

Sometimes you can get a cheap ticket by being a courier, but generally it isn't the great bargain that it used to be. Be sure to find out all the restrictions, and be aware that some of the companies don't allow you to take a suitcase. Information about courier companies changes very fast, but here are two telephone numbers in case they are useful: Courier Travel Services (071 351 0300) and Polo Express (081 759 5383) (send stamped addressed envelope to 208 Epsom Square, Heathrow Airport, Hounslow, Middx. TW6 2BL for details).

Protection against dubious agents

There are many rogues in the cheap-ticket business, and I've known plenty of people who have lost their deposits, or even their whole fares. The European Community promises more protection, but meanwhile I've tried to make some sense out of the existing complicated situation.

The agent Remember that the selling of discount tickets has become widespread and respectable, and it has become less necessary to go to that little agent on the fourth floor at the furthest end of the Harrow Road. Therefore if you have found your agent through a newspaper, visit it at an early stage to see whether it is suspiciously seedy.

If your agent is a member of ABTA (Association of British Travel Agents), you will – as the law now stands – be refunded if it goes bust. But all 'bonding' or guaranteeing rules are probably going to be changed by the European Community, so try to find out if your agent is guaranteed by whatever new *bonding* rules may have been enacted. At present most agents are members of ABTA, and if you want to check on the current situation, you could contact the association: ABTA, 55 Newman Street, London W1P 4AH (tel. 071 637 2444).

Charter tickets Membership of ABTA is not enough to give you protection for *charter* tickets. The company you book with should hold an ATOL (Air Travel Organizer's Licence). This means that the company is regularly investigated, and there will also be some type of bond to protect you in case the tour operator goes bankrupt. If the agent advertises, they will display both their ABTA and their ATOL membership. If you want to check they have an ATOL number, ring the Civil Aviation Authority on 071 832 5620 or 071 832 6353. Although a receipt from an ATOL holder means that you are protected, in the case of an 'agent' for ATOL holders you are not protected from fraud by the agent, and you remain vulnerable until the agent has paid the holder of the ATOL number. But, as I say, the European Community is likely to change all these rules.

Cheap scheduled tickets If your ticket is with an IATA airline, then you will be protected once you have the ticket in your hand. Therefore if you are booking with a small airline, check whether it is a member of IATA. An ATOL does not protect you for scheduled fares.

General rules You are usually vulnerable until you have your ticket in your hands. When buying a charter ticket, you are often obliged to pay in advance, but make sure you get the ticket within seven days. With a scheduled ticket you shouldn't really pay a deposit of more than 15 per cent. Always get a written receipt for any money you have paid. Ring the airlines direct to see if you are on the passenger list. If you are, this will be a comfort. If you aren't, this doesn't necessarily mean your agent is a rogue, but get back to him and ask why you aren't on the list.

If you pay for a ticket or holiday by credit card, you may (but see below) be protected if your payment was for more than £100. (At present this doesn't apply to charge cards such as American Express and Diners Club.) But if you aren't sure of the company's respectability, don't use your card over the telephone. If an agent refuses to accept credit-card payment, and doesn't offer an alternative bonding system, you should be suspicious.

When an airline goes bust, some credit-card companies try to wriggle out of repaying you. They claim they weren't liable because the credit voucher had been made out to the travel agent, not the airline. Sometimes it has been possible to pressurize them to pay up. I wrote to the National Westminster Bank to check this situation, and received the following reply:

In the case of a booking being made with a travel agent, and the travel agent goes into liquidation, then reimbursement for the cardholder by NatWest must be considered. If, however, the flight company goes into liquidation, then no cover will be provided by NatWest since the contract, which is between NatWest and the Travel Agent (i.e. the party which received the payment), does not extend to the flight company. The key point is that NatWest will only consider providing cover *if the party which received the payment via the NatWest Access card goes into liquidation (bankrupt).*

Inquiries, complaints, and disputes

Here are two addresses which may be of help.

The Civil Aviation Authority, CAA House, 45–59 Kingsway, London WC2B 6TE (tel. 071 379 7311)

ABTA, 55 Newman Street, London W1P 4AH (tel 071 637 2444) – they run a conciliation and arbitration service

The **Small Claims Court** is an excellent and cheap method of pursuing small sums of money (at the time of writing under £1,000), and there are no fees for lawyers. You can find your local Small Claims Court by looking under 'Courts, county' in the telephone directory.

Don't be bullied by any company into believing that their small-print clauses are gospel; British courts will reject any small-print clauses that are in contravention of the main spirit of a contract.

If you have booked the entire holiday through an agent, and you find any aspect of the living conditions unsatisfactory, take photographs. With photographic evidence, one friend of mine got 50 per cent of her money repaid immediately.

Airport tax

Travellers frequently spend the last of their money, and discover at the check-in counter that they have to pay an airport tax. This wretched institution is widespread in the Third World. And to complicate things, the tax may either be in dollars (which you probably won't have) or, if you do have dollars, the tax will be in the local currency (in which case you find yourself having to change a $50 note into a currency which will be worthless once you've left the country). As airport tax isn't levied at every airport, it is easily forgotten and a great nuisance. For this reason I try to find out about it in advance, and enter it in my security chart (see Fig. 2, Chapter 1). Increasingly often the tax is as high as $20.

Reconfirming tickets

Return tickets don't guarantee a place on the plane – even when the date and flight number are on the ticket. Often there is a rule obliging passengers to reconfirm more than three days before departure, and airlines are increasingly ruthless about dropping passengers who don't do this.

Three days before departure often turns out to be an impractical time to reconfirm. Even those who manage to remember may be out in the sticks, where there is no access to telephone or booking office. Until recently, I didn't realize that the best way of avoiding this problem is to reconfirm immediately on arrival; in fact the counsel of perfection is to walk straight to a ticket desk immediately after you have gone through customs and immigration (though one would usually be too cluttered and tired to bother to do this). But the first day of a trip would usually be an easy time to use the telephone or find a suitable office, and have done with this annoying little chore.

Previously I had believed that an early reconfirmation would be less effective than a later one, but friends in the travel business assure me that this is not true, and that the earlier you can do it the better.

When flying with a minor airline, it is worth checking that the reconfirmation has worked. In the Solomon Islands I once had to reconfirm five times before my name actually appeared on the passenger list.

At whatever stage you reconfirm it is little extra trouble to make sure that the flight schedules haven't changed.

Airlines are more frequently overbooked in the Third World than they are in Europe. This is often caused by the block bookings of VIPs and by other individuals reserving places on a large number of different flights before deciding which flight will be the most convenient. Confirming a seat can be extremely difficult, and occasionally a booking clerk announces there is no seat within days or even weeks of the desired departure date. Nevertheless, if you go to the airport on spec, you can often board the plane – and often find that half the seats are empty. On at least thirty occasions I have taken a chance by going to the airport, and nearly every time (but not always) I've got a seat.

CHAPTER 5

HEALTH

I'm not qualified to discuss medicine, and especially don't want to encourage people to treat their own ailments when they can go to a doctor. But health is one of the main concerns of those who are about to set out for the tropics, so I have tried to write about the more important aspects. Please remember, though, that tropical medicine is an enormous subject, and that my judgement is fallible. For more detailed information I list some good books about travel medicine in Appendix 1. In particular I should mention *Travellers' Health*, edited by Richard Dawood, because each section is written by an expert. I referred to it frequently when researching this chapter.

When describing medicines I have written the pharmacological name with a small initial letter, and the usually shorter brand names (by which they are often more commonly known) with a capital letter: for example, co-trimoxazole, which is commonly known as Bactrim or Septrin.

I have been helped enormously with this chapter by Dr Jane Wilson, Professor David Warrell of Oxford University, and Dr Larry Goodyer of the Department of Pharmacy at King's College; but any mistakes or wrong judgements are definitely mine.

IMMUNIZATIONS

Don't rely on advice from your local GP about this, as GPs are often inexperienced in travel medicine. At a conference on expedition medicine, I heard an eminent tropical specialist say that he had 'been struck by the astonishingly misleading, near-criminally negligent information given by doctors to expatriates before travelling'. It is best to contact specialist immunization centres; even they aren't always accurate. Three of them once told me that I needed a cholera immunization for India, when it definitely wasn't necessary.

You should start your immunizations well in advance; if this is your first long trip, and you therefore have to get a lot of immunizations, you could even need as long as two months. Some of the immunizations necessitate an interval between the first and second inoculation (rabies requires twenty-eight days), or there may have to be a gap between one type of immunization and another. You may suffer after-effects from an immunization (as I once did after a typhoid injection), and will want to recover before you leave. And as immunity may not develop for several days, your immunization may not become valid immediately. For instance, immigration officials will not accept the yellow fever immunization certificate until ten days after the vaccination.

A confusion about immunizations may result from the following simple misunderstanding. If a traveller from London asks the Indian Embassy whether a yellow fever certificate is necessary for travelling to India, the Embassy will say no. But the traveller has omitted to mention the various countries he will be visiting on his way to India, and therefore he won't be told that a yellow fever certificate is required for anyone entering from a yellow fever zone.

One very important point. Occasionally, after all your best efforts, you may still be in doubt whether a particular immunization is mandatory. In this case, because of the danger of Aids, it is always best to get it first, because a compulsory injection in those countries where fresh needles aren't always used could be a death sentence. People have also died from incorrectly stored cholera vaccine.

It is best to keep a note all the way through your life of immunizations: the effect of some of them is cumulative.

Pregnant women should always get special advice about immunization, or before taking any of the drugs mentioned in this chapter.

If you have been having any type of regular medical treatment, or if you have developed HIV, be sure to declare this before getting immunized, because if your immune system is suppressed, some of the immunizations with a live virus (such as yellow fever, polio, or one of the typhoids) could be dangerous for you.

Mandatory immunizations

Two immunizations may be mandatory when you visit particular countries. These are **yellow fever** and **cholera**.

Yellow fever is a highly effective vaccine, and lasts for at least ten years. Although the species of mosquito that carries the disease does live in Asia, yellow fever is found only in Africa and South America.

At the time of writing, the overwhelming body of expert opinion considers that cholera immunization is not very effective. (As usual in this book, I'm raising this more as a question than as a definitive answer, because the situation may change; and a new, more effective cholera vaccine may be on the way.) Even where cholera exists, the careful traveller is not likely to get it. The World Health Organization formally abolished cholera vaccinations as long ago as 1973. The Center for Disease Control in Atlanta logged only ten cases of cholera among American travellers during the first twenty years of an epidemic that began in 1961. A report by SmithKline Beecham has estimated that travellers were 800 times more likely to catch hepatitis A than cholera.

Cholera isn't nearly as dangerous for Westerners as has been generally supposed. It is true that death from cholera may occur within a few hours, but this is most unlikely. With prompt rehydration therapy, fewer than 1 per cent of cholera patients die; therefore, where there is a risk, carry your rehydration sachets or tablets (see page 167). Antibiotics shorten the length and diminish the severity of the illness, but they aren't as important as rehydration.

Unfortunately some countries still require valid certificates of cholera from all travellers, and others require certificates from travellers who are entering from an infected area.

Recommended immunizations

Some recommended immunizations are more important for your health than the mandatory ones. The following are the most likely to be recommended.

Tetanus   You should get the highly effective immunization. You are more likely to catch tetanus in the tropics, and the immunization is especially important if you are at risk of being cut or wounded. As the immunization booster lasts ten years, it is also very useful for protection at home.

Polio   This is a most unpleasant disease which can cause paralysis. The immunization is highly recommended. You can usually take it as a few drops on a sugar lump.

Hepatitis A   Protection against hepatitis A is very worthwhile because it is one of the commonest diseases among travellers; you are forty times more likely to catch it than typhoid. Backpackers are six times more likely to catch it than luxury tourists. The disease is especially widespread in the Third World; in one study in Bali, the blood of all 287 individuals tested showed that at some stage they had been infected with the disease.

Recently a new vaccine has been developed for hepatitis A. The two-dose course provides immunity for about one year; a booster dose, given six to twelve months after the first course, extends the immunity for up to ten years. This gives a far higher level of protection than the immunoglobulin immunization. (The development of the new vaccine took eight years, and cost $100 million dollars – which shows why we don't get new immunizations more often.)

I presume that this new vaccine will make gamma globulin out of date, except perhaps for short trips, when some people may be reluctant to pay for the more expensive immunization, or in cases when the traveller needs to leave in a hurry. The new vaccine takes ten days to produce an immune response.

If you do receive your gamma globulin immunization in Britain, there is no truth in the scare stories that you might develop Aids.

157

To double check this I wrote to several sources: the Public Health Laboratory Service, the School of Pathology at the Middlesex Hospital Medical School, the Department of Health, and the Medical Officer of the Radcliffe Infirmary. These letters confirm that the process which is used in preparing pooled gamma globulin kills the HIV virus (and also that of hepatitis B). However, as gamma globulin is a pooled blood product made from a number of donors, it is extremely unwise to get this immunization in any country where the strictest standards may not have been enforced.

Few travellers realize that they may already have had hepatitis A, which means they are lucky enough to have lifelong immunity. A test in the west of Scotland showed that some 60 per cent of blood donors aged between eighteen and forty had acquired hepatitis A antibodies.

This percentage is lower in other parts of Britain, but higher among those who are widely travelled, and also it is higher among older age groups. Up to about 40 per cent of adults who have travelled in the Third World possess immunity to hepatitis A. This rises to as high as 50 per cent among Oxfam fieldworkers. So if you are well travelled, it may be worth taking the rather expensive test to see if you can avoid getting injected.

If you have developed full-blown hepatitis A, you will be immune for life.

If you are likely to be a long-term traveller, and you aren't immune, then you would be very foolish not to get protection against hepatitis A, which is an unpleasant and debilitating disease.

Hepatitis B This is quite different from hepatitis A, and can be a more serious illness. It is caught in much the same way as Aids, through blood or sexual contact, but is far more infectious. In parts of the Third World about 30 per cent of prostitutes are carriers of the virus. Although for most people the risk of catching hepatitis B is less than for catching hepatitis A, the immunization is being increasingly recommended. It is a very infectious disease, and I know of at least two people who have caught it from dental treatment abroad. It can be caught from sexual intercourse even when you are wearing a condom, and is also easily caught from faulty medical treatment or dirty needles; it would be sensible to be immunized if you were spending a long time in a country where, in the event of an accident, you might get a transfusion of suspect blood. The immunization is considered very safe – Princess Anne has had it – and after the three (widely spaced) injections it gives at least three years' immunity, and probably much more. After the injections you must check that you have developed the antibodies, as this isn't always automatic. Hepatitis B immunization is about to be recommended as part of a childhood programme in the United States.

Typhoid This quite common disease can be dangerous. The immunization is therefore often recommended. At the time of writing there are now three alternative types of immunization, including a pill. Quite a number of people (especially if they are older than thirty-five) develop flu-like symptoms from some of the immunizations. At present it is the more expensive immunizations which are less likely to give you symptoms.

Rabies The disease was eradicated in Britain in 1902, when quarantine and import controls were introduced. Since then no one in Britain has died of rabies from an infection caught within the country. (Several, though, have become infected abroad.) There is now an effective vaccine without unpleasant side-effects. Travellers at special risk, therefore, should be immunized. Those generally considered at greater risk include some anthropologists, vets, zoologists, and cavers (bats may carry rabies, especially in the Americas). Also the immunization is advisable for anyone going to very remote areas where they won't be able to reach a hospital quickly.

I initially wrote that the vaccination did not seem worthwhile for many *ordinary* travellers, because when bitten by a suspicious animal you are still obliged to get treatment, even if you have had a vaccination. But when I sent this text to a professor of tropical medicine, he wrote to me:

159

I thoroughly disagree with you about pre-exposure (preventive) rabies vaccination. Having circulating antibodies against the rabies virus, and an immune system primed to produce lots more antibody very quickly, gives you a big advantage if you are exposed to rabies. Although a booster course is advisable, you won't need passive immunization (human rabies immune globulin or anti-rabies serum) and you have more time on your side, which may be important if you are a long way away from civilization.

After receiving this advice, I think that I would strongly consider vaccination for certain trips off the beaten track, and possibly for long trips in the Indian subcontinent, where rabies is rife. Check the cost of the vaccine first, as it can vary a lot, especially as in some travel clinics you might be able to share the cost of an ampoule.

The above covers the most frequently recommended immunizations. There are two others which are occasionally recommended for intrepid travellers visiting areas where there is an epidemic. The immunization for **Japanese B encephalitis** gives good protection for about three years. The risk of catching it is very small, but it exists through a large area of Asia, especially in Nepal. If you are going to an area where there is an epidemic (most likely during the monsoon), it is important to have the immunization, as the disease is potentially fatal. The immunization for **meningococcal meningitis** provides three years of protection within ten days of administration. (This strain of vaccine does not protect you against the variety of meningitis that is most common in Britain.) The chances of catching meningitis are small, but if caught, the outcome is usually very serious and often fatal, so it is well worth checking to see if you need the immunization. It is now quite often required for East Africa, and for the Middle East during the Haj.

If you want specialist advice about immunizations or health risks in remote areas, MASTA (tel. 071 631 4408) sell health briefs and personal immunization programmes; forms for these can also be obtained from Boots. Free advice can also be gathered from the immunization centres listed in Appendix 3, and from the hospitals mentioned under the section below on prophylaxis for malaria. In the United States information about specific regions can be got from the Center for Disease Control in Atlanta (tel. 0101 404 322 4555).

A booklet, entitled T4, 'Health Advice for Travellers Anywhere in the World', is available from post offices. You can also try ordering a free copy by ringing 0800 555 777. It includes an application for form E111, which enables you to get emergency medical treatment free of charge in most European Community countries, and the booklet lists other countries where the UK has reciprocal arrangements. Don't however, let the possibility of free emergency treatment deter you from taking out full medical insurance (see Chapter 1).

———————————

Malaria

The word malaria is derived from two Italian words meaning 'bad air'. For at least 2,000 years people have associated malaria with the air around stagnant water, but it wasn't until 1897 that Sir Ronald Ross discovered that the disease was spread by mosquitoes, which of course breed in the water.

The guilty insects are the females of the Anopheles genus, of which we have five varieties in Britain. Malaria existed here for many years before declining in the nineteenth century, but in theory an outbreak could happen here again. After the First World War, when soldiers returning from Greece and India were convalescing in Kent, the local mosquitoes picked up malaria. The resulting epidemic included 500 cases of malaria among Kentish citizens who had never left the country. In fact, malaria has now been eradicated through much of the temperate world.

Travellers visiting any part of the tropical or semi-tropical world, however, should be on their guard against malaria. Its increase has been dramatic. Some of the problem has been a resistance of the mosquito to insecticides, partly due to the erratic administration of eradication programmes, and partly due to the resistance of the actual parasite to prophylactic medication. Throughout the world there are now estimated to be nearly 200 million cases of malaria each year, with more than 1 million deaths. This is reflected in the numbers now treated in Britain: in the 1960s there were only about 100 cases a year, now there are more than 2,000 cases a year, which always include several deaths.

Prophylaxis   Wherever malaria exists you must take prophylactic pills. Even though they aren't guaranteed to protect you against malaria, they certainly reduce the likelihood of an infection; and in the event of infection, they will reduce the severity of the illness, and therefore possibly save your life.

Pregnant and breast-feeding women should be extra cautious about visiting malarial zones. Pregnant women are more likely to catch malaria (even when they are taking the tablets), and the disease can be more severe in pregnant women.

Travellers should make the most careful inquiries before choosing their prophylactic; one that is excellent for a particular area may be less suitable for another. Furthermore, the pattern of resistance to prophylactics is constantly changing, so a prophylactic that is considered effective one year may no longer be recommended the next.

Don't take the advice of either a tourist board or the embassy of the country you are about to visit. Many of them are recklessly dishonest with their advice, especially when they wish to encourage tourism.

Don't rely on your local doctor's advice about which tablets to take: GPs are often out of date. Ask the regular immunization centres, and check with any of the following specialists:

The Malaria Reference Laboratory, which gives recorded advice (for which you pay a premium rate) on 0891 600 350

The Nuffield Department of Clinical Medicine, John Radcliffe Hospital, Oxford (tel. 0865 741 166)

The Liverpool School of Tropical Medicine (tel. 051 708 9393)
The Unit for Communicable Disease and Tropical Medicine
   at the East Birmingham Hospital (tel. 021 766 6611)
In the United States you can ring the Center for Disease
   Control in Atlanta (tel. 0101 404 332 4555)

It is worth knowing that the areas of the world with very
high risks of the most dangerous varieties of malaria are usually
in low-lying tropical Africa. For instance, at the time of writing,
you are fifty times more likely to catch malaria in West Africa
than in most parts of South America.

The most common way of catching malaria is to forget to
take the pills after you have returned home. It is easy to do this
because once you are home the danger seems so far away. In fact
it is crucial that you take the pills for at least four weeks (some
authorities recommend six weeks) after you have returned, because the pills aren't effective until the parasite has been released
from the liver. And if a parasite does break through after you've
stopped taking the pills, it is likely to be a more severe variety.

Start taking your tablets a week before leaving; this gives the
medication a chance to enter your system, and also gives you the
opportunity of changing your pill in the event of being one of
the few people who react adversely.

When I have to take a weekly pill, I usually try to start on
Sunday, as this is easy to remember.

Symptoms   If you have the slightest symptom of any type of
malaria at any time *up to a year* after you have returned home,
then get a blood test, even if you have been scrupulously taking
the pills. Don't just discuss it with your local GP, *who may easily
diagnose it as flu, with the result that you could be dead within a few
days*. If you have any unexplained illness, or any illness with flu-
like symptoms, or any illness with the symptoms of jaundice or
diarrhoea, then insist on a blood test. This will usually diagnose
the problem, but remember that even a blood test isn't
conclusive.

The usual symptoms of an attack of malaria include a cold shivering stage, followed after an hour or so by a period of unbearable heat. Profuse sweating then ends the attack, restoring the usual body temperature some five to eight hours after it began to rise. The entire cycle takes about twenty-four hours and is repeated approximately every other day, but may be more frequent to begin with.

Falciparum malaria, which is the most dangerous variety, often begins with flu-like symptoms, including fever and headache; frequently the dominant symptom is violent diarrhoea, which can lead you to believe you have food poisoning or dysentery rather than malaria fever.

It is worth knowing that the symptoms of dengue fever (see page 185), which will clear up by itself, are similar to those of some types of malaria. Dengue fever is also caught from mosquitoes.

Treatment of falciparum malaria   Most books don't give advice about treatment of malaria, as it is far better that you should get correct treatment from a doctor. But because some strains of malaria are life-threatening, and because you may save your life if you have the right pills, it is wise to carry them when you are going on a trip that takes you out of the reach of doctors. Imperfect treatment is better than dying.

Most lethal cases of malaria are of the falciparum variety. And if malaria has broken through your prophylactics, then it is most likely to be of this type, especially if you are in Africa. So find out the most up-to-date advice about the most effective treatment for falciparum malaria: you will learn that very few pills are necessary. Traditionally a course of quinine followed by a few tablets of Fansidar have been recommended. Some strains of falciparum malaria are even resistant to Fansidar, so alternative regimes have to be used: for example, mefloquine (Lariam) or the new drug Halfan. But don't rely on any of this information; get **up-to-date advice** from a **tropical** doctor. It is worth knowing that many of the malaria remedies are toxic, and that they can cause quite a variety of side-effects (including psychiatric disturbances among a very small proportion of patients). But all of this is much better than dying.

Quinine is a very ancient remedy for malaria. Gin and tonic originated because the gin helped disguise the bitter taste of the quinine. If it is the only remedy you can get, you should know that it commonly produces side-effects, including deafness and buzzing in the ears. You may need to adjust your dose.

When you are getting advice about a regime for treatment, remember that a larger person will need a larger dose.

For the headache that accompanies malaria, take paracetamol.

Where malaria is dangerous, it is best not to rely on prophylactics, and you should adopt a belt-and-braces approach by using both repellents and insecticides. For more information about these, see the section on Mosquitoes in Chapter 6.

Diarrhoea

Most travellers suffer from diarrhoea at some stage. This is nearly always during the first part of their travels. Approximately 60 per cent of diarrhoea outbreaks occur within the first week and 95 per cent within the first two weeks. And you can be comforted by the knowledge that most of the outbreaks clear up quickly. In Dr Anthony Turner's *Traveller's Health Guide* (see Appendix 1) he concludes from his own and other surveys that approximately 80 per cent of cases clear up within three days. A few self-limiting diarrhoeas, though, may last for up to ten days.

Therefore, when you are struck by ordinary diarrhoea and feel reasonably well, there is no need to become too anxious. It is probably best to take no drugs, and to let nature take its course, apart from rehydrating yourself. After all, diarrhoea is a method of letting the body cleanse itself. In certain circumstances, diarrhoea remedies (apart from rehydration ones) can be harmful, as they merely prolong the disease and may even mask the symptoms of the infection.

There are circumstances, though, when you need to block yourself up. You may be going on a long journey in a canoe or a bus, when there is no access to a lavatory. So it is always best to carry a **blocking-up remedy**. Personally, I favour codeine-phosphate, which has long been considered one of the very best anti-diarrhoeal drugs. The pills (which have to be bought on prescription) are also practical because they are tiny, and because they usefully double up as an effective remedy for pain and headache (even more effective when taken with aspirin).

In the last edition I reported that the assembled experts at a meeting of the British Society for the Study of Infection had agreed that, after codeine-phosphate, the remedy of choice was diphenoxylate with atropine (trade name Lomotil). This is now disapproved of by several experts, which shows how fast expert opinion can change. The favourite over-the-counter remedy now appears to be loperamide (trade name Imodium or Arret). It is cheapest from Boots, where it is called **Diareze**. I also find that the anecdotal evidence from travellers seems to support this. It is safe, and doesn't turn your insides into solid cement.

I never travel without ispaghula husk, a remedy I discovered many years ago in India, when it cured an agonizing stomach pain within minutes. Instead of acting like a drug, it is a bulking agent with the remarkable distinction of being able to cure both constipation and diarrhoea. The Indian packets proclaim, 'It is an ideal agent for the treatment of constipation. Its substance aids the intestines to move fast and brings easy stool. Its mucilage contents pacify the cause of irritation thus giving relief in dysentery and diarrhoea'. A woman friend tells me that my recommendation of ispaghula husk has saved her from a lifetime's martyrdom to constipation.

We know that it was used by Persian physicians as far back as the tenth century, and was first discovered by the British towards the end of the eighteenth century in India. By 1868 it was listed in the *Pharmacopoeia of India*. Since 1931 it has been sold in Britain under the name Isogel, and is also available as sachets, under the name Fybogel. In India, it is often known as Sat Isabgol. When you take the husk with liquid, you must drink it immediately because it swells fast and becomes extremely sticky.

In whatever form you carry ispaghula husk, it is rather bulky; I usually find the sachets of Fybogel to be the most convenient, but you might want to decant it into something like a Redoxon tube.

Unfortunately it appears I must qualify my rhapsody for this remedy, as a knowledgeable doctor sent me the following comment: 'I would be wary of recommending ispaghula for diarrhoea caused by infection. It could worsen dehydration.'

Nearly everyone knows by now that clioquinol (trade name Enterovioform) is of no use for the prevention or treatment of diarrhoea, and can be harmful.

Many anti-diarrhoeal agents, including codeine-phosphate and loperamide (Arret, Imodium) may be a serious risk for children.

Don't drink milk or milk products during diarrhoea, or for a few days afterwards. On the whole, follow your body's instincts for plain food, which may include boiled rice, bread, and clear soup. Bananas are valuable, because they contain pectin, a binding agent, and are also a source of potassium (a valuable salt which you will have lost during diarrhoea).

Diarrhoea can increase the risk of your becoming pregnant, as it reduces absorption of the contraception pill. It may also reduce absorption of other vital pills, including malaria prophylactics.

Travellers, especially business travellers, have often demanded a prophylactic against diarrhoea, and formerly several remedies were recommended. But this isn't advisable: drugs interfere with the body's exceedingly complicated mechanisms, and shouldn't be taken unless strictly necessary. If you have a very sensitive stomach and are upset by highly spiced food, then try taking a sachet of Fybogel a day. As it's only a bulking agent, it won't do you any harm. Increase the dose, as appropriate.

Many tropical doctors consider that one of the greatest medical breakthroughs, after penicillin, was the recent discovery that the absorption of vital fluids and salts is greatly enhanced by the presence of sugar (or starch). The *Lancet* described this **rehydration therapy** as 'potentially the greatest medical advance this century . . . Glucose and sugar can act as the Trojan horse which opens up the intestinal wall to the absorption of twenty-five times as much salt and water as is possible without glucose.'

The therapy is necessary because diarrhoea and dysentery may cause severe dehydration, which is dangerous. You can fix the problem of non-absorption of liquids in your mind by thinking of a flower in a waterless vase – how fast it dies! Children are especially vulnerable: a Granada television programme claimed that 5,000,000 lives a year could be saved by rehydration therapy.

In the event of diarrhoea (and especially diarrhoea and vomiting) sip some liquid in which you have mixed salt and sugar – approximately 1 *level* teaspoonful of salt with 8 level teaspoonfuls of sugar in 1 litre of liquid. Sometimes it is more practical to remember one pinch of salt and 1 teaspoonful of sugar in a cup of liquid. If you are worried about proportions, follow the rule of not drinking the liquid if it is more salty than tears. Too much salt can be harmful. If you want to order a plastic spoon giving the correct measurements for salt and sugar, write to TALC, PO Box 49, St Albans, Herts., sending a stamped addressed envelope, and a donation to support their excellent health education work in the Third World.

In several circumstances knowledge of rehydration therapy could be life-saving. Rehydration is so important that experts say it is better to rehydrate with liquid that is suspect than not to rehydrate at all.

There have been recent reports that the absorption of liquid and salts is helped even more by the presence of starch, such as a thick, drinkable solution made from rice-flour, or the water in which rice has been boiled. But I have concentrated on sugar, because this is easy to remember and the most practical for a wide variety of circumstances.

When someone is severely ill with dehydration, give them a sip of rehydration fluid every five minutes, day and night, until they begin to urinate normally. A large person needs more than 3 litres a day. Give this to them frequently in small sips, even if they are vomiting. In fact, when someone is vomiting, a whole glass will usually induce a great puke, but if the patient sips, then some of the liquid will slip down. If dehydration gets worse, or the person doesn't urinate within six hours, you must find a health-worker who can give liquid in a vein (though make sure the equipment is sterilized, because of the risks of HIV and hepatitis B).

I don't imagine that one in a hundred travellers carry **rehydration mixtures** (in Britain the leading brands are Dioralyte and Rehidrat), especially as they are rather bulky and expensive. But I always carry them, for various reasons. Even with milder diarrhoea you will tend to feel better when sipping rehydration fluid, especially in a hot climate; this is probably because you are mildly dehydrated. I also find the rehydration fluids to be a very effective remedy for the worst aspects of jet lag (see Chapter 4), and for adjusting to unaccustomed heat in a new country. I'm convinced that quite a lot of the under-the-weather feeling of travellers can be avoided by their use. As well as ordinary salt, the rehydration mixtures include potassium (a salt massively lost during diarrhoea) and bicarbonate, which soothes an acid stomach.

The mixtures are available mostly in sachets, but Dioralyte market them in tablet form, which I find more convenient and less bulky. (Two of the tablets equal one sachet.) If you haven't brought any rehydration remedies with you, you will find that they are available over the counter in many Third World chemists.

Remember that diarrhoea is a symptom of numerous, very different diseases, including serious ones such as malaria, cholera, and dengue fever. All the various popular remedies only relieve symptoms, they do nothing to cure the actual disease. When you have a severe outbreak for more than a few days, or when the outbreak is accompanied by fever or blood in the stools, you must consult a doctor.

Dysentery

If there is blood (sometimes blood and mucus) in your stools, you may have a variety of amoebic or bacillary dysentery. **Bacillary dysentery** is the most common; it is usually indicated by a sudden attack of very acute diarrhoea, severe stomach pains, blood in the stools, and – nearly always – fever. It usually clears up within a week. **Amoebic dysentery** is rarer; it usually starts gradually, the diarrhoea is less acute and sometimes only intermittent, and there often isn't any fever. It can alternate with constipation. Amoebic dysentery can develop a long time after infection, occasionally even years afterwards. There is another type of dysentery, **giardiasis**, in which there is no blood in the stools. Instead they tend to be yellow, frothing or bubbly. The victims' bellies tend to be uncomfortable and swollen with gas, and they usually fart a lot. Only a small proportion of dysentery cases are caused by giardia, but they form a higher proportion of persistent cases after returning home, and the disease is on the increase. If you have a very long-lasting dysentery, it is likely to be giardiasis or amoebic.

If you are going to be entering areas without doctors, or where medical supplies are poor, ask your tropical doctor for a remedy for the main types of dysentery (see Antibiotics, page 195).

Heatstroke

Heatstroke is extremely dangerous, but is rare – provided travellers have drunk enough fluids, maintained their salt levels and worn sensible clothing. Its likelihood is increased by excessive drinking of alcohol.

The signs of heatstroke are usually a dramatic increase in body temperature to above 105°F (40°C), accompanied by a reduction in sweating, and sometimes nausea or vomiting. The condition is often caused by a failure of the sweating mechanism. According to the excellent health handbook *Where There is No Doctor* (see Appendix 1), a crucial difference between heat exhaustion and heatstroke is that in the latter the skin tends to be dry, red, and hot, while in mere heat exhaustion the skin tends to remain sweaty, pale and cool. In heatstroke there is often no moisture, even under the armpits.

Heatstroke must be treated as an emergency. The patient should be removed out of the sun, preferably to a cool room, then stripped naked and doused with cold water. Sponging and fanning the body should continue until the temperature has fallen to about 102°F (39°C); sponging should then cease. If you don't have access to much water, cover the victim with paper (or if not available, thin material) and pour on whatever liquid you have. As a victim can die within a few hours, don't be squeamish: if necessary, pee on the paper. Get the patient to a doctor as soon as possible.

Sunburn

A great many novice travellers get sunburnt. The innocent tourist on a beach thinks that one hour's exposure to the sun is quite safe. This isn't the case in the tropics, especially when the presence of water combined with salt can roast your skin. The main reason why such an astonishing number of tourists get sunburnt is that they don't feel the pain immediately: unlike an ordinary wound, the pain is considerably delayed. If you have a fair skin and have recently arrived in the tropics, ten minutes' exposure to the sun may be more than enough. After your skin has tanned a little, you can build up your exposure time very fast.

Bear in mind that a stretch of water reflects the sun twice as intensely as a green field, and that you can be burnt even when the sun is hidden by clouds.

Parts of the body with less fat tend to burn first: for instance, the nose, the shin and the collarbone. When you apply sun-cream, be sure to cover your nose and the backs of your knees, both of which get easily sunburnt. Sun-creams are discussed in Chapter 3.

If you do get sunburnt, aspirin is helpful because it relieves not only the pain, but also the inflammation. Otherwise it seems to me from strong anecdotal evidence that by far and away the most effective ointment for soothing sunburn is aloe vera, from the aloe vera plant.

Aloe vera is a very ancient remedy, and was certainly used as long as 5,000 years ago by the Egyptians. Later, Aristotle persuaded Alexander the Great to conquer the island of Socotra because of its abundant aloe vera plants, which were being widely used for healing wounds and for many other remedies. As early as 1596 it was introduced to Barbados, and it is now sometimes known as *Aloe barbadiensis*.

The plant looks like a cactus, though it isn't (all cacti, except for one, originate in the Americas). Where the plant is available, it is best to cut a bit off one of the fleshy leaves and rub the oozing segment on your burn; otherwise use commercial aloe vera gel. Pure gel (don't bother with any of the mixtures) is available in Britain from the Body Shop.

A friend of mine, who used the local plants in the West Indies, found the gel to be the only effective remedy for her child's nappy rash. I recommended it to another friend, who was a life-long sufferer from rashes, and her rash was cured immediately. It is worth trying for a wide variety of skin ailments.

Treatments for sunburn are too bulky for most people to carry, but I will mention two. Some people recommend witch hazel, which can be found in preparations such as calamine and witch hazel cream; and a reliable doctor has recommended After-sun, which is sold by Boots.

Skin cancer is an excellent reason to reduce your exposure to the sun. Its recent increase has been dramatic, and now more than 600,000 Americans get skin cancer every year. In Australia, two-thirds of the population have had at least one type by the age of seventy-five. Many skin cancers aren't dangerous, but more than 1,000 people in England die from them each year. Recently there has been even more convincing evidence that the ozone layer has been depleted, thus making the sun's rays more dangerous, so this is another reason to avoid long periods in the sun, or to protect yourself with creams.

People with white-collar jobs who usually have little exposure to the sun are far more susceptible to skin cancer if they don't protect themselves.

Because the danger from malignant skin cancers can be greatly reduced if you get them treated immediately, consult a doctor without delay if you develop a mole, or pigmented patch, which shows several of the following features:

Itching (though ordinary moles may occasionally itch)
An increase in size, especially when you are younger than thirty-five
Shadowy satellite moles around the edge of the original mole
An irregularly shaped mole
Colour changes (most malignant melanomas are a mixture of browns, black or red, and sometimes a blue-white tinge at the centre)
Inflammation or reddish edge
Crusting, bleeding, or oozing

Fungal infections

Dhobi itch, ringworm, and athlete's foot are all fungal skin infections. Dhobi itch is an infection of the crotch or groin, usually characterized by itchy brown (or reddish) areas. Ringworm shows itself as red circular patches, usually on the main body; athlete's foot, which is by far the most common, can cause painful irritation of the feet or toes. Fungal infections can take a long time to clear up; you may need to keep applying medicine for at least a month, and certainly continue for some time after the infection appears to have ended.

The overwhelming weight of anecdotal evidence seems to indicate that an old-fashioned remedy, Whitfield's ointment (compound benzoic acid ointment), is the best remedy. Apparently the full strength is too strong for most skins, and you should stipulate half-strength. It can be bought over the

THE TROPICAL TRAVELLER

counter, and it is cheap. The ointment isn't suitable for thrush, a fungal infection of the vagina. An excellent modern remedy for fungal infections is Daktarin (miconazole), and several readers have written to me in vigorous support of Canesten (containing clotrimazole), which is the treatment of choice for thrush.

Prickly heat

Prickly heat, an intensely irritating skin rash, bothers quite a few visitors to the tropics, especially when they first arrive. It usually happens when sweat has failed to evaporate, and therefore moisture has settled too long on the skin. To help sweat evaporate, wear loose-fitting clothing made of natural fibres (without even a small mixture of artificial material).

In the event of suffering from prickly heat, use a liberal amount of cold water to cool the rash, dab it dry rather than rubbing it, and cut down on your use of soap. A solution of bicarbonate of soda (if available) is sometimes recommended, and an antiseptic powder may be helpful. Numerous remedies have been suggested over the years but none of them is guaranteed to work.

In the first edition I wrote, 'In my opinion Westerners (and quite a few locals) use too much soap for washing.' A doctor who has since written to the *British Medical Journal* is of the same opinion:

Prevention is achieved by avoiding the use of soap. The average expatriate taking one, two, or more showers or baths in hot climates automatically reaches for the soap, as he has always done, and washes out the natural oils and waxes from the skin. The shower or bath without soap is equally refreshing and cleansing; soap applied to the crotch and axillas very sparingly and well washed off once daily is all that is needed.

Women who get thrush have often washed their vaginas too frequently with soap.

A doctor who had dealt with thousands of cases of prickly heat in the Far East wrote to the *BMJ* about the problem: 'The incidence can be reduced by wearing the minimum of clothing, and exposing the skin freely to wind, sun and water.' Another doctor has since written to me: 'From my extensive experience of treating colleagues' children, prickly heat can be effectively cured only by dramatically reducing the skin temperature – ideally air conditioning or tepid sponging and fanning.'

HIV and Aids

There is little point in additional pontification about the dangers of sexual intercourse with strangers or prostitutes – everyone who reads a newspaper must be aware of Aids. And they will also have read that in many areas, be it Nairobi or Bangkok, the majority of prostitutes are infected with the HIV virus.

The Aids goalposts are constantly moving. As I write, the majority of victims in Europe and the United States are male homosexuals, drug abusers, and haemophiliacs. In Africa, though, the overwhelming majority of victims are sexually active heterosexuals. No accurate statistics are kept in Africa, but, judging from a combination of anecdotal and written evidence, it is clear that the death toll through a huge part of Africa will be catastrophic, far worse than expected.

If you must have sexual intercourse with someone who isn't your usual partner, use a condom. Make sure the wearer squeezes the tip, before rolling it on. Don't use a petroleum or oil-based lubricant: it can dissolve the latex. The wearer should withdraw while he still has an erection.

Spermicidal pessaries used by women have some anti-Aids properties, so it may be best to use both a condom and a pessary.

But although this sermonizing about sexual activity may be unnecessary, it is well worth stressing the dangers of medical and dental treatment in underdeveloped countries. Unscreened blood, unsterilized needles, unsterile drips can all be a death sentence.

Because of the spread of Aids you should know the telephone number of your consulate (as mentioned in Chapter 1), so that you can get advice on the whereabouts of first-rate medical treatment. You should also know your blood group, so that if necessary blood can be ordered in advance. You can get a free notification of your blood group by becoming a blood donor.

If an expedition is going to an area (such as most of Africa) where hepatitis B and HIV are prevalent, it could be especially helpful if everyone in the expedition knows their blood group. Then if necessary an expedition member can donate blood to another member in the event of an accident requiring blood transfusion. Carry a packet of sterile equipment (as sold by MASTA, British Airways, Trailfinders, or Nomad: addresses in Appendix 2), preferably with a printed explanatory leaflet so that customs officers don't think you are a junkie.

Hepatitis A

Because travellers in the Third World are likely to catch hepatitis (if they haven't received the immunization), it is well worth knowing the easily recognizable symptoms (which are the same as for hepatitis B). After a few days of flu-like symptoms (sometimes accompanied by nausea and diarrhoea), the most well-known sign is yellow skin and yellow whites of the eyes; but a more obvious indication may appear before then – your urine will most likely turn the colour of Coca-Cola, and your stools will turn pale grey. It's helpful to know this, because if you have got hepatitis, no medical drugs will help you, and indeed they may cause considerable harm (because of the delicate state of your liver). It is important that you don't drink even a teaspoonful of alcohol; and you are probably best advised to give up coffee and chocolate.

As I've mentioned before, if you've had hepatitis A once, you will be immune for life.

Venereal diseases

Venereal diseases are rampantly on the increase, and are by no means caught only from bar-girls and prostitutes.

Should a man have sexual intercourse with someone likely to convey the disease, a condom will give a measure of protection, even though it isn't foolproof. It is also some help if he urinates soon after intercourse and washes his genitals with soap and water.

Some travellers take antibiotics immediately before and after having intercourse with a prostitute. This is a bad practice because it may only relieve the symptoms while you are still unwittingly harbouring the disease.

It's best to appreciate that there is no foolproof method of protection against the ever-increasing range of venereal diseases. This fact was jocularly demonstrated as far back as 1977 by an article in the *British Journal of Venereal Diseases* (Vol. 53, p. 346):

Venereal disease can be prevented if before sexual intercourse the man applies a condom, the woman an antiseptic cream, and if afterwards the man immediately passes water and anoints his genitalia with a prophylactic ointment while the woman has a prophylactic douche; both should then have a bath before spraying each other with antiseptic lotion, and they should visit a physician to receive 2.4 megaunits of procaine penicillin by injection plus 1.0 g of probenecid by mouth – which should prevent gonorrhoea and syphilis – plus a ten-day course of oral tetracycline to prevent non-gonococcal urethritis and a one- or two-day course of metronidazole or nimorazole against trichomoniasis – even with such commendable caution the risk is not entirely removed of infection from the viruses of Condylomata acuminata, Molluscum contagiosum or even that of hepatitis B.

If you do catch a venereal disease, self-treatment shouldn't be attempted; instead you must have a full laboratory test as soon as possible. You may have caught more than one type of venereal disease, and if you treat one, you may mask the effects of another. Besides, in many parts of the world there has been too much self-treatment, with the result that the diseases have become increasingly resistant to antibiotics. In some areas common antibiotics have no effect whatsoever on gonorrhoea. As the guidebook *Along the Gringo Trail*★ puts it: 'There are strains of Amazon clap that can drink penicillin for breakfast.' A local laboratory will know which medicines are the most effective in their area.

The signs of VD are more noticeable in a male than a female. The most common VDs, gonorrhoea and non-gonococcal urethritis, are both indicated for men by painful peeing and visible signs of discharge on their underpants.

★Jack Epstein (And/Or Press, 1980)

If a female traveller sleeps with a man who is not her regular lover, she should be checked by a specialist; as a result of her liaison she may later carry non-specific urethritis, gonorrhoea or syphilis, but be genuinely unaware of it. A regular lover would, we hope, tell her if he developed VD.

Should you catch a venereal disease, or even if there is a likelihood that you have caught one, it is wise also to visit a specialist clinic on your return home. For instance, the signs of syphilis may not develop for a considerable time after your exposure.

Small cuts

Never ignore the slightest cut or graze: in a tropical climate it can easily become infected, and it could turn into a very long-lasting tropical ulcer. Having washed your hands in soap and water, wash the cut thoroughly also with soap and water. Provided that there is no danger from dirt, some people like to leave the cut to dry out by itself. I prefer to put on some antiseptic powder, and find it practical to cover the cut with a plaster. Because immediate treatment is so important, I always carry some antiseptic wipes (see page 179).

An excellent antiseptic available in many tropical countries (and it can also easily be bought in chemists here) is potassium permanganate; dissolve a pinch of crystals in a third of a cup of clean water (*Where There is No Doctor* says dissolve a teaspoon in a bucket of water!), dab it on three times daily, and it will cure most early skin infections. You can use it for any cuts, grazes, and sores; and this excellent and cheap remedy has the advantage of being very drying. It is liable, though, to leave stains on skin and clothes.

Many people buy tins or packets of 'assorted plasters'; I sometimes find many of them to be too small, and often prefer to cut my own plasters from a **dressing strip**. Elastoplast, for instance, sell a useful strip that is 1 metre long; assuming that you have a pair of scissors, this can be cut to a wide variety of shapes and sizes. The cushioned protection is also useful. The disadvantage of a dressing strip is that it isn't sterile, and if it stays too long in your baggage, it tends to become grubby. I also keep a 'pocket pack' of Elastoplast's individually wrapped plasters in my shoulder bag.

When you are staying in a village, you are often expected to treat a multitude of cuts and sores, and here again the dressing strip is more useful, because an ordinary tin of plasters soon runs out.

Don't use waterproof plasters unless necessary, as they don't provide enough cushioning; nor do they allow the wound to breathe. They may be necessary, though, when you can't avoid immersing the wound in water.

Don't put any plaster down too tight. Give it a little ridge, so that some air can circulate underneath.

Provided there is no danger of opening up the cut, it may be best to change the plaster every day, especially if it gets damp or wet.

You should position a plaster on a cut in such a way that, when you have to take it off, you pull along the line of the cut, and not against it – which risks opening it up again.

It is an excellent idea to take some sachets of **antiseptic wipes**. You may have to cope with cuts in many situations when you can't immediately find clean water. For this reason, I never travel without some wipes in my shoulder bag. They are also a very useful (but extravagant) method of cleaning up when there is no water – if you have eaten a mango on a bus, or a child has been sick down your leg.

Travellers should also take some type of **antiseptic**. A remedy that is drying rather than greasy is often preferable, so take an **antiseptic powder**. Povidone-iodine preparations contain iodine, which is an excellent cleansing agent, useful both for bacteria and for viruses. Nor do they sting (unlike tincture of iodine, which has an alcohol base that may also damage tissue). One disadvantage of the most common povidone-iodine preparations (such as Savlon Dry) is that they are sold as sprays, and are therefore bulky. However, there is a handy puffer, marketed as Videne; most chemists don't appear to stock it, but they can order almost any pharmaceutical item, including Videne, within twenty-four hours.

Although these remedies will be more effective than the usual antiseptic creams, I still like to take a small tube of Savlon, as it can be useful to have a cream that soothes, and I have always found it excellent. (Savlon cream, by the way, does not contain the same active ingredient as Savlon Dry.)

In the Third World, antibiotic powders are often used on wounds. Don't do this: you may become 'sensitized', developing very severe reactions. If you need antibiotics, take them orally.

Larger cuts and wounds

If you have to treat a larger cut or wound, ordinary plasters are often not practical, and it is best to take **non-stick sterile dressings** (such as Melolin). These are bought wrapped in individual packets.

Also bring some **surgical tape** or fabric strapping, for keeping the dressing in place. Sometimes a bandage is helpful (see page 200). Because tape or strapping can fulfil quite a few functions, and because it is inconvenient to take more than one roll, I shall discuss the pros and cons of various types.

Waterproof tapes These can't usually be recommended, as they don't breathe. If you really need a very adhesive tape, then the best is Sleek, made by Smith and Nephew; doctors use it for securing vital intravenous drips and catheters to sweaty, feverish patients.

Fabric-strapping tapes (also known as zinc oxide tapes). I find these the most useful all-round tapes to take. Although not properly waterproof, they are very adhesive and are kinder on the skin. Because they provide a measure of cushioning, they can also be useful as a prophylactic against blisters (see Chapter 12). The tapes usually come in 1-inch or 2-inch sizes. Most people will use the 1-inch.

Micropore Quite a number of people get a bad skin reaction to fabric-strapping tapes. If so, they can use Micropore, which isn't as adhesive, but is far kinder on the skin. It also has

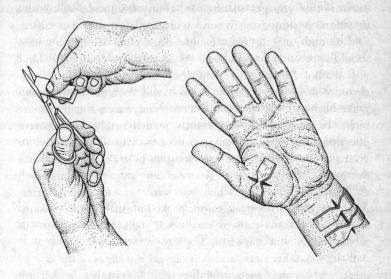

Fig 4. Butterfly system.

the advantages of being cuttable without scissors, and far less painful to peel off.

If your trip is in any way adventurous (including riding, for instance), it would be wise to take special **wound dressings** (BPC size 14 seems a good compromise). These can quickly and firmly be put in place, and will absorb a lot of blood; therefore this type of all-in dressing will be more useful for bad wounds.

Obviously, a wound should be attended to by a doctor; but if there is no doctor, you will have to treat it yourself. Having washed your hands in soap and water, wash round the wound also carefully with soap and water. Gently pour boiled-and-cooled water into the wound to wash away any dirt and the remains of the soap. Lift up any flaps of skin, and clear any dirt and grit out. If necessary use the tweezers from your Swiss Army penknife, having dipped them in boiling water first. It is essential that you get all dirt out, as any left inside will ensure infection. A clean fresh wound will mend fastest if it is closed. Old wounds, or bites from people, dogs, pigs, or other animals, should apparently be left open. As a general rule, you shouldn't put alcohol, tincture of iodine, or merthiolate (or mercurichrome) directly on a wound, as it will damage the flesh and make healing slower; use instead soap and water. But if you are bitten or scratched by an animal, which might cause severe infections, including rabies, then do use them. Gin, whisky, or vodka are suitable. If you are going to be trekking far from a doctor, you could take a povidone–iodine antiseptic liquid (such as Betadine) for times when you can't get to boiled water. Alternatively, antiseptic solutions packed in small sterile containers (Steripods) are easy to carry, and useful for washing out wounds when you don't have access to sterile water.

If the wound is clean, and you can get the edges of the skin to meet, try keeping them together with **Steristrips**, which are specially designed for closing a wound. If no Steristrips are available, do the best you can with your tape, using the 'butterfly' system (see Fig. 4). Hospitals are using Steristrips more and more instead of stitches.

If the wound is bleeding badly, hold a sterile dressing tightly in place, and, if bleeding continues, keep adding dressings (or in emergencies the cleanest available cloths and handkerchiefs) until the bleeding stops. Try to keep the bleeding part raised above the rest of your body.

When you are in a remote area with no doctor and the wound is deep, or still dirty, or caused by a bite, you should take a course of antibiotics – of the penicillin family, unless you are allergic, in which case try the non-penicillin alternatives such as erythromycin or co-trimoxazole (Septrin, Bactrim). In the case of dirty wounds, infection from tetanus could be life-threatening. For this reason you should already have been immunized.

Rabies

All mammals can carry rabies. A carnivorous mammal, however, is much more likely to give you rabies than a herbivorous one. Everyone knows that dogs are the most likely animal to infect us, but few know that in many countries cats are the second major source of infection for humans, and that they are an extremely efficient vector of the disease.

Rabies is transmitted by a bite or lick from an infected animal, nearly always through broken skin or a scratch. Avoid wild animals behaving in an unnaturally tame manner – particularly those such as jackals, foxes, or skunks. Never pick up a bat. If an animal is run over by a car, don't rush to give first aid: it may have been run over because it was reacting to the symptoms of rabies. Avoid any dog that you don't know well. In the event of being bitten by a jackal, a fox, and so on, presume the animal is rabid.

Because humans aren't particularly susceptible to rabies, the correct washing procedure may prevent infection after a bite; the virus is unstable and easily destroyed by heat and detergents. Flush out the wound with copious amounts of soap and water, directing any saliva away from the wound. If possible flush under a flowing tap for five minutes. If alcohol of between 40 and 70 per cent (gin, whisky, and vodka are suitable) or iodine is available, use it to wipe the wound. Then, leave the wound open, until you get professional treatment.

Although we aren't particularly susceptible to rabies, you must always have post-exposure prophylaxis as soon as possible, because once the symptoms of rabies have appeared you will die. If you are near a well-equipped modern hospital, you will receive the new human diploid cell vaccine, which is safe, painless, and effective. (Some British and US embassies abroad hold stocks of the new safe vaccine, or can tell you where to get it – another reason to know the address and telephone number of your consulate.) Just because you are a long way from hospital, don't give up. Although the symptoms may – very rarely – begin as early as four days after the bite, more commonly they come much later – usually somewhere between one and three months. So always go for post-exposure vaccination. However long it takes you to reach medical facilities, don't ever give up the idea of being vaccinated, as when rabies develops it is the most agonizing of all communicable diseases.

You must still get some post-exposure vaccination, even if you have had the pre-exposure vaccine. And you should get a tetanus booster after any animal bite.

If you can kill the animal safely, take its corpse to a laboratory, where they will be able to inspect its brain for rabies.

If you haven't killed the animal, and it is still alive after ten days, then it wasn't rabid. But don't wait for this news before beginning your post-exposure vaccination.

Bilharzia

Bilharzia (schistosomiasis) exists in more than seventy tropical and semi-tropical countries in South America, South-east Asia, and especially Africa. In parts of Brazil the majority of children are now suffering from it, and in large tracts of Egypt about 50 per cent of the population are infected. Throughout the world more than 200 million people suffer from the disease. The parasite responsible is a water-living worm which passes half its life cycle in the human body – where it lays a large number of eggs – and the other half in a fresh-water snail. The eggs are passed into the water by human excrement or urine. (Baboons have also been implicated in passing on the disease.)

Unfortunately many schemes intended to help the Third World, such as dam construction or irrigation schemes, have helped to spread the disease. Apparently, most reservoirs above dams are infected within ten years of construction.

The most common cause of infection by bilharzia is paddling or bathing in still (or slow-moving) fresh water. Always ask, therefore, for expert advice before entering any fresh water; in this case don't rely on the advice of locals, as they often bathe in infected water.

If you have had to paddle or bathe in potentially infected water, rub yourself with a towel immediately after bathing. There is evidence that this may help, because it has been found that the parasites or flukes burrow into the skin only after the water has evaporated. Washing with clean water may also get rid of the parasites.

A few hours after being in the infected water the bather may feel a tingling on the skin or experience a mild rash. The next symptoms of bilharzia don't usually appear for four to six weeks. The victim may then experience lassitude, loss of appetite, night-sweating, and a rash. This can be mistaken for the symptoms of typhoid or malaria. After a few months, when the disease is established, the most common sign is blood in the urine (Napoleon described Egypt as 'the land of menstruating men'). A less common symptom may be diarrhoea plus blood and mucus. However, because many people suffer no symptoms whatsoever, you should have a specialized check-up whenever you may have exposed yourself to infection. There is now a safe and effective drug, which with one dose can treat all three varieties of bilharzia.

Dengue fever

This is a common disease, but most travellers are unlikely to catch it. It is spread from person to person by the *Aedes aegypti* mosquito, which particularly likes to bite the ankles. The incubation period is fast, from five to eight days, and the initial signs of the illness are usually fevers, headache, and especially muscle pains (which gives rise to its other name, 'breakbone fever'). After a few days a rash appears over the body. The first bout of the disease lasts only a few days, but it usually recurs. In adults the disease isn't dangerous, and there are no particular medicines for self-treatment. If you can't get to a doctor, drink the usual rehydration fluids, stay in bed; take codeine or paracetamol instead of aspirin for the pain, as there may be stomach bleeding.

A few famous diseases which you are unlikely to get

Sleeping sickness is caught from the bite of certain tsetse flies in Africa. Those most at risk are travellers who have been on wildlife safaris. However, of the many thousands who go on safari, only very few get the disease. The first sign of the infection may be a boil-like swelling that appears five or more days after the bite on its site. Swellings that arise within a few hours are usually a sign of allergy rather than infection. Treatment should be given only by experienced doctors.

Chagas disease is a common disease found only in South and Central America. However, very few travellers catch it. The disease is caught almost exclusively by those living in mud adobe huts, and it is spread by the assassin bug, which emerges only at night. A frequent sign of the bug is cobweb-like dark-brown marks down the walls, which are its excreta. If you do stay in an adobe hut, try to sleep under a well-tucked-in mosquito net, which will keep the bugs out; otherwise keep a candle lit all through the night. Although it is most unlikely you will catch the disease, you should know that the first symptoms may not appear for years afterwards. It is dangerous in the long term, and it is best to identify it at an early stage, when a cure is possible. Anyone who has spent a lot of time living in villages in rural South America, or has had a blood transfusion, should get a specialist blood test so that early treatment can be given.

Filariasis is also spread by biting insects. Although this is an extremely common disease (about 300 million people are affected by it), you are unlikely to catch any of the three types of the disease. One of them is river blindness, found in West Africa. This is very rarely caught by foreigners, and it is safely treatable. The most common variety (but still very uncommon for travellers) is lymphatic filariasis, of which the first symptom may be painful swellings of the lymph glands either in the groin or the armpit, and often the testicles. The extreme examples are known as elephantiasis.

I know someone whose symptoms of filariasis didn't appear for a year, and this is yet another example of why you must get a specialist check-up, even when an illness happens a very long time after you have returned from the tropics.

Cholera Unlike the above diseases, which are all spread by various insects, cholera is spread through the faecal–oral route.

I've already mentioned that the immunization is unnecessary, and you are extremely unlikely to catch it: it is mostly a disease of the very poor. In areas where there is an outbreak, drink only safe water, and be especially careful of shellfish and seafood, which easily pick up the infection. Bear in mind that in most parts of the developing world untreated human excreta is deposited straight into the sea.

Worms

Only a small proportion of travellers get infected by worms. Nevertheless anyone who has lived rough for any length of time should get a specialized stool check-up on their return. Symptoms may not always be apparent, and worms can occasionally be very harmful. I will deal first with three types of worms which you might be able to see in your stools.

Tapeworms These grow to several feet long in your intestines and are picked up from uncooked or undercooked meat. The symptoms are mild, often including a slight stomach ache and loss of appetite. The signs are usually small, flat, white segments under ½ inch long in your stools or in your underwear. Treatment should be under supervision.

Roundworms About 1,000 million people are infested with roundworms, which are spread by food and water through the usual oral–faecal route. The worms are usually 8 to 12 inches long, and roughly the shape of an earthworm. They usually clear themselves up, but you should get treatment.

Threadworms (sometimes called **pinworm**) These are quite common and often caught by children. The first sign is an intensely itchy bum. They are under ½ inch long, white, and very thin.

The most popular worm medicine, Piperazine, works for threadworms and roundworms, but not for any of the others. Mebendazole (Vermox) is used for threadworms, roundworms, hookworms and whipworms. *Where There is No Doctor* (see Appendix 1) gives a local remedy for roundworm: collect 3 or 4 teaspoons of the 'milk' that comes out when the green fruit or trunk of the papaya tree is cut. Mix this with an equal amount of honey and stir into a cup of hot water. If possible, drink along with a laxative.

About 600 million people are estimated to be infected with **hookworm**, which is picked up through bare feet. In populated areas, therefore, don't walk barefoot except on sea-swept beaches. Hookworm will sometimes start with itchy feet (when the larvae enter the skin) and then develops into a cough (when the larvae enter the lungs). Then there may be no more symptoms, although the worms may live in the body for up to nine years. Occasionally they may cause debilitation.

Worms capable of causing ill-health may be ingested if you eat raw fish.

The World Health Organization is hoping to obliterate **guinea worms**, but in India, Pakistan, and eighteen African countries, there are still approximately 10 million cases a year. Travellers are extremely unlikely to be infected, because the worms are carried by large water fleas, which can be filtered out even by a handkerchief. Once picked up, though, guinea worms are very unpleasant: they can't be killed, and when they become 2 or 3 feet long they will exit very slowly from various parts of the body (usually below the knee, though it may be the eye). President Carter described in a newspaper article how in Ghana he had seen as many as a dozen worms exiting at the same time from just one victim.

Menstrual problems

About 80 per cent of women who travel and work in the tropics have problems with their periods. A VSO health handbook (now out of print) reported that it is not uncommon for volunteers to miss periods for up to six months after taking up their projects. This can also happen to any travellers whose lifestyle has dramatically changed, especially if they undertake any strenuous activity. High altitudes may also play havoc with menstrual cycles. Periods may last two or three weeks or more, and then return after only a few days. Women in early menopause may even start menstruating again, and the cramps may be persistent and excessive.

Women should carry generous supplies of tampons, as they might either not exist or be uncomfortable and ineffective. Even seventy years after its revolution, the Soviet Union still couldn't provide tampons for its citizens.

To avoid having periods while travelling, some women take the pill continuously, without the seven-day break in between packets, though it is best to consult your doctor before doing this.

There are reports that menstruating women may attract sharks, and that they are generally more likely to be attacked by wild animals. I can't confirm any of this, and I think many of the fears are probably exaggerated; but I do know that they should definitely beware of several habituated mammals, including dolphins and orang-utans. (It isn't only women who can suffer from the sexual advances of animals: recently a male diver in the Arabian Gulf was nearly drowned because of the relentless sexual attentions of a male sea-cow.)

Asthma

Asthma sufferers should be aware that the housedust mite is commoner nearer the Equator than in Britain. Bring appropriate medication.

Mountain sickness

When you travel direct from sea level to between 8,000 and 10,000 feet, there is a small chance you will feel unwell. At 11,500 feet, about 50 per cent of travellers feel unwell. At 14,000 feet, most people suffer some symptoms. (For comparison, Cuzco is at 10,600 feet, La Paz at 12,000, and Lhasa at 12,090.)

Headache, fatigue, undue breathlessness on exertion, the sense of the heart beating forcibly, loss of appetite, nausea, dizziness, a slow, irregular, sighing breathing in sleep, and waking up breathless are common symptoms. These are often not apparent immediately on arrival, but develop within the first thirty-six hours. Insomnia is often the most tedious symptom.

Acute mountain sickness (the correct medical name), though unpleasant, will usually clear up by itself. Should you suffer a headache, you could take aspirin or paracetamol. When you do suffer, it is vital not to go higher, and, if recovery doesn't take place, to descend to lower altitudes. The people who die of acute mountain sickness are usually fit macho men, who won't stop and won't come down.

The best policy is to ascend slowly, so that you become acclimatized to less oxygen. The Mountain Medicine Data Centre (see page 191) recommends:

It is reasonable for healthy people up to the ages of sixty-five to seventy to travel rapidly to 11,500 feet. Thereafter the speed of further height gained should be gradual and we advise taking a week before sleeping at 16,500 feet. This, for example, seems acceptable with a party of travellers in Tibet, when one flies to Lhasa (12,090 feet) and travels by road to the Everest Base Camp at 17,000 feet. Thereafter progress should be gradual, with at least a further eleven days before staying at 20,000 feet.

Although it is reasonable for healthy people to travel direct to 11,500 feet, many will feel sick. Ideally, they should first spend a couple of days at about 7,000–8,000 feet.

Diamox (acetazolamide) is sometimes recommended as a pro-phylactic against altitude sickness. But as altitude sickness is a self-limiting disease, and as drugs should be avoided whenever possible (most of them have side-effects), I personally wouldn't use the pills; but some good doctors recommend them for when you are ascending at comparative speed (i.e. by vehicle or plane).

When travelling at high altitudes, avoid any pills which tend to depress breathing (this includes sleeping tablets), and also be wary of the contraceptive pill, because of its effect on fluid retention and its tendency to increase the chance of clots (throm-bosis). Neither of these, though, are absolute rules.

Pregnant women, especially in the first three months, should beware of high altitudes.

Two complications of the illness are rare but dangerous:

High-altitude pulmonary oedema   This is most common at altitudes between 13,000 and 16,500 feet. It is less commonly experienced at higher or lower altitudes and is almost unknown below 10,000 feet. Severe breathlessness, frothy (sometimes blood-stained) spittle, and a permanent unproductive cough may all be symptoms. Crackling may be heard in the chest without a stethoscope. An important symptom is breathlessness at rest. The condition can cause death within a few hours, even to a previously healthy victim.

Cerebral oedema   This is caused by fluid retention within the head. Patients become iller than one would expect from ordinary mountain sickness. They become drowsy and confused over a period of hours, and their walking is unsteady, like a drunk's. Double vision may occur, and headaches or neck aches are common. The sufferer eventually lapses into a coma and dies.

The remedy for both pulmonary and cerebral oedema is immediate descent. Oxygen may be helpful, but less so than an increase in barometric pressure. Even a descent of 1,000–1,500 feet can save life. Recovery can be expected below 10,000 feet. Climbing higher, even for short periods, will make matters worse – an important point in event of evacuation by an unpressurized airplane (the plane might have to climb higher before descending).

Once recovery has taken place, it isn't then safe for the sufferer to try another ascent to higher altitudes.

The clearest literature I have found on mountain sickness was issued by Dr Charles Clarke of the Mountain Medicine Data Centre, to whom I am indebted for most of the above information. If you need further information about travel to altitudes over 13,000 feet, write to him at the Mountain Medicine Data Centre, Department of Neurological Sciences, St Bartholomew's Hospital, 38 Little Britain, London EC1A 7BE. It is the only centre in Europe which gives this type of information. It can also give advice about new potent drugs for the treatment of cerebral and pulmonary oedema.

Don't forget that, as mentioned in the later section on Water, high altitudes are very dehydrating.

Check-up

Those who have spent months travelling rough should consider having a thorough medical check-up on their return. It is a wise precaution, even though an infestation of worms is the most likely ailment to be discovered. One friend who had been canoeing in South America discovered that he was infested with a dangerous type of worm, even though he hadn't felt ill.

It may be worth going to a specialist tropical testing centre. One well-known, but non-tropical, laboratory missed my brother's infection of bilharzia, and on another occasion his infestation of roundworms.

You should give the doctors complete details of your medical record, and make a full confession if you have ever forgotten to take your malaria pills.

Even if an illness happens as late as a year after your return, you must tell your tropical doctor that you have been travelling. For instance, falciparum malaria – the one that can kill you – may take a year to develop.

THE MEDICAL BAG

I have already mentioned several items for possible inclusion in the medical bag:

   Rehydration salts
   Anti-malaria tablets
   Codeine-phosphate
   Diarrhoea remedies
   Dysentery remedies
   Fungal remedies
   Antiseptic wipes
   Dressings
   Antiseptic powders and creams

Surgical tapes
Plasters

I shall now list some other items the traveller may find useful.

First, it should be mentioned that it is often best to buy any medicines before you leave. Many fake medicines are sold in developing countries, and some of them are dangerous. According to an article by Dr Richard Dawood in the *Traveler*, the problem is widespread; in Nigeria and Pakistan it is possible that as many as 50 per cent of all medicines are fake. One hundred children died in Nigeria after taking paracetamol that had been diluted with an industrial solvent. If you must buy medicines abroad, take a hard look at all the packaging, and be suspicious of any medicines that are ludicrously cheap.

Motion-sickness remedies

I am fairly sceptical about many recommended folk-cures but I have collected a lot of anecdotal evidence that **ginger** is an excellent remedy for motion sickness. Apart from its uses for seasickness, I've known it to be successfully used for car sickness among children. And when I recommended it to a pregnant friend with bad morning sickness, it was immediately successful (though the success was only very short-lived for another pregnant friend). In a test on thirty-six people in California, ginger proved more successful at curing motion sickness than Dramamine. Some people recommend taking the ginger in powder form with hot water. In the case of my friend with morning sickness, she just chewed crystallized ginger. Glacé ginger can be bought in the cake-mixtures sections of stores. In most of the Third World root ginger is available, and you can grate some onto a sandwich.

Sea Bands are an elasticated cloth bracelet with buttons which exert pressure on an 'acupressure' point above the wrist. I was very sceptical about these, guessing that they were just an item of New Age nonsense, but after several anecdotes and written recommendations I decided to write to the company to see if they could provide any convincing evidence of the bands' effectiveness. A huge folder was sent to me, filled with surveys and reports, one of which had been published in the journal of the Royal Society of Medicine. All of this evidence was certainly impressive. But the doctors that I have personally consulted are very sceptical, and now I have bought a pair, I do have a niggle: why do they cost so much, when they must be so very cheap to make? I'm not yet entirely convinced by Sea Bands; but they can't harm anything but your pocket, and some of my friends are convinced they work.

If ginger or the wrist bands don't work for you, then try Stugeron (cinnarizine) pills, which were heavily tested during the Falklands War and were found to be excellent. An advantage of Stugeron is that it won't make you as sleepy as many of the other pills. They shouldn't, though, be taken by children under five, or by pregnant women.

Different motion-sickness remedies suit different people. One friend tells me that she finds Stugeron useless for hovercraft crossings, and – even though they are soporific – much prefers Avomine (which contains promethazine) and Dramamine (which contains dimenhydrinate), both of which she considers infallible. It is no good taking seasickness pills by mouth at the last minute, because you won't be able to hold them down. Start them at least half an hour before the journey.

Individual medicines

Travellers should anticipate any ailment to which they are normally prone, and then pack the appropriate medicines. I am prone to mouth ulcers, and therefore carry a tube of Adcortyl. (It is worth knowing that, if you get mouth ulcers, Paludrine/proguanil malaria tablets may be the cause.)

Antibiotics

This is a tricky subject to write about because in principle nobody should ever take antibiotics without qualified medical advice and supervision. The use of antibiotics can be counter-productive:

they are easily misused, can cause complex side-effects, and can destroy your beneficial bacteria.

Nevertheless, if you are going into areas without doctors, you will be sensible to take some antibiotics for emergencies, especially as they could be life-saving. Consult with a knowledgeable doctor, and discuss the possibility of choosing from the four (imprecise) categories of antibiotic that I mention below. This is not to say that you should take four varieties of antibiotics; two, or possibly three, may well be enough.

1. A penicillin-style 'anti-staph' remedy that will deal with infections from cuts and wounds (which have failed to respond to treatment with potassium permanganate, see page 178), and those producing pus. This is especially important for people travelling into damp jungle areas, as infections there can easily flare up from even the most minor cuts, leech bites, etc. On one large Borneo expedition over half the members needed antibiotic treatment. At the time of writing flucloxacillin is often recommended, unless you are allergic to penicillins.

2. A broad-spectrum antibiotic that will deal with respiratory infections (which are dangerous), ear and sinus infections, and infections of the urinary tract (common for women in the tropics). Co-trimoxazole (Bactrim, Septrin) is a current remedy.

3. An antibiotic for long-lasting dysenteries. At the moment tinidazole (Fasigyn) is the preferred remedy for giardiasis, and metronidazole (Flagyl) for amoebic dysentery. But either of these remedies (at a different dose) will cover the two. (For the different symptoms of these two long-lasting problems, see Dysentery, page 170.)

4. Possibly another broad-spectrum antibiotic, such as the expensive ciprofloxacin, which may be used for the bacillary dysenteries (as well as salmonella and paratyphoid), and would also cover other infections, such as those of the urinary tract. It would not work for giardiasis or amoebic

dysentery. An alternative to ciprofloxacin might be co-amoxiclav (Augmentin), which is very effective for treating wound and chest infections.

If you are likely to be treated with an antibiotic of the penicillin family, such as flucloxacillin or co-amoxiclav, it is especially important that you know you aren't allergic. If you have ever had any type of reaction, the next reaction might be extremely serious. Pills are likely to be less dangerous than injections. As a general rule, though, penicillins are very safe antibiotics, and even a surfeit will rarely do you harm. They can be taken in emergencies for middle-ear infections, other skin infections, chest infections such as pneumonia, typhoid, sore throat, abscessed teeth, and infected wounds.

If you are allergic to sulphonamides (signs include skin rashes, blood in the urine, or jaundice), don't take co-trimoxazole (Bactrim, Septrin). At present, trimethoprim is recommended as an alternative.

Get up-to-date advice about which antibiotics to take. Expert opinion changes fast, and the ones I have listed may no longer be recommended. I have only mentioned specific names because they may help in discussions with your medical adviser, and because these names might conceivably be useful in an emergency.

You should always complete the full course of antibiotics. Don't stop treatment just because the symptoms have gone away.

Don't take tetracyclines with any dairy produce.

Find out about the side-effects and cautions of any antibiotics you are carrying. For instance, drinking any alcohol while taking metronidazole will cause very unpleasant reactions. Taking any of the penicillins with food will result in poor absorption. Sulphonamides should never be taken if you are dehydrated.

It is sometimes wise to try to obtain a data-sheet on each of the antibiotics (and other medicines) carried; this would be particularly true if you were the medical officer for a group or expedition. Although data-sheets are somewhat technical, they may be of help to a doctor in countries where the particular medicine is little used; and they could be helpful if any customs officer is suspicious of all your pills. Your chemist should be able to provide the data-sheets.

Remember that antibiotics are of no use for the treatment of viral infections (which includes colds and flu), and if taken when you have hepatitis, they can actually damage your liver. (For symptoms, see Hepatitis A, page 176.)

Antihistamine tablets

Antihistamine tablets are taken for irritating skin conditions or allergic reactions. They can help soothe insect stings, rashes, jellyfish stings, etc., and may be important for hay fever victims, who are likely to suffer more in the tropics. Piriton (chlorpheniramine maleate) is considered by many to be the most effective, but the modern ones are less likely to make you sleepy. Antihistamine tablets aren't a necessary part of most travellers' medical kits, but might be advisable if you are prone to swelling.

Basic painkillers

The usual choice is between aspirin or paracetamol (called acetaminophen in the United States). The standard BP (British Pharmacopoeia) products are far cheaper than the brand names and often just as good.

Aspirin is a miraculous medicine, and we don't yet fully understand all its workings. Many people find it a slightly more effective painkiller than paracetamol. Aspirin reduces itching, lowers fever, and is a powerful anti-inflammatory; I have already mentioned that it is useful for sunburn, and that it may also help to calm a bad cough. There has been a lot of publicity about the potential hazards of aspirin, as it can be irritating on the stomach and can cause internal bleeding. You will probably know by now if it has an irritating effect on you, in which case you will have to use paracetamol (which can also lower fever). Aspirin shouldn't be taken after a snakebite, or if you have any stomach disorder. It shouldn't be given to children, as it may induce in them a disease that causes brain damage. Not more than one dose should be given to a dehydrated person till they can urinate well.

Soluble varieties of aspirin and paracetamol work faster, and are useful whether or not you have access to water. Personally, I like Codis, which is soluble aspirin mixed with a small amount of codeine. Water-soluble preparations of aspirin are less likely to irritate your stomach, and they also make an excellent gargle for a sore throat. They are also handy when you need to swallow them with little or no water.

I have already mentioned that **codeine-phosphate** tablets (used for the symptoms of diarrhoea) are useful and effective painkillers, and being so tiny, they take up little space.

More powerful painkillers

Travellers who are going to remote areas may want to ask their doctor to prescribe a few very powerful painkillers.

Eye ointment

Eye infections are more likely in the tropics; a tiny tube of antibiotic eye ointment takes up little room and could be valuable. **Conjunctivitis**, for instance, is quite common in hot climates, and may be very distressing. It is usually indicated by a sore, gritty sensation and a sticky discharge. In the event of infection, put a line of ointment under your eyelids several times during the day, and especially before going to bed. This should usually clear it up within a few days; if it doesn't, you may have viral conjunctivitis, in which case you will need expert attention.

Toothache

A minute bottle of oil of cloves will help toothache. When you don't have any, a dab of cotton wool soaked in gin or whisky may help relieve the pain, and so will an aspirin on the gum at the base of the tooth (some claim that this is liable to cause a mouth ulcer, but it never has for me). If you are desperate temporarily to plug a filling, try chewing-gum. If you have a dental abscess, and you can't get to a doctor, take antibiotics. When your face is swollen, the abscess should be taken very seriously, and you should seek early treatment, as there is a small but significant risk of a life-threatening spread of infection. Apart from antibiotics, try hot mouthwashes with lots of salt until you can get to a good dentist. Remember, though, that you may catch HIV or hepatitis B from the medical equipment of a dentist who isn't scrupulously careful.

Dental floss

Some people can't live without it. It can also usefully double up as string, or as thread to sew up torn rucksacks, or as a clothes-line, and so on. It is very strong.

Dental kits

These are being increasingly marketed, but as far as I can gather, it is usually far better not to muck about with your teeth, but instead to wait till you can get to a proper dentist. In March 1992 *Holiday Which?* published a report on six dental kits, and the magazine wasn't impressed by any of them.

Vitamin tablets

Although there is no scientific evidence of their usefulness when you are eating a healthy diet, they may be worth taking during a difficult expedition when your diet is unbalanced and your body is stretched. If you do bring vitamin tablets, you might as well buy ones with added iron, which may also be missing in an inadequate diet.

Vitamin pills can also be a useful placebo (see Medicine in the village, page 202).

Contraceptive pill

Remember that contraceptive pills may not be available locally, and even if they are, you may not get your particular type (especially if it is a recent one). Keep an empty packet with you, so that you have the generic name. Some varieties have as many as twenty different brand names throughout the world.

Be aware that if you get diarrhoea for more than a day, the pill may not be absorbed, and you may expose yourself to the risk of pregnancy. The efficacy of the pills can also be reduced by antibiotics.

If you catch hepatitis, you mustn't take the pill, and you must get advice before taking it again – which might be a long way ahead.

Bandages

Most independent travellers who are not on an expedition, won't take a bandage. If you do take one, take a crêpe bandage, because of its elasticity (washing reinstates this), which will be particularly helpful if you need to use it on an ankle – the most frequent site for a bandage. In the event of an ankle sprain, a long crêpe bandage, which stays on better than others, might prevent someone from being immobilized.

A piece of bandage can be useful for securing dressing, especially in the heat if sweat stops the strapping from adhering, or if the strapping irritates the skin. In emergencies you might find a Tubigrip useful (I've already mentioned its several other merits; see Index); it is a convenient elasticated tubular bandage which you can buy in different sizes to suit different limbs, and it can be doubled up for extra-tight support. It can be washed and used again.

Tiger balm

A small jar of tiger balm is popular with some travellers, especially in the Far East, where it is widely available. I can't really vouch for its usefulness, but one reader tells me 'it is the only thing that works as an anti-itch for mosquito bites'. Tiger balm fans claim that its many merits include the power to relieve a variety of itches, to soothe aches, to cure toothache, and, when rubbed on bed-legs, to prevent reinfestation by bedbugs. It is best to buy the colourless, non-staining variety.

Lip-salve

My guess is that, as with sunglasses (see Chapter 3), travellers are rather too quick to use lip-salve. Allow your lips a bit of time to adapt. If you start using it too easily, then your lips are inclined to get addicted. Just look at all those racks of lip-salve by the cash counter in chemists. Did our ancestors need them?

At certain times, though, you may need a lip-salve, and after driving round a desert in an open jeep, for instance, your lips may be agonizing. The best remedy for sore lips I have ever discovered is the jojoba moisture cream sold by the Body Shop. And one's lips don't seem to become addicted to it.

Packing the medical bag

Glass bottles are heavy and breakable, and many other containers are too large or heavy, so if you find a shop that sells plastic bottles, buy a stock of different sizes. At the time of writing the Body Shop sell a useful range of ordinary plastic bottles. Nomad stocks Nalgene bottles, which come in a wide range of sizes, don't leak, and are very strong.

If you take several different medicines with names such as co-trimoxazole or metronidazole, you may, after several weeks' travelling, forget their precise function. So write a full description on the label, and cover the label with a protective layer of Sellotape; otherwise the label will rub off, leaving you knowing neither the medicine's name, nor its dose, nor its use.

About every two weeks it is a good idea to tighten the tops of your bottles; they occasionally unscrew themselves with disastrous results. Sealing them with Sellotape helps. The new child-proof bottles avoid this problem.

If you open a tube of any type of cream above 10,000 feet, the contents are liable to shoot out, unless you ease the cap off gently.

In Table 1 (pages 70–74), in the section under Sponge-bags, I have mentioned that by squeezing a plastic bottle before screwing on its top, you can prevent its leaking (or exploding at altitude).

I like to keep a ready-packed medical bag for all my travels. It also includes other items of kit, such as pocket-knife, insect repellent, and a spare torch. I take it wherever I travel, and it gives me confidence that I have at hand almost anything I could need in an emergency.

MEDICINE IN THE VILLAGE

If you hike far away from well-developed areas, you will frequently be asked for medicines and medical treatment. This should be taken into account when you are buying medical equipment, because at the least you will certainly need to take extra stocks of mild pain-relievers, plasters, and antiseptic creams.

When you do give pills to genuine sufferers, you may also be inundated with requests from people who are clearly not suffering, but are wooed by the general attractions of pills. It is of course hard to judge the genuineness of these appeals, but it is best to keep a store of vitamin pills for those applicants who are clearly bogus. At least vitamin pills can't do any harm.

You may well be faced with difficult medical problems which you are in no way equipped to deal with. Obviously whenever practical, the seriously ill should be persuaded to take the long trip to a doctor. If you do have to administer medicine, it should probably be given in smaller doses than usual, for the patient may be unused to any type of drug.

If you settle in a remote area where there is no access to a doctor, you can hardly refuse to give some medical treatment. Nevertheless, an expatriate who effects only 'miracle cures' is not doing the locals any good in the long term. Many people are already far too impressed by the magic of pills (and especially the magic of injections) and they pay too little attention to the causes of illness. Another unfortunate result is the gross misuse of antibiotics: often they are sold (without prescription) at exorbitant prices, then taken in the wrong doses for the wrong length of time and for the wrong illness. In many areas common diseases have become quite unnecessarily resistant to the most useful antibiotics.

Expatriates are doing the locals a far greater favour if they teach them about the avoidable causes of disease – such as lack of sanitation, water pollution, and bad diet – and if they instruct them in elementary and understandable first aid.

If expatriates are obliged to give medical treatment frequently, they should know about the indispensable handbook called *Where There is No Doctor* by David Werner (see Appendix 1).

Remember that if a villager falls seriously ill or dies after you have given him or her medical treatment, you may well be blamed.

A medical officer

When an expedition or a group of people is travelling into the wilds, it is a good idea to appoint one of the party as a medical officer. He or she should then attend an appropriate first-aid course and learn some elementary medical techniques before leaving, such as stitching, injecting, artificial mouth-to-mouth ventilation, and external chest compression.

This medical officer should know the closest practical **telephone number for emergency medical advice**. It is quite likely that you will have access to a telephone before you have access to professional treatment, and the telephone may be very useful, because even an amateur can be given a surprising amount of medical help over the telephone – both for diagnosis and medical treatment. If possible make notes before telephoning about the following aspects of a patient's health:

Breathing
Pulse
Temperature (including records of changes in temperature)
Eyes, including the size of pupils (the black circle in the centre
 of the eye)

Skin condition
Urine
Faeces
Any known chronic diseases, such as asthma or diabetes
Number of days of symptoms
Rousability of the patient

British consulates keep a list of recommended English-speaking doctors.

FOOD

It is obvious that if you don't eat a nourishing and well-balanced diet, your body will be less resistant to infection. All the same, many travellers don't pay enough attention to their diet, particularly as they can often eat enough bulk very cheaply. A VSO handbook once crisply wrote: 'More volunteers become sick from inadequate diets than from any other cause.' Travellers usually eat enough vegetables and cereals, but they should make an extra effort to eat plenty of fruit, as well as some protein in the form of meat, beans, or fish.

Having said this, I must admit that, where the hygiene is suspect, I cut out meat and fish, and I'm sure this helps reduce infections. After all, when one smells a really disgusting smell (nature's way of warning us), it nearly always comes from meat or fish. How often do vegetables or fruit smell really bad? And in a hot climate, I don't think one needs as much protein as in a cold one.

Vegetarians, though, often aren't sufficiently aware that if you cut out meat and fish, then the *bulk* of your food must be vastly increased. I am not saying that a vegetarian diet is necessarily inferior, but weight for weight (and bulk for bulk) vegetables are not as nutritious as meat. If you don't believe me (and lots don't) think of herbivores (such as antelopes or cows) who keep their heads down all day: munch, munch, munch. Then think of tigers, who, having taken their carnivorous snack, can afford to rest for a couple of days. It isn't a coincidence that people who are doing strenuous physical labour often report an intense craving for meat, if they have access only to vegetables.

Don't eat watercress, local ice-creams, and raw fish (quite common in the Far East, but may infect you with flukes). Ice-cream is often especially rich in bugs, and may well have been made with contaminated water. Dr Bent Juel-Jensen, who has great experience of tropical medicine, has written:

All local meat whether flesh, fowl, or fish, and all local vegetables should be carefully chosen and prepared, and thoroughly cooked. Some meats are more dangerous than others. If you eat only partly cooked or raw beef, you will at worst get beef tapeworm that stays in your gut, but if you eat half or uncooked pig, you may get the pig tapeworm that migrates into your muscles and into your brain. This is the reason why Muslims, Orthodox Jews and Coptic Christians do not eat pig . . . If you must eat salads, choose some that are made from tomatoes and cucumber, but avoid lettuce like the plague. Weight for weight lettuce has a three to four hundred times greater surface area than cucumber or tomato . . . Many vegetables in Third World countries are raised with the aid of human excrement, and are likely to have lots of these germs on their surface.*

Apart from salads, shellfish are probably one of the greatest dangers, as they filter huge quantities of sea water and therefore pick up traces of human excrement.

Milk is a particularly favourable medium for the breeding of germs. All milk should be boiled before you drink it in order to avoid the danger of catching brucellosis, typhoid, dysentery or tuberculosis. Don't think that once you have boiled milk it is safe for ever; drink it as soon as possible after it has been boiled because germs will quickly start breeding again.

Some people believe that yoghurt and other fermented milks, such as dahi, are safer than milk; and in some parts of the world yoghurt is used as a remedy for stomach upsets. It is true that yoghurt is fairly acidic and is therefore a less suitable environment

* *Expedition Medicine* (Expedition Advisory Centre, Royal Geographical Society, rev. edn 1991)

for many pathogenic bacteria to survive in, so it is *relatively* safer than potentially polluted milk.

There are rumours that it is dangerous to eat watermelons because they can pick up contamination through their skins – especially if they are grown in fields manured by sewage. In the last edition I wrote:

As far as I can find out, this is untrue. The story may have begun during the Second World War, when many soldiers fell ill after eating melon; it was discovered that in order to increase the melons' weight they had been injected with water from a contaminated river.

Now two people have written to me to say that melons get soaked in dirty ditches to make them heavier; so be cautious about watermelons that are sold by weight.

In Iran, you are often given a raw onion with your food; Iranians believe that it disinfects your stomach and prevents upsets, and in parts of the Arab world onion juice is used as treatment for stomach upsets. I know of no medical evidence to support this, but many sensible people believe it to be effective.

Some nervous travellers stick to the more expensive hotels, and refuse to eat any food sold at roadside stalls. But hotels are often less safe; their food is likely to be left lying about (buffets are especially suspect), they misuse frozen foods, and the tropical heat is the perfect temperature for bacteria to multiply. *Holiday Which?* magazine investigated fifty-nine kitchens of starred hotels (in Tunisia, Majorca, and Rhodes) and found that fourteen of them had kitchens liable to an outbreak of infection. You are often safer eating a sizzling hot snack at a roadside stall.

Pawpaw

The pawpaw, or papaya (which shouldn't be confused with the American paw-paw, *Asimina triloba*), is a most useful and versatile fruit. Unfortunately some people are put off the fruit by its slightly offensive smell, but they should persevere, for it is an acquired taste. A squeeze of lime helps.

The pawpaw fruit is easily digested, rich in vitamins (weight for weight it has more vitamin C than an orange), and is known to have a beneficial effect in the treatment of stomach ulcers. Eating a slice of pawpaw each day is a great help in keeping your bowels regular. Mr J. F. Dastur, in *The Medicinal Plants of India*,* makes some interesting claims for it: 'Papaya is alterative, cholagogue, stomachic, digestive, and antiscorbutic; it is given in piles, and enlarged liver and spleen; the ripe fruit is eaten regularly for habitual constipation and chronic diarrhoea.'

The rind of pawpaw is used to relieve the stings of insects, jellyfish, and stingray, and it also has a beneficial effect in the treatment of sores and tropical skin ulcers (place pawpaw rind on the sore and change frequently). Apparently the enzyme in pawpaw helps dissolve the dead tissue.

Meat tenderizer made from the pawpaw fruit or tree is used all over the world. If you wish to tenderize meat yourself, prick holes in it with a fork, and rub it with the rind of a pawpaw.

If you are settling anywhere for more than a year, you should consider growing some pawpaw trees. They are particularly easy to grow, and will flourish almost anywhere with a hot climate and a reasonably well-drained soil. You will need both male and female plants. After approximately ten months the trees will start bearing fruit, and will continue to do so for about five years. Each tree can give you about thirty to forty fruits a year.

Salt

Only a few years ago, most travellers considered it de rigueur to take a bottle of salt tablets. Now the experts don't recommend them, but they are still carried by many travellers. Are they necessary? Do we need extra salt in the tropics?

The human body contains about 8 ounces of salt – enough to fill several salt-cellars. Salt is vital for the working of many bodily functions. It is involved in muscular contractions (including our heartbeat), in nerve impulses, and in the digestion of body-building proteins. Without salt the body goes into

(D. B. Taraporevala, Bombay, 1970)

convulsions and paralysis, and death follows. It may seem strange that the body, which has evolved so well in other respects, doesn't always acquire enough salt from its ordinary food intake. From a well-balanced, natural diet we get enough vitamins, amino-acids, iron, protein, and so on, but not necessarily enough salt. This is a major reason why salt has been outstandingly expensive at various moments in history, and why in West Africa it was once traded weight for weight with gold.

The explanation of our need to consume extra salt lies in our changing habits of eating food. When we were hunters, we assimilated enough salt from meat and fish, but when we became crop-growers our natural intake of salt diminished. Mungo Park, the West African explorer, described in 1795 how 'the use of vegetable food creates so painful a longing for salt that no words can sufficiently describe it'. Even for those of our ancestors who still ate meat, their intake of salt was reduced by changes in cooking, because raw and roast meat retain more salt than boiled meat. Those Masai, who still live on raw blood and milk, don't require additional salt.

From the time that we became cultivators (rather than hunters, gatherers, or pastoralists) salt began to play a crucial role in our religious and economic life. Throughout the world the words 'bread and salt' go together; Homer called salt 'divine', Plato called it 'a substance dear to the Gods'. In the early history of the Roman army an allowance of salt was made to soldiers, and in Imperial times this *salarium* became an allowance of money for salt, hence the word 'salary'.

Salt was also important for its preservative qualities, and its economic importance was indicated by the almost universal practice of salt taxes or government monopolies. This continued even to this century, and I can remember when salt was an Italian government monopoly and could be bought only in tobacconists.

The question of salt becomes important in the tropics, because you are losing it when your body sweats, and this has to be replaced. How should we replace it? The experts now agree that swallowing **salt tablets** is not the best method of increasing your absorption of salt. The tablets have been photographed passing right through the stomach without dissolving. So there is no need to carry an unnecessary bottle of tablets in your medical bag.

When you have been in a hot country for a week or two, you need only put some extra salt on your food. Our taste mechanism is sufficiently sophisticated to increase tolerance to (or desire for) salt, and you can adjust the salting of your food accordingly. There are no fixed rules, and it is best to use common sense. When taking severe physical exercise – and therefore sweating a lot – you should heavily salt your food, or even dissolve a small teaspoonful in a drink. You will be surprised by how much your tolerance to salt increases when it is needed.

On first arriving in a hot country, though, your taste mechanism doesn't sufficiently alert you to the need for extra salt. For the first fortnight be sure to add plenty to your food each day, especially during the first few days when you are dehydrated from a long flight. Personally, during my first couple of days, I always drink some rehydration fluid (see Index for several mentions of this). In the West, salt has had a very bad press recently, but when you are in the tropics, don't be too worried about excessive salt in your food, as your body's homoeostatic mechanisms will normally take care of any excess.

If you get leg cramp, you should immediately drink some rehydration fluid, as the cramp is often a symptom of salt depletion.

WATER

The key to avoiding the overwhelming majority of travellers' diseases is to have access to *plenty* of *clean* water. I shall deal first with the question of quantity and then the question of cleanliness.

Most of us have always had access to running water, and

therefore don't appreciate the crucial part that water plays in our lives. In fact, approximately 70 per cent of our body is composed of water (and this percentage is the same for most living organisms). Loss of only part of this water is extremely serious. As I point out in the survival section (see Chapter 12) we can manage for a surprisingly long time without food, but in a hot climate we die after only a few days without water. Many people also don't realize quite how much water is needed in a hot climate. When the weather is very hot, it is not unusual to drink 16 pints in a day. Besides, water is excellent for the health, and even at home many people should drink more of it than they do.

I have met several travellers who drink any water offered to them; they have often told me that when you drink impure water in small amounts, you gradually build up immunity to water-borne diseases. This is nonsense. You can catch a large number of diseases and infections from water, including polio, guinea worm, leptospirosis, typhoid, paratyphoid, cholera, bacillary dysentery, amoebic dysentery, infective hepatitis, roundworm, cryptosporidiosis, and giardiasis. It is impossible to build up immunity against most of these diseases.

When you are obliged to drink water which you suspect is impure, don't think 'In for a penny, in for a pound'. Remember that many diseases are dosage-dependent, and therefore the less you drink the better.

Don't forget that infection doesn't come only from *drinking* the water; you should use safe water for brushing your teeth and for washing vegetables or fruit. Avoid ice cubes that aren't made from sterilized water, because freezing doesn't kill disease organisms. In restaurants, ice cubes should usually be avoided because most owners laugh at the belief that they should be made from boiled water.

Bottled fizzy drinks are usually safer than bottled still ones, as the fizzy drinks are generally more tamper-proof, and the acidity produced by carbonation is high enough to kill some bacteria, such as the typhoid bacillus. In fact, just storing water in a bottle reduces bacterial counts, and after five days the water is *relatively* safe.

For the best method of rationing water when walking, see the section on Walking in Chapter 12.

If you don't have access to clean water, how do you make it safe to drink? The three methods of purification are boiling, filtration, and chemical sterilization. Before looking at these in detail, it is worth repeating that there is no use in purifying water if you then drink it from a contaminated container (see the section on water-flasks in Chapter 3).

Boiling

Boiling is the safest way to sterilize water. It kills all the major disease organisms. For how long should we boil water? None of the authorities seem to agree, but bunching all their opinions together, I reckon that a brisk boil for two minutes would be sufficient at sea level; and for every 1,000 feet above sea level add another minute. (This is because at high altitudes water boils at a lower temperature than 212°F and therefore it takes longer to kill disease organisms.) Some books claim that it takes as long as twenty minutes to destroy amoebic cysts. Because this would be inconvenient and often impractical, I wrote to check with Liverpool School of Tropical Medicine and the Department of Medical Microbiology at the London School of Hygiene and Tropical Medicine. They both agreed that at sea level the cysts would be destroyed by bringing the water to the boil, and that at any altitude they would be destroyed by boiling for five minutes. They also pointed out that as the cysts are comparatively large, they can also be easily filtered out, and that even tightly knitted socks would be sufficient in emergencies.

Although boiled water is the safest, it's worth knowing that very hot water does kill many disease organisms. For instance, the cholera bacillus is destroyed at 140°F. Therefore when you are sitting in an unhygienic restaurant, ask for tea or coffee; it will be safer than cold water, even when the water hasn't been boiled.

All the containers in which water is kept should be sterilized by pouring boiling water over them; and if you are keeping water in a flask, you should take care to sterilize its rim.

Filtration

Constant advances are made in the production of portable filters, and no doubt improved models will appear soon after I have written this. However, I would be inclined to treat them with an element of scepticism. Several times I have tried what has been described as the latest state-of-the-art model, and they have rarely proved satisfactory.

Before buying any filter, consider the following questions.

1. How bulky is it to carry? Many filters are too bulky for the ordinary traveller, and it is often easier to take a water-flask, and keep it topped up with boiled water.
2. If you haven't been vaccinated against hepatitis A, does the filter strain out this virus? Many filters don't, although this won't matter so much when you are going on an expedition into totally unpopulated areas, because hepatitis is transmitted by the oral–faecal route, and therefore is found only where there are human beings (or occasionally baboons).

   Expeditions, though, will often need a filter, as it is rarely practical to boil all the water that is necessary.
3. Does the filter need cleaning? And if not, how long will the self-sterilization process last? This is a very important question, as filters can be a perfect breeding ground for disease organisms.
4. If the filter isn't of the ceramic non-clogging type, ask how soon it will be likely to get clogged. A litre of apparently clear water may contain 100,000 million particles. A filter needs to catch all of these in order to filter out the disease organisms. Naturally this can block up the system quite easily; a 'filter straw', which I bought from a specialist mail-order company, clogged up during its very first use.

5. How long does the filter take to process the water? Some of the modern filters, which in theory are so wonderful, take too long to be practical. One widely sold modern filter takes half an hour to produce one glass. A filter that takes only ten minutes to fill a glass may be impractical for the backpacking traveller.

Because many of these questions aren't often answered satisfactorily, I remain sceptical about the use of filters for the ordinary traveller on the move. It is a different matter if you are settled in one place, as you will then be able to use one of the large filters which are more practical.

In the past many expeditions used to take Millbank bags, which are an easily packable cloth filter. But most people now consider that they take far too long to do their job.

Ideally, water should be filtered before being boiled. Apart from clearing sludgy water, the filter removes small, hard particles which can cause mechanical irritation in the intestines, which in turn can result in diarrhoea and subsequent infection. It is also better to filter before you boil, because it is possible that the filter may be contaminated. Unfortunately, in the real world this isn't always possible.

Chemical sterilization

Chemicals are not as effective as boiling, but they are much better than nothing. Most tablets sold in Britain are **chlorine**-based. The modern ones are a great improvement: they are much smaller than they used to be, and don't need additional tablets to take away the taste.

Many travellers are obsessed with amoebic dysentery and believe that water-purifying tablets don't kill the cysts which cause it. To check on this point, I wrote to the makers of Puritabs (a convenient small effervescent pill, widely marketed in Britain). They wrote back:

The tablets are formulated to release hypochlorous acid in solution, which is the active germicidal agent. They contain enough chlorine to kill the cysts of *Entamoeba histolytica* when used at the appropriate concentration, i.e. one tablet in 1 litre of water and left for ten minutes before use . . . as these tablets are chlorine-based they are active against most enteric water-borne infections.

The London School of Hygiene and Tropical Medicine was slightly more cautious: 'Chlorine tablets would kill most cysts in most waters if completely mixed and the temperature is high enough. They would render most water safe for practical purposes; the contact time should be as long as feasible, preferably about an hour.'

I have since written to the makers of Puritabs about the efficacy of the tablets against the cysts of giardia. Their Medical Information Officer gave the following, somewhat cautious, reply:

We have no direct evidence for the effectiveness of Puritabs against giardia cysts. However, published data suggests that at water temperatures above 10 centigrade, one tablet per litre of water with a contact time of ten minutes should be effective. At water temperatures of less than 10 centigrade, two tablets per litre of water for thirty minutes will be needed.

Chlorine does not kill cryptosporidiosis, one of the more recently identified causes of traveller's diarrhoea. This is yet another reason to prefer boiled water whenever possible.

Bear in mind that vegetables, fruits, or containers which have not been washed properly are just as likely as water to infect you with amoebic cysts.

Chlorine is convenient as a base for water-purifying tablets. It is reasonably safe (though there are an increasing number of people who are suspicious of it), and there is a rough-and-ready check on the correct amount of chlorination: if the water smells slightly of chlorine you have probably put in the correct quantity; if it smells strongly of chlorine you have probably put in too much. The extra amount shouldn't do you too much harm, but it tastes disagreeable.

Effervescent tablets, such as Puritabs, are effective faster than ordinary ones.

Some people prefer to use **iodine**, either as tincture of iodine or as iodine-based tablets. I have found it difficult to sort out the pros and cons of chlorine versus iodine. As usual the experts disagree. They aren't in agreement even about the dosage of iodine when it *is* used. I have read books which recommend as little as one drop per litre, and others which recommend as many as ten drops. (You probably won't go far wrong if you use approximately six drops per litre for clear water, and double for cloudy water, and then wait twenty minutes.)

As far as I can make out, the advantages of iodine are as follows. At low levels of concentration it may be more effective against some organisms, such as the cysts of giardia and amoeba. Many people prefer the taste of iodine to chlorine. One expatriate wrote to me to say that after washing vegetables in Puritabs for three months she was so nauseated by the taste that she happily changed to iodine. And tincture of iodine is far more space-effective than chlorine tablets, which will be important if you are stocking an expedition. I have also been told that, when there are other organic substances in the water, these can use up the chlorine in preference to killing the organism you are aiming at, and that this doesn't happen with iodine.

Some disadvantages of iodine. A broken or leaking bottle will stain everything in your rucksack. Iodine tablets will eventually deteriorate. And iodine shouldn't be used by pregnant women, the elderly, children, or anyone with a thyroid condition.

You will gather from the above that I haven't been able to be very categorical about the pros and cons of the different methods of chemical sterilization. But I don't think this is a disaster, as, although the pills are useful for emergencies or as an adjunct, you should prefer boiling and filtering.

If there is suspended matter in the water, this may protect disease organisms. When you are in the bush and unable to boil water before chemical sterilization, the ideal is to filter the water through a **filter bag**. These easily portable bags will filter out the hard particles already mentioned, and remove the suspended matter which protects disease organisms against the effect of sterilizing tablets. They also remove the cysts (such as amoeba and giardia) which resist low levels of chlorination. Supposing you don't have a filter bag, then filter the water by the best means available, using any tightly woven cloth that filters the water slowly. The slower the drip, the finer the filtration.

When the water still looks dirty after filtration, double the recommended dose of any sterilizing agent.

Chlorine and iodine won't be effective if put into very hot water. Wait until it has cooled.

Try to avoid drinking any chemically sterilized water for long periods, especially when iodine has been used.

Thirst

Under normal conditions, our thirst mechanism should let us know when we need liquid. For some reason this mechanism doesn't work efficiently in the tropics, and it has been estimated that in a hot climate a normal thirst makes you drink only about three-quarters of your body's needs. Get in the habit of increasing your fluid intake. High altitudes are also dehydrating and, again, our thirst mechanism doesn't tell us to drink enough.

Whenever you are in the tropics, keep an eye on your urine, and if you aren't producing at least two reasonably clear pints of urine a day, start drinking some more liquid at once. If your urine becomes tea-coloured, you are probably dehydrated. As one guidebook says, 'A few dark-coloured drops and a puff of steam are not enough.' Women are especially prone to urinary infections in the tropics if they haven't been drinking enough water. And there is another good reason why everyone should drink plenty: if you don't, you may develop kidney-stones, which are agonizing.

This is a good place to mention a separate thirst problem. When a seemingly unquenchable thirst isn't cured by gulps of cold water, it is usually quenched by hot tea.

Filling the bath

Not only is water essential for our health, it is vital for many other crucial parts of our life, such as the lavatory, washing, laundry, and cooking. The average English person uses more than 30 gallons a day; but not one of us ever wakes up in the morning, thinking how lucky we are to be blessed with running water (and even luckier – with running hot water); during most of the world's history people haven't had this wonderful benefit, and hundreds of millions still don't.

When revolution breaks out in a foreign city, canny journalists immediately fill their hotel bath: they know that if the supply is cut off (which often happens), the water will be invaluable for flushing the lavatory, washing, shaving, cooking, and, most important, drinking.

CHAPTER 6

ANIMAL HAZARDS

In the past many thrilling accounts have been written about the dangers from wild animals. When travellers walked through the bush, lions were waiting in ambush, while snakes dripped off every tree; around every corner an elephant was waiting to charge. In fact most of these dangers were exaggerated: large animals are frightened of human beings and usually prefer to keep well out of their way. As we shall see, by far the greatest danger comes from the insects.

The large cats

As a general rule the large cats, including lion, tiger, and leopard, aren't dangerous. We are not their natural prey, and they usually show no desire to attack us. With experienced guides I have several times walked close to lions, and haven't yet been charged. Sometimes, however, a few aberrant cats turn into man-eaters, and then they are exceptionally dangerous. A man-eating cat only has to sit behind a bush, and wait for someone to walk along a path. They also become extremely cunning, learning in some mysterious way how to detect a poisoned bait.

Man-eaters spread terror over a wide area, so you will nearly always know if one is about. Some particular areas, such as the Sundarbans in India, are consistently notorious for man-eaters.

Be careful about all **tame or 'half-tame' wild animals**, especially cats. It is doubtful whether any wild cat can be truly tamed — except for the cheetah (which, having unretractable claws, isn't strictly speaking a cat). The Adamsons' lions were probably the most famous tamed cats in the world, and yet they were responsible for at least one death and several mutilations.

(Gavin Maxwell's equally celebrated otters had to be condemned, having bitten off several fingers.) Beware, also, of half-tame primates, such as baboons, chimpanzees, and rhesus monkeys, which quite often seem friendly and then give very nasty bites.

Wild animals that are familiar with human beings have often lost their fear of us, and therefore tend to be the most dangerous. Thus lions that live in a game reserve or near a populated locality are likely to be more dangerous than those living somewhere really wild. Recently in the Masai Mara Game Reserve, a lion took hold of a camper by his head, pulled him out of bed and killed him. The camper was sleeping inside his tent, but he'd stuck out his head in order to avoid stuffiness. This incident would have been less likely in a more remote area.

In the event of **being charged by a wild cat**, don't run away. Wild cats are hunters, and by running away you will help trigger their hunting instinct. Although terrifying, it is much safer to face them. Over the years I have collected quite a weight of anecdotal evidence to support this. One acquaintance of mine was charged by a tiger in Nepal. His Nepalese guide rushed at the tiger, shouting and yelling. The tiger retreated. A Botswanan, who had many encounters with lions, told me that he has sometimes resorted to throwing a stone or clod of earth at a charging lion. As he pointed out, lions aren't used to their prey throwing stones at them, and this unnerves them. The fishermen of the Sundarbans, which probably has the worst man-eating problem in the world, have sometimes worn masks on the back of their heads, because they believe tigers are unlikely to attack someone who is facing them.

I can give the 'don't run away' advice with some confidence because running away is pointless: a cat is so fast that it will catch you anyway. Stand to face it, and you might have a chance.

Two more pieces of advice about wild cats. Never get out of a vehicle anywhere near them. This might seem unnecessary advice, but a surprising number of people, especially photographers, are seduced by the placid appearance of lions. Lions are unused to people getting out of vehicles, and therefore feel threatened, which makes them highly prone to attack.

If you are camping in lion territory, always carry a torch when you are moving within the camp after dark. Lions do come into camp (I have been within 15 feet of one), but they are far less likely to attack when a torch is shone in their face.

Hippopotamuses and buffaloes

Both of these are far more dangerous than lions. A hippo that is out of water is highly dangerous; and it is especially unwise to get between a hippo and its refuge in the river. Because hippos feed at night, the chief danger times for walkers are early morning and evening. Don't think that hippos aren't fast: they can move faster than Carl Lewis.

Despite a benevolent appearance, hippos are aggressive, and they are among the few animals that deliberately inflict severe wounds on each other. An extreme example of a hippo's aggressiveness was recorded on the Natal coast of South Africa, where a cow hippo plunged into the sea, seized a 300-pound shark which was lazing in the surf, hauled it onto the beach, and trampled it to death.

Although hippos will occasionally attack a small boat or overturn one by accident, they are generally safest when in water: they feel secure there. The famous wildlife photographer Alan Root spent many hours swimming among hippos at Mazima Springs; he was eventually attacked, but this may have been just bad luck.

Once when I was with a walking safari along the Luwegu River in Tanzania, we found the hippos a particular threat. Because the river was very low, they had to spend most of the day on dry land. On one sad occasion a hippo charged us and, when it was 30 feet away, our guide was forced to shoot it.

Buffaloes that are gathered in a herd are rarely aggressive. The danger usually comes from solitary, old ones which may have been kicked out of the herd, and spend much of their time feeding alone in thickets.

To avoid the danger from both buffaloes and hippos, don't go into any dense bush near a river. In fact you should try to avoid walking through any dense bush, because in game country it is always safer to walk in the open, where there is no risk of *surprising* any animal. Attacks from most animals are far more likely to be provoked by fear than aggression.

In the event of being charged by a hippo (or rhino) and getting no instructions from a guide, don't try to call its bluff. Although it is possible that the charge may be a false one (I have seen a hippo veer off at the last moment), it is not worth taking a chance. If there is a tree anywhere near, get up it. Fear will help you climb even the most difficult and thorniest. If you can't get up a tree, get behind one – people have been saved by dodging around a tree-trunk.

Elephants

I can give no confident advice about being charged by an elephant. Every expert I've asked has given a different opinion. And although many more elephant charges are bluffs than was previously believed, I'm still not sure that I would have the courage to face a charge.

On flat ground an elephant can move faster than a human, but if I were near a steep hill I would try running up or down it, because although elephants are astonishingly agile, a slope will slow them down. It is also worth knowing that elephants have an excellent sense of smell, but very poor eyesight. So you can usually remain unnoticed by staying upwind.

The safest advice of all is never to walk in game country without a trained guide. They nearly always have a superb understanding of the animals, and if you implicitly follow their instructions, you will be safe.

Surprisingly, elephants which have been caught in the wild and then domesticated are less dangerous than elephants born in captivity. During their playful youth, the latter have often knocked over a few humans, and therefore don't have the natural fear of their wild cousins.

Too often, people assume that because certain species are harmless in one place, they will be just as harmless in another. In the Savuti region of Botswana I have sat on a ledge where wild elephants have gently touched me with their tusks and trunks; I have also been to a wildlife reserve in India (Palamau) where the elephants are dedicated killers of human beings, even attacking pedestrians innocently walking along a metalled road. Wherever there are potentially dangerous wild animals, it is always best to ask local advice.

Hyenas

I know several people who regularly camp in areas where hyenas abound, and who have never been attacked. But I mention hyenas because they are a good example of animals which may be perfectly safe in one area, but lethal elsewhere. There are localities in southern Africa, for instance, where hyenas are killers, and have entered tents to bite at the faces of sleeping campers.

Wolves

Wolves are a good example of absurdly exaggerated reports of ferocity. Although it is possible that in extreme circumstances wolves (especially rabid ones) may have attacked humans, when you start investigating the thousands of reports of wolf attacks, it is almost impossible to find any reliable first-hand accounts. Indeed, some experts claim that there are no authenticated accounts anywhere in the world of fatal attacks by wolves upon human beings except – on very rare occasions – by animals maddened with rabies. In a twenty-five-year period of a wolf-control programme, the US Fish and Wildlife Service failed to substantiate a single reported unprovoked attack. A newspaper in Ontario, in an area known for blood-curdling tales of wolf attacks, offered a $100 reward for proof of an unprovoked attack, but the reward went uncollected. As I have said, the ferocity of animals may vary from one region to another, but it certainly appears that, at least in North America, wolves are relatively harmless.

Piranhas

Piranhas also have an exaggerated reputation for ferocious attacks. The original source for most of these stories appears to be President Theodore Roosevelt's *Through the Brazilian Jungle*, which was published in 1914. He claimed:

Piranhas are the most ferocious fish in the world. They will snap a finger off a hand incautiously trailed in the water; they mutilate swimmers – in every town in Paraguay there are men who have been thus mutilated; they will rend and devour alive any wounded man or beast.

Although piranhas have certainly been guilty of wounding some people, I have found it difficult to authenticate a single first-hand account of death from an attack. For instance, my friends Martin and Tanis Jordan, who made seven long trips on South American rivers, washing and swimming in the river almost every day, were never once bitten, nor heard any first-hand account of an attack. In *The Piranha Book*, the editor, Dr George Myers, while having no first-hand evidence, does give some credence to stories of danger from piranhas.* But on the other hand, one of his contributors, Harald Schultz, wrote that in his twenty years of studying Indian life in South America, he had never heard of a major attack. Among other rivers, he had travelled along the Rio Sao Francisco, which is often described as the most dangerous. He had also travelled throughout Paraguay, which is considered to have some of the most dangerous rivers.

During the years that Schultz spent in South America, he did, however, meet seven people who had suffered minor piranha bites, and he was himself bitten on the big toe when he entered a river to retrieve a net full of *wounded* fish. I have italicized 'wounded', because although piranhas (an imprecise word which covers several species of related fish) are less ferocious than believed, I would never enter a South American river if I was

---

* (T.F.H. Publications, USA, 1972)

anywhere near a struggling, bleeding, or wounded animal. Nor would I go into the river if I was suffering from a cut. And I have received a letter from an expert, Rosemary Lowe-McConnell, who takes a very cautious view of at least one variety of piranha:

The red-bellied piranha (*Pygocentrus nattereri*), common in savanna ponds, can give awful bites (taking pieces out like an ice-cream scoop, so no flap to heal over). If the piranhas started to bite the technique was to stay quite still, push the bitten foot down into the mud so blood would not spread, and signal to companions to bring a boat to take the bitten person from the water.

The same correspondent also wrote that her husband had worked in an area near the borders of Surinam where the piranha were said to be so dangerous that the experienced field-staff would remove water from the river only in buckets.

Certainly you should be cautious when fishing. Most piranha wounds have probably been caused out of water. Landed piranhas have the habit of flopping about, while gnashing their teeth. Be extra careful when removing a hook from one.

To sum up, piranhas are nothing like as dangerous as they are supposed to be, but, as usual, it is always a good idea to get local advice.

Candiru

Several minute parasitic catfish reportedly have a taste for urine, and thus are prone to swim up the urogenital openings of both men and women. The most notorious species is the candiru. These thin scaleless fish, not much thicker than a pencil lead, are equipped with erectile rear-pointing spines, which are allegedly raised once they have entered the urethra of a bather. This habit is often described, but although I have chased the story hard, I have again failed to acquire a convincing account. I wrote to a specialist on South American fishes (Dr John Lundberg of Duke University in North Carolina), but he said that, although he and his ichthyological colleagues had heard a lot of third-hand stories about the candiru, they had never come across any first-hand evidence.

I suspect that the stories about candiru are a nonsense; however, the idea of their danger is so horrific that, if the locals were to utter any warning, I would be tempted to wear tight protective clothing before entering the water.

Sharks

The danger from sharks has also been greatly exaggerated. There are several hundred varieties of shark, but very few of them offer any threat to humans. When the locals are swimming happily in the water, you will usually be safe, even when there are sharks in the vicinity. I have frequently seen sharks when swimming, and many divers have learnt to be very familiar with them.

Worldwide, sharks kill human beings at the rate of only about fifty a year; we kill more than a million of them each year, and several species (most of which play an important role in the oceans' ecological life) have been nearly exterminated – including the dogfish shark, which used to be the staple of our fish-and-chip shops.

Off the Californian coast (one of the worst places for shark attacks) there were only forty-one incidents in the thirty-two years between 1950 and 1982; and off the notorious Australian coast, recorded incidents have averaged only about three a year. Surprisingly, most shark attacks are not fatal, and of those forty-one people attacked off California only four died. In recent years there has been an increase in attacks off California, which can partly be explained by the increase in the sea-lion population. The sea-lion is the natural prey of the great white shark, and the combination of wetsuits, flippers (fins) and the modern, short surfboard is thought to make the swimmer look like a sea-lion.

It is worth quashing a few myths about shark attacks. They do attack at temperatures below 70°F. They do attack in shallow waters: a substantial proportion of attacks take place in water shallower than 4 feet. The largest sharks are not necessarily the most ferocious: some of only about 4 feet are man-killers, while some of the largest, such as the basking shark and the whale shark, feed only on plankton and small fish.

From what I have read about sharks, I have come to the conclusion that by far your greatest danger is to be anywhere near a wriggling fish. If you must indulge in spear fishing, don't keep fish attached to your belt: instead, put them into some kind of floating container towed behind you. Spear fishermen frequently notice that they can swim for long periods unmolested, but the moment they spear a fish, a shark appears, apparently from nowhere. For a long time it was believed that sharks were attracted by the blood, but the best evidence now seems to show that they are attracted by vibration from the wriggling of the fish. In one instance a shark even 'jumped out of the water and took off the arm of a man walking along a reef with a fish he was carrying'.*

When sharks are in your area, get advice from locals. And if the sharks are even remotely dangerous, don't swim if you are having your period; and avoid swimming in the evening or night, because some of the most dangerous sharks (such as the tiger shark) come into the shallows at this time.

Barracuda

Like the word 'piranha', the word 'barracuda' is also imprecise: it refers to about twenty different species of fish, most of them nothing like as dangerous as believed.

The general rule is that when the water is clear, barracuda are safe. We are, after all, not their natural prey. In cloudy water, however, it is safer not to wear any jewellery or rings, or carry anything glittering near you. Barracuda have been known to attack when attracted by a glitter which they thought came from a fish.

Three more warnings about barracuda. According to an excellent book, *Dangerous to Man*,† a solitary barracuda is more dangerous than one in a group. And, as with shark, you are in far greater danger when spear fishing. Also, like shark, they are

* *Shark Attack*, Victor Coppleson (Angus & Robertson, 1982)
† Roger Caras (Penguin, 1975)

attracted by thrashing in the water; so, however difficult, try to remain calm when barracuda are near.

Jellyfish and family

Jellyfish are a regular hazard for swimmers in the tropics. It is a good idea to ask advice before swimming, because their occurrence does vary according to weather and season, and the more dangerous moments are often avoidable. Jellyfish are easier to spot when you are wearing a mask.

Most jellyfish sting to some degree, though few are dangerous. Those with long tentacles tend to be the most painful. The box jellyfish of Australia (the world's most venomous animal) stings several hundred people a year, causing on average about three deaths. Most jellyfish are not as venomous as this. However, there is evidence of a recent increase in jellyfish stings, probably caused by a decline in the population of the turtles that eat them.

When stung, the instinctive reaction is to reach for the sting with your hands; don't – or you will be stung again. One reader sent me a description:

There was a little slime between my toes and a little on top of the foot. My first reaction was to try to wipe off the tentacles . . . hands down to wipe away – hands stinging – the pain – and in exclamation my hands went to my face and that also suffered . . . My companion had by now realized what had happened, and tried to wipe the tentacles off and was stung himself; it was at that point that I began to think the problem out. Cotton waste was used to wipe away the remaining slime . . . a petrol rag was used to finally get rid of the stinging cells . . . on talking to the locals there seemed to be no cure for the pain, the urgency is to get rid of the stinging cells. The method they used was rubbing with massive amounts of sand. I believe that petrol was an effective substitute in the absence of sand.

The stinging cells of the notorious box jellyfish can be entirely inactivated by liberal doses of vinegar. Unfortunately, to complicate things, vinegar can activate the stinging cells of some other jellyfish. Antihistamine tablets may be of help.

As with all other medical problems, if the victim stops breathing, use artificial mouth-to-mouth ventilation (see Chapter 8), which has proved life-saving for even the most severe jellyfish stings. Remember, though, that most stings are not life-threatening, and during the whole of this century only about seventy Australians have been killed by jellyfish.

Stingrays and other marine horrors

Always be careful where you put your feet in water, whether in the sea or in a river: there may be stingrays and other horrors, such as sea urchins and stonefish (which give one of the most agonizing stings in the world). Personally, I always wear rubber sandals in the sea, but they are no good against stingray spines.

Spines of **sea urchins** are one of the commonest problems of the sea. They are so brittle that it is impossible to extract them. I have heard of several methods of dealing with this problem, but I have never come across any reliable solution. A reader reports on a familiar second-hand version:

The locals light a candle and drip wax thickly over the infected area. Once the wax has solidified, it is peeled off, pulling the spines with it. Lemon juice is then squeezed on to the wounds. This is painful but the acidity acts an an antibiotic and also helps denature the toxins released by the spines.

In fact the spines of sea urchins are so brittle that I've never come across first-hand evidence of anyone getting them all out.

The spines eventually dissolve, and the wound will heal naturally. In many parts of the world, urine is used to speed up the process of dissolution, and in some areas the punctured flesh is first pounded with a hard object, such as an oar, to hurry things along. A reliable tipster, Moyra Bremner, wrote in the *Daily Telegraph* that plastering the wound with pawpaw helps open up the skin, making rejection of the spine material easier. Jack Jackson, an experienced diver and expeditioner, recommends dipping the foot in very hot water for half an hour, which softens the spines, making it easier for the body to reject them. He also points out that when you are not continuing to swim in sea water, it may be necessary to prevent the skin healing over, which would stop the spines from being rejected.

Because sea-urchin spines are such a real hazard – in contrast to so many of the hazards mentioned in this chapter – I would be very grateful for *first-hand* reports on the subject.

If swimmers cut themselves on **coral**, the wound is liable to go septic; so try to extract pieces of coral with fine tweezers, and treat the graze with antiseptic.

The **stingray** lies on the seabed and stings by flicking up its tail. It buries itself in the sand on the bottom of shallow bays, and is easily trodden on by unwary bathers. The pain is excruciating.

There is also fresh-water stingray, a particular problem in South American rivers. Wherever they exist, try not to paddle in shallows; if you must, it is best to shuffle forward which will usually scare them off. Don't believe stories that they lie only in sand – they also lie over pebbles.

The stings of many marine fish, including stingrays, weever fish, stonefish, catfish and firefish, can be greatly relieved by immersing the affected limb in the hottest water that you can tolerate (one doctor has described this to me as 'uncomfortably hot but not scalding'). Immerse the limb in the hot water for anything from thirty minutes to two hours – until the pain stops. The heat will decrease both the pain and the effects of the sting. Jack Jackson tells me that, when no other supply of hot water is available, the cooling water from an outboard motor can be used. You should follow up most of these wounds with an anti-tetanus booster and, when you can't reach a hospital, with antibiotics.

Don't ever touch any live cone shells. A few of them are extremely dangerous.

Following the most painful stings of marine animals (such as the stonefish) you may lose consciousness; so put all your determination into reaching the shore.

Scorpions

Although scorpion stings can be excruciating, most fit adults aren't at risk from them. Most scorpions aren't as dangerous as generally supposed. There are more than 400 known species, and some of them aren't dangerous at all.

Some scorpion stings are hardly more painful than that of a bee. When an old lady in Indonesia was giving me a massage, she was stung by a scorpion on her finger; she merely shook her finger a few times and continued. However, other scorpions deliver an excruciating sting, the effects of which may last for days. Children suffer most, as they have smaller bodies to absorb the venom. When you are living simply, or camping out in scorpion country, you shouldn't let your bedclothes trail on the ground, for a scorpion might climb up them. They also like dark corners, so it is best to get into the habit of knocking out your shoes in the morning – especially as there just could be a small snake lurking there as well.

In the Okavango Swamps in Botswana I met a lady who had been stung five times by scorpions within a year. On each occasion the scorpion had got onto her towel – probably attracted to it by the damp.

When camping in scorpion-infested areas, some people try to clear out the scorpions before pitching camp. Dr Bent Juel-Jensen has written: 'Scorpions burrow and have characteristic oblong holes. Insert a stick and dig down – the stick will help you find the course of the tunnel, which often changes direction ... Carefully upturn all stones by daylight; keep checking for new arrivals.' In a review of this book's first edition, Richard Snailham wrote: 'For scorpions I recommend the dousing of torches and the use of an ultra-violet lamp. Scorpions show up white, and the camp can easily be cleared with a pair of long tweezers.'

I have seen North Africans tease scorpions out of their holes by inserting a thin palm leaf. The aggressive scorpion attacks the palm leaf, and can be dragged out.

Snakes

You are far less likely to be bitten by a snake than stung by a scorpion. Snakes aren't nearly as dangerous as generally supposed, and extremely few travellers have been bitten by them.

ANIMAL HAZARDS

There are approximately 3,000 species of snake, of which not more than about 10 per cent are venomous, which means that many bites are not venomous at all. Even when a poisonous snake bites, it rarely injects a full dose of venom – in most cases not more than a tenth.

In Australia, for instance, where some of the world's deadliest snakes are found, there are approximately 3,000 bites a year, but in only about 300 cases is it considered necessary to give anti-venom.

And the mortality rate from snakebites is far less than commonly supposed. In the United States, with all its terrifying rattlesnakes, there are only about twelve deaths a year. In Australia there are now less than five deaths a year, and in the whole of Europe only about fifteen. In Britain only fourteen deaths have been reported during the last 100 years.

In the Third World, though, where many more children play in bare feet and many more labourers work bare-legged in the fields, there are many more snakebites. Some of the statistics are dubious, but even so we know that in Sri Lanka alone more than 900 deaths a year are reliably reported.

There are no dangerously venomous snakes in Ireland, Iceland, New Zealand, most Polynesian and Micronesian islands, the Galapagos, the Canaries, Malta, the Orkneys, the Shetlands, Madagascar, and quite a few other islands.

A South African survey showed that 74 per cent of snakebites were below the knee and 67 per cent below the ankle. Therefore it is sensible to wear boots and thick baggy trousers anywhere where snakes are liable to be dangerous. Even if the snake succeeds in biting through the trousers, the flow of venom will have been greatly reduced.

Snakes are mostly nocturnal: therefore be especially careful at night, and always use a torch. Remember that snakes can't hear ordinary sound-waves because their 'hearing' is restricted to ground vibrations.

Be especially careful when collecting firewood, picking up rocks, or putting your fingers in any crevice you can't see into.

★
231

Medical opinion on the treatment of snakebites changes constantly, and the experts don't always agree, so it is difficult to give confident advice. However, I will risk being categorical about a few 'don'ts'. Don't follow the traditional advice to make incisions at the point of the bite. This is a dangerous practice, which can damage delicate mechanisms of the body (especially fingers) and invite invasion by bacteria.

Don't rub in crystals of potassium permanganate. Don't give aspirin for pain: it may produce breaks in the lining of the stomach which can be dangerous for patients bitten by several species of snake. Instead use paracetamol or codeine-phosphate.

Don't administer anti-venom unless you are a doctor or you have been specially trained. Most amateur snakebite kits give perilous advice. Anti-venom is by no means always necessary and it may be dangerous: a number of people are highly allergic to it. A professional will always have an emergency drug, such as adrenalin, ready to deal with an allergic reaction.

Don't give alcohol: it can be fatal. (In fact don't resort to alcohol in the event of any accident. It usually causes more harm than good. It is mistakenly administered to ward off cold, but by increasing the flow of blood to the skin's surface it in fact exacerbates the loss of heat.)

As a general rule, don't use a tourniquet. It is true that for certain snakebites a correctly tied tourniquet may help. But how can the amateur be sure of correct identification? For instance, a tourniquet is recommended for most cobra bites, but not for that of a black-necked cobra. Furthermore, hospitals usually find that when a tourniquet has been used by an amateur, it is nearly always incorrectly tied. Tourniquets can be positively dangerous for some bites, especially those of the viper family.

Don't trust the widely published drawings of a snake's fang or teeth marks to judge whether you have been bitten by a poisonous snake. These drawings are unreliable, and whenever possible you should visit a hospital.

What should you do?

In the event of a snakebite, shock is a major medical problem;

many victims think they are going to die. Try to explain that the chances of death are minimal (see the statistics above).

Try to keep the bitten part immobilized, and splinting may be a help. Any sharp movement will hasten the absorption of venom through the bloodstream.

If victims vomit, lay them on one side so that they don't choke.

Although a hospital will not always judge it suitable to administer anti-venom, get the patient to a hospital as fast as possible, because correctly administered anti-venom can save life.

Don't avoid taking patients to hospital just because they appear quite well; often the symptoms are delayed, and this delay can kill. Remember that in many parts of the world there has been a remarkable improvement in anti-venoms, which in Australia, for instance, has dramatically reduced deaths from snakebite.

In the rare event of arranging the type of expedition during which there is real danger of a poisonous snakebite, get advice from local specialist doctors on appropriate treatment for the *specific* snakes that are dangerous in that area.

If there is a massive swelling near the bite, and you can't reach a hospital, then some people recommend the administration of antihistamines. However, their efficiency remains unproven.

When there is acute respiratory distress, some patients can be saved by mouth-to-mouth resuscitation (see Chapter 8).

If the snake has been killed, take it along with you to the hospital, so that they can identify the best anti-venom needed. But it is essential that you find some way to do this without handling the snake. Use sticks, and put the snake in a bottle or plastic box. Don't use bags: many people have been bitten through them. If you can't handle the snake safely (which is quite likely if there is no suitable tool and container), then leave it behind, because *snakes can sham death very convincingly*. And I have read about more than one case where even a severed head has bitten someone. 'A male adult took the severed head of a black mamba which had just been shot and placed it in his pocket – he wanted to use it to fortify a tribal remedy. A few minutes later, he removed it to show his friends and was promptly bitten.'* Dr Laurence M. Klauber once decapitated thirteen rattlesnakes of six different races to determine the reaction of severed heads. He found that up to forty minutes after decapitation the fangs would erect at the approach of a hand, and the pupils would contract, and at forty-three minutes one head still bit and discharged its venom into a stick which the doctor put in its mouth. (The heart of one of the snakes was still active after fifty-nine hours.†)

A controversial question is whether to suck a snakebite. Here is what I wrote in the last edition:

Some of the experts advise against it. Others advise that it may be of help if done immediately. In theory there should be no danger from the venom (except possibly a cobra's) so long as you don't have cuts on your lips or mouth. Venom can't hurt you through unbroken skin. (Even the Romans knew this: the poet Lucan wrote 'Mixed with blood, the serpent's poison kills/The bite conveys it; death lurks in the teeth/Swallowed it works no harm'.) All the same, spit out the venom, and rinse out your mouth.

Since then I have consulted two trustworthy British experts, and they both advise against sucking. They say that it just might be dangerous, and that it could cause infection at the site of the wound.

At least one company has started marketing kits that produce a powerful suction by using a vacuum. A friend in Botswana thinks that one of these kits helped save his brother from a lethal mamba bite. If these kits really work, then they will be invaluable, as they are cheap and light and easy to use. But I was somewhat sceptical because good news doesn't hang around, and if they really were marvellous, wouldn't everyone know about them? To find out more about the kits, I wrote to the manufacturing company in South America, asking if they could offer any

* *Snakes and Snakebite*, John Visser and David Chapman (Centaur, Johannesburg, 1982)

† *Rattlesnakes, Their Habits, Life Histories and Influences on Mankind* (University of California Press, 1973)

proof of their kits' efficacy. I got no answer. So, I then wrote to two reliable snakebite experts in Britain. One of them replied:

Snake venom removal kits. Forget it!!! It's in, it stays in. Venom is injected via a very effective hypodermic system and it then spreads in the tissues and both the blood and lymphatic systems. It would be as difficult to remove as a tetanus toxoid injection given by your local GP.

The other expert wrote: 'Vacuum pumps can cause quite severe damage to the core of tissue which has been subjected to low pressure. They have not been adequately tested on human patients and, in my opinion, should not be recommended.'

Should you be far away from treatment and a snakebite starts putrefying, or becomes gangrenous, take a course of antibiotics. Don't take antibiotics when you can reach a hospital.

Sea snakes

The bites of *all* sea snakes are highly venomous, but your chances of being bitten are infinitesimal. In one survey of a large area of South African coast, where sea snakes are abundant, no one was bitten during fifty years. Very occasionally a fisherman gets bitten when pulling a snake out of a fishing net.

Crocodiles and alligators

You are unlikely to be troubled by crocodiles. Again, they feature more in travel stories than in real life. Nevertheless, when there are crocodiles about, always ask the locals' advice, because in some areas they are very dangerous.

The most notorious are the estuarine (sometimes called salt-water) crocodiles, which range from southern China and the Malay Archipelago, through India and Sri Lanka to northern Australia, New Guinea, the Philippines, and the Solomon Islands. Recent evidence appears to show an increase in deaths caused by estuarine crocodiles (sometimes caused by human encroachment into their territory), and they are especially notorious in northern Australia.

The African Nile crocodile (not only found in the Nile) can

also be dangerous – and may kill as many as 1,000 people a year. One crocodile 15 feet and 3 inches long, shot in the Kihange River, Central Africa, was supposed to have killed 400 people. And reliable anecdotal evidence has reached me of crocodiles being extremely dangerous in parts of Zimbabwe, even apparently taking people who were walking by a river.

American alligators have sometimes been know to be dangerous. Other species, such as the Indian mugger, might attack, especially if provoked.

Dogs

When approaching some villages on foot, you are beset by ferocious dogs. This is terrifying. It is crucial that you don't run away: if you turn your back you may well be bitten. Face the dog, look as fierce as you can, and bend down – as if to pick up a stone. This is what the locals do, and surprisingly the dog nearly always shies away, often before you have even picked up the stone. The dog probably has unpleasant memories of rocks being bounced off its head. Should it still be gnashing its teeth, forget the British attitude to dogs, and lob a few stones at it. This nearly always works, and is usually much better than using a stick. If it doesn't, then arm yourself with a stout stick, hold your ground, be prepared to hit it hard on the muzzle, and wait until someone calls it off.

Remember that rabies is common through much of the Third World, and a hostile dog often becomes temporarily affectionate when afflicted by rabies – tempting humans to stroke it, and thus increasing the chances of a successful bite. If you get bitten by a rabid dog, and don't get treatment in time, you will die (see Chapter 5).

Dogs aren't only a problem in the developing world. In the United States, there are more than a million dog-bites a year that require hospital attention.

Bees

Don't squeeze out a bee sting – there is a small sac on the end

which will inject more poison. After you are stung, this sac
keeps pumping in poison, and it may continue doing this for as
long as fifteen minutes; so flick it out sideways with a fingernail;
don't delay by searching for a knife to scrape it off. Don't panic
too much about being stung – in September 1964 a young
Rhodesian set a world record when he was stung 2,243 times by
a swarm of bees. To everyone's astonishment, he made a complete recovery after five days in hospital. But, of course, stings
can be very serious for those who are allergic.

In the last edition I wrote: 'Bee stings are better soothed by
the stronger alkali of dissolved bicarbonate of soda; however, the
alkaline stings of wasps need vinegar. This is easy to remember:
*B*ee stings need *B*icarbonate, *W*asps stings need *V*inegar.' I had
read this in so many books that I thought it must be true. But I
now learn that it is complete rubbish, for the venoms of bees and
wasps are both acidic. In fact it is doubtful if any remedy administered on the surface will be of much help, though an ice cube
might bring relief. Beekeepers take aspirin when stung, because
it is anti-inflammatory as well as being effective at relieving the
pain.

I was once attacked by bees, and my experience may be a help to
others. When I was looking for honeyguide birds in Botswana, I
had the frightening experience of being pursued by angry bees.
By the time I had been stung five times, I was in a panic: I
thought they might never stop stinging. My guide said, 'Look,
this is going to be difficult, but do as I say. Sit down, take your
hat off your head, put it over your face, and remain entirely
still.' I obeyed him, terrified by the noise of thousands of bees
buzzing angrily around me. However, once I was still, I was
stung only one more time. After fifteen minutes the noise had
considerably diminished, so my guide said we could move slowly
away – which we did without any further trouble.

On consideration, my guide's advice was logical. First, there is
no point in running away – the bees can fly faster. Second,
covering one's face is essential: the stings I received on my face

(before putting my hat over it) were far more painful than those on my legs; also, bees are apparently attracted to a sweaty, shiny face; finally, the face is the most vulnerable area for dangerous or unpleasant stings.

Mosquitoes and other small biting insects

By far the greatest danger in the tropics comes from small insects, and probably the most dangerous of these is the mosquito. I have already mentioned that more than a million deaths a year are caused by malaria. Unfortunately, mosquitoes are prevalent throughout the tropics: some areas, such as the South Pacific islands, used to be free of them, until they were carried there as larvae in the water-butts of sailing ships.

If a mosquito bites by day you probably won't catch malaria. It is the Anopheles species of mosquito that carries the disease, and generally they bite only after dusk. As usual the female is the deadlier of the species – the male can't carry the disease, and often doesn't even bite. Several other varieties of dangerous mosquito also bite only between 5 p.m. and dawn, so this is the time to take the most careful precautions.

Few people realize that the mosquito is also the carrier of some eighty other diseases, including yellow fever, dengue fever, filariasis, and Japanese encephalitis. Guidebooks instruct you to wear long sleeves, long trousers, and long socks in the evening. This isn't always practical, and anyway they don't offer a guaranteed defence. When sitting on a mosquito-infested balcony, however carefully dressed, your most pressing requirement is a good insect repellent. For recommendations, see Chapter 3.

The most crucial fact to remember about repelling insects is that the repellents last far, far longer on material than they do on your skin. A few points related to this are worth mentioning.

Because the more powerful repellents are to some extent toxic, this is an additional reason to put them on clothes rather than skin.

Normally I just plaster my clothes with repellent. Aerosols are more effective for covering clothes, but I don't take them as they are too bulky. A very effective and cheap method is to soak your clothes in a solution of Deet. At present the advised solution is 12 teaspoons of pure Deet in half a pint of water. If you can keep these clothes in a plastic bag, the effect will last for weeks, but even if you can't, the effect will last a very long time.

At night I often put repellent on my sheet, as well as on myself.

Many species of mosquito like to bite the ankles. It is often, therefore, a good idea to wear socks which have been soaked or rubbed with repellent. This may deter mosquitoes more than you think, because many of them begin their investigations as close to the ground as possible, and the repulsive smell of Deet may push them off on to someone else before they try investigating any higher.

It is often useful to kill mosquitoes as well as repelling them. For this, **permethrin** is increasingly being used. Its advantage is that it is pleasant to use (unlike Deet it doesn't smell vile nor dissolve plastics); it is biodegradable (unlike DDT it doesn't persist in the environment); it is considered to have low toxicity for mammals; and it works fast. It could be used to spray any surfaces on which noxious insects might land. But it is especially useful for soaking mosquito nets: one soaking will last for months, and it is such an efficient killer that a soaked net will be fairly effective even when it has holes. (The insect will usually land on the net first, and thus be killed by contact with the insecticide.)

Despite permethrin's many advantages, it still doesn't replace a traditional **repellent** for clothes, because it doesn't actually release a repelling vapour. Therefore the insects will most likely bite you, before they are either irritated or killed by contact with the permethrin.

If you are going to be walking in tick-infested country, though, permethrin-soaked clothes have a proven effect.

ICI claim that they are going to be marketing an insecticide (Icon) that will be even better, so ask shops about the most up-to-date long-lasting insecticide.

*

Where the threat from malaria is bad, it is best when possible to adopt a belt-and-braces-and-anything-else approach: use a residual spray on the walls, a knock-down spray in rooms every evening, a mosquito net (preferably impregnated). And, from dusk onwards (when malarial mosquitoes are most likely to bite), try to wear long sleeves, trousers, and socks that are impregnated with repellent.

As an additional help, mosquito coils are useful for keeping mosquitoes at bay for most of the night. Buy a reputable brand (local advice is usually best), as not all of them contain an effective ingredient, which is usually pyrethrum.

Mosquito coils break easily, but some of their tin supports have small indentations in the side for inserting broken pieces of coil. When they don't have this, the pieces can be burnt by balancing them on top of a bottle. Mosquito coils have caused many fires, so keep anything remotely inflammable away from them. I have mentioned in Chapter 3 that you can buy excellent little gadgets that dispense insect-repelling fumes. They have to be plugged into electricity.

If for some reason you don't have any repellent, here are some remedies for the desperate. The Dinka use ash from cow-dung fires. Mud can be quite successful, and can be improved by the admixture of tobacco juice. (Chew up some tobacco and spit the juice into the mud. Preferably use strong local tobacco.) Coconut oil is quite effective, and is sometimes used for head-lice.

I have seen pictures of banquets in East Africa where they have put branches of the neem tree around food; I don't know whether it is effective, but I know that the leaves are also used in clothes drawers to repel insects. Reports welcomed.

In Chapter 3 I have discussed various types of repellent, and the different concentrations of Deet.

You should always be mosquito conscious – aware that within quite a small region there are places more populated with mosquitoes than others. Hotel A may be infested, but Hotel B a short walk away may be almost free of them. This distinction becomes even more important when you are renting a house: before renting, you should study the prevailing breezes, the altitude, and local breeding grounds (always in water).

You will notice that houses are built on stilts in many parts of the tropics. There can be several reasons for this, but one of them is to avoid certain types of biting insect, including sandflies and certain species of mosquito. Mosquitoes prefer to hunt at ground level and go up only if they can't find anything near the ground.

What is certain is that the higher the altitude, the less likely you are to meet any mosquitoes or to catch malaria. The malaria parasite needs an average temperature exceeding 59°F for at least one month in the year. You are less likely to catch malaria above 5,000 feet and far less likely above 6,000 feet. The Anopheles mosquito cannot survive above 10,000 feet anywhere in the world, and its maximum altitude declines rapidly with distance from the Equator.

If you are settling for a long time in one place, you should arrange to spoil all watery breeding places, and remember that mosquitoes can breed even in the water collected on the top of a thick bamboo pole. If there are ponds or ditches near the house, try to introduce fish that will eat the larvae. The minnow gambusia and the guppy fish are particularly effective.

If mosquitoes get past all these defences and are sitting on the walls of your room, then swat them. This will be easier if you wet the end of your towel, which gives you the advantage of crucial extra speed; although textbooks say that mosquitoes have minimal eyesight, they seem remarkably good at spotting a threatening towel.

Mosquitoes are far more attracted to some people than others. Clearly our smell makes a big difference. This makes me believe that some day someone will discover an edible ingredient to repel them. Some say that eating Marmite is a help, others recommend taking vitamin B tablets. I am rather sceptical of both remedies, because if either really worked, then I'm sure the good news would have spread with the speed of a bush fire. But if anyone has done any kind of controlled testing, I would be delighted to hear from them.

Condé Nast Traveler recently carried a letter from a man who had been on a camping expedition in an Indian reservation. The writer said that he noticed that, although the Indians were never bitten, all the visitors were. He said that after they realized that the Indians used sweat baths, not soap, the visitors started using only plain water, claiming that the mosquitoes never bit them after this. I am not convinced this will work, but I mention it because it fits happily with my belief that many travellers use too much soap anyway (see Washing, Chapter 8).

I can add another gloss on the aspect of mosquitoes leaving locals alone. On one occasion in south China I entered a mosquito-infested roadside café with my guide. He correctly predicted that he wouldn't be bitten; but I was bitten, continually. He said that we were in the place where he had been sent to work during the Cultural Revolution, and that when you have spent a length of time in one area, the mosquitoes ignore you.

If mosquito bites are itching badly, I can offer some remedies that have been sent by correspondents. One strongly recommends toothpaste (since then, several others have praised its efficacy); this is worth remembering, as toothpaste will nearly always be at hand. Another correspondent claims that soap infallibly stops the itching after two minutes (this makes sense: soap is alkaline, which is good for many insect stings, which tend to be acid). Another strongly recommends tiger balm. Another correspondent recommends another alkali – urine. A tropical doctor has advised me: 'You have missed out on one of the best medical discoveries of mankind. Eurax (crotamiton) is a marvellously effective counter-irritant which replaces the most devastating itch with a warm glow.' It is especially valuable for children, as it stops them scratching. However, I did try experimenting with Eurax on nettle stings at home; I stung both legs, and then applied the ointment to only one of them. I couldn't distinguish any difference.

Botflies and tumbu flies

The maggots (in fact larvae) of certain flies in tropical Africa and Latin America are able to burrow into human skin, eyes, or the nasal passage. I've never suffered from one, and it is extremely unlikely that you will, but I mention them because if you do pick one up, then this can be alarming.

The tumbu fly is found in many parts of East, West, and Central Africa. It lays its eggs on clothing that has been hanging out of doors, and the eggs hatch on contact with human skin. The larvae burrow into the skin, and produce a boil that contains not pus, but instead a developing maggot. In areas where this is a problem, it is best to iron clothes to ensure destruction of the eggs. The problem is quite common with expatriate babies in West Africa – the fly especially likes to lay its eggs in their nappies.

The word 'botfly' is imprecise but is generally used to cover several species of fly whose larvae are parasitic on mammals. One of these botflies produces larvae that can go up your nose. This is very rare, and apparently they can be removed by gargling with salt water. A commoner form of botfly, sometimes called the warble fly (*Dermatobia hominis*) is found in the warmer parts of Latin America. Its maggot is usually first conveyed to humans in egg form by a mosquito. When the eggs have hatched, they burrow under the skin and mature in two or three months, by which time they may be about the size of a pea. A hard mass forms around the grub and this can become infected. As I write there is an epidemic of a similar botfly in Libya.

There has been a correspondence in the *South American Explorer* about how to deal with them, but there is no simple solution. One correspondent, Barb McLeod, gives an allegedly foolproof solution, but it is so complicated that it's not worth repeating. Before he had perfected this method he'd tried the following: glue, peanut butter, toothpaste, nail polish, lard, sno-seal and nicotine extract. He said the latter will kill the beast, but only by sending it into convulsions that are extremely uncomfortable for the patient.

In *BBC Wildlife* magazine Mike Linley, a *Survival Anglia* producer and adviser, wrote about a botfly larva he had picked up in Costa Rica:

I doubled over in agony because the thing had moved inside me. I rang the School of Tropical Medicine in London and told them I'd picked up a botfly, and they said, 'Very exciting', and quoted me some home cures: 'Keep a raw steak over the hole for a couple of hours and the larva will burrow to the surface to breathe and then you can take the steak away . . .'

I was staying in a hotel and so I rang room service for a raw steak, which arrived with a flower in a vase and a piece of lemon on the side. I watched television for a couple of hours with this steak on my tummy, and nothing happened. So I phoned again and they said, 'Try putting a blob of Vaseline over it.' That's difficult because Vaseline melts and slithers everywhere, and it didn't work. So they said, 'Paint nail varnish over the hole and it will kill the larvae by suffocation' . . . I spent half an hour painting layer upon layer over the hole and went to bed, and in the morning took two hours picking the varnish off, because I'm quite hairy, and then the damn thing moved again.

Eventually he went to Norwich hospital to have it removed by surgery.

If you do suffer from a botfly in the wilds, though, don't give up at once: it is worth dabbing your skin with paraffin or a Vaseline-like substance, as this just may bring the larva to the surface, in which case you could grab it with tweezers.

Back at home, most doctors think that a lump caused by a botfly larva is merely an infected sebaceous cyst. But if you've been in the Americas and been bitten by mosquitoes, tell them that it might be a botfly larva.

Chiggers

They are the larval forms of minute skin-burrowing mites, which are picked up from walking in long vegetation, or by going barefoot. The mite feeds on you for a period of one to ten days, but the itching continues for longer. Nothing can be done about them.

Jiggers

These are not to be confused with chiggers. A jigger is a type of
flea which burrows into your feet or toes. It can grow to the
size of a pea, but you should use a sterile needle to hook it out
before it gets to this stage. I have been told that if a jigger
burrows under your nails, it can be suffocated with clear nail varnish.

Jiggers can nearly always be avoided if you don't go barefoot
in the tropics, especially near human habitation (sea-swept sand
is safe). There are several other reasons why you shouldn't go
barefoot, including the danger of catching **hookworms**, which
are common throughout the tropics.

Human fleas and bedbugs

I have already mentioned that travellers living very simply
could take a small container of flea-powder, which will kill
nits, crabs, fleas, and bedbugs. If a mattress is infested with
bedbugs, try carrying it outside and laying it in the sun; a
sleeping bag is also easily rid of bedbugs by this method. One
correspondent has sent me the following remedy, which could
be useful:

A good way to get rid of fleas en masse from all your clothes, sleeping bags, etc. – just hang everything up in a room, prepare some
chopped red chillies, then heat up using a stove, then leave roasting
for an hour with all the room closed off. Repeat after about three
days.

Bedbugs can't fly, and compensate for this by being excellent
wall climbers. When sleepers take the precaution of standing
bed-legs in tins of paraffin, the bugs may cross the ceiling to
drop accurately on to the bed.

Sandflies

Sandflies, which are much smaller than mosquitoes, and can get
through most mosquito nets, carry leishmaniasis, so they are
another good reason for using repellents.

Ticks

These are usually picked up walking through thick grass. Some people just pluck them off, but others warn that, when pulling them off, one is inclined to leave behind the mouth parts, which are then likely to cause infection. Several people say that the best way to remove them is with paraffin (kerosene) or alcohol, which loosens them, then to use tweezers, then to dab the area with an antiseptic. Others have suggested using gaffer tape instead of tweezers. I have read suggestions that one should use the burning end of a cigarette, or that one should light a match, and then use its head while it is still hot. Here is a comment on this from Dr Richard Dawood, contributing to the Panama section of *The Mexico and Central American Handbook*:

It is said that ticks should be removed by holding a lighted cigarette close to them, and we had an opportunity to put this old remedy to the test. We duly unwrapped a pack of American duty-frees that we had preserved carefully in plastic just for such a purpose, while our Indian guides looked on in amazement, incredulous that we should use these prized items for such a lowly purpose. The British Army expedition to Darien in 1972 carried 60,000 cigarettes among its supplies, and one wonders if they were for this purpose! The cigarette method didn't work, but caused much amusement. Further discussion with the experts indicates that the currently favoured method is to ease the tick's head gently away from the skin with tweezers.*

Dabbing them with permethrin might be very effective, but I have not had a chance to test this yet.

When you have been badly infested with ticks, feel round your backside, as they like to hide there. Some ticks carry diseases, so be sure to tell your doctor if you've fallen ill after suffering an infestation.

Ants and termites

These can be a great nuisance, and certain species eat their way through almost everything. Where there are heavy infestations,

* (Trade and Travel Publications, 1993)

stand the legs of tables and other furniture, especially bookcases, on bricks in basins of water and paraffin. The latter is to prevent evaporation, and to stop mosquitoes breeding there. White ants don't like eating through thick polythene, so sometimes campers put polythene under their beds. Most ants don't like walking over wood ash.

Spiders

It is extremely unlikely that you will be bitten by a spider. All spiders are venomous, but most aren't large enough to give you a dose of their venom; very few can give a bite anywhere near as dangerous or painful as a wasp.

Even the notorious black widow hasn't caused as many deaths as believed. Out of the 1,291 reported bites in the United States between 1726 and 1943, only fifty-five were fatalities. Most of these were children, invalids, or old people. In healthy adults the bites may cause severe pain and prostration for between two and four days, but complete recovery almost always follows. Only the female causes the trouble, and the likely occasions for a bite are now much rarer: nearly half the black widow bites reported in medical literature during the first four decades of this century were inflicted on male genitals by spiders lurking under outdoor lavatory seats.

'Tarantula' is a fairly loose word, covering about 300 species of spider. A few are dangerous, but most are calm, docile, mildly venomous animals of no great menace. When angry, though, they can flick off their body hairs, which may cause intense irritation.

Leeches

Leeches may be a disagreeable nuisance, especially in the damp forests of the Far East. I remember the shock of my first encounter: when I happened to glance at my trousers, I saw that they were half-covered in blood. The saliva of leeches contains an anaesthetic and an anticoagulant, so I hadn't felt anything happen.

Most guidebooks instruct you not to pull leeches off your skin because they leave their mouth parts behind, with resulting infections. You are supposed to remove them by touching them with a hot pin, raw tobacco juice, salt, the burning end of a cigarette, etc. I have often found it impractical to obey these rules, and haven't yet had an infection; though I do rub the bites with antiseptic. Many locals just scrape the leeches off with a machete. However, as there are many different types of leech, the guidebooks may sometimes be right; certainly, during the Second World War, some British jungle fighters suffered from bad ulcerations on their legs, probably caused by a mixture of leech-bites and malnutrition.

It is astonishing how leeches attach themselves to walkers' legs – despite stout shoes, long socks, and long trousers. Your best hope is to try smothering your socks and trousers with an effective insect repellent (even better, use pre-soaked socks – see Mosquitoes, pages 238–9). A very high proportion of Deet will be best; 75 per cent may not be enough. Also coat any boots with insect repellent to discourage the leeches from crawling through the lace-holes (though be aware that Deet can rot the stitching of some shoes). Roll your socks over your trousers. If you wipe the repellent only on your skin, it will be washed off either by your sweat or by any rivers you wade through. Experiment with permethrin (and let me know the results). Leeches can't make their way through Tubigrip, and you could try using Tubigrip like spats.

There are many myths about leeches. When visiting leech-infested country, you are told that they are likely to enter your penis, vagina, or rectum. Even remedies are described: 'In the event of a leech entering your penis drink plenty of salted water.' Before the last edition I had asked several tropical doctors about this, but never discovered an authenticated case. But a doctor has since confirmed to me that: 'Aquatic leeches certainly can enter the vagina of females bathing in fresh water. In Thailand there were a number of cases of unexplained vaginal bleeding in little girls, which had resulted from this infestation.'

Travellers' tales often include stories about leeches jumping off bushes or hanging from trees waiting to fall on passers-by. They certainly do end up on walkers' hair, as has been confirmed to me by a correspondent from Kalamintan. However, Mr B. E. Smythies (writing in the *Sarawak Museum Journal*) took a very dim view of the idea that they can deliberately jump:

Leeches can and do attach themselves in a split second to a passing foot with a lightning dab of the front sucker, but during twenty years of experience in the Himalayas, Burma and Borneo, including some of the leechiest country in the world and the wettest times of year, I have never seen a leech jump so much as a millimetre . . . also bald statements about leeches dropping on to travellers from trees are common enough in travel books but never with sufficient corroborative detail to carry conviction; their ability in this respect has probably been greatly exaggerated. Stand close to a leech perched some feet above the ground on a leaf or twig and what happens? He will advance to the edge of the leaf and wave excitedly about in your direction; sooner or later he will hang head downwards, visibly relax and become limp and drop. He hesitates for so long, however, that he would never be able to drop on a person walking or riding past underneath . . . that leeches deliberately climb trees, in order to lie in ambush and drop down your neck, must be regarded as a myth.

CHAPTER 7

TRANSPORT AND ACCOMMODATION

TAKING A CAR

Some disadvantages – and advantages

Don't rush into the decision to take a car. The idea is superficially attractive, but there are several disadvantages worth considering.

Any vehicle creates a barrier between travellers and the country through which they are travelling. If the travellers are so self-contained that they sleep in the vehicle, they will have even less contact.

Many countries have regulations stopping you from selling the car, which will reduce the flexibility of your plans. You can't, for instance, simply decide that you are going to drive to India and leave the car there – Indian regulations prevent you selling or leaving the car in the country without paying huge import charges.

There are also plenty of practical problems. Shipping can be expensive and difficult. Thieving causes headaches for car-owners, and is rapidly increasing in most of the world. Vehicles are a prime target: unless converted into mobile fortresses, they are easily broken into when left unguarded. Formerly, they were mostly robbed for the valuable booty left inside, but now they are increasingly robbed for machinery or instruments which can be sold as spare parts. Hubcaps, petrol-tank caps (take a lockable one), and wing mirrors are all vulnerable; in Colombia, windscreen-wipers are left on the windscreen only when it is raining. There are also minor problems such as lack of good service facilities, low-grade petrol, and breakdowns caused by heat, or dust, or bad roads.

Another deterrent to drivers is the possibility of an accident. Roads in the developing world are far more dangerous than those in Europe. If you are involved in an accident in which someone is injured, even though the fault may not be yours, the ensuing problems will be nightmarish.

Nevertheless, taking a car needn't be one long catalogue of woes. You have far greater mobility, which encourages you to explore areas you wouldn't otherwise visit; you can take almost any luggage or equipment you desire; and some car-lovers are gratified by the joy of taking their own vehicle.

Decision about cars

I'm so ignorant about vehicles, that I'm not equipped to lay down the law about any aspect of a car journey. I did once drive from England to India (I shudder to remember how ill-prepared I was), but any advice of mine would now be second-hand and, by the time you've read this book, probably out of date. Therefore, for those determined on going by car, I've tried to concentrate on all the major *questions* that should be considered. These questions can then be best resolved by reading specialist publications (I mention several), inquisitioning manufacturers, and – best of all – talking to people who have completed a similar trip.

Even if you are going on an unadventurous trip, and are therefore not using a four-wheel-drive vehicle, inquire if your vehicle has good ground clearance. I once travelled along the main roads of Yugoslavia: several hundred miles of these were not metalled, and they were sometimes deeply rutted. A low ground clearance would have been disastrous.

Bear in mind that your problems will be reduced if you take a standard car with a standard engine. Even with the ubiquitous Volkswagen, engines and bodies can vary between countries. So when you've decided which countries you are visiting, check with your manufacturer about the likelihood of easy servicing and spares in those countries.

Do you want a long- or short-wheelbase vehicle? Smaller vehicles will probably be more manoeuvrable, cheaper to buy, and cheaper to run. But they are no good for carrying large supplies, or for sleeping in at full length.

Do you want four-wheel drive? Many do manage without four-wheel drive. The Volkswagen Kombi, for instance, is in use in almost every country, and is the most popular motor vehicle used by overlanders. It has more space than a long-wheelbase Land Rover or Land Cruiser. Jack Jackson has written (in *The Traveller's Handbook*, see Appendix 1) that although the Kombi lacks the four-wheel-drive capability,

it partly makes up for this with robust independent suspension, good ground clearance and engine weight over the driven wheel. With experience and astute driving, a Kombi can be taken to places that will amaze some four-wheel-vehicle drivers . . . The Syncro version, which has an advanced fluid-coupling four-wheel-drive system, is now available – but at a price. The low-stressed engines are reliable, simple to maintain and, being air-cooled, have no water pump, hose, or radiator problems. Mechanics with Volkswagen knowledge can be found almost anywhere. With the use of lengths of chicken wire fencing as sand ladders, plus some helpful pushing, a Kombi can get through quite soft sand.

If you decide to choose a four-wheel-drive vehicle, then I strongly recommend the *Off-Road Four Wheel Drive* book by Jack Jackson (see Appendix 1). In it he lists, in great detail, all the available four-wheel-drive vehicles, and gives many valuable tips. As the terrain of every journey has different requirements, this will help you choose. He is still of the opinion that, despite some weaknesses, Land Rovers are the most durable and reliable four-wheel-drive small vehicles on the market:

Their spartan comforts are their main attributes! Most of their recent challengers are too softly sprung and have too many car-type comforts to be reliable in hard, cross-country terrain. There are plenty of spare parts available worldwide and they are easy to work on with most parts bolted on . . . Range Rovers, Land Rover Discoverys, and other short-wheelbase vehicles are not specialist enough nor have the load-carrying capacity for use on long journeys.

He has driven some fifty different Land Rovers during the last ten years over difficult terrain in Africa and Asia, as well as almost every other four-wheel-drive vehicle. Some people prefer a Toyota Land Cruiser. Toyota are the world's largest-selling four-wheel drives and have a standard of reliability by which all others are judged. They are particularly reliable in hot climates. Jack Jackson describes their off-road performance as being 'great in open scrub country, but poor in deep ruts, mud and soft sand due to high weight, poor ground clearance and long overhang'.

For further information on intrepid car trips abroad, here are some more sources (publication details are given in Appendix 1):

The Sahara Handbook – this has a useful section on cars
Land Rover Limited Public Relations Department in Solihull (tel. 021 722 4242) – they produce a booklet called *A Guide to Land Rover Expeditions*, and a *Land Rover Manual for Africa*
Brownchurch Limited in London (tel. 071 729 3606) – they are specialist safari operators for Land Rovers and Range Rovers
Land Rover Owner Magazine in Diss, Norfolk (tel. 0284 750 652) – they include a monthly column about safaris

For a general overview on taking a car abroad, there are thirty-nine very useful pages in *The Traveller's Handbook*, and *Desert Expeditions* (published by the Expedition Advisory Centre of the Royal Geographical Society) covers the subject for intrepid drivers in the desert.

Petrol versus diesel

Again, what I'm writing could easily become out of date, because diesel technology seems to be advancing in leaps and bounds. I shall, however, quote again from Jack Jackson, who has raised the most relevant questions:

Weight for weight, petrol engines have more power than diesel engines, but for hard usage in Third World areas, they have several disadvantages. In hot countries there is a considerable risk of fire and the constant problem of vapour lock, which is at its worst on steep climbs, or on long climbs at altitude. Dust, which often contains iron, gets into and shorts out the distributor. High tension leads break down, and if much river crossing has to be done, water in the electrics causes more trouble. A further problem is that high-octane fuel is not usually available, and low-octane fuel will soon damage a sophisticated engine. However, petrol engines are more easily repaired by the less experienced mechanic.

Diesel fuel does not have the fire risk of petrol and outside Europe is usually about one-third of the price of petrol. It also tends to be more available, as it is used by trucks and tractors.

Diesel engines are heavier and more expensive to buy, but are generally more reliable and need less maintenance, although a more knowledgeable mechanic is required if they do go wrong. An advantage is that extra torque is available at low engine revolutions. This allows a higher gear in the rough, which improves fuel consumption and means less weight of fuel need be carried for a section without fuel supplies. This improves fuel consumption still further. There's also no electrical ignition to malfunction where there is a lot of dust or water. Against this is the fact that diesel engines are noisier than petrol engines, which can be tiring on a long trip.

A second filter in the fuel line is essential to protect the injection pump from bad fuel in the Third World.

Which tyres?

The choice of tyres is important, and if you are venturing into different types of terrain, the final decision may have to be a compromise. If you are spending a lot of time on soft sand, you will need special tyres. The choice is usually between radial and cross-ply. An advantage of radials is that they are easier to remove from the wheel rim with tyre levers when you get punctures away from help. Remember that the two types should never be mixed.

Tubeless tyres are impractical for off-road work, so always use tubed tyres and carry several spare inner tubes. A vehicle travelling alone in bad terrain should carry at least one extra spare tyre, as well as the one on the spare wheel. *The South American Handbook* recommends you should take at least one locking wheel-nut per vehicle.

Paperwork preparation

A **carnet de passage** is often essential. It is a device used to prevent you selling your car within countries which have high import duties, and therefore provides you with exemption from the payment of the import duties for a temporary period. Should your car be stolen, the customs authorities will claim duty from the organization issuing the carnet. Find out further details from the AA or RAC. These organizations will demand some type of guarantee, which can be a huge sum of money. This can sometimes be mitigated by taking out an insurance indemnity – they will give you the details. Apply for your carnet well in advance, as it may take weeks.

Most countries outside Europe (except a few such as Morocco, Tunisia, and Turkey) are not covered by the green card system, which makes life so much simpler within Europe. Therefore you must take great care over **insurance**. Check very carefully the extent of personal liability. In the United States, for example, this may be limited to $100,000, which would be nowhere near enough there, and should be more like £1,000,000. When investigating insurance, it may be best to investigate **third-party insurance** separately from your **accident damage, fire, theft, and collision-damage insurance**. Although third-party insurance is a legal requirement in most countries, it is not automatically offered at the border, and you may need to take some trouble to obtain it. The Association of British Insurers advises that you ring the relevant embassies of the countries you are visiting to find out what specific insurance they require.

Find out if you need an **international driving permit**, as well as your **national driving licence**. You will also need an **international registration distinguishing sign**, which indicates the country in which your vehicle is registered. Always bring a **vehicle registration certificate**. Before leaving, take two photocopies of all your documents. Keep one lot with you, in some locked area, and leave one set behind at home.

Kit for a car trip

Anyone contemplating an intrepid car journey should consult the books I've mentioned. But even if the going won't be especially rough, you should probably carry a **fanbelt, spark plugs,**

tow rope, fuses, a **set of bulbs**, a **distributor cap, two break-down triangles** (which are a legal requirement in several countries), a **lockable petrol cap** and a **pair of jump leads**. Make sure you have a **jack**, of course, and it is usually best to have a **foot-square piece of strong wood or iron** to give the jack a sensible base area. You should also take spare **inner tubes** and a **tyre pump** (get the most up-to-date advice about a tyre pump – it needn't necessarily be the foot-operated variety). Many books recommend a **puncture kit**, but though it's still always best to take one, Jack Jackson says it is better to take several **inner tubes**, and then get the puncture repaired over a hot vulcanizing machine, which is definitely superior for hard-worked off-road tyres. Drivers who are going into remote areas should first learn how to remove tyres with tyre levers, and also how to mend them. You should also take a comprehensive **workshop manual**, preferably illustrated. A workshop manual is not the same as your usual car handbook. A **laminated windscreen** is strongly recommended: they are safer than other windscreens, and they don't shatter every time they are hit by a stone. In some countries a **fire extinguisher** is mandatory, and it is definitely best to take one anyway. **WD40** is invaluable; it is an oily fluid used for lubricating hinges and bolts, freeing seized threads, and dispersing moisture from electrics.

Spare fuel cans which have been emptied and resealed at altitude will *implode* at sea level. If the cans have been emptied at sea level, and then taken up to a high altitude, they will *explode*. If the can is strong enough it will not actually burst. You should probably buy metal cans, even though they eventually produce granules of rust inside. The main problem with plastic cans is that many of them are made with material which is porous to petrol; for use with fuel they must at present be made of Polypropylene.

Before opening a fuel can, touch it against the bodywork to short out any static electricity built up due to wind. This will avoid a possible fire with petrol. Remember that empty fuel cans contain an explosive mixture and are therefore more dangerous than full ones.

I like to travel with a **car compass**, which is especially useful in the Third World where signposts can be very rare (or often in an indecipherable script). The massive increase of car thefts in the West has spawned a new range of **anti-theft devices**. Investigate them.

A few more tips about cars

If you are going on an adventurous trip, consider going on a car maintenance course. Apart from the possibility of saving your trip, you will learn information that may remain useful for life.

As almost all our roads in Britain are metalled, we aren't fully aware of the hazards caused by dust. An easily remediable hazard is the clogging of the air filter, so it's worth learning how to unclog one.

If you want some cheap travel in the United States, try looking up in the *Yellow Pages* under 'Automobile Transporters and Drive-away Companies'. Sometimes people are looking for drivers to move cars around the country, and you might get some long journeys for little more than the cost of petrol.

Luxurious trappings in expedition vehicles are usually a mistake. They often can't withstand rough treatment. Fridges are a classic example: they very rarely continue functioning in extreme heat, and, if gas-fired, can be dangerous.

When stuck in sand or mud, make everyone get out of the car, and try getting the vehicle out by going into reverse, with the passengers also pushing. This often works, when going forwards won't. If it doesn't, and you don't have the appropriate kit (sand ladders, etc.), try laying branches under the tyre.

If you are driving in dusty country, the car's steering lock can jam up, which can be disastrous for expedition use. Get the steering lock removed in advance. If the steering lock hasn't been removed, leave the key in it permanently when in dusty areas.

It is usually possible to tell if the hole in the petrol cap has been clogged by sand, because when you take the cap off, there is the symptomatic hiss of a vacuum being released.

Bars in front of the headlights may be a good idea, but remember that you must be able to clean the glass by hand: in most places there won't be hoses.

Car hiring

Don't think that just because you are hiring a car from one of the major companies, you will be getting a reliable product. This is frequently not the case. Often the local car-hire companies are merely agents of the parent body, and as the parent body has little control over them, they may hire you a dangerous car. This has often happened to me. *Business Traveller* published an alarming article about the hire of an Avis car in Turkey. At the end of the article, Avis (who had been given right of reply) wrote: 'I would like to state, categorically, that Avis Europe PLC do not exert influence over Avis Turkey.'

One advantage, though, of using a major company is that you are less likely to be cheated. One alarming feature of hiring cars is that you are nearly always required to hand over your credit card, which is then imprinted on a blank sheet, which can then be used by unscrupulous companies to increase the agreed charges. I was once cheated in this way by a car-hire company in Dublin.

When hiring a car, it's very difficult to tell whether it will be reliable, but it is still worth checking one or two things. In a recent report *Holiday Which?* found that, out of the sixty hire cars they tested in Spain and Greece, twenty were dangerous, of which nine were considered to be very dangerous. Make sure the horn works, as it's used far more in the Third World, and can be crucial. One friend of mine experienced a tractor driving straight into his car: the tractor's load had obscured the view of its driver, and my friend found too late that his horn didn't work. Check that the tyres have sufficient tread and are sufficiently inflated; look to see if there are visible bulges in the rubber, indicating that the inner fabric of the tyre has been split, which makes it liable to a blow-out. Check that all the lights work. Check that there is a spare wheel (and there often isn't), and a manual, and a wheel-changing kit. I have often found faulty brakes, so check these immediately you start driving. Take a good look at all the bodywork, in case an unscrupulous company tries to charge you for damage that has already been done.

The hirers of four-wheel-drive vehicles often remove a propeller shaft (to lessen damage by hire drivers), which means that the four-wheel drive isn't fully connected. Therefore, if you will be going through difficult terrain where a breakdown might be dangerous, it is advisable, though very tiresome, to get the vehicle checked by an expert.

It is tempting to hire a car when you arrive at an airport, but this can be hugely more expensive than hiring one from a local firm in the city. The firms with booths at the airport have been known to charge twice as much. Before leaving home, find out how much it would cost to book a car. Sometimes special discounts are offered, particularly when you book a car with an air ticket.

Your hired car (especially with a map on its front dashboard, indicating you are a tourist) is a great target for thieves. It is sometimes wise to ensure your car has a boot, as this can hide your luggage. The boot, however, isn't a guarantee of safety: it is believed that in certain countries thieves have keys for all the rented cars.

Although it is a boring task, always check your insurance very carefully. Check both the extent of the **collision-damage waiver** (which covers you for damage to the hired car) and **third-party insurance** (for when you hit someone else). Unfortunately, these insurance contracts can be very misleading; check the small print doesn't include a punitive 'excess' clause, which may force you to pay as much as the first £750 of damage to either car. When you are negotiating a car rate, always ask in advance about the costs of both third-party insurance and collision-damage waiver, because between them they may add up to a very large part of your total bill. Car-hire companies are adept at bumping up profits through insurance wangles. They may also try to sell you **personal-accident insurance**, which could be as much as an additional £3 a day; but if you have normal holiday insurance, you should already be sufficiently covered.

It is nearly always cheaper to hire the car on an unlimited-mileage basis, or you might be surprised by how the miles add up.

Should you need to hire a car, a credit (or charge) card is almost essential, because it releases you from having to pay a large deposit.

In some countries it is scarcely more expensive to hire a car with a driver. Make inquiries about this, because if you have a driver, the responsibility for accidents and breakdowns will be his and not yours. Besides, when you hire a car with a driver, you are usually given a more reliable car. A driver can also be a tremendous asset: apart from local knowledge and his ability to guard your luggage, he may be a godsend as a translator.

If you are going to be in a country for a long time, you can sometimes save yourself a small fortune by buying a car, and selling it at the end of your trip.

Night driving

Third World roads are far more dangerous than those in the West, and those in Africa are especially dangerous. In Nigeria 234 people per 10,000 vehicles are killed each year as opposed to three per 10,000 in Britain. Even people who go on adventurous expeditions are more likely to die in a road accident than from any other cause. You can take one major precaution: whenever possible avoid driving at night.

The number of road accidents greatly increases after dark. Roads are liable to be cluttered with unlit bullock carts, bicycles without reflectors, deaf geriatrics, and hidden potholes. These hazards are even harder to spot when drivers dazzle you with undipped lights. Lorries which are missing a light hurtle towards you; they often look like motorbikes. Few vehicles boast the full range of correct lights. One survey in Delhi showed that nine out of ten buses were equipped with dangerously faulty lighting.

Another serious hazard at night is the increase in the drunkenness of drivers. I have seen drivers so drunk that they have hardly been able to get into their cars.

If you must drive after dark, ensure that you have adjusted your headlights after loading up the vehicle – otherwise the car may be tilted in such a way that your lights illuminate only the tree-tops.

Car-itis

Car-itis, a common disease, is an obsession with driving from point A to point B to the exclusion of almost everything else. It appears that most people (including myself) who travel by car are to some extent liable to catch this disease. Once drivers are bowling along at 50 m.p.h., they tend to become deeply reluctant to stop; they have to force themselves to go for a walk in a beautiful valley or to explore an interesting market. It is the pedestrian, not the car-driver, who bumps into a wedding or is invited to a feast. Unless drivers make a determined effort not to remain trapped in their mobile cocoons, they are likely to cut themselves off from the people, the sounds, the sights, and the smells of the country through which they are travelling.

CYCLING

Cycling is one of the most enjoyable ways of exploring the countryside. Your speed is fast enough to provide variety, but slow enough for you to savour the landscape. There is no noise to drown bird-song, the exercise is stimulating, and you breathe fresh air.

Within the last few years the development of **mountain bicycles** has transformed the possibilities for cyclists. In the 1970s these bikes were developed in California for off-the-road cycling, and by the mid-1980s were being widely sold in Europe. They are the cycling equivalent of a Land Rover; with a mountain bike you can comfortably ride for hundreds of miles along unpaved tracks. I once listened to a fascinating talk by someone who spent a holiday cycling along the disused railway-lines of Yugoslavia.

Mountain bikes can now tackle the steepest gradients: Hallam Murray, who cycled 17,000 miles from California to the tip of South America (and who has given me much advice for this section) says that winds, rather than mountains, are now the main enemies of the cyclist. Another advantage is that mountain bikes are extremely tough. Hallam used one for the second, 7,000-mile, leg of his trip, which was mostly on unpaved roads, and didn't get a single puncture, whereas during the first part of his trip, on a touring bike, he suffered more than a hundred.

Mountain bikes are expensive. Second-hand ones are available very much cheaper, so, provided you can get advice from an independent expert, investigate the police auctions and specialist magazines.

A mountain bike isn't necessarily the best for all journeys, as it is designed for unpaved roads. If your journey is only along paved roads, then you're probably better off with the usual **touring bike**, which is lighter, and therefore less hard work. However, manufacturers are developing interesting hybrids, so these may be worth investigating.

Another possibility for some very particular trips may be a **folding bicycle**, although the recent spread of cycle hire (see below) has made them less likely to be useful. Obviously, folding bicycles can't be as satisfactory as normal ones, but their great advantage is that they can be stashed in a very small area. Two Bickerton bikes, for instance, can be squeezed into the boot of a Mini. Some intrepid people have used them for remarkably long distances: Christian Miller★ used a Bickerton to cycle right across the United States.

Don't be tempted by a bike that is too high-tech. Get one which has little to go wrong, and is easy to mend. Ideally, its spare parts should be available in at least some places along your route. In Appendix 2 I mention two shops which, at the time of

★ *Daisy, Daisy* (Routledge & Kegan Paul, 1980)

writing, can offer useful advice on buying bikes for foreign touring.

A crucial piece of advice. Whichever cycle you choose, it is essential you try it out for at least a month before departure. You should become completely familiar with it, and let the bike work out all its teething problems.

Hallam Murray says that the chain (a piece of technology that has hardly changed since Victorian times) is the Achilles' heel of a bicycle. Learn how it works. Take some **spare links**. Learn how to lubricate it. You should be attending to the hidden parts: by and large the exposed links shouldn't be lubricated (the oil picks up too much dust).

Take a **tool kit**. The most crucial tool is a spanner for removing the pedals – often necessary when a bike is taken by plane or train. Removing the pedals is a delicate job, because it is easy to damage the threads. So learn to do it before your departure.

It may be worthwhile to upgrade your **tyres**. Most mountain bikes bought in Europe are (like Range Rovers) used mostly on paved roads, so they aren't necessarily equipped for rocky tracks. Those unpunctured tyres of Hallam's included an ingredient, Kevlar, which was allegedly used in President Reagan's bullet-proof vest. You should also investigate puncture-resistant **inner tubes**.

Many cyclists prefer a **horn** to a **bell**, as pedestrians usually pay more attention to a horn. It sometimes acts as a helpful alarm, too, as anyone who is mucking about with your bike can rarely resist squeezing it.

Your body loses a lot of liquid when cycling, so strong leak-proof **containers** for drinking water are important. They should be bought before you leave, because local ones are often unreliable. Paul Vickers (see page 264) recommends attaching $\frac{3}{4}$-litre bottles in near-indestructible Zefl 'cages' to the frame of the bicycle.

Good **panniers** are essential. You shouldn't cycle with a ruck-sack, for it changes the centre of gravity, and is dangerous. Although you may not use a **mirror** on your bicycle at home, it will probably be a great help on a trip. Most people cycling any distance use **toe-clips**, as they greatly increase your energy efficiency. If your trip is likely to be very mountainous, discuss suitable **gearing** with your bicycle shop.

Long-range cyclists dislike plastic **saddles**. Hallam Murray used suede, which is very comfortable, but disastrous when water-logged. Ordinary leather saddles are also comfortable, but need breaking in (sometimes with the use of oil) before leaving. Many saddles are available in different shapes for men and women. Traditionally, airlines have transported bicycles free of charge. But with the increase in international cycling, the situation is changing. Check. Don't forget to reduce the pressure in your tyres before loading it on a plane. A 50 per cent reduction is enough; don't entirely deflate them or the rims may get damaged if the bike is wheeled along the ground.

When cycling with a heavy weight on unpaved roads, the back tyre tends to wear out before the front one, so swap them at suitable intervals.

Cyclists carry a wide variety of weights. At one extreme Hallam Murray carried 50 pounds on his South American trip. Another very adventurous cyclist, Nick Crane (who has cycled along the Himalayas) sometimes carries as little as 18 pounds.

If you have problems getting insurance for your bike, consult the Cyclists' Touring Club in Godalming (tel. 0483 417217). For further information about bikes, consult *Richard's New Bicycle Book* or *Richard's Mountain Bike Book*; Nick Crane has written a useful section on cycling in *The Traveller's Handbook*, and another useful one is by Hallam Murray in *The South American Handbook*. The Expedition Advisory Centre publishes *Bicycle Expeditions* by Paul Vickers. (For publication details of the above books, see Appendix 1.)

Cycle hiring

I have noticed that within the last few years there has been a tremendous increase in the possibilities of hiring local bicycles.

Be on the lookout for this, as cycling is a delightful way to see the countryside, and often the hire is very cheap. Recently I hired a bicycle in China for as little as 20 pence a day.

Taxis

Should you be staying in an expensive hotel, try to avoid its taxi rank. In effect you are paying for their waiting time, and most likely for a fee/bribe which they have had to pay for the privilege of queuing there. The taxis you find a little further down the road are usually far cheaper: in the Yemen, a five-minute walk brought me to taxis which were a quarter of the price.

Hitch-hiking

It is important to know that in many Third World countries it is customary to pay for lifts. Where this is so, negotiate in advance or you will find yourself paying more than you would for public transport. When the fare is demanded in advance, don't pay the full amount: pay half then and half on arrival.

Find out which signals are used by local hitch-hikers. Jerking your thumb forward may not be the local practice, and is sometimes considered rude.

A sign showing your destination (and possibly your nationality) is often a help. Sometimes it is advisable to write a destination that isn't too much further on: a close destination may encourage potential lift-givers, and it also gives the hitch-hiker an earlier option of leaving the car when a driver is obnoxious or dangerous.

One great advantage of hitch-hiking is that, although you meet your fair share of bores, it is a short cut to making local acquaintances.

I have mentioned elsewhere that I have come to the reluctant conclusion that a lone woman shouldn't hitch-hike. In some countries a woman is probably safe in ninety-nine cases out of a hundred. But when you think what could happen on that hundredth occasion, is it really worth the risk?

Buying tickets on public transport

Travellers who are accustomed to Western systems of ticket-buying should be aware of the complexities of other systems. Different seats in the same vehicle are often charged at different prices and, if you haven't studied the system, you will most likely be landed with the most uncomfortable seats. The window seat in the front of a bush-taxi may cost more than a seat in the middle of the back row, and the seat in the cab of a lorry almost certainly costs more than a place in the back among the sacks of maize.

When buying a seat on a bus or train, consider which side will be blasted by the sun. Seats near the front of a bus are usually more comfortable.

In some places you needn't feel shy about booking more than one seat: this may be the common practice. After an arduous journey you may want the extra comfort of two or three seats, particularly when you want to keep your luggage nearby. I once bought no less than six seats for a long journey in a motorized canoe: the small extra cost enabled me to carry a supply of pure water and to stretch out my legs when I slept. In countries where taxis are shared for long distances, it is often the custom to squeeze two passengers into the front seat. You can ensure comfort for yourself by buying both tickets, which usually isn't very expensive.

Hotels

I am surprised at the number of travellers who accept the first hotel room on offer. They stay in the most dingy rooms when something far better is available at the same price. After you have discussed the price of a hotel room, always ask to be shown the room on offer. This is a precaution against being given an unacceptable room, and an elementary method of ensuring that you get offered the best room available. When you don't bother to do this, the hotel may be sensible enough to put you in the worst room, so as to keep better rooms free for more discriminating travellers.

Experienced travellers soon become expert at checking the important items in a hotel room. Does the tap work? Is the fan noisy? Are the sheets clean? Does the light bulb work? And so on. Depending on the price, you may want to demand luxuries such as soap or a towel.

When a hotel doesn't provide a towel, it may be best to use a bedsheet on your last morning. This prevents packing a damp towel, which soon becomes smelly and mouldy in your luggage.

When you want to live cheaply, and are going to cities where there are few cheap hotels, get lists of hostels from the YMCA (Young Men's Christian Association) and YWCA (Young Women's Christian Association). Both of these organizations offer accommodation in many countries, some of them surprisingly pleasant, and not necessarily exclusive to one sex. They tend to be more comfortable than those run by the Youth Hostels Association. If you are prepared to live simply, then get the relevant booklet from the Youth Hostels Association. For the addresses of all these, see Appendix 3.

If you are anything like as absent-minded as I am, there is a good chance of leaving something behind in your hotel room. When you have kept your luggage to the minimum, every item tends to be indispensable, so try to invent an unvarying routine of searches: my own routine when I leave a hotel includes searching

For my wash things
For shampoo (and universal plug)
In drawers and cupboards
Behind the door on hooks
On top and underneath the bedclothes, which I strip off
Under the bed (sometimes a cornucopia of other people's treasures)

Try to get into the habit of packing according to a regular plan, so that every object has its allocated place. This also enables you to find anything you want in the dark.

Readers write to tell me that we should pack all clothes into rolls: they take up less room and don't crease. As my own luggage is always a mess, I can't confirm this.

Having stayed in a hotel you particularly like, don't just remember the name of the hotel, but take a note of your room number. Often it is the room that is especially nice, not just the hotel. When you recommend a hotel to friends, they are usually put in a dismal room at the back of the ground floor, and wonder what you made all the fuss about. Even when you have stayed in a bad room, take the trouble to find and note the good rooms if the hotel is at all promising. Your friends will bless you for this valuable information.

Every seasoned traveller knows that you can bargain with simple hotels; few realize how often you can bargain with more expensive ones. Managements are obsessed by occupancy rates, and if a hotel room hasn't been taken by evening, it is clearly in their interest to retain the casual traveller by agreeing to a reduced rate.

Don't be embarrassed by asking for a cheap room; there are plenty of devices which save both the receptionist's face and your own: 'Do you have a cheap room without a bathroom?' 'Do you have any attic bedrooms?' 'Is there a discount for paying cash?' 'Do you have a "late-booking discount system"?' At the famous Norfolk Hotel in Nairobi, when I asked if they had a cheap room, I was offered a remarkably cheap one in an old wing. It was much more pleasant than a modern one, but was available cheaply because it didn't have its own bathroom. At one of the world's most expensive hotels, the Crillon in Paris, Evelyn Waugh dispensed with even these tactics: 'I asked for the cheapest bedroom and bathroom they had. There was a very nice little one for 180 francs said the man at the reception counter. I said I wanted a cheaper one. He said I could have the same one for 140, so I took it.'* At the time of writing, you can hire a bathless room at the Basil Street Hotel (a grand hotel next

* *Labels* (Duckworth, 1930)

door to Harrods) for £56 a night, while a room with a bath would cost £105.

Don't be too easily bamboozled into staying in the hotels recommended by cycle-rickshaw or taxi drivers, who are almost certainly on commission. Indian friends who own small hotels tell me that they are always obliged to pay a commission of at least 15 per cent of the daily room-rate (even when the customer has pre-booked), and that some hotels are forced to pay as much as 50 per cent of the daily rate. Because this is a fortune to drivers, they will push very hard to get you into the hotel of their choice. When they do make their own choice, most travellers fall into the lazy mistake of staying only in hotels mentioned by guidebooks. Other hotels are invisible to them. It takes quite a mental struggle to avoid this trap; but remember that the guidebook has probably been written by an ordinary traveller who may have spent only a couple of nights in the town, and certainly won't have tested all the hotels. Most guidebook authors are obliged to scrounge complimentary lodgings, and their verdicts may be biased in favour of hotels who comply (the majority don't). Also, the average guidebook is well behind the times: the authors may have researched it as long as a year before the actual writing, then the book may have taken another year to publish. When some months later you are reading the guidebook, it may be nearly three years out of date. And if any hotels are strongly recommended, the owners have usually become lazy, so the hotel will be spoilt before you arrive. The famous *South East Asia on a Shoestring* has sold more than half a million copies since 1975. Imagine the easy life for any hotel recommended by it!

Use a guidebook, perhaps, when you arrive exhausted in a town; but next day investigate any hotel signs, and ask local advice. You will relish making a discovery of your own.

CHAPTER 8

SOME PRACTICAL HINTS

This chapter consists of a hotchpotch of information that hasn't fitted into other chapters.

Swimming

Travelling is far less dangerous than most people suppose, but the sea, which is an alien environment, can be a real threat.

After being tempted by an idyllic stretch of beach, swimmers can be dragged out to sea by fierce currents, which cause them to panic and drown. In many parts of the tropics, long stretches of the coast are lethal. Even when you see other tourists swimming, this is no guarantee of a beach's safety. The dead body of a tourist is a normal occurrence on the beaches of Ghana, and as many as 300 people are drowned each year off the beaches of Australia. Be especially careful when a beautiful beach is deserted: there may be a reason.

You should always ask for local advice before swimming. This is not just because of treacherous currents; there may also be danger from jellyfish, stingrays, and (very rarely) sharks. Jellyfish and stingrays are the most likely problem, and local advice is especially helpful because the worst danger from these horrors is often seasonal.

Advice should be sought before swimming in fresh water as well. Rivers, too, have hidden currents; and both rivers and lakes may harbour noxious animals and bilharzia.

If you are pulled out to sea by a strong current or riptide, don't thrash away in a futile attempt to swim against it. I know how easy this is to do, and have panicked myself, but such panic has caused many unnecessary deaths. In tiny Costa Rica there are approximately 200 drownings a year, and most of these are caused by riptides. *Remember that you can last a very long time in a tropical sea, and that riptides will pull you out but not under.*

Try to get out of the current by swimming parallel to the shore, and then, when you are out of it, try to swim back to the beach. Don't try to beat the current, as you will pointlessly exhaust yourself. Sooner or later it will be possible to swim sideways out of a current. If you are not a strong swimmer, and are forced to swim great distances, it is my impression (after experiments in my local swimming pool) that by using a casual backstroke one can swim almost indefinitely with minimum effort. This is because the water is supporting one's head, which is the heaviest part of the body (see Crossing rivers, in Chapter 12).

In the event, though, of being capsized in cold water, it is better to cling to some wreckage than to swim; in this case your main enemy is loss of body heat, which is exacerbated by swimming.

Try not to swallow any sea water while swimming. When you are anywhere near human habitation, the sea is almost certainly contaminated with excrement. A report on the Spanish coast showed that 15 per cent of swimmers in the sea had stomach upsets, compared with 3 per cent of non-swimmers.

Swimmers, especially snorkellers, should consider wearing shoes or flippers to protect their feet from various spiky animals and from coral cuts (which infect very easily).

Third World fishermen often kill fish by dynamiting, an environmentally destructive but effective method of catching them. I have heard (but been unable to check) that it is dangerous to swim within a mile of people dynamiting fish, as you may be deafened. This is likely to be true, for sound carries extremely fast and efficiently under water.

Swimmers who are staying near a sandy beach are often bothered by sand getting into their rooms, where it gets into every crevice including the bedclothes. All this is avoidable. Put a bowl of water by the door; a quick rinse of your feet will get rid of all the sand. I can't think why all seaside hotels don't do this.

Artificial resuscitation

As drowning is quite a common hazard in the tropics, and as a person knocked unconscious in a relatively minor accident may also temporarily stop breathing, a basic knowledge of artificial resuscitation may help save life.

Your must act fast; every second counts. A brain deprived of oxygen for five minutes will be permanently damaged.

Place your face close to the victim to listen and feel for air moving through nose and mouth. If in doubt, take action: you can't do any harm and you may save life.

Your immediate job is to ensure the victim has a clear air passage: place one hand under the neck, and the other hand on the forehead, tilting the head so far back that the top of the head is touching the ground. This will open the air passage. Without delay, clear the mouth of vomit, debris, and false teeth. The casualty may then start to breathe.

If this doesn't happen, pinch the casualty's nostrils, and seal your lips around their mouth. Make four quick breaths to partially inflate the chest. If the chest fails to rise, assume the airways aren't open, and try adjusting the position of head and jaw. After this, give one breath approximately every five to six seconds, taking about two seconds to actually blow air into the casualty. Most amateurs try to breathe too quickly, thus exhausting themselves prematurely. The resuscitation may need to continue for a considerable time, possibly even more than an hour. Try to synchronize your own exhalations with the casualty's own efforts to restart breathing.

If mouth-to-mouth resuscitation isn't practical, close the casualty's mouth, and try mouth-to-nose resuscitation. A child as young as seven can effectively resuscitate a full-grown adult by this method, as it is easy for them to make a 'seal' over the nose. It is also the only effective method (though still very difficult) of resuscitation for most people in water.

After resuscitation, try to keep casualties on their side, so they don't choke on vomit. To keep them in this 'recovery position', it is often necessary to tuck their lower arm behind them. Get them to hospital as fast as possible, continuing to keep their airways clear by tilting the head back and holding the jaw forward. Restart resuscitation whenever necessary.

If mouth-to-mouth ventilation by itself has been unsuccessful and the casualty's heart stops beating, you must perform external chest compression in conjunction with the mouth-to-mouth resuscitation. Check if the heart is functioning by feeling in the hollow of the neck, which is more reliable than at the wrist. *External chest compression must never be attempted if the heart is still beating, even faintly, and any pulse is felt.*

It is difficult to manage external chest compression without being taught; but I shall mention the basics, as they just could be life-saving. Lie the casualty on their back on a firm surface. Put the heel of one hand just above where the breastbone meets the ribs, and cover this hand with the heel of your other hand, and interlock your fingers. Your shoulders should be directly over the casualty's breastbone and your arms straight. Press down on the lower half of the breastbone to compress it about 2 inches. Complete fifteen compressions at the rate of just more than one per second. (To find the correct speed, it may help to count: one and two and three, until you reach fifteen.) Move back to the casualty's head, reopen their airway and give two breaths of mouth-to-mouth ventilation. Continue with the cycle of fifteen compressions, followed by two full ventilations. Check the pulse at the neck after the first minute, and then after every three minutes. As soon as the pulse returns, stop compressions immediately. Continue with mouth-to-mouth ventilation until natural breathing is restored. Resuscitation is illustrated in Appendix 9.

Snorkelling

The exhilaration of snorkelling over a good coral reef is hard to explain to someone who hasn't done it. It is one of the great pleasures of the tropics. If you expect to have the opportunity, it is well worth bringing your own snorkel. Don't on any account rely on being able to hire one. For details on buying a snorkel, see Chapter 3.

Many swimmers take a deep breath before diving with a snorkel. This is a mistake, because it makes the body so buoyant that you dive with difficulty. It is best to take a couple of deep breaths, and then a normal relaxed breath in order to inhale enough air for the dive. Don't take repeated deep breaths before diving because this can be extremely dangerous, possibly leading to anoxia, which causes unconsciousness without warning.

The backs of many snorkellers get badly burnt, because being so absorbed in the world below, they forget about the dangers of sunburn. Clouds don't necessarily protect you from the rays of the sun, nor does the sea. It is best to wear a T-shirt, which will also save you from having to use too much sun-cream. A T-shirt won't, however protect the back of your knees, which are also very prone to getting sunburnt.

There is no need to use elaborate devices to keep the inside of the mask clear: you only have to spit on the inside of the glass, rub it all over, then rinse it.

If you go **scuba-diving** it is crucial that you avoid a dramatic rise in altitude (including going up mountains) for at least twenty-four hours after you have been diving. Remember that small inter-island planes aren't pressurized, and even large airlines may depressurize. Recently five British holidaymakers were paralysed because they flew in a plane too soon.

When you start scuba-diving, you should definitely be taught by an approved sub-aqua school, as there are some very important safety precautions to be learnt.

Windsurfing

In recent years there has been a dramatic growth in windsurfing. It is a wonderful sport: no engines, no noise – just you alone with the wind and the sea. It can be a misery to learn, but don't give up – you suddenly get the hang of it, just like riding a bicycle.

Bring some plastic or rubber shoes for windsurfing as the board is often covered in sun-cream, which makes it slippery. Also, when you fall (which beginners frequently do) you might get nasty coral cuts.

Don't windsurf out of other people's sight. The wind can change, causing you to drift fast and frighteningly out to sea. If this does happen, the golden rule is never to abandon your board. The recognized – in theory – distress signal is to wave your arms slowly from side to side.

While windsurfing you are exceptionally prone to sunburn. For more on this problem, see Chapter 5.

Watching animals

Most people watch animals in entirely the wrong way. The worst time to watch them is while you are on the move – whether on foot or in a car. Unless you are in a well-visited game park, the animals are likely to rush away or remain hidden.

But when you keep still (and preferably hidden) the situation is transformed. For a start you can savour your surroundings – enjoying the smells, the animal calls and the bird-song (none of which can be appreciated from a moving car). You can watch the animals behave naturally, and you will be astonished at those which appear. I have seen elephants emerge from wispy thickets which you would think could hardly hide a jackal. And when you remain still, you will be surprised at how close many animals approach. Unlike human beings, many of them don't have stereo-scopic vision and many don't see colour in the same way as us, so they find it hard to distinguish something that isn't moving. Occasionally gazelle have walked almost within touching distance of me.

Two other important points must be remembered for remaining unnoticed by animals. Although many of them, such as elephants and antelopes, have poor eyesight, this is often compensated for by a prodigious sense of smell; so you must position yourself upwind. The other crucial point is that *most animals will*

275

spot you if you present a silhouette. This is avoided by keeping as low as possible, or, when you can't keep low, by ensuring that there is a background *behind* you. This may be every bit as important, sometimes even more important, than camouflage in front of you. I have even found this true even when fishing: when you wade quietly in a river, trout can be caught within just a few feet, because, unlike a fisherman on the bank, you are presenting no silhouette against the sky.

On some safaris you aren't allowed to get out of a vehicle, and therefore won't be able to build yourself a hide. If this is the case, you must still be insistent that you don't rush about all the time; instead, ask to be driven to a water-hole before dawn, then turn off the engine, and just watch. You will have a wonderful time seeing the different animals arriving at their different times of day; and you will also see them interact with each other, something they will never do when they are keeping an eye on a moving car.

If you are about to disturb the animals with a sneeze, then rub your nostrils up and down. This is a wonderful remedy – far better than the popular one of pressing your upper lip.

Receiving and sending mail

If you have mail sent to the **poste restante** department of a post office, you should carefully instruct the senders in the best methods of addressing the letters. In some countries the surname is customarily put first, and there are other sources of confusion. A letter which is sent to 'Mr John Shaw' or to 'John Shaw Esq.' might be filed under 'M', 'J', 'S', or 'E'. It is best to write the surname in capitals, underlined, and placed first. Thus a letter to John Shaw is best addressed: *SHAW* (John).

If you have an American Express card or use their traveller's cheques, you are entitled to use their mail facilities. This is often easier and more reliable than using a poste restante. However, be careful: according to their rules, they keep mail only for thirty days, and some of the offices are strict about this. It is also best to ensure that your mail is forwarded only to their own travel offices. A large quantity of my mail was lost after it was sent to the institution acting as their agent in Djakarta. It is best to ring American Express on 071 930 4411 to check whether the relevant offices can receive client mail. Also, you should know that for security reasons their offices don't accept parcels, packets, or registered letters.

When sending mail from countries that don't have a reliable postal service, I have nearly always found that letters are more dependable than postcards; the latter can be very unreliable. Where letters are unreliable, use the special pre-printed airmail letters; if you have to use an ordinary letter, try to see that the stamps are franked in front of you, so that you can be sure they aren't peeled off for resale.

On the rare occasions when I have arranged for shops to send goods direct to my home, they have always arrived. But anecdotal evidence has made me believe that these agreements now tend to be far less reliable – either the shop or the postal service lets you down.

Telephoning home

In case you need to telephone home from any of the countries connected to the international dialling system, here are some easily memorable rules. (In some countries you may be able to dial only from major cities.)

1. When you dial out of a country the **international access code** is always the same. Thus, when you dial to any foreign country from Britain, you always begin with 010. Dialling to any country from Australia, you begin 0011; from the United States 011. You will see in Appendix 3 that '00' is the most common exit code (being used in more than thirty-two countries), and that '011' is also very common.
2. You then need to know the **country code** of the country you are dialling. Wherever you are dialling from, Britain is always 44, Australia is always 61, and the United States is

always 1. If you can't find out how to dial Britain, it would always be worth trying '0044' or '01144'.

3. In many countries the area codes have an initial digit (or more rarely digits) which is used for long-distance calls within the country itself but not for international calls. One (sometimes two) of these digits often needs to be omitted when making international calls. In Britain, as in many countries, the dispensable digit is 0.

Therefore to ring a British number (071 228 5000) from Australia, you would dial 0011 (the international access code from Australia, always the same), then 44 (the British country code, always the same), then 71 (the British area code minus the dispensable 0), then 228 5000 (the subscriber's number).

Hotels often profit by a scandalous mark-up on telephone calls. London hotels are among the worst offenders, often charging a mark-up of 250 per cent, sometimes as high as 400 per cent. Hotels levy the same rapacious mark-up on faxes. Some hotels even charge for calls which haven't connected. In New York this charge can be as high as $8 for each unsuccessful call.

If you must ring from a hotel, it is often worth persuading the recipient to ring you back. Or it may be worth braving the rigours of a post office.

Recently there have been two developments – the arrival of UK Direct lines and BT charge cards – which will help avoid hotel mark-ups, and be a great help in emergencies, when you have lost your money.

UK Direct is a system by which you can call (free of charge) an operator in the UK. You can then ask the operator to credit your charge card (see below) or make a reverse-charge call (often now known as 'call collect'). All the credit-card companies will accept a reverse-charge call for reports of lost cards.

A joy of the UK Direct system is that it avoids the language problem of having to speak with a local operator. In theory you should be able to order a free booklet listing UK Direct numbers by ringing a freephone number (0800 800852) and asking for the pamphlet 'Telephoning Home from Abroad'. However, it took me three months and eighteen telephone calls to get the pamphlet out of British Telecom; therefore, because these numbers might be useful in an emergency, I have put the most up-to-date list in Appendix 4.

BT charge cards, which are issued free, enable you to make telephone calls while charging a particular number. (It's necessary only to remember the card's number; you don't have to take it with you.) This, too, could save high hotel mark-ups. When you aren't in a country attached to the UK Direct system, you can (in theory) use your BT charge card by calling the local international operator.

If your children are travelling abroad, and you want the comfort of knowing that they can easily telephone you from countries connected with the UK Direct system, you can get them to reverse the charge via the system, or you can give them a BT charge card, which can be restricted for use only to your own home number.

Letters to newspapers

When you see unnecessary environmental damage, consider writing a letter to the local English-language newspaper. Obviously, people don't want to be bossed by impertinent foreigners, but if you phrase the letter very gently, beginning with lyrical praise about the country, you shouldn't cause any offence. I try to write when I see the destruction of coral reefs and forests, or the sale of animal skins; my letters have always been published.

Hotel fires

When people die in a fire, they have nearly always been killed or immobilized by smoke before being burnt by flames. Therefore, if you are trying to escape from a fire, whether in a hotel, house, or aeroplane, try to remember one important point: *keep as low as you can*. Smoke rises, and therefore you may be able to escape beneath it. And when you crawl close to the ground there will be more oxygen, and (because heat rises), it will be cooler. You will also be more likely to spot dangerous hazards such as holes in the floor. When the fire brigade go into a burning house, they crawl on their stomachs.

Very punctilious people get into the habit of automatically making a mental note of the nearest fire exit to their hotel room, so that they could find their way to it in the dark.

Embassies and consulates

An embassy handles the diplomatic representation of one government to another. It is the **consulate** which is charged with the welfare of its nationals. So if you get into trouble, don't contact the ambassador; instead ask for the Consular Department. The embassy and consulate are usually, but not always, in the same building. It is a good idea to have noted in advance the consulate's address and telephone number (see Fig. 2, Chapter 1): addresses can be surprisingly hard to find when you need them in emergencies. To find out addresses of consulates, look in the Diplomatic Service List at your local library, or ring up the Travel Inquiries number of the Consular Department (tel. 071 270 3000).

Only in extreme circumstances, and only under the strictest safeguards, will consulates give you a loan. They usually refuse. Here is what they can do.

They can issue emergency passports; they can contact relatives and friends in order to ask them to help you with money or tickets; they can advise on how to transfer funds; in emergencies, some consulates can advance money against a sterling cheque, up to the limit of your banker's card; they can provide a list of local lawyers and interpreters. In my opinion, one of their most important functions is to be able to recommend an English-speaking doctor; this function may be life-saving.

Newspaper addicts also might like to know the address of consulates (and sometimes British Councils), because in nearly every capital city there is a consulate or embassy which provides a reading room equipped with British magazines and newspapers. Considering that a Sunday newspaper may cost several pounds, this can be a useful saving.

Diary

Although it is no business of mine to recommend that every traveller should keep a diary, I think that you should consider it. Even those people with a retentive brain will forget many interesting conversations, incidents, and observations, unless they have written them down. When looking at the few diaries I have kept, I am always astonished by the startling incidents which I had completely forgotten.

If you find diary-keeping a chore, don't work too hard at it, but write in it only when something interesting happens. This way it ceases to be a chore, and you probably end up with a more detailed chronicle of the interesting periods.

All the same, it is a good idea to record mundane facts such as the cost of local wages or hotel rooms; these may seem dull at the time, but are fascinating when you read them years later. Also be sure to write the current exchange rate in large letters at the top of a page. Several times I have looked at my diaries to learn that a guide cost, say, fifty pengulus a day; but this isn't so interesting when you have no idea what a pengulu is worth.

It is also worth recording practical information which may be helpful if you or a friend ever return to the same country. The names of good hotels, guides, and restaurants are always useful.

When you keep a diary, letter-writing becomes much easier. You can just copy out chunks of your diary, which you hope make interesting letters, and then if your diary gets lost, you have a safe copy at home. My diary has been stolen twice with my luggage.

Antiques and crafts

Exotic antiques are usually cheaper in the salerooms of London than they are in the country of origin. For many years, gullible travellers were buying Persian carpets in Iran, while the Iranians themselves were coming to Britain to buy them.

Travellers and colonial officials have been collecting curios, artefacts, and antiques for the last 200 years, and they have usually brought their acquisitions back to Europe – particularly Britain, the mother country of a huge empire. Britain is still a treasure-house of exotic antiques which regularly surface in auctions. Some years ago I bought a collection of Balinese paintings at Christie's in London; they were painted in the 1930s (the best period) and are as good as the paintings in the museum in Ubud. Today they could not be bought at any price in Bali; and yet they cost me only £3 each.

There is a scarcity of old artefacts for sale in most Third World countries; if they haven't already been collected, they have been destroyed either by owners, by conflict, or by climate. But the locals realize that foreigners are obsessed with 'antiques' and they make sure the gap is filled. Enterprising artisans have discovered that they can buy a small modern statue, distress it, pee on it, bury it for a few weeks, dig it up, and, hey-presto, it is worth five times what they paid for it. I once looked round the famous 'antique' market in Solo, Indonesia. Crowds of tourists were buying 'colonial' Dutch lamps and 'ancient' Indonesian daggers. But I don't exaggerate when I say that the only genuinely old objects in the entire market were to be found in the section devoted to motor-car spare parts.

One important reason why Westerners are such keen collectors of antiques is that the skilled crafts of Europe have declined: nobody today is capable of imitating a sixteenth-century tapestry or seventeenth-century marquetry, and very few of our modern products are hand-made. But travellers should rid themselves of this bias towards antiques, because many Third World crafts are still flourishing, and many artefacts are still made by traditional methods in traditional materials. If you ignore the massive amounts of junk turned out for tourists, you will find that many modern products, whether traditionally made or not, are most attractive; and if they are made for sale to the locals, they are cheap – unlike any article which pretends to be antique.

Don't fall into the trap, though, of thinking that it is easy to bring back foreign goods, and then sell them for a profit at home. If there is a market at home, someone else has usually discovered it; the tendrils of capitalist trade are far more efficient than most people realize. If you do find some crafts which you think can be profitably resold, bring back just a few specimens to test the market; you can then return having discovered the most saleable designs and the price you can afford to pay.

In my earlier years of travelling I wasted far too much time on shopping sprees: like so many travellers, I felt it was almost obligatory to spend hours shopping for antiques, clothes, and local knick-knacks. I then reacted against this and always returned home empty-handed. Now it amuses me to search for just one object which best captures the spirit of the country I've visited.

Disabled travellers

Arthur Kavanagh, an Anglo-Irishman of the last century, was born with only the rudiments of legs and arms – in their place he had stumps and flaps. He had to be carried round on the backs of servants, and when he went riding, he was tied to the saddle. Despite his disabilities his parents made few concessions, and in 1846, when he was fifteen, his mother took him on a journey to the third cataract of the Nile. At the age of eighteen he travelled overland through Russia to India, where he went tiger-shooting. Running out of funds in India, he had to undertake the arduous job of being a King's Messenger. He then returned home to Ireland, where he got married and settled down as a benevolent landlord. Later in his life he published a lively account of a yachting trip off the coast of Albania.

Kavanagh wasn't only courageous; he was also remarkably unselfconscious about his missing limbs. After arriving by train at a country house, he told his host, 'You've got a remarkably intelligent station-master. He recognized me even though I haven't been here for years.'

The physical and mental bravery of many disabled travellers is astonishing. The Rough Guide series has published a 550-page book, *Nothing Ventured* (see Appendix 1), which is a collection of accounts by disabled people of their travels. It is a wonderful and fascinating book, and sometimes very funny. Some of the contributors' stories are amazing: paraplegics, even quadriplegics, who have zoomed around the globe; a wheelchair-bound spastic who went swimming in Crete; a blind woman who went alone on a holiday to Spain.

An especially moving aspect of the book is the repeated kindness of strangers in foreign countries. One expects it of the more humane races, such as the Italians or the Irish, but I was repeatedly surprised by the others. Personally I had always regarded Singaporean taxi drivers as an unlovable bunch, but they were delightful to Susan Preston, who had muscular dystrophy. I had thought that every inhabitant of the souk in Marrakesh was a fiend out of hell but they were angels to Ivy Leach, who was in her late seventies and severely lamed by arthritis.

Facilities for the disabled are gradually improving: Terminal 4 at Heathrow, for instance, now has a special check-in counter. But disabled travellers still meet many problems. After reading the accounts in *Nothing Ventured*, it was clear to me that time and again the great stumbling blocks are the lavatories, both in planes and hotels. It is usually a great problem for disabled people to get from their seats to the plane's lavatory, and even the special aisle-wheelchairs will rarely fit. (Virgin, as usual ahead, are pioneering improvements.) The technology of incontinence aids is also improving, so these might be a help for some people during long flights.

Disabled travellers mention time and again that they can't get their wheelchairs into hotel bathrooms. Often hotels claim to have facilities for the disabled (and often display a disabled logo), but these claims may mean little more than that the hotel's front door is wide enough for a wheelchair. The bathroom-door problem is so frequent that I strongly recommend any disabled traveller to ask their potential hotels to measure the door in advance.

Don't necessarily believe the large British travel companies who claim they cater specially for the disabled. On many occasions they have let people down. Anecdotal evidence from friends will always be more reliable than claims in a brochure.

Unfortunately, the history of specialist travel companies for the disabled has been an unhappy one. However, Virgin Holidays have recently linked with a revamped Threshold Travel, which is now under new management (80 Newry Street, Banbridge, Co. Down, N. Ireland BT2 3HA; tel. 08206 62267). Their brochure gives details of all hotel entrances, widths of doors, height of switches, etc.

More information about travel for the disabled can be gathered from the following sources. RADAR publishes a book called *Holiday and Travel Abroad – A Guide for Disabled People*. This can be ordered from RADAR (25 Mortimer Street, London W1 8AB; tel: 071 637 5400). The AA (Fanum House, Basingstoke, Hants, RG21 2EA; tel. 0256 20123) publishes a useful ninety-six page booklet called the *World Wheelchair Traveller* by Susan Abbot and Mary Ann Tyrrel.

In addition to its travellers' accounts, *Nothing Ventured* has detailed factual information at the end of each geographical section.

Information can be requested about almost any country from the Jewish Rehabilitation Hospital (3205 Place Alton Goldbloom, Laval, Quebec, Canada H7V 1R2; tel. 0101 514 6889550), which specializes in information for travellers with a mobility handicap. The medical librarian, Irene Shanefield, has told me that she is very happy to receive telephone calls about information, and is prepared to send up to ten information sheets free of charge.

The Holiday Care Service (2 Old Bank Chambers, Station Road, Horley, Surrey RH6 9HW; tel. 0293 774535) has many information sheets on holidays abroad for disabled people. Their most comprehensive information is on Europe, but they do have some pamphlets on more exotic places, such as Morocco and Tunisia. Check first on the telephone. It is essential you send them a stamped addressed envelope. The Paul Vander-Molen Trust (Model Farmhouse, Church End, Hendon, London NW4 4JR; tel. 081 203 1214) is a small one-man charity which gives grants to help disabled people go on adventurous travels.

Finally, many people who are not wheelchair-bound but have difficulty in walking find it a great help to take a collapsible stool or a carousel stick, which is light and opens up to quite a solid seat.

Sex

At the time of writing, Aids in the United Kingdom is mostly caught by drug addicts using needles and homosexuals; there is controversy about the extent to which the disease is likely to spread into the heterosexual population. But there is no controversy whatsoever about the extent of Aids among heterosexuals abroad, and in Africa it is an appalling catastrophic plague, which is even worse than newspapers tell us. The disease appears to be spreading quite fast into Asia, and large numbers of Asian prostitutes are now infected with the HIV virus. All prostitutes are also likely to carry the hepatitis B virus, which is far more infectious than HIV.

We still know comparatively little about Aids, and only a few years ago it was unheard of. Who is to say that it may not adapt, and spring yet more traps on us? Unfortunately we must presume that all unprotected sex is dangerous.

As mentioned in Chapter 3, it is best to buy your condoms at home, as foreign ones may not be sufficiently strong and in some areas may be too small.

The etiquette of sexual relations changes from country to country, from region to region, and even from clan to clan. There are many places where every single girl will remain a virgin until she marries; there are others where everyone is exceptionally free and easy. Don't be misled by newspaper reports: a city such as Bangkok has become celebrated as a sexual paradise, but almost all the erotic encounters of its tourists are based on financial transactions. Does that really make it a paradise? And in some places, such as Cuba and Iceland, where prostitution hardly exists, the inhabitants are extremely permissive.

Travellers are perfectly capable of working out the local sexual etiquette for themselves. But I will point out three areas where customs of the Third World tend to be different from ours.

First, courting is often first done through a third party. This is a useful device, because it saves loss of face on either side. It may also prevent a traveller from unintentionally making some appalling gaffe.

Second, specific sexual practices may vary from ours. Kissing as a sexual act is, for instance, unknown throughout large parts of the Third World. In extensive parts of Africa it is actually taboo. For some people in the Far East, the head is the holiest part of the body, and is therefore not used for any sexual purposes.

Third, confusion often arises from the blurred line which divides prostitutes from other women who also expect some reward. I mention them because, although they exist in all types and levels of society (think of our word courtesan), travellers are often encountering them for the first time. They can be especially common in the nightclubs of larger towns and cities. When a man has slept with a local woman, there are often embarrassing scenes – even when she isn't really a prostitute – if he has failed to realize she expects some type of 'present'. Some of these women have ordinary office jobs, and may only expect dinner in a restaurant or a trip to the cinema; others expect more substantial gifts.

The issue is frequently confused even further by ordinary prostitutes who pretend at first that they are only in quest of fun. After a man has slept with one of them, she demands a payment; and if he complains, he faces a hysterical row – and probably a few male relatives. This is especially common in Africa.

A number of travellers have been confused in another way, when their slinky prostitute has turned out to be a man. Some protestations of surprise can be taken with a pinch of salt, but the unexpected does happen. If you pay attention to the prostitute's voice, hands, and, above all, Adam's apple, you are unlikely to be deceived.

★

If a man is keen for a liaison in rural areas, his best method is to use a third party for courting (as mentioned above). If the man wants a pick-up in a city, his most promising destination is nearly always the local discotheque. Even if you are shy, the pick-up procedure is in theory quite simple – though maybe not in practice. At first look for eye contact. If a woman's eye connects for a micro-second with yours, presume that you have reached stage one. She hasn't come to the discotheque to do her knitting. Stage two is to talk. Explain that you are a stranger in the vicinity, and that you would like to buy something for her to drink while she gives you some local advice. There are so many tones in conversation, that within two minutes you will know whether there is a possibility of the friendship going any further, and she can easily give you a gentle brush-off – without loss of face on either side. The final stage is touch. The advantage of a discotheque is that, while dancing, it is always possible to sensitively gauge any level of physical response. There is never any need for an embarrassing lunge.

Homosexuality

The incidence of homosexuality varies widely from being common, as in the Philippines, where bisexuality is widespread, to being almost unknown, as in Central Africa (although I have collected a cutting about lesbian orgies at Gayaza High School in Uganda).

Quite a high proportion of European expatriates are homo-sexual. Even though some of them live in areas where homosexu-ality isn't widely practised, I have never heard of any of them being given a hard time by the locals on account of their sexual preferences. Either the locals have tolerant sexual attitudes (usu-ally the case), or they think that homosexuality is yet another example of the curious and eccentric behaviour of Europeans.

Absurdly, many travel articles still presume that the custom of men walking hand-in-hand indicates homosexuality. This is rub-bish. The authors of the articles should know that this widespread custom (which is usually most common in areas where walking hand-in-hand with a woman is taboo) rarely implies homosexuality. Indeed, in areas where there is minimal homosexuality, men and women are often less self-conscious about physical contact with their own sex. Nigel Barley, an anthropologist who worked in the Cameroons, has written:

The truth seems to be that homosexual practices are largely unknown in West Africa except where white men have spread the word. Dowayos were incredulous that such things were possible. Such behaviour in animals was always interpreted as 'They are fighting over women'. Males will have much more physical contact than is normal in our own culture but it contains no sexual overtones: friends walk hand-in-hand; often young men will sleep entwined together but this is not thought to involve sexuality. Dowayos who had not seen me for some time would often sit in my lap and stroke my hair, amused at my embarrassment at such behaviour.*

Detailed country-by-country information about the laws on homosexuality, and on gay meeting places, is provided by *Spartacus Guide for Men* and Gaia's *Guide for Women*, which are usually available in large bookshops; if not, the Gay Switchboard (071 837 7324) can advise on availability.

Drugs

An embassy's cultural attaché in Delhi once told me that he was 'high' for three days after a sitar recital. Travellers should aim for just such a natural 'high'; a drug-induced stupor is usually a confession of failure.

There are more than a thousand Britons in foreign gaols for drug offences. You are a fool if you ever cross a frontier with the smallest amount of drugs. You should think twice about driving a stranger across a frontier. You should never offer to take someone else's package across a frontier on a plane. Remember that there are countries, such as Turkey, where possession of a small amount of cannabis may bring you a sentence of ten years or more.

* *The Innocent Anthropologist* (British Museum Publications, 1983)

THE TROPICAL TRAVELLER

Within some countries some drugs are socially acceptable. In parts of India opium is drunk (never smoked) at traditional ceremonies, and in some Italian cities ganga shops openly sell an astonishingly hallucinogenic brew. But don't presume that acceptability in one place implies safety in others: in Allahabad, hippies are regularly hauled off the trains and charged for drug offences.

On the hippie grapevine it is often said that although it is unsafe to buy drugs from a local (they may be a police stooge), you are safe when buying from a fellow foreigner. This is untrue. There have been several instances of foreigners acting as police stooges, sometimes to get off their own indictments.

In a few countries police who hope to be bribed or rewarded are in the habit of planting drugs on innocent travellers. The most notorious countries for this are Morocco, Thailand, Turkey, and most of South America (especially Colombia). If you look 'straight', you are less likely to be a victim.

Washing

In most parts of the developing world, even when the surroundings are scruffy, the inhabitants are clean. The filth of public places is no indication of the level of private hygiene. Although the locals may spit on restaurant floors or tip rubbish into the streets, their own bodies and clothes will most likely be scrupulously clean. It is not surprising, therefore, that they are so shocked by travellers who rarely wash and wear dirty clothes.

Foreigners often consider many of our personal habits to be disgusting, including blowing noses into handkerchiefs, and sitting in our own dirty bathwater. If they live in modern houses, they usually prefer to take showers, if they live in traditional houses, they pour water over themselves.

In several Far Eastern countries this water comes from an open-topped, tiled water-tank (usually about 3 feet high) in the corner of a bathroom. The tank is kept filled by either a tap or hand-carried buckets; the water (which isn't as hot as water kept in a roof-tank) is scooped out and poured over the body. This is a cooler method of washing than taking a shower. It would be a boon if this system were used in the parts of the tropics where piped water is always breaking down; the tank, which is constantly topped up, guarantees a supply of water for washing – and, sometimes more important, for keeping cool.

A few travellers commit the gaffe of mistaking this reservoir of water for a bath. When jumping in it, they cause offence by polluting the water.

In my opinion many people use too much soap for washing. In the tropics you may need to wash several times a day, but there is no reason why soap should be used every time. A good rub with water is often sufficient to clean away sweat and feel fresh. Too much soap disturbs the natural oily protective film on your skin. And if you don't use too much soap, you are in the long term less prone to smell of sweat. Some people claim (but as yet I have no first-hand proof) that if you cut out washing with soap, then you are far less bothered by biting insects.

The lavatory

Several hundred million people don't use lavatory paper; some use stones, sticks, leaves, and so on; most use water with their *left* hand. Furthermore, many people who have heard about our Western methods consider them disgusting. As long ago as 1681, Robert Knox recorded (in his *Historical Relation of Ceylon*) how the Singhalese were disgusted by foreigners not washing themselves properly after they 'had gone to stoole'. There is no doubt that paper alone can never completely clean you.

I mention this subject, which is often glossed over, because I think that all travellers should at least know about the water method. Travellers do get caught in emergencies without lavatory paper, and if there is access to a river or water supply, their problems are diminished, provided they are prepared to change their habits. If done carefully, this method is not quite as unhygienic as it sounds, particularly when there is a good water supply and you are in the crouching position. In many parts of Europe there is, of course, the tradition of bidets.

The universal use of water instead of paper at the *actual* site of the lavatory can be noticed as close as Turkey, where most lavatories are equipped with a small additional waterpipe at the back of the lavatory bowl. Egyptian lavatories have a system which incorporates the best of both worlds and should be universally copied: next to the lavatory there is a separate tap, which sends water down a flexible tube. With this tube people can clean themselves efficiently without having to use their hands; and the system saves you from having to shift to a bidet.

In Chapter 3, I have already mentioned that flip-flops or rubber sandals are invaluable for wearing in slimy lavatories, showers, and bathrooms.

In parts of South America and Africa, you will find many lavatories furnished with a bin, which is there for used lavatory paper. This may come as rather a shock. It is there, however, because either the plumbing or the sewage system can't cope with the lavatory paper, and therefore is essential.

HEAT

Acclimatization

If travellers are flying from a temperate to a hot tropical climate, they shouldn't be surprised at feeling a little washed-out. There are no hard-and-fast statistics on acclimatization, but it is generally agreed by medical experts that most people take about one week to become reasonably acclimatized, and that after about two weeks they are nearly fully acclimatized. Men apparently acclimatize faster than women because the male hormone, testosterone, stimulates sweating. If you do feel under the weather during your first few days, take rehydrating salts (see Chapter 5). I'm convinced they help.

Your clothing should be as thin and loose as possible, and will be cooler if made of pure cotton. Many locals, both men and women, try to keep cooler by cutting their pubic hair, and many Muslims consider the removal of pubic hair to be a religious obligation. Although a lack of pubic hair is definitely cooler, its effect is quite scratchy.

Getting up in the morning

The easiest way to avoid the worst of the heat is to get up early in the morning. Guidebooks write about evenings and mornings, as if they were both equally cool; but they aren't. Mornings are far cooler, for the obvious reason that there has been a whole night without sun. And tropical mornings, with their beautiful light, are almost always the most magical time of day. Although at home I find it impossible to get up early, in the tropics I often take breakfast in the dark so that I can get out of doors at first light.

Air-conditioning

Travellers who find acclimatization difficult may be tempted to spend extra money on an air-conditioned hotel. On the whole I think this temptation should be resisted. Air-conditioning slows down your acclimatization, for there is too great a disparity between the heat (and sometimes the humidity) outside and the cold (and dryness) inside. This may be a partial explanation for the colds and coughs suffered by so many customers of international hotels.

Provided you have access to water, and can find some breeze (whether natural or artificial), you should be able to tolerate all but the hottest temperatures (see Evaporation, below).

There are some circumstances, however, when an air-conditioned hotel-room is a boon: for instance, if night after night the heat prevents you from sleeping; or when you are suffering from prickly heat; or, perhaps most important, when you can't escape from biting insects.

Evaporation

The most effective way to keep cool in a hot dry climate is to douse yourself with water; if you want to feel really cool, stand in a current of air while you are still wet. Even the slightest breath of wind will do the trick. And if you want this wonderful cooling to last longer, then pour water over your clothes. If you can't do this, a wet hat, or a wet handkerchief tied round your neck or forehead, will still be a great help (large ones sold as 'bandannas' in America are useful for this).

It is the water evaporating which makes you feel cool; it is performing the same function as sweat. There are plenty of other ways in which evaporation is utilized in hot climates (provided the air isn't so humid that evaporation can't take place). In some places water is cooled by being kept in slow-leaking canvas bags; in other places, porous pottery jars fulfil the same function. Egyptians use pottery jars – identical in shape to ones used 3,000 years ago – which are tall and thin, thus maximizing the area of evaporation in proportion to the volume of water. Some water-flasks are sold with cloth jackets, which can be dampened, and, if you are forced to carry water in a plastic canister, you can wrap a damp cloth round it in order to keep it cool. In dry areas, Indians sometimes block windows with screens made of cut thorn bushes; water is dripped through the screens, and the breeze which passes through them is delightfully cool and fragrant.

Indoor heat

A surprising number of tropical houses, especially modern ones, aren't well designed for hot climates. Although few readers will be building themselves a house, it is worth explaining some principles behind the construction of a cool house, as this will help you choose cool places to stay.

The top of the building should provide some measure of insulation. A corrugated-iron or asbestos roof, especially without a ceiling underneath, does exactly the opposite. The heat under these roofs can be appalling. If a roof has to be made of a material which absorbs so much heat, then it should be covered with something like thatch, which will not only look better, but also deaden the noise of rain.

Roofs should overhang buildings by a wide margin, so as to

form a covered balcony. This prevents the sun beating down on the walls of the house; hot walls not only turn the house into a cauldron by day, but also keep it hot at night. A wide balcony will also provide a protective layer of coolish air around the house. There should be nearby trees to produce shade, and grass should be planted beyond the balcony so as to reduce radiated heat and dust. During one evening in Rajasthan I was astonished to notice the difference that grass can make: when I moved my chair just a few yards from bare earth to lawn, the temperature difference was dramatic. Pavements and roads also radiate heat, and cities may be 13°F hotter than the surrounding countryside.

The most important factor in keeping a house cool and pleasant is a **through-draught**. Provided that a house is designed so that there is a through-draught in the living rooms and bedrooms, there is very rarely any need for air-conditioning. (The exception is houses in very hot dry areas, where you may want to keep out hot daytime winds.) Even in places where there is little breeze in the daytime, there is often a breeze at night.

Before a house is built, the site should be carefully chosen with regard to microclimate, as there can be dramatic differences within a surprisingly small area, especially where there are hills. A tiny difference in altitude can make a considerable change in temperature. Prevailing winds and breezes should be studied; often there are predictable winds near the sea – sometimes going out to sea at night, and in the opposite direction by day.

Rooms should be built as tall as possible, and the windows best placed to catch the breezes. Ideally the windows should be on two or three sides of a room, so that the draught can blow right through. This can apparently be encouraged by building on the leeward side windows that are larger than those on the windward side. If there are no windows on one side of a room, a draught can be encouraged by making large ventilation holes at the top of the walls.

Provided you have electricity, an artificial movement of air can of course be made by a fan; but it is nowhere near as refreshing as a current of fresh air.

CHAPTER 9

PHOTOGRAPHY

The most important issue is **whether or not to take a camera**. There are single-minded travellers who maintain it is much better not to take a camera at all. Their argument is that the process of photography obscures the real appreciation of the country you are visiting. Much of this is true. Some people, when watching a magnificent village dance, don't appreciate the music or enjoy the spectacle. Instead they are fretting, 'What is the best camera angle? Where is the best source of light? Is my film going to run out?' Photography cuts them off from the country they are visiting, and in places where there is a suspicion of cameras, it creates a barrier between them and the locals.

If you aren't careful, photography can dominate your travelling far too much. Some people remember Kandahar only as the town where they snapped a good photograph of a sunset, or the Spice Islands as the place where they lost all their film.

Camera tackle is a nuisance. Although your camera may be quite small, the whole outfit, including film-rolls, takes up valuable space. And your equipment is a hostage to fortune: you have to protect it against thieves, and are made miserable when it breaks down. Without a camera you can travel with less bulk and more freedom. You also save money.

Nevertheless, I must admit that, although all this may be true, I usually travel with a camera. I like to have a record of what I've done and where I've been. And if I'm not carrying a camera, I'll inevitably stumble on a dramatic scene, probably a python swallowing a goat. Besides, I happen to enjoy taking photographs. Being somewhat restless, photography gives me continual excuses for diversions. I may climb a hill to get a better view, walk an extra few miles to watch a festival, or hire a boat to get a better angle. Surprisingly, a camera can sometimes cure me of restlessness: I may wait an extra two hours to catch a special light across a temple gate; or stay an additional hour by a lotus pond in the hope that a kingfisher will once again fly across it.

Sometimes it becomes almost rude not to have a camera. Unless you are in a very remote area, everyone now knows about cameras and photographs. Although there are places where people distrust them, more frequently they *expect* photography from travellers. If someone has led you for three hours through the jungle to look at a waterfall, they sometimes feel let down if you don't produce a camera. If a remote village has organized a special dance, the villagers may be eager for you to photograph it; and when you've stayed with a family, it is often polite to photograph them – and sending photographs after you have returned home is a nice way of returning hospitality.

EQUIPMENT

In earlier editions I was perhaps too eager to recommend specific items of equipment. I hadn't fully realized how fast they become discontinued, and how fast specific models become outdated. Therefore, as in many parts of the book, I shall try to concentrate mostly on key questions. With these, potential buyers can interrogate friends and camera shops, and then make choices of their own. Try not to rely only on the advice of shops, as the assistants may be on a commission (with bonuses to sell slow-moving or about-to-be-replaced products).

Choice of camera

Much has been written about the advantages of taking an **instant-picture camera** – in particular that photographers can win easy popularity by giving people pictures of themselves. Instant-picture cameras are also useful in areas where locals are nervous of being photographed: seeing pictures of themselves, they often lose their camera-shyness. However, instant-picture cameras aren't usually worth taking: they are too large, the film is very bulky, and the photographs are inferior. When films run out, you will have a problem replacing them, and if you hand out photographs, you will be besieged by others insisting on yet more photographs.

An instant-picture camera is more useful if you are settling in one place. Then the bulk doesn't matter so much, and after the first few days the requests for photographic presents should dry up.

The **35mm camera** is still the most popular model for travellers. Its film-size is sufficiently large for good prints, and is widely used by professionals. There is a wide choice of cameras, many of which are versatile, light, and sometimes very small. The most popular models of 35mm cameras are the SLR (single lens reflex) models. With these, the photographer can see the exact image that will be exposed, and they are very easy to focus. The camera can be fitted with a very wide range of interchangeable lenses. Among the more famous makes of 35mm cameras are Canon, Nikon, Minolta, and Olympus. Nikons have been the most popular with journalists because of their reputation for reliability. In the past many models were heavy, though now they are becoming lighter. During the past few years I have been using a Nikon camera, the FE2 (needless to say, discontinued), which has been a godsend because it has survived the most brutal treatment. Twice I have dropped it on to a stone floor, and it has survived. I have never tested Canon cameras with such rough treatment, but I have always found them beautifully designed and a joy to handle.

Try to choose a model with a manual facility that can be used in the event of battery failure.

Modern cameras are equipped with an increasing amount of electronic wizardry. Be cautious about this, because every extra bit of wizardry is something extra to go wrong when the camera is treated roughly. And electronic cameras can seize up extremely fast in a tropical rain forest. As a general rule, travellers are best advised to buy a simple but strong camera, rather than one which is too sophisticated.

Many cameras are now equipped with automatic wind-on and automatic rewind. But these can be heavy on batteries. Although battery performance is improving, I don't think that the advantages of these automatic facilities as yet outweigh the disadvantage of excessive battery use.

Cameras are increasingly made out of plastic materials rather than metal. The joy of plastic is that it is incomparably lighter, and therefore the cameras are much nicer to use. The manufacturers swear that these plastics are every bit as reliable and strong as metal, but I notice that many professionals still insist on using metal ones. So if your equipment is going to get rugged treatment, get the best updated advice on the pros and cons of plastic versus metal. My latest advice, which I am near to trusting, is that these modern light plastics are now genuinely getting to be very strong. If this is true, it will be a great joy, making reliable cameras so much lighter.

Some automatic cameras work on a shutter (speed)-priority system, others on an aperture-priority system. Find out which you prefer, because it makes quite a difference. I prefer shutter-priority, for with aperture-priority I am absent-mindedly liable to photograph at speeds that are too slow.

Manufacturers have developed excellent **smaller (non-SLR) cameras**; the leading makes are usually Olympus and Minox. The principal disadvantage of these cameras is that you can't use them with interchangeable lenses, and this denies you the versatility and artistic possibilities of the larger cameras. However, before I took photographs for magazines, I used the small Minox on several trips, and found it excellent, with a remarkably sharp lens. I was tired of being festooned with heavy cameras, and therefore was greatly relieved to be carrying only a tiny one. It can be carried effortlessly in a pouch attached to your belt. The latest miniature Olympus (the MJU-1) is a lovely little camera for taking snaps. Because carrying these small cameras is hardly a chore, you can have one with you all the time, and therefore take many photographs which would otherwise be missed.

Those who will be photographing in very wet or dusty conditions will need a **waterproof camera**. There is now quite a range from about £70 upwards. At the top of the range is the Nikonos, but you must be sure to experiment with it before using it for any special trip. I once hired one for photographing dolphins, and discovered only afterwards that its viewfinder was completely misleading.

Those who are serious about photography should strongly consider taking two camera bodies. This has important advantages. The main one is that you can put a different lens on each camera, thus saving time when you need to take photographs quickly. Also, if one camera breaks down (probably when you are about to photograph a levitating fakir), then you will have a spare. An occasional advantage is that you can put a different type of film in each camera: a fast one and a slow one; or black-and-white in one camera and colour in another. In dusty conditions a spare camera might save you from having to open a camera.

Whatever type of camera you buy, you must always test it before you go abroad. Therefore don't, as many do, buy your equipment just before your departure. Your camera should be given time to develop any inherent faults, and you should have plenty of time to feel comfortable with it. At the very least, always put a roll of print film through your camera. There is now no excuse to avoid this important little chore, because instant-print-developing shops have opened everywhere, and within just a few hours (in some places, in under one hour), you can see if your camera is working properly.

Video cameras

Many more people are now taking video cameras. Formerly they were too cumbersome, but now they can weigh less than 2 pounds. Every other aspect of their technology, including sound-recording, is also improving. Personally, I am still prejudiced against them. A video camera is yet another bit of clutter that makes you less of a free agent; they use a lot of battery power, and the batteries will need frequent recharging (though this can now sometimes be done even from a car's cigarette lighter); in places where the cameras are unfamiliar, they will draw crowds; the equipment is fragile (with plenty to go wrong), and likely to be damaged by excessive heat; the resolution on the final films isn't as good as the normal picture on our televisions. (If you want really good resolution, you will need to take a proper cine camera, but this is nearly always too expensive and difficult for non-specialists.) Finally, it is noticeable that when novices take moving films, the results are nearly always amateur-ish, but when they take still photographs, they may be lucky enough to get a picture which will rival that of a professional.

Having never taken a video camera, I know very little about them, and because the technology improves at great speed, it is difficult to give precise advice. But here is a list of questions that will be helpful when selecting a camera, and when choosing between the two main systems: Video 8mm and VHS-C.

How long do the tapes run? At present those for Video 8mm last much longer (ninety minutes, as opposed to twenty minutes), which is a great advantage.

How bulky are the tapes?

Can the tapes be played straight on to a television? Will an adaptor be needed?

How easy is it to edit the tapes? Does the sound system make them near-impossible to edit?

How long will the batteries last? How easy are they to re-charge?

What is the camera's capability in low light? There can be a big difference between cameras.

What is the zoom capability? It is worth knowing that the widest angle of videos tends not to be very wide: for instance, it is often the equivalent – on an ordinary still camera – of only 40mm, which often isn't wide enough for landscapes, large buildings, or the inside of rooms.

If you are serious about buying a video camera, then consider hiring one to find out which aspects are important to you. Some shops offer a hire-before-you-buy scheme, whereby if you decide to buy, the rental cost is deducted from the final purchase price.

Video-users should be aware that there are three very different types of television system, which are not interchangeable. If you buy a video camera abroad, you must be sure to get the correct system for your home country. The British system is called Pal B.

Choice of lens

The choice of lens is very much a personal one, and will depend on the nature of your travels. The only certainty is that whatever combination you take, you will wish you had chosen another one. It is impossible to provide for everything without weighing yourself down with heavy lenses.

I usually travel with three lenses: the 28mm (wide-angle), 50mm (standard), and 180mm (medium telephoto).

For my **wide-angle lens** I prefer the 28mm to the more popular 35mm. The 28mm is better for taking interiors, which rarely fit within the view of a 35mm lens; and if you are already carrying the standard 50mm lens, the 28mm offers more of a difference than a 35mm. Some people prefer the 24mm to the 28mm, so have a look at it. For my own taste, it exaggerates the wide angle to such an extent that the photographs look unnatural.

The 50mm **standard lens** approximates to what you see with the eye. Once, when I left it behind and travelled with only a 28mm and a 135mm, I badly missed it. In fact, the more I use this lens, the more I like it: the lens is very sharp and its photographs have a certain intimacy and naturalism that is lacking with other ones. You can also buy a standard lens with a **macro facility**, which is useful for those who wish to take close-up photographs of insects, flowers, and so on. Apparently you will get even better close-up results by reversing your normal lens, and special reversing rings are sold for this purpose.

A **semi-telephoto lens** is superb for portraits: you can sit in a quiet corner and snap good photographs of people without disturbing them. Some people prefer the 105mm to the 135mm; some people like the 180mm, so find out which one suits you.

When photographing animals from a vehicle, you can often get close enough for any of these portrait lenses to be adequate. But if you are walking (when you rarely get as close to the animals), you will need one of a longer focal length. Photographs of birds are extremely boring unless you have a proper telephoto lens. Remember that with any lens longer than 135mm camera-shake may be a problem. The usual rule is that the slowest reasonably safe shutter speed is the nearest fraction of a second which corresponds to the focal length of the lens, i.e. $1/125$ of a second for a 135mm lens, or $1/250$ of a second for a 200mm lens. With the development of faster-speed films, you can more often take photographs at a fast speed, and therefore lenses of a longer focal length are becoming more practical.

In my opinion auto-focus lenses are still too fragile to be reliably useful for anyone travelling off the beaten track.

Whatever you do, don't burden yourself with too many lenses. Fiddling about with lenses is often a distraction from the real job of taking photographs. It is much better to become properly familiar with just a few lenses: you will then feel at home with them, and you will learn exactly what they can do for you.

One way of cutting down on the number of lenses is to buy a **zoom lens**. In the past they have often been insufficiently sharp and too light-consuming, and sometimes changed the colour cast. The technology has improved, and zooms have become very popular with amateurs; but I notice that many professionals still disdain them. Nikon, Canon, and Angenieux do in fact make some zoom lenses that professionals will use, but they are tremendously expensive – three or four times the cost of a normal zoom lens. Because the technology of zoom lenses is improving, it is worth checking on the latest situation, but always be sceptical and get up-to-date advice.

Some photographers use **teleconverters** to gain extra focal length. A 2 X teleconverter turns a 100mm lens into the equivalent of a 200mm, a 180mm into a 360mm, and so on. Therefore they are a space-effective way of greatly increasing your telephoto power. However, any teleconverter will reduce the sharpness of your pictures, and a photographic writer once described a typical teleconverter as having the optical quality of the bottom of a milk bottle. But like much photographic equipment, teleconverters have been improving in recent years, and they are increasingly used by professionals. Buy only a well-known make, and be sure that it matches the specific lens you will be using it with.

FILM

Black-and-white or colour?

The choice between black-and-white or colour is a personal one. But don't base your choice only on your experience at home: there are many photographers who never use colour film at home, but can't resist using it to catch the extraordinary colours of the tropics.

There is a great difference in technique between black-and-white and colour photography, and some photographers are much better at one than the other. In my own case I have concentrated so long on looking at colour and light that I can usually produce some satisfactory colour photographs; but my black-and-white ones are laughable.

Prints or slides?

Many people are allergic to slide-shows. A good album, which anyone can look at when they like, is often more desirable. Photography is an expensive hobby, but the principal expense may not be buying the camera, or buying the film, or getting the films developed, but having to give your friends a sufficiently good dinner so that they can be bribed to watch your slides.

If you are an unambitious photographer who wants only to fill albums with holiday photographs, then ordinary print film is still your best bet. If, however, you take transparencies to the average printer, their equipment can't cope with the many shades of colour, and the resulting prints will have too much contrast. However, the technique of making prints from slides is improving enormously, even with ordinary printing. And the best prints are usually made from transparencies, if you are prepared to spend more money. Cibachrome prints are now superb, and have the advantage of not fading. (If you hang ordinary colour prints on a wall, they will fade disappointingly fast.)

Most keen colour photographers take transparencies. And as a general rule, if you wish to sell colour photographs in Britain, transparencies are greatly preferred. If you ever wish to market photographs through a photographic library, they will also want transparencies.

Newspapers, who mostly use black-and-white illustrations, usually want 10×8 inch *glossy* prints. If you get an extraordinarily good photograph, though, on a negative film, don't despair, because modern technology enables a magazine to make a good illustration from a print.

Choice of film

When you are buying a large quantity of film, shop around because great savings can be made. When I last inquired in London, Tecno shops sold Kodachrome 64 for 20 per cent less than Dixons.

You may also be able to save money by buying abroad. Depending on currency movements, film in Hong Kong and Singapore may be sold at half the British price. Be careful, though: in some countries the price of slide film doesn't include processing (there won't be a capital P after the reference number on the packet), and you should look closely at the expiry date, because a film nearing the end of it may have been stored for too long in heat and humidity. Hong Kong has the reputation for stocking the world's cheapest film, but much of that was sent there on long ship journeys with no air-conditioning.

Heat hastens the decay of film both before and after you have exposed it. Try to store it for as little time as possible. While the film is still in its film canister it is protected from humidity (but not heat); but once you have opened the canister it is no longer protected, and you should expose and develop it as soon as you can.

When choosing your film, the important characteristics are grain, speed, stability (both before and after use), ability to cope with contrast, and quality of colour.

We would all like to use film with the fastest possible speed, because that would give us the possibilities of taking photographs in dim light. But there is an invariable rule: the faster films produce grainier results. The very fastest films produce grainy results even when the photographs haven't been enlarged. Therefore these fast films aren't always suitable. The slowest commonly used transparency film is Kodachrome 25. This has very little grain, and the photographs can be enlarged to a considerable size with great clarity.

At present, the most popular transparency film for ordinary professionals is Kodachrome 64. I have found this an excellent film and have sold many photographs taken with it. Being quite a lot faster than Kodachrome 25, it gives more latitude in difficult light conditions, and there appears to be little difference in quality between the two. Some purists, though, still prefer the Kodachrome 25. Fuji have also produced a slow-speed slide film, Velvia, which doesn't at present handle contrast as well as the Kodachrome, but is liked by some for its punchier colour.

If you will be taking prints, buy the standard print films made by Fuji and Kodak (they are usually about ISO 100), and try taking a few photographs at home to see which you prefer.

Recently Kodachrome have produced a 200 transparency film. Considering its speed, it has a very high quality, and therefore is useful. But, unlike the difference between Kodachrome 25 and 64, I definitely do notice the quality difference between 64 and 200. Where light conditions permit, I would still recommend using the 64.

Although it is best to stick to slow film whenever possible, I always like to take a few of the fastest films, because they can be very useful in bad light, and graininess doesn't always matter, occasionally even adding to the atmosphere of a photograph. When buying very fast films, you should experiment as to what suits your taste, as their character varies a lot. As an experiment I have just shot a roll of Agfa 1000, Fujichrome 800 and Ektachrome 800, and on this occasion I preferred the Agfa film. However, there is such strong competition between the companies, that new improved films will almost certainly be developed, and you should make experiments of your own.

One great advantage of the slow Kodachrome films is that they have been proved to be very stable both before and after being developed. This is extremely important when you are travelling in the tropics, where heat can be very damaging to film. I once left some Kodachrome films on the bottom of a car, little realizing that they would be roasted from beneath. I was mortified, for they were very precious; but they nearly all turned out to be fine. Kodachrome is also at present thinner and more flexible than other slide films, so it is less likely to tear in hot or cold weather.

Many slides from high-speed film aren't stable for long periods. Some types have a shelf life of only a few years, which is disastrous if you are putting your slides into a photographic library. Kodachrome slides are very stable, and I'm still selling some of mine twenty-five years after they were taken.

Always take more film than you think you need. If you find you have taken too many films, there is always a chance you can sell them for a high price at the end of your trip. In many countries you can't buy satisfactory film, and in some countries you can't buy any film at all. I reckon that as many as half of travelling photographers run out of film. Some of them are heartbroken.

Films are bulky and take up far less room if you unwrap them from their square cardboard boxes; by doing this you may also prevent an officious customs officer demanding import duty. However, don't unwrap all the films, because the ones you may want to sell should still be in their packets.

POTENTIAL DISASTERS

X-rays

Many photographers' films have been ruined by being passed through the X-ray machines at airports. This has happened so often that by now most people are aware of the danger. However, at modern airports the old X-ray machines have been replaced by new 'safe' ones. Photographers have given me conflicting advice about these machines, so I wrote for advice to Fuji and Kodak, who cleared up a number of misconceptions.

Some of the modern machines are safe for many films, but the result of exposure to X-rays is *cumulative*. It isn't possible to be precise about how many times it is safe to allow your films to be X-rayed, because this will depend on the particular model of the 'safe' machine.

The safety will also very much depend on the speed of your film. Films of a higher speed are more susceptible to damage. If your films are ISO 400 or higher, try to avoid allowing them to be X-rayed in all but the most reliable machines; and even with these try to avoid repeated X-rays.

Specially lined X-ray-proof photographer's bags are on sale for travelling photographers. They aren't entirely reliable: the person who is controlling the X-ray machine might spot the obstruction and turn the X-ray dosage up till it penetrates the bag.

Colour negative film (for prints) is far more susceptible to X-ray damage than black-and-white or colour reversal film (for slides).

Many people don't realize that unexposed film, as well as exposed film, is subject to X-ray damage.

Because of worries about the X-ray machines I always carry my film in a **transparent** bag. I find the cheap wash-bags sold by the Body Shop to be very useful for this. Normally (but not invariably) a courteous request enables my films to be hand-inspected.

You don't have to worry about the archway metal-detectors

or the hand-held devices. Neither will damage your film. Nor need you worry about processed films, for they can't be harmed by X-rays.

If you send home a package of unprocessed film, there is a danger that they might be X-rayed, and therefore damaged. However, films sent in the individual special mailing-envelopes aren't usually X-rayed.

Very occasionally a customs officer insists on opening your camera, so be careful not to leave a precious film inside. Anyway, if you leave a film in your camera, you might forgetfully allow it to be exposed to a non-safe machine.

Most people remember about the problems of non-safe machines when they are taking international flights. The real danger time is during internal flights. For some reason these are the occasions when it's easy to forget to ask for a hand-inspection, and it's at the small local airports where you are likely to encounter X-ray machines that will fog your film.

More hazards

In the tropics it is easy to let your camera and film get too hot. Even if the camera is in its case, take particular care when you are on the move. You might easily leave it on the sunny shelf of a car, or in the scalding boot of a bush-taxi. Once I carefully packed my film on the bottom of an overnight bag so that it wouldn't get hot in the event of the bag being left in the sun. After the ensuing journey I discovered that the floor of the van was piping hot and the heat had roasted the film.

Don't rush into photographing bridges, airports, police stations, or anything within miles of an army camp. Developing countries tend to be extra-sensitive about these places, and you can get into trouble photographing the most innocent-looking bridge.

If a magazine or publisher wants to buy photographs of yours, always insist on a signed receipt which says that the photographs are insured for at least £200 each. Make sure the receipt covers damage as well as loss: several magazines have used photographs of mine, which they have then returned unmounted, greasy, and scratched.

Distorted readings

A camera's meter most often distorts readings when it is influenced by a strong light-source, which results in important parts of the photograph being underexposed. This is a common problem for novices. If you are inside a house and your camera is pointed anywhere near a window, the light from that window will prevent the camera from giving an accurate reading for the rest of the room; or if you are photographing a landscape, and a large part of the viewfinder is filled with bright sky, then the reading will probably be wrong for photographing the land. Many cameras now have a 'backlight switch' which compensates for backlight by increasing the exposure by one and a half or two stops. Even so, you should get into the habit of taking a reading off the darker parts of your potential photograph.

When photographing a landscape, point the camera at the ground, and notice the difference between this reading and the reading for the whole photograph; or if you are in a window-lit room, don't take just a general reading, but take an additional one off the wall. Many better modern cameras have a centre-weighted system, which takes a reading only from the central part of the lens; this makes accurate readings much easier.

Photographing black people provides the classic example of the problems inherent in light-reading. Quite a number of photographers come back from Africa with photographs of silhouettes. Black skins are efficient absorbers of light; if, without compensating, you take a photograph of a dark African against a bright sky, you get a photograph of only a featureless black shape. For the same reasons, black people are good subjects for flash photography – there aren't the ugly reflections you get from white skin. Oriental skins are excellent for both daylight and flash photography.

ACCESSORIES

Filters

You are mad if you don't always keep a filter on your lens. If your lens gets scratched or damaged, you lose a lot of money, and are bereft of a vital piece of equipment. If a filter gets scratched, you've lost just a few pounds, and can easily replace it with another. For this reason always travel with spare filters, and keep one in your shoulder bag.

Don't economize by buying an inferior filter; it will nullify the quality of your lens. If you are taking colour transparencies, the usual standard filter is the Skylight: it doesn't distort natural colours, and it reduces the blue haze caused by UV rays.

Obsessive photographers take a great battery of filters. I'm against this because it can lead to unnecessary fiddling, which detracts from concentration on good photography; and I particularly dislike the artificial tints and colours that many filters produce.

However, my photography dramatically improved after I started carrying a **polarizing filter**. The photographer twiddles this filter, cutting out varying degrees of reflected light. In the right conditions (often with the sun at a right angle to the camera) it enhances the true colours of your picture. This filter is particularly useful when photographing the sea (cutting out the glare) or cloudy skies (emphasizing the contrast between blue and white). And it is invaluable for extending the useful hours for photography. During much of the day in the tropics the light has become too flat for good colour photographs; it is then that the Polaroid lens often enables you to take pictures that would otherwise be impossible.

Take care when you use a polarizing filter with a wide-angle lens. If the filter is too thick, it will cause 'cut off' (dark corners on your photographs). The problem is not noticeable through the viewfinder, and I have twice been caught out in this way.

Many types of filter often get jammed on the lens. If this happens, wrap an elastic band round the lens, and then twist while gripping the elastic. This works like magic.

Camera case

Many ludicrous camera cases are sold which are sealed only with Velcro. Dust is the greatest enemy of your camera, and therefore any container holding your camera should be closeable with a zip.

Although **soft cases** don't protect your lenses as well as hard ones, they take up far less room, and therefore I prefer them.

Cleaning equipment

I don't think it is practical to travel with an aerosol for blowing air; and I'm not too keen on camera brushes. They tend to pick up the dirt, and occasionally they leave a hair inside the camera, which is disastrous.

For the inside of the camera, I just give it a good blow every time I change my film. Each time you open the camera door, check that there are no dust specks on the film pressure-plate (which you will find on the inside of the camera door), as any dust or grit on this can scratch a film disastrously. As for the lens, I blow with a *dry* breath to remove any particles before cleaning, and I then blow on it with a *humid* breath before cleaning it with a cloth. Don't ever forget to give the lens a really good blow before wiping it. I once ruined a filter by wiping a piece of grit all over it.

A professional friend of mine recommends using the large blowers that are used by watch-repairers, and a large camel-hair brush for all non-glass surfaces.

Some professionals prefer to use tissues rather than a cloth, because a fresh one can be used each time. However, the modern micro-fibre polishing cloths (such as the one sold by Pentax) are greatly improved, and I find them extremely practical. They can be washed, so there is no reason for them to become too dirty; in fact they should be regularly washed in order to get rid of the grease from your fingers. Don't use *ordinary* tissues, which will scratch the lens.

These modern cloths claim to get grease off the lens as well.

Although this is often true, I still consider it essential to take some special ointment, as you are in trouble if your cloth can't remove the grease. I find that in the tropics there is a certain type of grease that gets onto the lens (I think from sweat) which is impossible to remove with only a cloth. Because of this problem I carry a few foil-wrapped tissues in my shoulder bag; but it is best not to rely on them, as they can dry out before being unwrapped. Try not to use cleaning fluid too often on a lens, because it can degrade the lens's coating.

Camera straps

Some people find wide camera straps more comfortable than thin ones. Ensure that the strap is attached to the actual camera, not just to the leather case that holds the camera.

Lens hood

Because of lateral glare, you will often need a lens hood. An additional advantage of a hood is that it will help protect your lens from scratching when you shove your camera into your shoulder bag without replacing the lens cap. Be careful that the shop hasn't sold you the wrong size of lens hood (another reason to make a pre-trip test of your camera), because they often do this. Also don't, as I have, be a sucker for the frequently sold dual-purpose lens hood which is adjustable for both ordinary and wide-angle lenses. When I was taking wide-angled photographs of some gorillas, my hood had been pulled out by some branch, and all the photographs were ruined.

Flash

I have quite often been too lazy to take a flash, and quite often regretted it. Sophisticated photographers use them a fair amount during the day for 'filling in'. This is useful, for instance, for portraits when the sun is high in the sky, or for compositions with extreme contrast. As mentioned before, I make sure that my flash batteries are interchangeable with my torch batteries, so that the spares can do for either. If you get serious about flash photography, investigate rechargeable packs.

Tripod

Not wanting to become burdened with an excess of photographic paraphernalia, I have never taken one. And I have discovered that it is often possible to take photographs at speeds far slower than the textbooks allow you. (I take several to spread the risk.) However, because so many interesting photographs aren't taken in bright conditions, a tripod will make a great difference to a keen photographer. A **monopod** isn't as effective as a tripod, but takes up far less room, and can still be very useful. I have been recommended tripods and monopods made by Gitzo.

Camera battery

If you use an electronically controlled camera, a spare battery is easily forgotten; and when your only battery packs up, you are in real trouble. Some camera straps have a useful attachment for carrying a spare battery. Always keep the battery sealed and free of contamination in its original packet.

If your camera unaccountably doesn't work, don't despair – it may just be the connection with the battery, especially if you are in a humid area. Take the battery out (ideally in an air-conditioned room), dry it, and rub it with a pencil rubber if you have one. Don't handle the battery with your hands, which may cause it to discharge or leave a film on it. This may do the trick; if not, try cleaning the battery chamber with lens-cleaning fluid. Where humidity is a great problem, it can be worth sealing the outside of the chamber with tape.

Spare lens cap

Lens caps are easily lost, so bring some spares. Not quite so necessary when you are using protective filters.

Silica gel

Many books advise you to take packets of silica gel, but I'm not quite so sure. Film in canisters is protected against humidity until opened. So the only point of the silica gel is to protect your cameras against humidity. But to do this you need to keep the cameras very securely sealed, and this sealing must be done in a dry atmosphere, along with a sufficient amount of silica gel. This isn't usually practical; besides, it is quite hard to buy sufficiently large bags of silica gel. The packets can only soak up a limited amount of moisture. Almost every time you break the seal, the silica gel must be reactivated by being dried out in an oven.

Accessories bag

I find one of the cheap transparent wash-bags from the Body Shop useful for carrying bits and pieces of kit. And being forgetful of the most obvious advice, I always put in my bag an instruction manual for both the camera and the flash.

PHOTOGRAPHING PEOPLE

Human beings are the subject of the majority of interesting photographs, and this causes a problem: many people aren't willing to be photographed.

Nevertheless, some photographers click away regardless; they push their cameras under people's noses, and treat them like performing animals. Apart from being uncouth and insensitive, this behaviour may well be putting the photographer in danger. Some more sensitive photographers give up the battle, and confine themselves to snapping buildings or landscapes. A wise photographer, however, by learning several techniques, can take many photographs of people without causing any offence.

There are two sides to the problem: some people are merely shy and nervous; others have a superstitious fear of being photographed. (Some, of course, are shy and superstitious.)

When you show respect and are prepared to take your time, shyness should not be a problem. When you first walk into a village, the locals may be wary, but if you don't alarm them by taking photographs straightaway, they nearly always relax. When you actually stay in a village, you can usually take almost any pictures you like, provided the people aren't actually superstitious.

Both shy and superstitious people can have their fears calmed if you let them hold the camera and look through it. Allow them to take a photograph of you, and perhaps one or two of each other. This is when an instant-picture camera would be useful.

Wide-angle lenses can be very useful for taking surreptitious photographs. With my 28mm lens, I can be pointing the camera at a door while, in fact, photographing an interesting woman at the side of the door. And because of a wide-angle lens's considerable depth of field, you don't have to be so careful about focusing. This enables you to take very hurried photographs, and sometimes to photograph without putting the camera to your eye. It is also possible to take quick pictures without putting the camera to your eye by pre-focusing.

A telephoto lens is obviously a great help for photographing people. Often they don't realize that someone at such a distance is capable of taking photographs. If you go to a busy place, seat yourself in a suitable corner and don't take photographs for at least quarter of an hour. If you have dressed unobtrusively, everyone soon recovers from your novelty value, and you can usually take photographs without worrying them. Markets are perfect for photographing in this way, because people are so absorbed in the business of buying and selling that they aren't bothered by a quiet photographer.

I used to be very sniffy about demands for money when photographing people: I thought it degrading for both the photographer and the subjects. Now I've changed my mind. After all, the photographer is getting some benefit, so why shouldn't the people (usually impoverished) get some as well? Once, in some remote bleak uplands of Guatemala, I photographed villagers dancing in the costumes of conquistadores. They asked for money, and I was delighted to pay it: as they had saved all year to be able to hire these costumes, it seemed right for me to contribute.

Even when there is no need to take photographs by stealth, many amateurs believe that posed portraits are necessarily bad. Not so. They can be very interesting. And if your subject is willing, don't be shy about going up very close in order to take only a head shot: an interesting face makes a wonderful photograph.

When taking portraits at full length, the most common amateur mistake is to cut off the feet. In fact, as the mounts of transparencies often cut off some of the picture, always allow plenty of margin all round.

PHOTOGRAPHIC SENTIMENTALITY

In an interesting article in the *Traveller*, Robert Holmes wrote:

I often spend a great deal of time waiting for a person dressed in jeans and a T-shirt to move out of frame in an otherwise perfect shot of local people; but should I do that? Sadly, jeans and T-shirts are as ubiquitous as Coca-Cola. I believe that those of us who are privileged to photograph some of the more remote places in the world have a duty to show the place as it really is . . . if most of the people wear jeans, then show that. Selecting your pictures to show only the image that fits with your preconceptions is, in my opinion, misrepresentation.

I quote this because there is a lot of truth in what he says. And in the chapter on Culture Shock I describe having met many educated foreigners who are irritated that we concentrate so much on the folksy (and often unrepresentative) aspects of their countries. I must admit, though, that my own photographs are usually biased in favour of the picturesque. Unfortunately, almost everything modern in the Third World is, to my eyes, tawdry and ugly, while almost everything traditional is aesthetically pleasing. The same is often true even in Europe. Compare the traditional Italian vineyard (muddled terraces, interspersed with olive trees and wild flowers) with the grim columns of regimented vines which have replaced them. And if you do catch traditional life in photographs, you have gained a record of something which one day will certainly disappear.

GOOD PHOTOGRAPHS

The secret of taking good photographs is to take lots. The problem is the expense! You would be astonished by the number of films that professionals use. Amateurs usually take too few photographs. They take one photograph of each subject and expect them all to be good. They would do better to take as many photographs as they can afford, and on returning home edit them right down.

During your first few days in an exotic country, it is especially important not to be stingy with your photographs. It is at this time that your eye is at its keenest. After a while you become less sensitive to what, after you have returned home, will seem colourful, strange, or dramatic.

When you see an interesting subject, take a photograph straightaway. Don't start looking about for a better position or fiddling with your camera. Many good photographs are missed in this way: a cloud passes in front of the sun, a new person wrecks the composition, or a car arrives to obstruct your view. When you've taken the first photographs, then look about for variations.

One of the keys to good photography lies in recognizing the value of these variations. The photographer must consider every possible angle, speed, background, and light; and that is one reason why it's necessary to take so many photographs. Ignore, for instance, the advice that you should always stand with the sun behind you; some of the best photographs have their subjects backlit by the sun. Don't always take photographs in the conventional standing position – everyone is used to these, and the lack of variety can be dull. For instance, try bending your knees and photographing people at this level, instead of always at eye level. Ask permission to go on a roof to catch a different view of a street scene. Always look for the *fresh* angle. The novice may think that good photographs are taken only in the sun, but some of the best are taken in abominable weather. Never be content with the average and the ordinary: endlessly experiment with every possible variation.

You should sometimes inject artificial variety into your photographs by altering the speed or aperture controls from the conventional dictates of your light meter: if the meter shows that the aperture should be f 8, then also try taking photographs at f 5.6 and f 11 (or you could change the aperture by only half a stop). This technique, which is known as 'bracketing', is also a good insurance against the meter giving a distorted reading. Sometimes you may prefer to bracket with a speed setting, but as you have to alter this by a whole stop, you don't get quite such a fine variation.

I slightly under-expose all my slide photographs by a minor misadjustment of the camera's film setting. Thus, if the dial should be set at ISO 64, I set it instead for ISO 80. For my own taste, I find this gives slightly better colour saturation, and I prefer photographs that are slightly under-exposed to those that are over-exposed. (A professional photographer has recently told me that the camera dials are adjusted for negative films, and that it is anyway correct to under-expose slide films – of the same apparent speed – by three-quarters of a stop.) Also, when you are printing a photograph, it is always possible to remedy a mild under-exposure, but nothing can be done about over-exposure.

Unfortunately there are very few hours for good photography in the tropics. Often there are hardly two hours after dawn, and maybe only one hour before sunset. And if you want really first-rate photographs, you often won't have as long as this. Light conditions often change so fast that half a minute can make all the difference. Although this comment may appear pretentious, it is no exaggeration.

A key ingredient in memorable photographs is often some **added element**. This could simply be a human being who brings interest and adds composition to what might have been an ordinary architectural photograph. Sometimes the added element is an unexpected one. I remember seeing on the front of a Sunday colour section a brilliant photograph by Ken Griffiths of a mounted Spanish bullfighter dressed in all his glorious tinsel. The bullfighter had a cigarette dangling from his lips, and for some reason it was the unlikely cigarette which transformed the photograph from being merely good to being remarkable.

Finally, if you want your photographs to hold attention at home, you must accept the harsh fact that a mundane photograph of 'The living room of my friends, the Dawangas' will be considered more interesting than one of 'Dappled light in a rain forest'. Unless you are an outstanding photographer, you won't hold your audience unless a reasonable proportion of your photographs include people.

CHAPTER 10

HUMAN HAZARDS

Perceptive travellers are usually more surprised at the abundance of honesty, rather than the extent of dishonesty. Once outside towns and cities they find that most people are trustworthy, often despite biting poverty. Instead of worrying about losing property, travellers – especially in remoter areas – are more likely to be embarrassed by the quantity of food and presents thrust upon them by people who can hardly afford to give away anything. If you choose guides and companions carefully, you will find that they are nearly always honest. I have always entrusted guides with both money and possessions, and have never yet lost a penny.

Many people are also surprised to discover that they can roam most of the world without the slightest fear for their physical safety. Thieves are usually after your chattels, not your body. Travellers who leave Europe for the first time are for the most part struck by the lack of malice and the absence of physical fear – far more important than worries about the loss of mere possessions.

Nevertheless, there are problems, and I catalogue them in some detail, since it is a pity to spoil a journey for lack of a few simple precautions. It is better to expect the worst, and to end up being pleasantly surprised.

Theft

Theft really is a problem: it has massively increased both in Europe and in the Third World. In some countries, such as Colombia, crime has reached epidemic proportions. At one stage *The South American Handbook* felt obliged to offer the direst of warnings: 'Hardly anyone goes to Bogota without losing something . . . *never* walk into a crowd . . . take your glasses off if you can see without them . . . armed attacks on pedestrians are quite common . . .'

Up till a few years ago I never locked a suitcase because I was more frightened of losing my key than my possessions. But now if you return to the same country after a long gap – whether Bulgaria or Madagascar – you will be staggered by the increase in crime. On Bali, thefts were almost unknown until a few years ago; and possessions could be left unguarded by the road. Now, if you aren't drowned by the dangerous currents of Kuta Beach, you will be drowned by the tears of Australian girls who have been robbed of all their possessions.

The reasons for this massive increase in crime are complex, but one or two are discernible. One obvious cause is the frantic increase in urbanization: cities and towns have grown at an unprecedented speed, and many of them have quintupled their population during the last few decades. Country people are lured by the meretricious charms of urban life, and migrate in the hope of instant Utopia. More often than not, their ambitions aren't realized and they grow disillusioned. At the same time they are released from the village codes of loyalty, hospitality, and honour.

Another reason for the increase in thieving is a change in attitudes to foreigners. Many localities are being visited by an unprecedented number of tourists and travellers. If some of these are 'hippies', the respect for foreigners has usually diminished (this is discussed at greater length in Chapter 11); at the same time it is realized that even poor-looking foreigners are comparatively wealthy. A scruffy traveller gets robbed, and £150 is found in his shoulder bag, which in many countries is equivalent to an agricultural wage for two years. News about the £150 quickly spreads, and travellers are robbed time and again by thieves hoping to hit another fabulous jackpot.

In several parts of this book I have emphasized that the countryside is far safer than the town. This is true; but unfortunately you should be aware that crime is increasing in rural areas, and I was once robbed in the depths of the countryside in Mali; the thief took a bag which was actually touching my body while I slept.

The most unlikely regions are riddled with thieves. You might imagine that a relaxed and charming country such as Indonesia would be relatively free from crime, but let me quote from Bill Dalton's invaluable guide:

There are thieves the width and breadth of Indonesia – snatch thieves, pickpockets, cat-burglars, and on the buses on Sumatra, travellers have even been drugged in order to make them easier to rob. Take all imaginable precautions because practically everything you have, they want. Indonesians themselves are very rarely stolen from. At night they accord their motorbicycles the ultimate honour: they put them in their bedrooms. The best precaution is to travel through the islands without jewellery, watch or camera. The less you travel with, the less there is to be stolen, the less resentment is aroused, the less restricted your bargaining position . . . never take a room without strong bars on the window. If you do, either take all your valuables with you when you go out, or hide them very well . . . as much as you'd like to trust the Indonesians you're staying with, the word that a whitey (connotes 'rich') is in town spreads instantly throughout the whole kampong. Quick and quiet, thieves will enter your room through the window while you sleep and steal the camera from the hook above your head, and backpack from under your very bed . . . wet washing is stolen from the line . . . Indonesians borrow things – surf-boards, sunglasses, rings, guitars, books, and 'forget to return them'.*

Problems with thieving will always be worst where there are tourists. I know of a couple who lived for more than two years on three tourist-free Indonesian islands, and nothing of theirs was even stolen.

Never underestimate the ability of thieves. One British traveller, who had heard a lot about crime in South America, always took sensible precautions, being careful during bus journeys to place his feet on his rucksack. At the end of one journey, however, he discovered his rucksack was half empty: someone had

* *Indonesia Handbook* (Roger Lascelles, 1984)

wriggled under his seat and razor-slit it. In East Africa, thieves are skilful at manipulating long poles through your bedroom window; your possessions can disappear without anyone entering your room.

Many backpackers keep their valuables tucked 'safely' down the bottom of their sleeping bags while they are sleeping. Don't do it: thieves are well aware of this hiding place, and will razor-slit the sleeping bag.

Be sensible about your hotel window; thieves aren't frightened of climbing in at night. They might not even have to enter the room: in Malaysia I met someone who had had his watch removed while sleeping under a window. Lock your hotel bedroom at night, but leave the key in the door in case of fire.

A locked hotel bedroom used to be a safe place to keep possessions during the day, and hotel staff were usually reliable. Now this is less true. When I think hotel-owners look reliable, I sometimes leave my *real* valuables – passport, tickets, and traveller's cheques – in their keeping. It is the loss of these three that could ruin your journey, so they need special protection. In large hotels, credit cards have occasionally been illicitly used for fraudulent transactions, but generally you will be safe.

I have mentioned in Chapter 3 that a locked hard-sided suitcase can be a mild protection against hotel sneak thieves, as they are unlikely to lug a large case out of the hotel.

Since being Travel Editor of *Harpers & Queen*, I have frequently stayed in expensive hotels, which quite often have small safes in the room. I use them and find them very convenient. But I have heard of even these being robbed. And don't believe that main safes of hotels are necessarily secure; I have also heard of these being busted, and of the victims not being offered any compensation. Forgive me if I'm inducing paranoia!

It's not only the locals who steal. I have met many travellers who have been robbed by their fellow foreigners (though not usually by their compatriots). Be wary of travellers who suggest sharing a room to save money, and be wary of any who camp nearby when you are sleeping outside.

Luggage in a car is a prime target. Try to keep your cases in an enclosed boot, where they can't be seen. Even this isn't entirely safe: a friend who had had his luggage stolen from the boot of a car in Portugal was told by the police that local thieves had keys for all the rented cars.

Unfortunately, in some countries you should beware of the police. One acquaintance of mine travelled for several months around South and Central America. He was robbed three times, on each occasion the police were the culprits.

Be cautious about anyone who describes himself as a plain-clothes policeman; he may have forged identification. *The South American Handbook* says that you should be extra suspicious if you aren't asked for your passport. Don't let anyone who claims to be a plain-clothes policeman search you (an excuse for finding your wallet) or lead you away from the main streets.

Some people leave their suitcases in hotel storerooms when they are going on a side trip with only a backpack or overnight bag. Occasionally, other foreigners claim the suitcases as their own, so it is best to tie a label on any luggage you leave in a store. If you are extra fussy, stipulate that the suitcase should be released only on presentation of a specified passport.

It is no good hiding your valuables under your mattress. All hotel staff know about this obvious hiding place. A surprising number of travellers use it, and an astonishing number forget, and leave their money there. In one Guatemalan hotel I learnt that the honest chambermaids had handed over four lots of money in the previous week.

When you need to hide something in an emergency (such as when soldiers are looting), use gaffer tape to strap it to the underside of a piece of furniture such as a cupboard.

I first read in *The South American Handbook* about travellers being **drugged** with sweets. Because this sounded like a character-istic scare story, I wrote a sceptical letter to the editor, who assured me that he had received several first-hand accounts. Since then the *Handbook* has confirmed many more instances, and now advises that nobody should ever accept offers of food on a

Colombian train. I have also read of travellers being given drugged cups of tea on Indian trains, and of tourists being drugged and robbed in Istanbul.

At first I also disbelieved reports about travellers being **gassed** and robbed in trains. Unfortunately, the reports turned out to be true, and there have been frequent reports of gassing even in European trains.

Almost everywhere in the world beaches are a magnet for thieves. Be extra careful when swimming, as even your towel and humblest clothes may disappear.

Be especially careful if you are dallying with a prostitute. Cheap films and novels often contain stories of clients being robbed by prostitutes and their accomplices. For once, fact and fiction coincide; a prostitute's client is often naked and distracted, and therefore he is an easy victim.

If you are robbed, you must report the theft to the police within twenty-four hours, so that you can claim on insurance; and you must report to the issuing companies the loss of any traveller's cheques or credit cards. For this, try to use the UK Direct system (see Appendix 4, and Telephoning home, Chapter 8). Once you are connected to the UK operator, you can ask for a reverse-charge call to the various numbers. If you must carry several credit cards, then consider a scheme such as the Card Protection Plan (tel. 071 351 4400) or Sentinel (tel. 0705 4864440), which will cost only a few pounds. One call to them will cancel your cards. If you are stranded without cards and insufficient cash anywhere in the world, Card Protection Plan claim to be able to rush you £750 emergency cash and an air ticket. They will also cover you against fraudulent use of cards (up to £1,000) before you notify them.

When thieves steal documents that are valueless to them but valuable to you (such as a passport or an air ticket), don't give up your chance of finding them. Explain to the police that you aren't bothered about the loss of other possessions, but that you badly need these documents. Offer a good reward. The corrupt elements among the police often have good contacts with the criminal fraternity, and you may get your documents back. At the same time, spread the news of your reward to anyone else who may have the slightest contact with criminals, such as guides, touts, and taxi drivers.

As a precaution against theft, always keep a separate list of your air ticket numbers and your traveller's cheques (see Fig. 2, Chapter 1). Carry your passport number in your head.

Bag snatching and pickpocketing

Those who stay at home in Britain will most likely go through a lifetime without having their pockets picked; but in many parts of the world pickpocketing is rampant. At one stage the *Lonely Planet Update* (sadly now defunct) was reporting that half the travellers on the Inca trail were having their bags razor-slit. The problem is also bad in some parts of Europe: when the Royal Ballet visited Barcelona, they suffered twelve bag-snatches on the first day.

Pickpockets and snatch-thieves nearly always work according to a similar formula, and an understanding of this may help you avoid becoming a victim. Their basic ploy is *distraction*. Instead of working singly, as generally supposed, they nearly always work in pairs or in small groups. This enables one of them to distract you while the other grabs the goods. A pedestrian may 'bump' into you in the market, and while you are rebalancing, your wallet disappears. In a typical trick an accomplice will drop ice-cream over your clothes; this brings friendly faces to mop it up – meanwhile, your shoulder bag is razor-slit. Sometimes more imaginative methods are used. An old lady 'drops' a bunch of coins: you scrabble to help retrieve them, and when you turn round, your luggage has disappeared.

Because of the great skill of pickpockets and snatch-thieves, you should obey one golden rule of travel: *never carry any valuable item in a shoulder bag*, especially your passport, air ticket, or money. Shoulder bags are a prime target, as they are easy to pull off, easy to razor-slit, and often easy to pickpocket. If you are walking along a street, or even sitting on a cycle-rickshaw, snatchers on motorbikes can yank the bag away – sometimes hurting you in the process. I have also met travellers who have lost the contents of their shoulder bags without feeling anything; a thief has walked alongside them, all the while slitting the underneath of the bag with a razor. I wouldn't have believed this if I hadn't seen the razor-slits with my own eyes. In fact razor-slitters are so skilled that some of them can slice through a shirt to your money-belt without you feeling anything.

So where should travellers carry their money? As I find money-belts uncomfortable, I once had trousers specially made with a back pocket defended by a zip, and the zip was hidden by a flap. Those expensive pockets were picked four times. My first mistake was to underestimate the skill of pickpockets, and my second was to keep any money in hip pockets – which are the most vulnerable. If you insist on carrying cash in ordinary pockets, use the ones in the front of your trousers. As mentioned in Chapter 3, a pocket sewn on the inside waist of your skirt or trousers is often an effective and practical anti-pickpocket device.

Money-belts are still the most popular place for hiding your cash, but in the more dangerous regions, thieves do know about them. Eager to find an alternative for money-belts, I was impressed by a money-belt that was designed to be used around the calf of the leg. After briefly using one I was struck by the idea of using **Tubigrip** as a cheap and comfortable replacement.

Tubigrip is an elasticated bandage on sale in most chemists. Doubled up over the calf, it makes an excellent hiding-place for your passport (especially the modern thin one) or money. You can wear it all day – and even sleep in it – while hardly feeling anything. Luckily the legs aren't a very sweaty part of the body, and all sizes of Tubigrip are now made in 100 per cent cotton.

The calf of your leg is generally a far more secure place for money than your midriff, especially as there are so many places where thieves know about the conventional money-belt. And if you are standing in a crowded bus (a prime place to be pickpocketed), your leg is a much more awkward place for a thief to get at.

Quite a number of travellers have told me that my Tubigrip idea has saved them from losing large sums of money and on occasions it has saved a whole trip. Unfortunately some travellers have behaved idiotically – openly getting money out of their Tubigrip during the day. As a result, this hiding-place is beginning to get known, and I've had my first report of a robber who has searched someone's leg (in Istanbul). So please keep your ordinary shopping money in a pocket. If that's pickpocketed, it is not the end of the world; but it will be a tragedy if Tubigrip no longer remains a safe way of hiding money.

You can buy it in widely different sizes, so experiment to find one reasonably tight enough to be secure. Tubigrip comes in two colours, flesh and white; both are washable, but I choose the flesh-coloured one because it looks less grubby after frequent use.

Tubigrip isn't a good place for hiding wads of money when you are crossing frontiers, because it will be found by guards when they frisk you for guns.

When walking through wet undergrowth, anything in your Tubigrip needs to be wrapped in a plastic bag: on a jungle walk in Rwanda I stupidly never considered this, with the result that my passport and banknotes were sodden.

A few manufacturers make trouser-belts which have a secret compartment for hiding paper money. (At present Go Products sell an excellent canvas one that can be found at airport shops.) These aren't convenient for shopping or day-to-day money, but they are really excellent for keeping cash reserves for emergencies. Because you are probably wearing the belt every day, this emergency money is nearly always with you.

Mugging

In most parts of the world you are unlikely to be mugged. In my case it has only happened once – in Trinidad, where mugging is in fact quite rare. I was walking down a brightly lit street when the one other pedestrian asked me the time. While I paused, he grabbed hold of my shirt and demanded my money. When I told this tale to Trinidadians they said I should have resisted him. In a way they were right, as I could have kneed him in the crotch, yelled for help, or run away. I think yelling would have been the best. But surely it is better to carry only a small sum of money and a cheap watch, and then one can hand them over with a smile. The safety of one's body is so much more important than any amount of cash.

It is often said that you should always carry *some* money to prevent a disappointed mugger becoming vicious. This appears to be sensible advice.

Cautious guidebooks recommend their readers to stay away from the poor, bustling districts of some Third World cities; but this isn't good advice, for although crowded places are the worst for pickpockets, they are as a general rule freer from any violent type of crime: local people will usually help and protect a foreigner in trouble, and in many places any thief who is caught (whether he has robbed a foreigner or a local) will be beaten to a pulp. It is the empty, deserted streets – even in wealthy districts – which are often more dangerous.

Having probably induced excessive paranoia, I better now repeat that, although thieving is a major problem for travellers in the Third World, there is very rarely any danger of violence – and certainly far less than in most American cities. Thieves want your money, they don't want to harm you. After my incident in Trinidad, I asked the mugger for my house keys back, and he gracefully returned them. And I was cheered to read in the *Lonely Planet Update* about the following incident in Larache, Morocco:

Clad in only my swimsuit, I was walking through the dunes carrying my clothes, car keys, and money in a plastic bag, when suddenly the bag was snatched by a young man disappearing into the trees. There I was, 50 miles from my hotel, practically naked and with no money. But soon I heard someone calling me over. The bag came sailing through the trees, minus the money of course, but thankfully with my car keys in it; so I was able to drive back to the hotel.

American Express have analysed the methods used in traveller's cheque-theft throughout the world. The most common cause is sneak-thieving from hotel rooms. Next highest is theft from cars, then unarmed street theft, then theft from the home. Only 1 per cent of theft was due to armed robbery.

Other dishonesties

Wherever other tourists have been, you are likely to face a number of ingenious attempts to separate you from your money. An exhaustive list of these potential dishonesties would be boring and too long, but a description of a few may encourage you to be on the alert.

One tedious incident in Niger is worth mentioning because it shows how almost every transaction is subject to abuse. I telephoned from my hotel's reception to a contact about 12 miles away, and spoke for about two minutes. After I'd finished, the receptionist rang the operator for the price, and then asked me for £17. My suspicions were easily aroused, for the manager had called the operator by his name, and they were clearly conniving in a regular ramp on tourists. The ensuing negotiations lasted for an exhausting half-hour, but I managed to get the bill down to £4, which was still too much.

Unless you actually see the stamps on your mail being franked, they are sometimes steamed off for resale.

Although it is a boring little chore, you can save money by checking bills whenever you are in tourist areas. Brian Moynahan describes the problem:

In Paris, open season is tacitly declared at Easter and runs till the end of September. Resident once in the City of Light, I was not cheated for four straight months in winter. Come April, more than three-quarters of the meals and drinks I ordered in English were overcharged by an average of 30 per cent. The rate dropped to a quarter by ordering in

French, but the mark-up remained the same. This was true of restaurants right across the price range.*

A favourite Parisian ruse is to give you change for a smaller note than the one you have put down. The waiter has nothing to lose (if you notice the mistake, he only has to apologize) and plenty to gain. Once the banknote has been pocketed, you can't possibly prove what you gave. Get into the habit of mentioning aloud the value of any high-denomination note you hand over.

An admirably clever ramp runs as follows. A youth tells an English traveller that he is a coin collector. The good-natured traveller digs up a few English coins from home. The youth accosts the next traveller, 'Are you English?' If the traveller replies 'Yes', the youth says he has some coins which are of no use to him. Would the traveller be kind enough to change them into local currency?

During some long trips I'm approached about once a month by confident and well-educated men who say something along the following lines: 'Would you mind, dear friend, lending me £5? My wife is ill, and I don't have the money for a taxi home'; or, 'I've just had my pocket picked. Could you lend me £6 for my train ticket back to La Badia?' These con-men are so artful that it is almost impossible to refuse their requests, especially as it is difficult to distinguish them from genuine cases of hardship. Should you refuse them, they make you feel like a monster. On the other hand, it is infuriating to give them quite large sums of money, when there are genuine beggars who could feed themselves for a week with the same sum. One of the psychological tricks used by con-men and touts is to choose a critical moment for saying to a traveller, 'Don't you trust me?' The well-intentioned traveller usually answers, 'Of course I trust you', and this puts the tout in an advantageous position. A better answer is, 'No, I'm sorry, I don't trust anyone unless I've known them for ten years, and I've only had the pleasure of knowing you for five minutes.'

* *The Tourist Trap* (Pan, 1985)

Harassment of women

Throughout most of the tropics women are considered as second-class citizens. I once stunned a family in the Upper Volta by revealing that the British were ruled by two women – the Queen and Mrs Thatcher. After they had recovered from the shock, they asked me what the husband of the Queen did for a living: *'Est-ce qu'il est fonctionnaire?'* In Sarawak, I once pointed to a poster of the Queen, and asked the house-owner who she was. He replied, 'I think she must be the wife of King Philip.' In most parts of the Third World parents yearn to produce boys instead of girls, and the richer families (who can afford to check) are aborting babies of the wrong sex. Women are frequently expected to walk behind their husbands, and often have to do most of the manual work; in many parts of Asia and Africa women are sent out of the house when they are menstruating. In Muslim areas their second-class status is also enshrined in religious custom. Muslim intellectuals like to make debating points about how their women are cosseted, but in practice, the more fundamentalist the country the more women are kept subdued. And in Chapter 4 of the Koran (considered the infallible word of God), we are told:

Men have authority over women because God has made the one superior to the other, and because they spend their wealth to maintain them. Good women are obedient. They guard their unseen parts because God has guarded them. As for those from whom you fear disobedience, admonish them and send them to bed apart and beat them.*

Because women are expected to marry young, stay at home, and devote themselves entirely to family, women travellers are often treated with mistrust. And in many countries (including European ones, of course) they suffer from sexual harassment.

Nevertheless, although some women's travels are spoilt by harassment, thousands of others travel with great enjoyment; many of our most famous travellers have been women, several

---

* *The Koran*, translated by N. J. Dawood (Penguin, 1990)

of them in those Muslim countries which are supposed to be so difficult. Sometimes women have an advantage over men, because there are more people who are prepared to help and protect them.

Even when it's not possible entirely to ignore sexual harassment, there are many ways of diminishing it. So I am setting out a whole menu of possibilities. No single one of these will solve the problem, and a remedy which may be effective in one area may be useless in another. But a novice will find some of these ideas helpful, and anyone can mix and match according to circumstances.

The most important advice is to dress appropriately. It is not fair to complain about harassment if you have offended local sensibilities by wearing tight T-shirts with shorts. Although there are resorts where the local people are accustomed to this type of clothing, there are many more areas where they aren't.

Find out which parts of the body cause the greatest offence (often not the same as in Europe). Legs, for instance, may be far more shocking than breasts. Exposing the knees, elbows or shoulders, even occasionally the ankles, is often considered taboo.

Nor is it necessarily enough to cover up your bare skin. It is often the bulges or curves that should be covered; therefore in conservative regions you should wear loose clothes that hide your figure. The same is true for men: trousers (and especially shorts) that are too tight in the crotch are usually considered vulgar and offensive.

Although trousers cover all your leg, they aren't always considered respectable for women, and in Malawi are actually illegal.

Skirts are often considered more respectable. They can also be an aid to discreet peeing. If you stay in traditional houses, skirts should be large enough and loose enough for sitting decorously on the floor, and ideally long enough to cover the soles of your feet (which may be taboo to expose).

In many Muslim countries you will dramatically reduce harassment if you wear a headscarf. Try it. In countries such as Turkey, where many people are pale, you might almost pass as a local. Even if not, you will earn extra respect for having tried. (Although it is arguable whether the Koran requires women to cover their face, there is no doubt about its injunction for them to cover their hair).

Several women who have travelled to the East told me that they have worn the salwar kameez – a Punjabi costume of loose baggy trousers and a pyjama-style top. This is cool, practical, and may diminish harassment in difficult areas. Unlike the sari, which nearly always looks graceless on Western women, the salwar kameez can be worn with some dignity. It is still obvious, of course, that you are a foreigner, especially if you don't wear the dupatta, which covers the head to show modesty and is draped around the shoulders to conceal the bust.

Sunglasses can be a great help, for they enable women to look in any direction without making eye contact.

Be very wary of empty beaches, especially during evening and night-time. Judging from anecdotal evidence, beaches are favourite locations for rapists. And anecdotal evidence is often all we can judge from, because holiday destinations tend to be very careful about hushing up rapes.

As I've said in Chapter 7, very reluctantly I have come to the conclusion that a lone woman shouldn't hitch-hike. In some countries a woman is probably safe in ninety-nine cases out of a hundred. But when you think what could happen on that hundredth occasion, the risk isn't worth it.

When travelling on public transport be aware that there are often unofficial (or sometimes official) seating areas for women. The front (or back) of a bus, for instance, may be the preferred place, and this will be helpful because other women will protect you.

Harassment is almost invariably worse for a single woman. Locals just can't believe that she isn't game. Depending on the area, harassment may in varying degrees be reduced when a woman travels with another woman. It is nearly always dramatically reduced (but not infallibly) when she travels with a man, even if that man is her son. Locals wouldn't normally dream of insulting a woman with a man, because they would be offending the honour of that man.

If you aren't travelling with a man, it is sometimes still wise to wear a wedding ring (though this isn't recognized universally), and to invent a husband and three children. If you are travelling with a man who isn't your husband, then it may still be best to describe him as your husband, or you may be considered a loose woman.

It can be very helpful to know a few appropriate words in the local language. A friend of mine bothered to learn the Turkish for, 'Fuck off, I'm old enough to be your grandmother.' Several women have reported that it is effective to know the local word for 'shame'. Know the local word for police (usually 'police'!). In some countries, however, you will learn that the police are as bad as any of the other men; but in some other countries people are so terrified of them that they will stop harassing you.

On the whole, though, a few polite words in a foreign language are more effective, and they will slightly alter your status from 'fair-game tourist' to 'civilized foreigner'.

If you are actually groped, it may be necessary to show anger, as otherwise the groper may presume you like it. Try to call other women to your help; they will often be effectively abusive.

In the section on unofficial guides and touts (page 338), I have mentioned that it is often convenient to pretend ignorance of any well-known language. This prevents any conversation at all. Once you've begun dialogue, it is hard to extract yourself.

Having dealt with a number of practical points I shall now mention some psychological aspects of avoiding harassment.

Although it may sound unlikely, a particular woman might walk down a street with no harassment, but five minutes later a similar woman, similarly dressed, might walk down the same street and be harassed all the way. The first woman has learnt to walk with confidence; she is carefree and she doesn't show fear.

To a surprising extent, people treat you as you expect to be treated.

It might be easier for you to hype yourself into confidence if you consider that harassment isn't necessarily inevitable – after all, *in most places the locals don't harass their own women.* That is one reason why it may be helpful to wear a scarf in Turkey.

Showing anger or annoyance only excites your tormentors, so I will try to make some excuses for your tormentors, and therefore hope to make you feel a little less angry with them. Remember that in most areas of harassment there is a strict rule that women must be virgins when they marry. Therefore sexual opportunity for young men is severely limited and usually restricted to the expensive local brothel; a visit to a prostitute in Istanbul costs nearly a week's wages. Also remember that a man often can't afford a bride until he is entering middle age. When you consider all this, and when you take into account that Western women are considered to be loose – partly because of Western films and videos, and partly because of the behaviour of a few women travellers – then it is not surprising that the local men hope you are Mae West on the loose.

When facing any type of problem (including sexual harassment) with strangers, it is nearly always best to go laughing and smiling on to the offensive rather than retreat grumpily into your shell. The indomitable Dervla Murphy has argued this excellently in an article in the *Traveller*, so I will quote her at length:

When dealing with animals, we invite attack if we are afraid. When dealing with men, women may invite harassment if they are always on the defensive – aware of, and scared by, the possibility of sexual assault. They are then, in a sense, unconsciously challenging the men around them. And as often as not, their attitude initially provokes resentment rather than lust, though this resentment may be expressed by aggressive sexual advances . . . Teasing lone Western women, and watching them over-react, has become a sport in many cities on the beaten tourist track. To mistake this irritating, but harmless, hobby for unbridled lust is an error that merely spurs young men on to further displays of mock lechery. The best antidote is to make a joke of the incident. If the

337

molesting male receives a broad grin and a friendly teasing remark, instead of an indignant reprimand, an icy stare, or a terrified shriek, he is likely to be completely disarmed. Having only made the pass to annoy, and having failed to provoke the desired effect, he may quickly repent, and declare himself your good (platonic) friend. I have spent many relaxed evenings with men who, on first acquaintance, were striving desperately to seem like the local sex maniac. And sometimes they have admitted, as chaste goodbyes were being said, that talking to foreign women is actually far more interesting than fornicating with them.

The solitary woman can be viewed as a soft target for revengeful persecution by men who have no intention of ever laying a finger on her. These men get their kicks out of taunting, frightening and degrading this representative of a race which, for centuries, treated non-Europeans with a certain lack of consideration. However, this situation may be quite easily defused. If one shows no fury, outrage or panic, surprising developments are possible – especially in Muslim countries. By ignoring the sniggers, jeers or filthy gestures, the woman appears to be preoccupied or puzzled. She can then ask her antagonist for advice, guidance or help – anything that will arouse his sense of responsibility towards the stranger in his land . . . This technique of suddenly changing one's status from 'tourist' to 'guest' almost always improves the atmosphere. Many a man finding his 'aggro' unnoticed, and his victim frankly showing dependence on him, suddenly reverts to normal. You may well find yourself spending the evening talking to him, instead of being trapped in some drearily safe tourist hotel.

Half the Earth (for further details see Appendix 1) is a collection of women's experiences of travel worldwide. At the end of each geographical section the book gives additional travel notes.

Unofficial guides and touts

Touts of various types are a regular human hazard of the tropics, and in some areas they are so maddening that they can spoil holidays. By general agreement the worst are in Morocco. However, once you know how to deal with the problem, they need never be a major problem; here are a few hints on coping with them.

The first and easiest solution is to hire one. Touts have their own communal etiquette, and once one is hired, no one else will bother you. If you choose well, they can take you to interesting places and generally be useful. You will have gained benefit for yourself, and meanwhile spread some money into the local economy.

The great problem with touts is that once you've hired them, they want to lead you into endless shops, where they will get commission on purchases. This problem is easily dealt with. Once you've agreed your daily rate, say $5, then explain to your guide that you will pay him a bonus of $2 at the end of the day *on the strict condition that he on no account leads you into any shop*. He will still probably have one attempt at leading you into a shop, but if you remind him that he is about to lose the bonus, you shouldn't have any more trouble.

If you don't want a guide, or if you want to stave them off until you have chosen a suitable one, then the trick is to speak not a single word of a known language. Once you have answered a single tout's question (usually, 'Where are you coming from?') you are hooked. Instead, when the tout first talks to you; give him your warmest smile, and reply in an invented language or a remote dialect of Albanian. When the tout realizes that he can't communicate, he soon gives up in despair.

When you do answer questions, you will be asked if you are travelling alone. Women should err on the safe side by never admitting to being entirely alone; if necessary they should invent a local contact.

Adulteration

A minor problem is the adulteration of food and goods. Travellers aren't likely to be bothered by the widespread adulteration of cement (unless a ceiling falls on their heads), but they will be affected by the adulteration of food, especially if they are doing their own catering, or buying provisions for an expedition.

While I was in Colombo, the city analyst, Mr da Silva, tested 782 different food samples. He found that 386 of them were adulterated. Of the eighteen milk samples, thirteen of them were adulterated. All of the gingelly oil samples had been mixed with coconut oil. None of the three arrowroot samples contained a trace of arrowroot; they were made up of wheat and maize starch. Mr da Silva pointed out that arrowroot is normally recommended for children suffering from diarrhoea, and that such adulteration would aggravate their illness.

If food bought by a discerning public is so frequently adulterated, imagine what goes into those drugs which are sold in quick covert deals to itinerant hippies! When I was in Afghanistan I heard that a junior member of the British Embassy had sent a sample of hashish for analysis to a laboratory in England. The puzzled answer came back that they couldn't identify all the ingredients, but one of them was conclusively identified as the pulverised grounds of 78 r.p.m. records.

The most dangerous type of adulteration is that of illegal home-brewed alcohol; occasionally this kills people by the dozen.

Misinformation

In some parts of the world you are safe from thieving, but you are never safe from misinformation. Even the most experienced travellers are occasionally misled. When I was searching for the offices of Royal Brunei Airlines in Manila, a helpful travel agent convincingly assured me that they were managed by TWA, who had their offices in the Hilton Hotel on Boulevard Roxas, which was the third street on the left. It turned out that Boulevard Roxas was not the third street on the left; when I found it I discovered the Hilton Hotel was elsewhere; when I arrived at the Hilton, it didn't house TWA; and when I finally reached TWA it wasn't a total surprise that they didn't manage Royal Brunei Airlines.

It is hard to explain why misinformation is disseminated with such panache. It is partly due to a desire never to refuse to help, partly to a reluctance to reveal ignorance, partly to politeness. Most of it is inexplicable. It is not surprising that anthropologists so often accuse each other of having been hoodwinked.

Even straightforward facts can be hard to pin down. In South-east Asia I noticed many cats with docked tails. The first person I interrogated said it was done to make the cats good mousers; elsewhere I was told that the Chinese cut the tails off so that the cats wouldn't jump over a dead body (thus turning it into a zombie); a travel book informed me that the tails were cut off to provide a valued ingredient for medicines; and a guidebook claimed that butchers cut off cats' tails if they had stolen meat. A resident Englishman, the owner of a tailless cat, told me that his cat had given birth to four kittens – all of them without a tail.

Although myth-making is common, it is far more prevalent in some areas than others, and one's scepticism can be reduced or increased accordingly. I once spent two weeks interrogating some Chinese about how they fished with cormorants. Among the many facts they told me, I never discovered a single inaccuracy, and they never once indulged in the types of tall story that are encountered in so many parts of the world.

If you wish to avoid misinformation, the crucial rule is *Never ask a leading question – never put words into someone's mouth*. I consider this one of the golden rules of travel. Inexperienced travellers frequently ask a question such as, 'Will the train for La Badia leave at 5.23?' The answer will always be, 'Yes.' The correct question should be, 'Where is that train going?' If this is answered by, 'La Badia', you then say, 'What time will it be leaving?', which you hope will be answered by '5.23.' Similarly, a prospective fisherman should never ask, 'Are there many fish in this river?', for the answer will always be, 'Yes, very many.' He should ask, 'Has a fish been caught here during the last year?' If the answer is 'Yes', then he should ask, 'When was it caught? Who caught it?'

Another important defence against misinformation is to check the reliability of your informant. Thus, if you want to know the distance from La Badia to Marimba, first ask him the distance from La Badia to Baramba, which you already know to be 200 miles. If he answers 20 miles, you will have an idea that he's not entirely reliable.

Bribery

The first point to realize about bribery is that it is immoral. Foolish people say, 'It has always been the tradition. When in Rome, do as the Romans do. It is best to adapt to the local customs.' But bribery isn't just a quaint custom; anyone who stops to think about the implications of bribery will realize that it is one of the most grievous blights of the Third World. Bribery is the champion of the rich against the poor, and of the strong against the weak. If a wealthy landowner wants to take over the small plot of a miserable peasant, he has only to bribe the relevant official in the land registration departments. Bribery ensures that large building contracts go to the corrupt contractor who builds with adulterated cement, and that substandard tractors are imported by the monopoly importer who has bribed the relevant minister. Where there is bribery there is inefficiency, and in the Third World inefficiency equals suffering and degradation. So whenever possible, travellers should avoid encouraging such an insidious disease.

If you do succumb to the temptation to bribe a tiresome immigration officer, you also make life much worse for all the travellers who follow behind you. Once officials discover bribery as a source of easy money, they make the lives of travellers a misery.

The countries most afflicted by bribe-hungry officials tend to be those which have been most visited by nylon-shirted businessmen. Nigeria is the worst example. Although there is quite a lot of corruption in some Asian countries, this rarely causes problems for outsiders. A journalist who has worked for years in many Asian countries told me that he has never once felt obliged to pay a bribe (although on occasions it might have made his life a little easier).

Despite my pious lecture on resisting bribery, I must admit there are occasions when it is almost essential. In West Africa I have met miserable travellers who have been forced to make 100-mile detours because an immigration official has found a 'fault' in their visa. They hadn't realized he was fishing for a bribe, and a gift of £3 (or sometimes even a tiny present, such as a lighter) might have saved them great expense and trouble.

It can be embarrassing giving bribes, but you soon get the knack, and the recipient rarely seems to suffer shame. A well-known dodge is to put a few notes inside a passport (or whatever document you are handing over); though this is rather obvious, it does enable you to deny you ever knew the money was there. Another method is to say, 'In my country we usually pay an on-the-spot fine, is that appropriate here?' If this is followed by a friendly gleam in the eye, you know a bribe is in order.

The South American Handbook sensibly warns:

Never offer a bribe unless you are fully conversant and up to date with the customs of the country . . . Do not assume that an official who accepts a bribe is prepared to do anything else illegal. You bribe him to persuade him to do his job, or to persuade him not to do it, or to do it more quickly, or more slowly. You do not bribe him to do something which is against the law. The mere suggestion would make him very upset.

Obstructive officials

When you have a difficult time with officials, keep your temper. This may seem obvious advice, but many travellers exacerbate problems by falling into impotent rages. Always remember that once you have been abusive, you have lost the option of sweet reason. And it is usually a disaster if your angry words make someone lose face. If you start with sweet reason at first, and it fails, then you still have the option of losing your temper. Even so, any tantrum is usually counter-productive; in fact I have noticed time and again that even the most tense situations can be defused by a joke.

When you are completely in the right, and an official is being vicious outside his legal powers, you must threaten. The one threat that terrifies most officials in developing countries is the prospect of losing their job: too many sisters, brothers, uncles, and children are dependent on their salary. Make sure you know in advance the name of a government minister, so you can say to the official, 'Mr Addima is a very good friend of mine; unless you behave correctly, I will report you to him, and you will lose your job within the week.' This usually works. When a customs officer at Kinshasa Airport seized £200 from me, I told him that I was a friend of Mobutu's daughter (I had shaken her hand in London), and that if he didn't return the cash immediately, he would lose his job. I could see he didn't believe me, but the cash was handed back. He couldn't afford to take the risk.

Don't feel in awe of officials; if you are reasonably well dressed you should have confidence. When you are about to have dealings with them, shake them by the hand. Not only is this a friendly gesture, but it helps reduce their automatic position of superiority. I find that shaking hands (though in some countries not with women) is appreciated in many circumstances – even when it isn't the local custom. In this respect the British should learn to behave more like the French.

Beggars

It is impossible to give money to every beggar, but don't believe absurd stories about them all being secret millionaires. In countries without social security, tragedies such as loss of land, famine, or widowhood can force people into beggary when they have no relatives to support them.

If you have enjoyed your travels, you can ease your conscience by giving money to a charity active in the Third World. To my mind one of the best is the Royal Commonwealth Society for the Blind (Grosvenor Hall, Bolnore Road, Haywards Heath, Sussex RH16 4BX; tel. 0444 412424), which each year restores sight to more than quarter of a million people.

When leaving a country I make a habit of giving all my loose change to the lavatory attendants at airports. If they have such an awful job, they are unlikely to be secret millionaires; and one's coins are valueless after returning home.

A caution

I hope all the alarms I have sounded in this chapter only make the traveller cautious – not paranoid. In hot climates it is all too easy for travellers to wind themselves up into a state of tension and misanthropy. It is better to be cheated than to live in a constant state of worry and suspicion.

Once in Bangkok, when I was particularly exhausted and fed up with being cheated, a taxi driver appeared to give me the wrong change for a 50-baht note. He claimed I had given him only 20 baht. I politely asked him for the right change; he refused. I lost my temper (which in Thailand is considered gross bad manners), and lectured him at length about dishonesty; but my tirade produced no change. I made him empty his pockets, which was also unsuccessful. As there seemed no end to the dispute, we stalked into the hotel to find someone who could speak better English. The receptionist, who fulfilled this function, explained to me that I couldn't have given the driver a 50-baht note because – at that time – there was no such thing. I still blush to think what would have happened if there had been a 50-baht note. I would have harangued the innocent man for hours, and in desperation he might have given me some of his own hard-earned money.

CHAPTER 11

CULTURE SHOCK

On the first page of his book about being a Peace Corps worker in Ecuador, Moritz Thomsen wrote: 'The final discovery, that we are all ultimately alike, is a hard-earned revelation. And it is well worth the trouble.'* Although a thousand travel writers have echoed his sentiments, what he wrote isn't true. Unsentimental travellers will discover that the differences between cultures are so fundamental that it is almost impossible for people to fully comprehend another culture unless they have been immersed in it during childhood. In fact a full reading of Moritz Thomsen's otherwise perceptive book shows that there was an insuperable gulf between him and the coastal people of Ecuador.

Although travellers are treated almost everywhere with friendliness, many of them have difficulty adapting to the rhythms of another country. A few hours' flight takes them to a land where the ways of thinking and patterns of behaviour are often quite different – even when disguised by a veneer of Westernization. When you walk on land after several days on a boat, you feel giddy and unbalanced, because you have subconsciously adapted your gait to the rolling of the sea. In a similar way, the effect of a new culture is disorienting even for the most easy-going. The endless variations in behaviour, customs, and manners in different countries often cause a culture shock, which has a disturbing effect on one's equilibrium.

Culture shock, combined with the effects of a hot climate, often results in severe mental stress, especially for the inflexible. Psychiatric problems are a common reason for costly repatriation

*_Living Poor_ (University of Washington Press, 1969)

of employees and families from tropical and subtropical areas. Almost a third of overseas employees give up their jobs before the end of their contracts. And even many of the expatriates who manage to survive in the tropics seem slightly unbalanced; some develop bizarre eccentricities; some become alcoholics; and a few seem to hate the local people with a quite irrational passion.

The worst problems can nearly always be avoided by developing harmonious and rewarding relationships with the local people. This chapter is an attempt to highlight the obstacles that might hinder these relationships, and to give a few hints for enhancing them.

If you still get a fit of gloom, be comforted by the knowledge that this is common among travellers. Personally I find that, though I remain mostly cheerful at home, the exhilaration of travel is occasionally interrupted by brief, unaccountable, and severe depressions. It is also very common for travellers to get bouts of depression after returning home from a long trip. This is probably also caused by culture shock.

Language

Learning some of the local language will make a huge difference in the quality of your travels. Even a few words will enable you to communicate quite effectively, and your efforts will be appreciated. Once you have learnt a few sentences you will be told you speak better than a native. And when you are in areas filled with tourists, you will be marked apart and treated better.

Most travellers make the mistake of not learning a language because, despite efforts by the French, English has now won the battle to become the lingua franca of the world. English is the agreed language for 156 out of 168 of the world's airlines; even the Russian pilot of an Aeroflot jet talks to the Moscow control tower in English. Half of all business in the Netherlands is negotiated in English, and in India alone there are 3,000 English-language newspapers.

But don't let this encourage you to be lazy about learning a foreign language, because even a few words can make a crucial difference. I will give an example. After landing at Guilin airport in southern China (a few days before the Tiananmen Square massacre), I was keen to discover what the ordinary Chinese thought about their government. Unfortunately, my taxi driver spoke only Chinese. I wanted to ask him, 'Do you think Deng Xiaoping is a good man or a bad man?' This was difficult, because I had found Chinese very hard to learn, and I had already forgotten the word for bad. So I was reduced to asking, 'Deng Xiaoping, *hao? Bu hao?*' (Deng Xiaoping, good? No good?) The answer was an emphatic, '*Bu hao*', repeated several times during the journey. When I got to my hotel, I asked the porter. The answer was the same. Next morning, a straw-hatted young woman tried to sell me a puppy. I asked her and got the same answer. In fact everyone had the same answer. So, with just two words of Chinese, I was able to gauge the opinions of a quarter of the world's population.

I have attempted to devise a universal survival list of approximately forty words which, along with the numerals, will cover a huge amount of situations in any country. I have listed them in Appendix 5.

I write these words down on one side of a blank postcard (which can be shoved in the back of a book), and on the other side I write the numerals. I keep this with me, and when there are any moments of longueur (bus-stops, and so on) I learn a few more words, or test my memory. It is even better to learn them before you leave home, for it isn't difficult to spend ten days learning only four words and four numerals a day.

Although this list of approximately forty words is aimed mostly at survival and muddling through, you will be astonished at quite how much conversation you can have with them. They also make an excellent springboard for a second stage of learning, which becomes much easier once you can distinguish a few of the more common words.

A few points about **learning the language**. Even if your vocabulary is excellent, you won't be understood unless you pronounce the words correctly. Stress is also very important: apparently it is very difficult for us not to stress part of a word, but it is worth knowing that in some languages the delivery is neutral. It is also helpful to know that in many languages the stress is often in the same place (unlike in English): for instance, in Italy the stress is usually on the second to last syllable; in Finnish it is always on the first one. In order to get your stress and pronunciation right, go through your vocabulary list with someone local, making phonetic notes. Preferably, you will have used some language tapes before you have left home.

Good **language tapes** are a wonderful help. They can be used during wasted times, such as driving; and they are the most effective way of getting your accent right. The best method of learning is to use the accompanying manual as well as listening to the tapes; the value of the two combined is greater than the sum of their parts. When you have struggled with certain words on the tape, and then read them in the manual, they somehow become fixed in your brain. The manual alone doesn't have the power to drum the words into your subconscious. I also like tapes because, if I ever need to return to the same language, then, by listening to them once again, the words I have forgotten can be miraculously resurrected from the hard disk of my brain.

With good tapes, it is possible to learn the rudiments of a language remarkably quickly. Although I have a bad memory and no ear for languages, I learnt (within a fortnight before departure) enough Spanish to manage basic conversation in Peru, even risking a simple discussion about the Falklands War. The tapes I used were from the excellent BBC courses *Get by in Spanish* and *Digame*. Be careful with your selection of tapes, for there is a big difference between them. Check that they lead you *gently* into the language, and that the initial conversations are simple ones which will definitely be useful, such as, 'Where is . . .', 'How much is . . .?', 'I cannot speak Spanish . . .' Some of the courses begin with, 'My uncle, Pedro, is cutting logs', 'I go out for a walk in the neighbourhood each day.' On the whole, the BBC beginners' tapes are excellent (though the Arabic one is a bit muddling). However, their *phrasebook* tapes are in my experience nowhere near as useful as the *Get by in* ones.

The BBC have recently produced language video tapes, which might be a good way of learning the rudiments of a language. For further inquiries about any types of BBC language courses, telephone 081 746 1111.

Should you need further information about learning languages, or should you need to learn one of the rarer ones, such as Hungarian or Punjabi, contact CILT (The Centre for Information on Language Teaching and Research. Regent's College, Inner Circle, Regent's Park, London NW1 4NS; tel. 071 486 8221).

In Chapter 3 I describe how you should choose your pocket dictionary. A phrasebook might be helpful as well.

Grant & Cutler (55 Great Marlborough Street, London W1V 1DD; tel. 071 734 2012) stock the best collection of language-learning books in Britain.

If you are ambitious to learn more than my survival list of forty words, try to start learning your language as far in advance as possible, because it is better and more enjoyable to learn the language little by little. It has been said that learning a language is like making mayonnaise – if you put in too much at one go, the whole lot curdles. Instead you should learn just a few words every day, and keep repeating them to yourself while chopping onions, sitting on a lavatory, standing on a tube platform. Sir Richard Burton, one of the greatest linguists of all time, wrote that he tried never to learn languages for more than quarter of an hour at a time because 'the brain loses its freshness'.

An effective and enjoyable way of improving your fluency is to read the local comic-strip magazines.

Remember that the vocabulary used by uneducated people is comparatively small (various studies of farm labourers and fruit-pickers have put their everyday vocabulary at no more than 500 words), so even a few words a day over a longish period will give you a good working knowledge of a language.

Because my memory is exceptionally bad, I have to resort to mnemonics in order to improve my vocabulary. Anthony Burgess, in *Language Made Plain*,★ claims he can use mnemonics to memorize any word in any language:

I have no very special linguistic aptitude; moreover, I have a very bad memory. And so I resort to the most fantastic of mnemonics. The word for 'if' in Malay is '*kalau*'. This is easy enough. Kipling wrote 'If'; 'Kipling' rhymes with 'stripling': a stripling is a callow person; 'callow' is close to *kalau*. The two other, more literary, words for 'if' are '*likalau*' and '*lika*', easily remembered when one has planted the strong mnemonic root of the basic word. Some mnemonics are essentially personal. '*Kawan*' is 'friend': I had a friend called Cowan. Others are ultra-ingenious. '*Bernastautin*' is borrowed from Arabic and means 'to settle in a country, be domiciled'. I formed an image of a stout-drinking Scotsman lying in somebody else's bed, saying 'Ah'm settled here. Bear ma stout in.' To remember '*mualif*', another Arabic loan-word meaning an editor of a newspaper, I had to make a tortuous rhyme: If you've been drinking, chew a leaf/of mint before visiting the '*mualif*'. This had to be pinned down in my head with an image of a hard-drinking newspaper reporter. I pride myself upon being able to devise mnemonics (some of them so childish as to be shameful) for any foreign word in existence.

Russian is a language which, though it belongs to the Indo-European family, contains many hard words, hard to learn and to remember. We can dispose of words like '*brat*' meaning 'brother' (my brat of a brother), and '*sad*' meaning 'garden' (A flowerless garden is a sad sight) with little enough trouble, but have to think hard with words like the following:

Nozh – knife (try – Eat your nosh with a knife)

Voda – water (try – Mr K is so fiery he turns water into Vodka)

Karandash – pencil (try – get into the car and dash off that note with a pencil)

Sobaka – dog (try – that dog is so much of a barker)

Activities

Most travellers, whether rich tourists or budget backpackers, usually tour a country by visiting the appropriate sights. They

★ (English Universities Press, 1964)

351

study the guidebooks to establish a programme, and this programme is organized around a framework of beauty spots,
beaches, nature reserves, or archaeological remains. This is inevitable because most Westerners are fidgety, and their fidgetiness
can't be sated by pot-luck excursions to a patch of countryside
where there might be nothing to do. There is, though, a problem
with sightseeing: everyone reads the same guidebooks, and therefore visits the same places. The popular destinations rapidly
assume a different atmosphere to the rest of the country, and
after visiting them, a traveller with an inquiring mind is depressed
by never having got to grips with the place. In *Riding the Iron
Rooster* Paul Theroux has described sightseeing as, 'Primarily a
distraction and seldom even an amusement. It has all the boredom
and ritual of a pilgrimage and none of the spiritual benefit.'
Elsewhere he has described it as 'the saddest pleasure'.

One way of avoiding the constraints of sightseeing is to involve yourself with any other activity, especially those bringing
you into contact with the people of the country.

If you collect butterflies, study plants, or watch birds, you
visit areas where the average tourist never goes; a railway engine
enthusiast has an excellent reason for visiting new corners of
India and making new friends; a musicologist studying harps in
West Africa will have insights denied to even the most adventurous travellers. In China I spent a fortnight studying cormorant
fishermen (for an article), and during that time I learnt more
about the Chinese character than I would have done during a
whole year on the sightseeing trail. Hallam Murray's bicycle ride
of 17,000 miles through South America would have been comparatively sterile if he hadn't had an obsession with pottery. This
gave him a good excuse to make numerous detours, and to share
enthusiasms with remote villagers. Fishermen, too, have excuses
to visit the most unspoilt stretches of countryside – whether the
hill streams of Kashmir or the idyllic rivers of New Zealand.

If you don't have a hobby, try to think of any diversion that
will take you away from the usual tourist beat. In an English-
speaking country a trip to the law courts might be interesting; in

both South Africa and Ghana they gave me a fascinating insight into the character of the countries.

Working abroad

Working is one activity which will certainly involve you in communicating with the local people.

Voluntary work is a possibility if you are staying away for a long time. Volunteers have no opportunity to indulge in sentimentality (see page 356), but this doesn't prevent them forming strong ties of affection with local people. In most Western countries there are organizations which recruit volunteers for the developing world; in Britain the most famous is VSO (Voluntary Service Overseas) which at any one time sends more than a thousand volunteers between the ages of eighteen and seventy to work in more than forty countries. Their range of projects is enormous, and more than seventy different skills can be used; but VSO, like similar organizations, is reluctant to accept those who don't have special skills that can be passed on to a local person; their intake is mostly from an older age group than those previously accepted. A charity that doesn't require them is Earthwatch, an organization which uses volunteers to work with a very wide variety of overseas projects, mostly concerning the environment and wildlife. These projects include tagging sharks, monitoring lemurs, and experimenting with solar ovens. The volunteers pay (high) fees, and can join projects for periods as short as a fortnight. In Appendix 1 there is a list of publications giving details of overseas projects and voluntary work, and in Appendix 3 a list of relevant institutions.

Even business transactions offer some type of authentic communication with local people. I met a volunteer who had set up a T-shirt printing business; it was highly successful and he could never keep pace with demand. Unfortunately, if you are on the move, opportunities for making money are limited. A few travellers, however, are resourceful, and I have read of two travellers who were able to travel round Latin America because of their skill at mending typewriters. It was a skill that could be used in any city, and the necessary equipment fitted into a small case.*

Those who are seriously considering financing their travels by working should read an excellent publication, *Work Your Way around the World* (see Appendix 1), which covers a wide variety of jobs from teaching cricket to packing fish. (It also includes useful sections on voluntary work.) The refreshingly unsentimental author doesn't flinch from admitting that certain jobs, such as grape-harvesting, may be both dull and back-breaking.

We are incredibly lucky that English has become the lingua franca of the world, and unless you have some other special skill, **teaching English** is usually by far your best hope of getting temporary employment abroad. There are countries, such as Japan, where you could easily become an English teacher even though you would be most unlikely to find any other job. Teaching will also give you the opportunity to meet local families who would never normally talk to a tourist.

Having decided that you would like to teach English, your next decision will be whether to get a Teaching English as a Foreign Language (TEFL) certificate. Although you might shrink at the idea, it is well worth considering. A one-month TEFL course will almost certainly guarantee you a job in a great many countries, and your training academy will probably have very good overseas contacts for obtaining jobs. The courses are also valuable for reminding you of grammar (which you will have forgotten) and instructing you in teaching (which you have probably never known). Susan Griffith points out that there is sometimes a moral obligation to take a TEFL course: your students have often invested a lot of money in hiring you, and it isn't fair if they know more about the subjunctive than you do.

The most recognized certificates abroad are the ones under the auspices of RSA/UCLES (University of Cambridge Local Exam-

* *World Understanding on Two Wheels*, Paul Pratt (privately published edition, 1980)

ination Syndicate). The main rivals are the qualifications under the auspices of Trinity College London. Susan Griffith comments:

If the RSA qualifications are as internationally well known as, say, American Express traveller's cheques, the Trinity College qualifications are more like National Westminister Bank traveller's cheques. They serve the same function and cost about the same, but are less instantly recognized. Trinity prefers to compare itself to Avis with their famous slogan 'We try harder', and says that in a few years' time the order may be reversed.

The disadvantages of the TEFL courses are that they are extremely hard work, and that they are expensive. They usually last for a very intensive four weeks. Some colleges of further education and universities hold state-run courses where prices are very cheap. These are nearly always offered on a part-time basis only, usually one or two evenings a week for the academic year. They tend to get very booked.

If you do decide to undergo a TEFL course, your best source book will be the 320-page *Teaching English Abroad* by Susan Griffith (see Appendix 1). As well as being useful for listing the courses, it also has chapters on finding jobs, problems at work, and an invaluable country-by-country guide. A comprehensive guide to all the courses on offer, both in Britain and abroad, revised annually, is published by EFL Ltd (64 Ormly Road, Ramsay, Isle of Man; tel. 0624 815926). A guide to the RSA/UCLES courses is produced by UCLES (Syndicate Buildings, 1 Hills Road, Cambridge, CB1 2EU; tel. 0223 61111). For information about Trinity College courses, contact the Group Administrator (Language) (16 Park Crescent, London W1N 4AH; tel. 071 323 2328). A free brochure (*Teaching Overseas*) about the role of the British Council in the world of TEFL is available from the Overseas Education Department (10 Spring Gardens, London SW1A 2BN; tel. 071 389 4931). Some TEFL courses are available abroad; and there are also some shorter introductory courses, which don't offer you a full certificate or diploma. There are many cowboys in the business, so consult *Teaching English Abroad*.

Sentimentality

If you have worked in a country, or if you know enough of the language to have really communicated with local people, then at least you won't come back talking the tosh which is perpetrated by so many returning travellers. I have met dozens of people who, before apartheid ended, came back from South Africa saying that it wasn't as bad as painted. If they had taken the trouble to ask black servants how often they saw their wives and children (who would have been living hundreds of miles away in a 'homeland'), or if they had visited the sections of Cape Town where non-white families were still being bulldozed out of traditional homes, they would have got a different picture.

Even shoe-string travellers, who in theory live far closer to the local people, are liable to sentimentalize. I remember one of them pointing to a village nestling under some coconut palms and saying: 'They sure are happy there – no hassles, no hang-ups; we've so much to learn from them.' It is true that we may have something to learn from them, but that traveller wasn't going to learn it, for he didn't speak the language, and knew nothing of their lives. I did have a small insight into their lives because a friend of mine worked there. He told me that this idyllic village was the scene of a vicious land dispute which had meant that during the last ten years one half of the village hadn't spoken to the other; most of the husbands had been obliged to leave the village for work elsewhere; most of the few remaining males were alcoholics; dysentery was rife; and several children had gone blind through lack of medical attention. Even when people aren't groaning in a gutter, their lives may still be troubled.

The serenity of Sinhalese villages is often applauded by foreigners who don't realize that one-third of the children are stunted for life by malnutrition. In Egypt almost half the population suffer the wretched effects of bilharzia; in much admired Tanzania about 40 per cent of the population is severely debilitated by hookworm, bilharzia, or filariasis.

Travellers are especially liable to become sentimental about countries which are difficult to visit. When China was almost impenetrable, the Chinese were described as models of honesty. Numerous journalists and writers recounted tales about discarded razor-blades being returned by ultra-honest hotel staff. In fact the hotel staff knew perfectly well that the razor-blades had been discarded. The credulous visitors never seemed to notice that the Chinese always locked their bicycles, that walls were topped with splintered glass, or that iron bars were installed in first-floor windows. More perceptive travellers discovered that an infallibly successful present was a padlock.

Bali is constantly described as a paradise on earth, both by writers and by expatriates who live there. What they never mention is that in 1965 the Balinese slaughtered more than 100,000 of their compatriots merely on account of their alleged political beliefs. The very few guidebooks which mention this massacre try to sentimentalize it by claiming that the victims dressed up in white robes before calmly awaiting their executions. I talked with one of the executioners, and he told me that the victims were dragged whimpering from their beds and were hacked to pieces with savagery.

Potential gaffes

This isn't intended to be a geographical guide to the gaffes of the world. That would take up far too much room, and I wouldn't have the knowledge. Besides, it would be too complicated: what may be taboo in Kano may be acceptable further south in Ibadan, and so on. However, it is worth covering the subject because a list of some potential gaffes will make you more *aware* of the various ways of causing offence; and some customs – which may be unknown to you – are so widespread that they are worth mentioning. Once you have been alerted to typical problems, you will be able to find out for yourself the relevant customs in the countries you visit.

Before discussing gaffes in more detail I must make a defensive point. I am aware that this chapter is filled with even more

357

generalizations than the rest of the book; I'm also aware that people get very hot under the collar about generalizations. But if one gives up generalizing, a lot of useful things get left unsaid; and it is dreary to qualify every statement that can be qualified. If I say that the French are better cooks than the Russians, this doesn't mean that I'm not aware that there may be plenty of dazzling Russian cooks – and plenty of hopeless French ones; but it is still a reasonable statement.

Here goes with my first generalization about gaffes. In large parts of the Third World it is rude to eat with your left hand, or to give or receive anything with it, because the left hand is used for lavatory purposes. (This is an additional reason why cutting off the right hand is such a grievous punishment: for ever after the criminal will have to eat alone.) I have so impressed upon myself the importance of always giving something with the right hand that I subconsciously do this even in Britain.

In many parts of Africa, the Middle East, and Asia it is still the tradition to eat with the hands, and many sophisticated people do so. Don't think, though, that there isn't an etiquette about eating with your hands, or you will be like the many Westerners who manage it so inelegantly. The Duke of Pirajno, who during the 1940s was a doctor in Libya, wrote about a chiding he received:

One evening after coffee it seemed the mother could no longer contain herself. She spoke in a low voice, and in order to make the pill more palatable she called me 'my son' instead of addressing me by my professional title.

'Listen, my son. Has no one ever told you that you eat like a camel herdsman? You use both hands, and look what a mess you are in. Your mouth is covered with grease – and even your nose. And you have stained your shirt. My son, whoever taught you your table manners?' She was as shocked and pained as an old duchess who, having invited the bailiff of her estate to dinner, sees him eat peas with a knife.

So it was from her that I learnt to take my food with the right hand only (at table the left hand is non-existent, since it performs the 'secret ablutions') and not to use more than three fingers. I learnt how to make little balls of semolina, rice or meat of the right size using only my thumb and first and second fingers, without dirtying the other fingers, or the palm of my hand. From her I learnt (seated cross-legged on the carpet) how to lean from the hips towards the central dish, just close enough to take a mouthful, without dropping grease either on the mat or on my clothes. I also achieved the art of two-finger eating, of popping the ball of food into my mouth without touching my lips, thus avoiding a greasy mouth or nose.*

In many areas you should remove your shoes before entering a house. Many people, quite rightly, think we are barbaric to bring the dirt from the street into our houses. Sometimes the removal of shoes is due to respect. In a Brahmin household in Calcutta I saw many shoes in the doorway, and therefore took off mine. The father of the house told me that it was only the servants who are obliged to take off their shoes.

Be careful about praising children. In parts of Africa and Asia, this is considered very unlucky, and likely to bring down the wrath of the gods.

In many areas, including much of the Muslim world and Africa, launderers will be insulted if they are given female under-wear.

Taboos about exposing flesh are usually far stronger than ours, and those who flaunt them cause unimaginable offence, and may even put themselves in danger. At Lake Bandi-i-Amir in Afghanistan naked bathers have even been shot by enraged local villagers. In Chapter 8 I have already mentioned that women should often be modest; but men must also be careful. Even in hammams (public baths/Turkish baths), it is the custom for men to keep their private parts well covered; in the streets of the Yemen, or the bazaars of Afghanistan, you won't see a man exposing even his arms.

It is rarely acceptable for a man and a woman to show physical affection in public.

In some countries we are considered eccentric – to say the least – for using a handkerchief for blowing our noses and then

* *A Cure for Serpents* (André Deutsch, 1955)

putting the dirty cloth back in our clothes. In Japan it is considered exceptionally shocking to blow your nose in public; the correct etiquette is to wait until you can do it in private.

The offensiveness of behaviour like farting greatly varies in different parts of the world. In Botswana I was accompanied by a white guide who used to proudly announce his forthcoming farts. In some countries it is still considered a disastrous breach of manners: on the island of Lamu in Kenya there is a man known as 'The man whose grandfather farted', and I have read of a traveller being forcibly ejected from a shop in Afghanistan on account of an involuntary fart.★ Many customs found in the Third World often existed at some stage in our own history, and the fierce taboo against farting is no exception. The seventeenth-century antiquary John Aubrey claimed that the Earl of Oxford emitted a fart when bowing to Queen Elizabeth I, as a result of which he felt obliged to go travelling for seven years. On his return, the Queen welcomed him with the words, 'My Lord, I had forgot the fart.'

In Europe we still bow to royalty, which is a survival of putting one's body in a lower, submissive posture. Most of this **physical etiquette** has now died out in the West, but it is often still important in the Third World. People tend to be far more aware of the height at which you are standing or sitting. It is often considered extremely rude to loom over someone, and when walking through sitting people, it is often the custom to bend your body. You will notice that people of inferior status will often take great care to sit at a lower level than their superiors; if other people are sitting on the floor, think twice before sitting in a chair.

In many parts of the Middle East and Asia it is bad manners to point your feet at anybody. Great care must be taken when sitting on the ground, and men are usually expected to sit cross-

★ *Overland and Beyond*, Theresa and Jonathan Hewat (privately published edition, 1976)

legged. When sitting on a chair, however, it may be rude to cross your legs, as this is more likely to expose the soles of your feet in someone's direction. In photographs of Arab dignitaries you never see them crossing their legs.

In many parts of the world, as far from each other as Fiji and Indonesia, it is rude to point a finger. Even the bushmen of South Africa point with their thumb. It may be rude to beckon with your palm upward (rather than downward).

I have read (but not yet succeeded in fully researching) an interesting example of physical etiquette. In Britain, when making one's way along cinema seats, one tends to face away from the other occupants. This is also true in France and Italy. But, apparently, in Germany and Sweden it is considered very rude to face someone with your bottom, and you would move along the row the other way round. Because Japanese customs are often the opposite of ours, I asked a nephew in Japan to investigate, and he confirmed that the Japanese follow the German style rather than ours.

Many of the traditional Chinese customs are also the opposite of ours. J. D. Vaughan, who in the last century documented the habits of the Overseas Chinese, wrote:

Many of the Chinese customs are just the reverse of ours – we mourn in black, they in white; we propel a boat with our back to the bow, they with their face to the front; we make the north point of the compass the chief point, they the south point. We take off our hats and shoes as a token of respect, they keep them on for the same purpose, we fan our faces to cool ourselves, they fan the antipodes to produce the same effect; in our names the surname is placed last, in theirs they place the surname first; their place of honour at table is on the left side, ours is on the right; they mount their horses on the right side, we on the left; their books are written from right to left, ours left to right; in speaking of dates they mention the year first then the month and lastly the day of the month; we give the day first then the month and lastly the year.★

★

★ *The Manners and Customs of the Chinese of the Straits Settlements* (Mission Press, Singapore, 1879)

Although a traveller obviously wouldn't adopt all the local customs, it may be appreciated if you try to adopt some. For instance, in India, when you want to give a gift of 20 rupees, or 100 rupees, it is more auspicious to give 21 rupees or 101 rupees. In a few countries it is polite to give something with *both* hands. In a very wide variety of countries (including parts of India, Botswana, Tanzania, Zaire, and Fiji) you will notice a remnant of this: traditional people will often touch their right arm with their left arm when handing you something.

A reader has sent me the following interesting comment:

It helps to avoid inter-cultural resentment by being aware of different time-keeping practices. In Britain and Germany one is expected to arrive five to ten minutes after the stated time for a social engagement; although many British these days seem to turn up an hour or more late, and still expect to be welcome. In North America one is expected to be exactly on time, a minute or two early is fine. Better early than late. An Indian family will not serve dinner until two or three hours after the time of invitation; have a snack at home before leaving. An essential when receiving Arab hospitality is to leave *immediately* after finishing the last course; run for the door as you are chewing the last mouthful. To stay any longer implies that you are waiting for something more.

I will end this section with a far more obvious breach of manners. It is self-evident that it is always offensive to say anything derogatory about someone's family or country, and I wouldn't bother mentioning the possibility if travellers weren't frequently lured into making this mistake. In Britain individuals sometimes refer disparagingly to their family – 'My sister is a perfect ninny' or 'My father is almost ga-ga'; but when someone agrees with them, they are invariably offended. Similarly, when Ghanaians say, as they are prone to do, 'We are a poor country – so corrupt, so inefficient, so many mistakes have we made', don't think this gives you carte blanche to say what you like. Despite whatever they have said, the Ghanaians are still likely to be devoted to their country. Remember, also, that in some places it is the custom to refer to possessions (including wives) in terms of eloquent – but feigned – disparagement.

Another snare

When walking through the ancient covered bazaar in Aleppo, I was delighted to see that many of the goods were still delivered by donkey. Every time a donkey appeared I couldn't resist taking a photograph. Later I was ashamed of these photographs, for Syrian friends asked me if I was going to be publishing the usual hackneyed photograph of a donkey in the bazaar. They were irritated that foreigners concentrate so often on the impoverished and archaic aspects of their country, rather than on those which are modern. My friends were right to be irritated, because one could spend days in Syrian cities without seeing a donkey; a dual carriageway would be more representative.

The problem is that many of us crave for the exotic, the antiquated, and the unusual, especially now that they are disappearing so fast. Even those donkeys won't be there for long. There is not much hope of expecting travellers to spend much time looking at new schools and factories; but I mention the problem because my Syrian friends weren't exceptions. I have noticed that educated people in the developing world are often intensely irritated by our obsession with the folksy and old-fashioned aspects of their countries.

A little ceremoniousness

In Britain we are accustomed to communicating curtly with strangers. When I want directions from a policeman, it is sufficient to ask, 'Could you please tell me the way to Broadwick Street?' In many foreign countries, though, it is wiser to approach strangers in a manner that is more formal and elaborate. Thus, when asking the policeman for directions, you would do well to say, 'Good morning. I am sorry to disturb you', before continuing with your request. As *The South American Handbook* puts it, 'A little ceremoniousness is much appreciated, and is certainly useful in dealing with officials of any description.'

This can also be true closer to home. I had always found Parisians insufferably rude until I read *Paupers' Paris*, in which the author encourages his readers to approach Parisians with extreme formality, taking care to use the words Monsieur, Madame, Mademoiselle.* After reading this, I experimented by treating Parisians with exaggerated, almost comic, politeness. At once they ceased to be rude. Even those who wished to be surly were wrong-footed by my salvo of courtesies.

If you get into the habit of taking more time over transactions, you will be combining good manners with pragmatism. This is a difficult matter to pinpoint on paper and can never be fully or clearly explained; but it has always been learnt by experienced travellers. Thus, if you want a favour from a district-officer, it may not be polite to walk into his office, request the favour, and walk out immediately; it is often the custom to take plenty of time over such matters, and, depending on the circumstances, it may be wise to indulge in a little general conversation.

When you need to elicit information, it is also nearly always best to manoeuvre as slowly as you can. Once when I was making inquiries of a shopkeeper to find out if there was an English-speaking guide in the neighbourhood, the shopkeeper insisted there wasn't. After this we chatted to each other, and after about half an hour he said, apropos of nothing, 'By the way, should you ever need an English-speaking guide, I have a cousin . . .' This time lag for information can't be explained by the shopkeeper testing either my manners or my suitability as an employer. A partial explanation may lie in an instinctive reluctance to reveal *any* information without considerable wariness. The story is worth recording only because similar incidents, with similar delays in the surfacing of information, have happened to me time and again.

Eye contact

A failure to look you in the eye doesn't necessarily imply surliness or shiftiness. I had thought the Punan in Borneo were a grumpy

* Miles Turner (Pan, 1982)

lot until I was told they considered it disrespectful to look a stranger in the eye. In 1983 *The Times* reported that Asian doctors newly arrived in Britain were being given lessons in looking patients straight in the eye.

I have already mentioned that in many areas women who make eye contact are considered promiscuous. In a large part of the Arab world a politely mannered man will, on meeting a friend's female relations, look anywhere but into their eyes.

An anthropologist, Martin Stokes, wrote an interesting letter to me about eye contact in rural Turkey.

In many parts of rural Turkey, smiling at or greeting a man on the rare occasions when he is seen in public *together* with his wife is taken as a serious insult, often implying and in some cases taken as evidence of adultery with the wife. This of course is a direct challenge to the man's honour, which is most often simply and frostily ignored, but more serious action might be taken against a single male committing this error. I was frosted out on many occasions on my first visit to rural Turkey, and it was only a comment about this in June Starr's book *Dispute and Settlement in Rural Turkey* that alerted me to this. The converse is also true: where less tourists are seen – mainly in the north of the country – when travelling with a girlfriend I've been ignored (though stared at); attempts to look friendly by smiling were met in return with blank stares. In the same town on my own, I would be stopped on every street corner and showered with all kinds of friendliness and hospitality: I hadn't realized that their previous coldness was simply out of respect to my sense of honour.

At the risk of sounding sugary, I would strongly recommend one form of eye contact: try smiling more than you would at home. It is wonderfully rare that your smile isn't returned. Even where the local people appear to glower at you, the glower is often only an intense scrutiny; when you smile at them, they nearly always smile in return.

Clothes, hippies, and cleanliness

When you consider that there are regions where a detail of turban or sarong can indicate precise status, and that in most countries people struggle really hard to keep their clothes clean, it isn't surprising that travellers are judged so much by their appearance.

It is a strange fact that 'hippies' are generally disliked throughout South America, Africa, and Asia. (When a child in Buenos Aires or a customs officer in Calcutta uses the word 'hippie', they mean anyone with unkempt clothing or long hair; therefore this is the sense in which I use the word here.) You might expect hippies to be unpopular with officials, such as customs officers and the police, but they are also disliked by many sections of society. The dislike is strongest in the areas where people have had experience of hippies, but you hear them being maligned in regions where a hippie has never been – rather in the way that the Irish in Donegal are alarmed by future 'waves of immigration'. In view of the unpopularity of hippies, it is best to wear clean, tidy clothes, and men should keep their hair short. Besides, short hair is cooler and needs washing less often. Beards, even closely cropped ones, are unpopular in some South American countries, and may get you harassed by the police.

You would often expect hippies to be more appreciated than conventional travellers: hippies aren't deliberately arrogant and in theory they live closer to the local people. Nevertheless, conventional travellers are usually preferred. I've questioned people in many countries about this, and an expression that frequently occurs in their answers is 'mutual respect'. They say that hippies have forsaken the right to respect because of their dirt, clothes, and behaviour; and they also say that hippies don't show sufficient respect for their local way of life. Sometimes this is a legacy from colonial days: although people may be sensitive to any hints of arrogance from foreigners, they still expect them to dress in a pukka way. A Malaysian district officer once said to me, 'They don't dress like that at home, why do they show their contempt for us by dressing like that here?' I failed to persuade him that many hippies were just as messy everywhere.

Some travellers, having been misled by *public* squalor, don't seem to appreciate how much trouble the local people take to keep their clothes and bodies clean. Very few people in the

Third World are dirty, and those that are, such as Tibetans, tend to live in cold regions (please remember I'm still generalizing!). Where there is access to water, most people in the tropics are far cleaner than Europeans.

Misunderstandings

Two Indian women of my acquaintance, having come to Europe for the first time, went on an organized bus tour round France and Italy. They made good friends with the other passengers, most of whom were English. At the end of the tour, the Indian women disappeared without saying goodbye, and the other passengers were probably hurt by this inexplicable behaviour. The Indian women had noticed with horror that all their new-found friends were kissing each other goodbye. They found this repugnant, and in case they should suffer the same fate, they had rushed off. This story is a classic example of an unfortunate misunderstanding which can arise between people from different cultures.

I expect that misunderstandings arise far more frequently than any of us realize. In the United States I once read of an example which, if true, shows that even the most mundane interactions are liable to misinterpretation. The writer claimed that when a black man spots a white acquaintance approaching in the distance, his instinct is to greet him at once. The white man, disliking contact at this range, tends to avert his eyes. When the black man is closer, the white man turns to greet him, but his black friend, thinking he has been cut, in turn averts his eyes.

Because misunderstandings are probably far more common than realized, it may be best to presume at first that any coolness you encounter is caused by a misunderstanding rather than irrational hostility.

Speech is also frequently misunderstood, and one of the commonest misunderstandings concerns the word 'yes'. In a large part of the world the majority of people either consider it rude to say 'no', or like to give pleasure by saying 'yes'. As a result the question, 'Is this train going to Zarabia?' will be answered by 'Yes', even when the respondent knows quite well that a train hasn't gone there for six months. The simplest solution (as mentioned in Chapter 10) is never to ask the type of question that can be answered with a 'yes'. Thus, don't ask, 'Is this train going to Zarabia?' Instead ask, 'Where is this train going?' This is one of the cardinal rules of trouble-free travel. You should also be aware that there are fifty different tones for saying the word 'yes', and when you are on the alert, you will recognize when 'yes' isn't said with the necessary ring of confidence.

A variation of this problem sometimes happens to strangers in the Indian subcontinent. The question 'Are there any trains to Bangalore?' is answered by a shake of the head, which inquirers interpret as 'No.' They soon learn that a special style of head-shaking in fact signifies 'Yes.' Just to confuse things, in parts of the Middle East, head-shaking can mean, 'I don't understand.'

The English language abroad doesn't carry the same meaning everywhere, and confusion happens even when an American talks to a Briton. When Americans speak of a 'vest', they refer to our waistcoat; their 'purse' is our handbag; their 'closet' is our cupboard; and their 'third floor' is our second floor. When I was staying on a farm in California, the daughter of the house offered to take me for a ride. When I asked for a few moments to put on some appropriate clothes, I thought she looked at me in a quizzical way; it wasn't until we had driven a long way that I remembered that a 'ride' just means a drive in the car.

There are possibilities here for offence as well as confusion. 'Homely' is mainly a flattering word in Britain, but implies ugliness in the United States. 'Cheap' in Britain usually only means inexpensive, but in the United States it means cheap and nasty. When Americans talk of a woman's 'fanny', they are referring to her buttocks.

A disastrous confusion between Britons and Americans can occur over the question of dates. If you read '2/5/93' in the United States, this doesn't mean 2 May; it means 5 February.

There are some verbal misunderstandings which are common to a surprisingly wide variety of countries. I have noticed in places as far apart as the West Indies, Egypt, and Indonesia that the word 'too' is synonymous with the word 'very'. Thus, 'There are *too* many people at the ceremony' probably means 'There are *very* many people at the ceremony'.

The word 'popular' often means 'common' or 'frequent'. Sometimes this meaning is clear: when someone says, 'Malaria is popular in Zarabia', you presume that Zarabians aren't baring their flesh every time they spot mosquitoes. On the other hand, 'The English are popular in Zarabia' could be interpreted in two ways, but it usually means, not that the English are especially loved in Zarabia, but that they are numerous there. The words 'brother', 'sister', 'cousin', and so on are all subject to different interpretations. This is my 'brother' may refer to an actual brother, but is just as likely to refer to a cousin, or even a friend; 'uncle' may indicate any senior male relative; and 'cousin' might mean a cousin, but is often used to describe anyone from the same family, tribe, or clan.

When you offer a drink, and the answer is, 'That's all right, thank you', your friend quite likely means, 'Yes thank you', not, as you might think, 'No thank you.' Many English-speaking West Indians and Africans use this confusing expression. When Spanish-speaking (and some other) people say '*gracias*' (thank you), they often mean 'No thank you.'

This may be the place to make the important point that in many cultures it is considered polite to refuse something on the first few occasions. Always persevere politely with the offer of any gift, just in case.

The words 'please', 'thank you', and 'goodbye' don't feature in quite a few languages and, even when they do, it is not always the custom to use them as much as we do. This can give an unfortunate and misleading impression of abruptness, especially when you have just handed over a handsome present. The sense of rudeness may be aggravated if you don't know that in some countries, such as Japan and China, it is rude to open a present in front of the donor.

The non-use or lesser-use of 'thank you' is more widespread than you would expect. I have often noticed in Italy that it is not the custom to say 'thank you' for gifts; even closer to home, there was until recently no tradition in Brittany of saying 'thank you.'* I can't produce a complete geographical list of courtesies, but I know that few people say 'thank you' in Bangladesh, nor in Bali; in the Middle East thanks aren't given for a formal present, nor for a trifling service such as picking up a dropped pen. The Punan of Borneo don't have a word for thank you, though they have forty words for one variety of the sago palm.

Other misleading impressions of abruptness can be caused by differences of behaviour. In Bali I was a little shocked to see that a husband didn't greet his wife, even after returning home from a week's absence. Later I discovered that this was their custom. Since then I was intrigued to read† that Zulu migrant workers don't greet their wives, even when they have come back to their kraal after a year away.

Pleasant relationships can be spoilt by a different type of misunderstanding. When travellers think they have struck up a spontaneous and genuine friendship with someone local, they don't mind at first paying for the odd drink or meal, because they are after all richer than their new-found friend. When, however, they are dragged off to a cousin's batik parlour, they start to smell a rat; and when they are asked to contribute $50 to an aunt's medical expenses, they become hurt and angry because they think they have been hoodwinked by someone who pretended friendship. When travellers have been stung a few times, they become reluctant to attempt new friendships.

I think it is important to realize that genuine friendship can be

* *The House of Pride: Life in a Breton Village*, Pierre-Jakez Helias (Yale University Press, 1978)

† *Move Your Shadow*, Joseph Lelyveld (Sphere, 1987)

combined with cupidity. Of course there are plenty of professional spongers; but on the other hand, someone who in good faith cherishes your company may not feel it wrong or embarrassing to ask for money, especially if they think you can afford it. The alleged friendship can easily be tested by studying reactions when you refuse the request. An extreme but believable example of this situation is related in Joyce Cary's brilliant novel *Mister Johnson*. A servant, who professes loyalty to his employer, actually steals from him. The normal presumption would be that the servant is both treacherous and ungrateful, but the novel makes it clear that, despite the theft, the servant still loves his employer.

An interesting misunderstanding

I will quote at some length an anthropologist's example of a particular type of misunderstanding, because it illustrates so clearly how alertness is necessary for tuning in to another culture:

To begin with I was distressed to find that I couldn't extract more than ten words from Dowayos at a stretch. When I asked them to describe something to me, a ceremony, or an animal, they would produce one or two sentences and then stop. I would have to ask further questions to get more information. This was very unsatisfactory, as I was directing their answers rather more than sound field-method would have prescribed. One day, after about two months of fairly fruitless endeavour, the reason struck me. Quite simply Dowayos have totally different rules about how to divide up the parts of a conversation. Whereas in the West we learn not to interrupt when somebody else is talking, this does not hold in much of Africa. One must talk to people physically present as if on the telephone, where frequent interjections and verbal response must be given if only to assure the other party that one is still there and paying attention. When listening to someone talking, a Dowayo stares gravely at the floor, rocks backwards and forwards and murmurs, 'Yes', 'It is so', 'Good', every five seconds or so. Failure to do so leads to the speaker rapidly drying up. As soon as I adopted this expedient, my interviews were quite transformed.*

I suspect that this method of conversation is common to a

* *The Innocent Anthropologist*, Nigel Barley (British Museum Publications, 1983)

large part of Africa; it certainly holds true for the Masai, who live thousands of miles away from the Dowayos.

Since writing the above, I was interested to read the following in an etiquette guide to Japan:

Another important aspect of language etiquette in Japan is the constant use of *aizuchi*, or what can be loosely translated as 'agreement interjections'. This refers to the Japanese custom of regularly and systematically agreeing with or acknowledging the comments of other persons by nodding one's head and/or saying such things as *hai*, *so dsu car?* and *asho?* during the course of conversations. These *aizuchi* interjections are expected and needed by the Japanese. If they are not forthcoming, the speaker knows immediately that something is wrong. He knows the other person is angry or disagrees with him to the extent that the person is deliberately breaking a sanctified custom. Japanese-speaking foreigners who are not familiar with the importance of *aizuchi*, and who fail to follow through with the appropriate interjections, may unwittingly send unintended messages.*

Contacts

When you look at the hordes of miserable tourists who flock round Piccadilly Circus, you wonder whether they enjoy themselves and whether they learn anything about Britain. They wait in endless queues at the Tower of London, search for the non-existent glamour of the West End, and rubberneck round Oxford, whose discreet charms will remain hidden. The interest and enjoyment of their holiday would be immeasurably increased if they were lucky enough to have contacts. Imagine their different perceptions of Britain if they stayed with a doctor in Surrey, a landowner in Yorkshire, or a miner in Wales! The only times I have felt that I've got under the skin of a country are when I've been able to stay with local people.

Even if you can't actually stay with a local family, any introductions to expatriates will still make a big difference; and even the most tenuous contacts are better than none at all. Assuming the expatriates have lived in the country some time, they provide a

---

Etiquette Guide to Japan, Boye De Mente (Tuttle, Tokyo, 1990)

short cut to its enjoyment. Far better than any guidebook, they will tell you which areas are worth visiting, the best ways to get there, and what to avoid. Above all, whether your contacts are natives of the country or foreigners, they will enable you to have an experience of the place that is denied to most tourists. Therefore you should make a great effort to dig up some introductions before leaving home. Ask every friend and acquaintance whether they have a friend in Zarabia, and as such contacts may be rare, start asking months in advance.

Contacts who live in the countryside are often preferable to those living in cities. The city-dwellers often have ordinary nine-to-five jobs and evenings filled with social engagements. Country-dwellers are rarely so constrained by routine, and are often far keener to meet strangers.

Collecting the names is only half the battle; the other half is in your manner of approaching them. Not everyone is happy to entertain all the travellers who are given their address. You should treat your contacts with the same caution and finesse that you would use to bridle an untethered horse on an open moor. Once you have alarmed the horse, there is no hope of catching it. The same is true of contacts. Don't ring up from the airport with a breezy, 'Hello, I'm here.' This can frighten them into saying, 'Oh dear, we are so fond of Dorothy, and we would have loved to have met any friend of hers; but sadly we are leaving town tomorrow morning.' Once they have told this type of lie, you have no further opportunity of meeting them.

The approach should be quite different. The first rule is to make sure your friend at home has written to them; this will get them over the initial shock, and you hope they will have been told how much they are going to like you. Instead of ringing them up from an airport or station, move into a hotel so they don't think you are trying to force them into providing a bed. Even when you have moved into a hotel, an unheralded telephone call may not be the best tactic. Whenever possible it is best to send (or deliver by hand) a letter explaining that you have arrived and giving some idea of what you intend to do.

This letter doesn't panic them into telling lies, and instead gives them time to decide what they may like to do for you. They may decide to set aside a day for showing you round, or they may arrange to meet you for a meal. This way, they get a look at you, and if you aren't obnoxious, they can then do more, or possibly have you to stay.

The value of contacts lies in making your journey more enjoyable and interesting – not in saving on hotel bills. In fact, unless you stay with people for a long time, they will rarely save you money. By the time you've given them a present and – if they live in a city – taken them out to dinner, you have often paid more than the price of a modest hotel. Remember, also, that you only go to Zarabia once in a lifetime, but your Zarabian contacts have a way of coming to England once a year – and expect entertainment every time.

CHAPTER 12

TAKING THE PLUNGE

As a short cut to the real enjoyment of a country, there is nothing like taking the plunge and walking in areas beyond the reach of cars. It is here, more than in the cities, that you are likely to get a genuine experience of a country's culture. And once in real countryside, you break into a different world: no fumes, noise, beggars, or neon lights; instead tranquillity and beauty. You are refreshed by the stimulus of exercise, and warmed by the friendliness which is customary among country people. Nearly all my happiest travel memories are of walking tours in countryside, and I have noticed that few travellers have regretted even their most arduous tours in remote areas.

Mounted or on foot?

Many travellers who go off the beaten track are attracted by the idea of making the trip on the back of a horse, mule, or camel. Such journeys have been glorified in many books, and the idea is romantic. In practice, however, these journeys may be more difficult and uncomfortable than you would expect.

A considerable problem is that you rarely get offered a satisfactory animal. A good horse, for instance, is usually in constant use, and its owner is unlikely to keep it hanging around for the occasional traveller. Furthermore, if the owner treasures his horse, he may be reluctant to hire it to someone who might not look after it. The quality of saddles presents another problem. The novice traveller may expect a hired animal to come complete with comfortable saddles and suitable stirrups; but locally made saddles are often agonizing, and the stirrups useless or non-existent.

The terrain will be a deciding factor when choosing whether to hire a mount. There are flat grasslands where it would be monotonous to walk, and there are tracks in the hills which are inaccessible even to mules. Where there is an evenly balanced choice between walking or riding, I prefer walking: it isn't always slower, and it is often more comfortable, less restrictive, better exercise, and cheaper.

If you do hire a mount, first insist on a day's trial run, which will give you the opportunity to test the saddle as well as the beast. Look to see if a horse has got a saddle sore, for even a lay person can spot this; once the sore exists, it is very unlikely to mend.

Most people who hire an animal ride much too far on their first day. They use rarely exercised muscles, which become tired and painful. Once you have over-stretched yourself, it is difficult to recover during the journey, which may be unnecessarily spoilt. Although two hours may seem a very short time, it is probably more than enough for the first day's riding. From then on, the period can be considerably increased each day.

Walking

When walking, as when riding, the temptation is to go too far on the first day. Many walkers are less fit than they imagine. If you overstretch your muscles, they will take days to recover, and if your feet aren't used to hard treatment, they may develop disastrous blisters. Four hours' walking is plenty for the first day, especially when you are not in top condition, or when the terrain is difficult.

When walking in hot climates, many people wonder whether it is better to drink a lot of water before setting out, or to drink sip by sip while walking; most of them decide on the latter. I have experimented many times with both methods, and am convinced that it is best to drink deeply before you leave, and then to resist the temptation to drink. If I have to drink again, then I don't just sip, but instead take a long deep drink and have a rest. This was certainly the method used by famous big-game hunters, and most pundits seem to agree with it. In *Stay Alive in the Desert,*★ K. E. M. Melville wrote:

In most novels and stories of adventure where the hero is lost in a desert, or adrift in an open boat, you will find that he rations his water supply very carefully, dividing it into small, infrequent sips, trying to preserve it as long as possible. *This method of consuming a water supply has been proved to be entirely wrong* [his italics] . . . very soon after you drink, you will start sweating, and if you are only having small sips you may actually sweat out more fluid than you have drunk . . . the correct thing to do is to abstain from drinking as long as you possibly can; when your thirst can no longer be ignored, then drink as much as you want.

When you are walking through thick forest with a guide, you may notice that he chops the bamboo diagonally with his machete; this is because many types of bamboo resist being cut horizontally. Even when it's not necessary to clear a path, he continues using his machete so that you have a trail to return by if you lose your way. Should you ever have to walk in thick forest alone, you would be well advised to follow this example.

A surprising number of people get lost when leaving camp, even on brief visits to the lavatory. If you look behind frequently, this will help fix the track in your mind. When in doubt, break a few branches so they hang down, or scrape some marks in the earth.

Occasionally I have walked on hillsides which were perilously slippery. Locals advised me to walk barefoot, which did seem to improve my grip.

When climbing steep hills, the general rule is that it is better to use a shorter stride, as if shifting into a different gear. If you can zigzag (as animal paths always do), this will also help for the same reason – you are obviously making less of an effort with each step.

Like most people, I find walking more pleasurable when carrying a **walking stick**. It is also a considerable help for climbing hills, descending slippery slopes, crossing rivers, and occasionally for repelling aggressive dogs.

★ (The Jerboa Press, 1970)

Many continentals and Japanese go trekking with a ski-stick. Most British would feel like idiots if they were equipped with one, but a ski-stick has the merits of being collapsible and of a more useful length.

Leaving no litter

I would have thought it an impertinence to plead with people not to be litter louts, if I wasn't aware of the amount of rubbish that trekkers have strewn along the beautiful trails of Nepal. Non-biodegradable trash, such as plastic bags, is one of the visual curses of the modern world. In any beautiful area I always make a point of clearing up some of this rubbish in front of the locals; most of these gestures are a waste of time, but we have got to start somewhere, and if many travellers did the same, it would eventually have some effect.

In dry tropical climates even biodegradable rubbish may not decay for a very long time. Orange peel notoriously lasts for ever. Paper lasts for a long time, and the disgusting sight of used lavatory paper has become far too common. When you are camping, try to bury all evidence of your defecation.

While I'm sermonizing about the glaringly obvious, let me mention that all travellers should play their part in trying to protect the environment. For instance, don't cut living trees for firewood; don't buy shells, skins or ivory; don't eat rare animals (a common activity in China); be particularly vigilant about coral reefs, which are disappearing at an alarming rate; and if you notice any type of trade in endangered animals, write both to the local English-language newspaper (see Chapter 8) and to CITES (Convention on International Trade in Endangered Species of Wild Flora and Fauna) via the Conservation Monitoring Centre (219c Huntingdon Road, Cambridge CB3 ODL; tel. 0223 277314).

Blisters

Most blisters are avoidable, and should be avoided, for they can ruin a trek. Boots that are too tight, too loose or too new are the commonest cause. Don't wear nylon socks, which overheat the feet.

The moment you feel the slightest indication of an incipient blister, take action. Cover the sore spot with Moleskin (or some type of adhesive tape designed for blisters). Cushioned Elastoplast is a reasonable second-best, but the free-standing part of the dressing may allow rubbing, which is the original cause of the blister. If you are even slightly prone to blisters, carry patches of Moleskin or other adhesive tape – in your pocket, not deep in a rucksack, or hidden in saddle-bags. When the tape is tucked away, you tend to put off remedial action, and therefore fail to catch the irritation in time. One trek leader tells me that, because she bullies her group into early treatment of sore spots, none of them ever gets blisters.

For those who are especially vulnerable, I quote from a letter from a correspondent, Dr Paton:

When I and friends started serious trekking fifteen years ago, we were plagued by the usual blisters and abrasions on the feet. One of our members recommended a simple measure which we've used ever since with results that can only be described as miraculous. Before starting, a 1-inch or 2-inch width of zinc oxide tape or Elastoplast is applied over the balls of the feet to include the toes, over the heels and around the back of the ankle – three in all. They can be left for as long as a week (and don't come off in the bath) or changed if they become too filthy. We have used them from the Pennines to the Himalayas and can attest to their efficiency, yet I've never seen the method described in any book.

Those who are prone to blisters caused by friction between their toes often find that a coat of Vaseline prevents this.

When walking in Scotland, I've never had blisters since wearing two pairs of socks (one thin and one thick).

If you get a blister, don't tear off the protective loose skin. Opinion is divided about whether or not to prick the blister. If you do feel the need to prick it, use a sterilized needle on its edge, and afterwards cover with an antiseptic powder. Any opening in a blister is prone to infection.

Two specialist remedies are now being more widely marketed.

Spenco Medical and Compeed both sell a blister dressing which the manufacturers claim will aid healing and enable you to continue normal activities. I haven't been able to test either of them on an actual blister (as I rarely get one); Compeed is the simplest to use, and I have experimented with their dressings on wet feet in leaky boots. The dressings survived quite well. I have experimented with both makes of dressing by swimming with them, and can report that although 'waterproof' they won't withstand prolonged exposure to water.

Crossing rivers

In his booklet *Advice for Small Expeditions in Tropical Rain Forest Regions*,* Roger Chapman warns, 'More tragedies occur from river crossings than from any other actions on jungle patrols, because people continually underestimate the power of water.' I am also covering the subject at some length because travellers who attempt even modest walks will quite often have to cross fast-flowing rivers.

When you have a backpack attached to your back, crossing a river may be dangerous because its weight can push your head under the water. Therefore, at least adjust the straps so that the backpack can be immediately jettisoned in an emergency. If the river is life-threatening, it is best to try to float your (hopefully waterproofed) pack, as it will be a severe handicap if your feet slip. Better to lose your backpack than your life.

Because river crossings are dangerous, time spent on a recce is never wasted. Look out for recovery points on either side of the river which you will be able to strike out for (or float to) in the event of being upended.

Launch out a bit of wood to see what the current does with it, and unless in an emergency never cross near any type of eddy (which is like a whirlpool), as there is probably a very strong current nearby.

* (Expedition Advisory Centre, Royal Geographical Society, revised edition 1990)

Before making any crossing, take the likelihood of a down-pour of rain into account if you are going to have to return across the river. Tropical rivers can rise several feet in an hour, and yet take more than a day to subside.

A stick is a must for crossing any river. An army officer, who spent four years crossing rivers in Borneo, told me that he would never let any of his men cross a river without a stick. He also said that even the local tribal people would always cut themselves a stick before crossing an unfamiliar river. A stick is both a third eye – you can prod in front to test depth in opaque water – and a third leg. Think of the stability of a tripod stool (or the instability of a two-legged stool!). For the same reasons of stability, don't bring your two legs together; take one step, and then don't move the other foot until you are quite sure that the first one is secure and stable. Don't step up on to a submerged rock, it is hard to keep your footing when you step down again. Then gently edge the other foot towards the first one, but still keeping the legs well apart. Try to keep something of the tripod position with your stick and your feet. Provided the depth of water permits, cross over on a long downstream diagonal.

I will now quote advice from Hugh Falkus on how to survive an upset in fast waters. I quote him because he hasn't copied his precepts from other textbooks, but drawn them from his experi-ence of thousands of hours spent in fast-flowing rivers. His advice has saved at least one life.

There is no immediate danger. But you must not throw up your arms and shout. If you do, you will sink, swallowing water as you go down. Pay no attention to those stories of drowning men coming up three times. If you ship enough water first time down, you won't come up at all. But if you keep your mouth shut and your arms at your sides you will soon resurface. Remember, when vertical, the body sinks. When horizontal, it tends to float. So – lie on your back, arms stretched at right-angles, legs on the surface, head right back in the water. This is the 'crucifix' – the classic safe floating position. Once in this attitude you can start shouting for help . . . Don't try to swim against the current. Drift with it, feet first. Then it is your boots that may strike a rock, and not your head. Kick with your legs, paddle with your hands and gradually edge in towards the bank. Don't keep feeling for the bottom with your feet. As your legs go down, so will your body.*

I have tested Falkus's advice in a swimming pool, and found that what he said was true – the moment I raised my arms, my body began to sink. Remember also that the head is heavy (between 10 and 15 pounds), and unless supported by water it tends to press you down.

Sleeping outside

Before setting off, you obviously have to decide whether you will be sleeping out of doors or staying in villages. If you are going to sleep outside, you need to take considerably more kit (see Chapter 3). Some walkers prefer to sleep under the stars, do their own cooking, and be free of local interference. In this book, I have only briefly covered the kit for camping (stoves, tents etc.) because I know little about it, and the subject is well covered by specialist books. I myself prefer to stay in villages: there is activity and human interest, access to boiling water, and a feeling of safety. When staying in a village, you are nearly always protected by a code of hospitality, but when you sleep out of doors, you are fair game for meddlers and predators. On the other hand, camping out in a beautiful wild place can be one of the great highlights of travel.

If you do decide to sleep outside, remember you need as much protection under your body as above; when the weather is cold, the ground – especially if damp – will suck the heat out of your body.

Sometimes it is very tempting to sleep without a tent, but remember that by morning you may be entirely covered with dew. A bivvy bag may be a good compromise.

Your body may sweat as much as a pint of liquid each night, so you must dry your bag out thoroughly in the sun each morning.

Aim to pitch camp well before sunset, so you don't have to

* *Sea Trout Fishing* (Witherby, 1975)

finish your chores after dark or hurry your choice of campsite. It is alarmingly easy to lose your way when you leave camp after dark, so always take a torch, and, as mentioned before, keep looking behind to memorize your route.

Don't ever camp in the bed of a dried-out river or on the edge of one. Although the weather may seem Sahara-dry where you are camping, rainfall further upstream can cause the river to rise at an astonishing rate. This may be dangerous, and recently campers have drowned, even in Crete. For the same reason, it is often unwise to camp on the edge of any river in tropical forests, for a river can easily rise 10 feet in one night. Because dried-out river beds and the edges of rivers make attractive places to camp, even veteran campers have woken up to see their equipment floating downstream. Some friends of mine, who specialize in South American travel, have had their camp swept away three times.

An evening change of clothes

A soldier who had fought in the Malayan campaigns once told me that a key factor in maintaining the soldiers' morale had been a clean and dry change of clothes in the evening. Time and again I have found this to be true, and an appreciation of this point is invaluable for anyone hiking away from modern comforts and laundries.

Even when you are carrying very little, it is possible to take a clean set of clothes for the evening; one pair of trousers and two shirts usually suffice. If you keep these strictly for evening use, they will almost never need washing. During the evenings the temperature is cooler and you move about less, therefore your shirts don't become sweaty and foul.

After travelling all day in damp, smelly clothes, it is a great comfort to luxuriate in clean, dry ones. And when you are well dressed, you create a much better impression in a village. In the event of visiting or staying with a headman, it is usually considered very rude to wear dirty clothes.

When you wake up in the morning and find yesterday's

clothes are still damp, it is tempting to dress in your spare, dry ones. Resist this temptation, and put on the wet ones again; after only a few minutes you will get used to them. Somehow, dirty or wet clothes are not too disagreeable during the day; they are much worse when you have to sit about in them after dark.

A few **plastic bags** are invaluable when you need to wrap your wet clothes. They are also useful for covering anything that needs protection against rain or dust.

Packing your backpack

The secret of packing your backpack is in the sensible use of strong plastic bags. Plan your packing so that you never have to get out much more than you need. Thus one plastic bag could hold the clean, dry set of clothes mentioned above; another could hold your wet, dirty clothes; another your night-kit and wash-bag, and so on. These plastic bags will also help protect their contents from dust and rain. The items you need during the day should ideally be in easily reachable rucksack pockets.

Guides

In the developed world few people have servants, and therefore most travellers recoil (or don't even consider) the idea of using a guide for a few days. Besides, it is often possible for enterprising travellers to explore the countryside without a guide. Many of the hiking guidebooks written or published by Hilary Bradt are aimed at just such travellers.

However, although guides may not always be necessary, they can provide an excellent short cut to the enjoyment and understanding of a country's culture. In particular they may be invaluable as translators, for if you don't speak the local language, how else are you going to learn about a country? I remember a woman ridiculing me for suggesting she hire a guide in Bali; later, I regretted not asking her if she spoke any of Bali's three languages.

If you are going off the beaten track, then guides may serve plenty of other purposes. They can follow tracks that would be indistinguishable to you; they know the safest places to cross hazardous rivers; they know which berries and fruits are safe to eat, if you are stranded; they know the fastest way to fetch help, if you break an ankle; when you return to populated areas, they can safeguard your luggage.

Guides can also make your trip more interesting and enjoyable. They can teach you the language, explain the life of the villages, find out about special events, and by countless other services help you become part of a community instead of an unaware alien. When I rode for several days along the south coast of Haiti, my guide was a popular singer, and therefore each evening we were surrounded by crowds who came to enjoy his singing. The same journey would not have been half as much fun without him.

In some areas a guide will offer a measure of protection against robbery. I hired one for a day to take me up to the top of Pacaya volcano in Guatemala. After returning in the evening, we discovered robbers had held up at gunpoint all the other foreigners who had climbed the volcano on the same day. I'm convinced that my guide's presence had deterred the robbers, probably because they didn't want to be recognized by someone local.

Because the character of the guide makes such a difference to the journey, he should be chosen carefully. If you hire one on spec, you are asking for trouble; instead he should be tested by giving him a short trial run before you commit yourself. Ask the guide to accompany you for a day's journey to some local tourist site. This should be long enough for you to decide that you don't want him because he's infuriating and ignorant, or you will hire him because he is amusing and reliable. You can also find out if he's knowledgeable enough to read animal tracks, know the names of plants, and give an accurate interpretation of local customs.

Should you hire a guide for a specific purpose, such as boating, fishing, or driving, first test his basic proficiency. In *Travels with Myself and Another*, Martha Gellhorn recounts a hilarious episode when she had to drive her sullen and useless 'driver' for hundreds of miles round East Africa.★ She had hired him to drive, but owing to his clever prevarication, discovered too late that he had never touched a steering wheel.

Don't expect a first-rate guide to walk up and offer his services; even if someone approaches you, he may be the wrong type. It is usually better to ask the advice of a hotel proprietor or another local contact. Don't ever risk hiring a guide whose face you don't like; if you are more than about thirty years old, you will most likely be competent at physiognomy. *First* impressions of a person's trustworthiness are usually correct.

If you don't know the level of local wages, the imagined cost of hiring a guide might deter you, and your fears are likely to be confirmed when you inquire about cost of the first guide who offers his services. But provided you take time to find the right person and negotiate sensibly, the cost of a guide is within the budget of many travellers. I have often paid less than £3 a day for a guide and even today I find they are often very good value.

Before negotiating wages, find out the local rates for household workers, farm labourers, and shop assistants. Expect to pay more, because knowledge of English makes your guide a skilled worker, and besides, guiding is not regular employment.

Quite apart from your guide's negotiated wages, set aside a reasonable sum as a bonus. Explain that you will pay this money at the end of the trip, provided you have been happy with his services.

Should you need porters, you will find them much cheaper, because they don't have any special skills such as speaking English. They are usually best hired through your guide, even though he may take a commission on their wages.

Provisions

Because it is neither wise nor fair to rely entirely on villages for food, provisions should be discussed in advance with your

★ (Allen Lane, 1978)

guide in order to find out what will be available during your walk, and what should be purchased in advance. If most of your food is going to be provided by villages, then you should ask which luxury supplies you can best bring for sharing out at mealtimes.

If you are carrying most of your food, it is a good idea to think in terms of buying a bulk food which fills you up (and gives a measure of energy), plus a variety of more nutritious foods.

Don't underestimate the importance of bulk. It is possible to put too much emphasis on attempting a nutritionally perfect diet, but except on a long trip, this won't be of supreme importance. Bear in mind that bulk is very important to maintain your energy, to make you feel good, and to induce a life-enhancing shit in the morning.

The bulk food par excellence is porridge (don't get oatmeal that is too refined). It is, of course, excellent at breakfast, but can be eaten at any time of day, or mixed with other food. Even when you are trekking it supplies you with energy for four or five hours. It is the favourite bulk food of the SAS, and when they have got bored of it, they have been known to eat it curried. Rice is also an invaluable bulk food: it is available almost everywhere, is easily cooked, doesn't spoil, and can be mixed with almost anything. Just a small addition of fish or whatever can make it palatable and nutritious. Because of the minimal moisture content of uncooked rice, it is weight-effective. Lentils are also useful when you can get them: they have many of the virtues of rice and contain much more protein. Obviously, bulk foods are not sufficient, and your diet should be varied. Dates, currants, sultanas, and raisins all have a high calorie content, and don't need cooking; they are all strongly recommended for expeditions, and are very useful for giving instant energy when needed – especially dates, which are full of sugar. Nuts, especially peanuts, have an even higher calorie content. If weight and space aren't a problem, copy the locals and take live poultry – thus ensuring a supply of fresh meat. During an East African safari I was surprised to see that hens were released and allowed to roam around the camp; they never strayed and at night flew up to roost in the trees. If they become too tame, though, it takes a hard heart to kill them.

Hot chocolate and cocoa give you more sustenance than tea, though they are heavier to carry.

When weight isn't a problem, onions are useful: they are tough, long-lasting, and very adaptable in cooking. According to folk wisdom, they relieve the symptoms of mountain sickness, stomach troubles, and excessive heat. Unfortunately, they are not very nutritious.

Because weight is usually an important factor, almost anything with a high water content is impractical. This rules out most tins. An exception might be made for tins of sardines, which are sold almost universally; they take up little room, and the oil is nourishing. (But don't forget your can-opener, because tins' own openers often fail.) I'm told that the best tinned meat is corned beef, as it holds almost no water.

Dried foods are long-lasting and light. Martin and Tanis Jordan, veterans of South American river trips, often take dozens of packets. But I have heard a report from Jack Jackson, who has led umpteen expeditions, that they are not suitable as the chief food during strenuous treks: after three weeks of walking, members of one of his groups could hardly put one leg in front of another, having fed almost exclusively on dried food. When clearing away their stools (as all good expeditioners do), they noticed that these were filled with undigested dried food. (After inquiring, I have since heard other reports of this.) They descended immediately to the nearest village, where they fed on scraggy chickens and condensed milk, and their energy was restored immediately.

Avoid taking too many local packets with monosodium glutamate; after a while it will irritate most Western stomachs.

Dried meat is usually about one-third the weight of fresh meat; it is far more nutritious than any vegetable equivalent, and can be eaten raw or cooked. (I don't know whether, like packet food, it isn't fully digestible, but I suspect that enough is digested to justify taking it.) Should you succeed in killing a large animal, the flesh can provide a valuable source of food for weeks, provided it is dried or smoked; if the meat isn't preserved in this way, you won't be able to eat it all before it goes bad. During their war against the British, the Boers were supposed to have greatly benefited from biltong (strips of dried meat), which kept them in rations when no other food was available. Various methods of drying meat in strips have been frequently used in many different parts of the world, and the word 'buccaneer' derives from *'boucanier'*, a producer (or trader in) dried meat.

Biltong is still popular in southern and eastern Africa and is made from a variety of flesh, from ostrich to antelope. Even kosher varieties are available. Here is a Kenyan recipe which can be adapted for emergencies:

You select your large steaks of raw meat – the best coming from the back legs – where the rump steaks are cut away in large, clean hunks. With a very sharp knife you cut strips with the grain down the muscle; these strips should be cut with one stroke as long as the meat allows and approximately 1 inch wide by $\frac{1}{2}$ inch thick. If the conditions are hot, dry, and sunny, you can cut the strips $1\frac{1}{2}$ inches wide by $\frac{3}{4}$ inch thick. Place all the strips in a bucket – sprinkle with salt and pepper liberally, leave to soak for six to seven hours, and shade-dry by hanging on a line between two trees. (Some Afrikaners put a cup of vinegar in the basin when the meat is soaking, which makes superior biltong.) Drying takes anything from five days to two weeks. There must be no fat on the meat.

When I received this recipe from friends in Kenya, I wrote to ask why shade-drying was necessary, and also how the fly problem was dealt with. They replied:

If dried in the sun you get a hard skin forming and drying is too quick, thus not allowing the inside to dry (it could even go bad). The ideal is a slow drying in a dry climate (it does not dry out before going bad if the climate is humid). The brine or salting and peppering of the meat seems to keep most of the flies away. However, if the climate is dry, flies only go for it when it is still moist – once it has dried off after a day or so, flies leave it alone. The salt keeps all infection away. However, the fastidious usually dry it under a mosquito net. So the ideal is a slow shade-drying in a dry climate, letting the centre dry out at the same time as the rest. The reason for cutting it in long, thin strips is to get the inside dry as well as to facilitate hanging it up. When drying, no two portions should touch; if they do, you hinder drying, and it is the ideal place for flies to lay their eggs.

If you need to speed the process, or if the climate is not hot enough to cure the meat, you should smoke it. The meat should be cured by the smoke and not the heat. Use the smoke of a wood fire – on no account the smoke of leaves or greenery. If you catch a surfeit of fish, they can also be sun-dried or smoked, but this must be done immediately.

Africans, Scandinavians, and Eskimos all carry dried fish. In emergencies you can try making your own, remembering of course that the fish will need to dry much faster than meat. Therefore put them out in the full sun (preferably on hot rocks), having gutted and split them. Score the inner flesh to speed up drying. In many places tiny fishes are just dried whole in the sun.

Fat provides twice as much energy, weight for weight, as protein or carbohydrate. For this reason long-lasting cheese is also valuable. Because meat and fat are so much more nutritious than vegetable products (see Food, Chapter 5) you might also consider taking some type of vacuum-packed sausage, such as Pepperami. It is unlikely that you would find this or the cheese locally, so if you want either, buy them before leaving home (see Snacks, Chapter 3).

Britons addicted to tea often take along some condensed milk. This is not always practical; the tins are heavy and, once opened, have a remarkable attraction for ants. It may be better to wean yourself off milk and convert to limes. One lime will flavour many cups of tea, and only a few drops freshen up a glass of water.

Provided you are staying in villages, you don't need to take much equipment for eating. A large mug may be bought locally, and is useful for eating rice, or for drinking tea, coffee, or soup. A plastic, rather than a metal one, is less likely to scald your lips when sipping hot drinks; though try to get a strong plastic, otherwise it will crack easily. A spoon is essential.

Don't forget to bring salt, especially as you will need extra amounts when walking.

Remember that any extra equipment you need to buy can easily be sold again. For a trip on a motorized canoe I once bought a large cushion, a huge pottery jar for carrying pure water, a tin mug, and a blanket. At the end of the fourteen-day journey I sold them all at a loss of only about 10 per cent. After two months of being on the receiving end of, 'You are my very good friend, I give you very special price', I enjoyed retaliating with similar sales techniques.

Water

The principal mistake of novice travellers is to underestimate the amount of water that they will need. When you won't have access to fresh water, you must always take more water than you think you need for normal requirements. This is one of the few pieces of advice in this book which should be taken without any questioning.

About 70 per cent of the human body is made up of water. If you weigh 12 stone, the water content of your body is 88 pints. Water is involved with almost every aspect of your body's crucial functions. Few realize that in a hot desert you may *want* to drink 20 pints of water a day, that you may need to drink at least 14 pints a day, and that even in emergencies you shouldn't be drinking less than 9 pints a day. If you aren't in a desert but are exerting yourself, you will still need a lot of water. Cyclists, for instance, may need to drink more than 20 pints a day. When an emergency cuts you off from regular provisions, it is water – not food – that is the vital commodity. In 1920, Irish hunger-strikers managed to live for ninety-four days without eating, and survivors in the wilds have been known to manage for more than a month without food. (It is said that after four or five days the hunger pains disappear.) But in a hot, dry climate you won't live for more than two or three days without water.

Many travellers in desert conditions not only underestimate the quantity of water needed, but make no allowance for unforeseen delays (or breakdowns, when travelling by car). When taking into account how much water to carry, consider another important factor. *You* may estimate your water requirements accurately, but what about the idiots you meet who haven't? When crossing deserts, or even travelling on their fringes, you are likely to encounter people who are either running out of water or have completely used up their supplies. It is hard to refuse their urgent appeals. Europeans are the worst culprits but, surprisingly often, locals are also guilty.

In Chapter 5 I have discussed in detail the various ways of purifying water.

Survival

Several Japanese soldiers who didn't surrender after the last war continued to live off the jungle for more than thirty years. If for some reason you are separated from regular provisions, there is no reason to become hysterical. As long as you have access to water, your chances of survival are high – especially in a warm climate. Nevertheless, when walking off into remote areas you should take three elementary precautions.

1. Always carry a writing implement and paper. This may seem trifling, but should an emergency arise, you will have the means to send a message for help; and if, for example, you fall ill, you can write down the symptoms so that someone can send the relevant medicines. In the unlikely event of being unwillingly detained, you may be able to bribe someone to take a message giving details of your predicament.

2. Study a map of the area you will be visiting to ascertain and commit to memory one suitable feature you can aim for in the event of getting lost. Thus, for instance, you should know that if you walk, say, due south, you will eventually reach a particular river; or if you walk due west, you will arrive at a particular road. This will help if you lose your map; most people, even if they can't handle

a compass, are aware that the sun rises in the east and sets in the west.

If the sun is high in the sky, making it difficult to judge directions, put a stick in the ground (or use an existing shadow), and place a stone at the tip of its shadow. Wait half an hour, and put another marker at the tip of the new shadow. A line drawn between the two will be an east–west line, with the later marker being in the east. Or, as Martyn Forrester puts it: 'Put your left foot on the first marker and your right foot on the second. You are now facing south.'★ When there is a vivid moon you can do the same at night. If there isn't a moon, you can work out compass points from the stars; but as the necessary stars aren't always visible (especially when I try), and as the method is different depending on whether you are in the northern or southern hemisphere, I shall instead repeat Martyn Forrester's rough-and-ready method of direction finding:

Push two sticks into the ground about 2 feet apart. The stick nearer you should be shorter than the other. Now lie down on the ground and sight along the stick tips on to any star in the sky. Watch closely for movement: if the star dips, it is in the west; [if it rises, it is in the east;] if it moves left, it is in the north; if it moves right, it is in the south.

If all else fails, it is often a good policy to aim for the nearest river (obviously not at night, when you might stumble into a ravine), for if you walk downstream, the river should sooner or later lead to human habitation; and it will guarantee you a supply of water.

3. Conserve water. As I've just written, in a hot dry climate you won't live for more than two or three days without it. When your water supplies are running low, be sure that you don't lose any unnecessary liquid through sweat or evaporation. Therefore keep out of the sun, reduce movement to the minimum, and keep any necessary exertions

★ *Survival* (Sphere, 1987)

until the cool of the evening. When the air is hot and dry, keep your immobile body covered in clothes (as the locals do) to reduce evaporation. When your liquid intake is low, reduce food consumption (especially of dried foods and proteins), because your body uses a lot of water for digesting them.

I think almost everyone knows that if you are stranded at sea, drinking sea water will shorten your life. The kidneys are forced to extract extra fluid from the body to excrete excessive salt, and dehydration is accelerated. If you are on a boat with cooking facilities, then hang some material in the steam created by boiling salt water; the material will absorb the purified moisture.

If you have to search for water, study the regular flight times of birds, especially if they are grain-eating ones, such as pigeons, doves, or sand-grouse. They tend to drink at dawn and dusk. Desert bats also drink at these times.

It is possible that animal tracks may lead to water, but don't follow them too far, because the likelihood of finding water may be outweighed by water loss through exertion. *Always remember that in any survival situation, water takes priority over food.*

Where there is no surface water you may have to dig; always look in areas where the water might naturally drain. The dried-up beds of rivers are usually by far the best places, especially under likely-looking plants. Try the lowest possible sites, and if in a desert, try the base of the steep side of a sand dune.

When you think there is going to be a dew at night, leave out some clothes to absorb it. If you haven't done this by the time of the morning dew, drag some clothes through the damp vegetation, and wring them out.

Similarly, when there is going to be rain and you don't have enough containers (for instance, on a capsized boat) then put out all your clothes.

In the last edition I never mentioned the often described solar

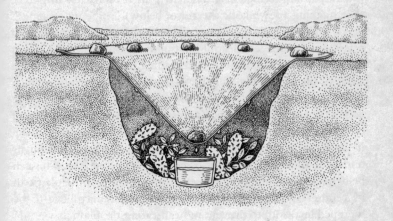

Fig. 5 Solar still.

still, which enables you to gather water even in areas that are very dry. I had read descriptions of the stills in many survival books, but presumed that the idea had been copied from one book to another and that in practice the still probably wouldn't work. Nor was my confidence increased when I noticed that some survival handbooks claimed that the still worked better by night, while others claimed that it worked better by day. Clearly, some of the authors had never tried one. When, however, I mentioned my scepticism to an ex-member of the Special Boat Services with whom I was staying in Devon, he marched out into the garden, dug a hole in the earth, and constructed a still. Within two hours we had collected some drinkable water, even though the experiment was in the middle of an exceptionally hot, dry summer, and the soil was completely parched.

I was so impressed by this miraculous production of water that I can't resist including a description and illustration of a solar still (Fig. 5); though I still presume that the energy used in constructing one will rarely be justifiable, and unless you are on a vehicle expedition, you are most unlikely to have the necessary kit. If you are going on a desert trip in a vehicle, it might be worth taking a few plastic sheets (see below).

To make a solar still, dig a hole in the ground approximately 3 feet wide and 2 feet deep. Place some type of collecting can (a mug or a saucepan) in the centre, then cover the hole with a sheet of plastic; ideally this should be transparent plastic (which makes it easy to see where to position the can). Weigh down the edge of the sheet with stones, and try to seal the edges with sand or earth. You should place a weight on top of the sheet to make it sag in such a way that the evaporation which collects on its underside slides down and drips into the collecting can. This can be helped by running your finger from the edge of the plastic to its centre. (If you use a stone as a weight, it may have to be wrapped in a cloth to prevent its heat searing the plastic.)

John Wiseman (see below) says the still is especially effective in regions, such as deserts, where it is hot during the day and cold at night, and he says this kind of still can collect at least 1 pint during a twenty-four-hour period (the still also works at night). The still can also be used as a primitive distillery in order to purify brackish water; put the water in shallow containers next to the collecting can. You can also increase water distillation by putting green vegetation at the bottom of the pit.

The still should be dug in places – such as dry river beds – where there is likely to be moisture, and it mustn't be in the shade.

I have no first-hand experience of survival and therefore much of this section of the book is gleaned from other handbooks or other people's advice. For this reason I haven't gone into great detail, but I have judged it worthwhile to pass on basic information, because it could be useful in emergencies for people who would never dream of reading the more informative specialized books. For instance, I can be fairly confident in offering the comforting information that the flesh of almost everything that walks, crawls, swims, or flies can be eaten in emergencies. In different parts of the world the most surprising animals, be they cats, dogs, snails, or snakes, are a regular feature of the local diet; and (as explained in Chapter 5) animal food is – weight for weight – usually far more nutritious than vegetable food. It is often much more worthwhile for a survivor to search for animal nutrition than to waste their energies on finding suitable plants and fruits.

All birds' eggs are edible and nutritious, provided they are fresh. If there is water about, it should be easy to catch frogs, which could be a very useful source of food. I wondered whether to leave out this advice, because of the fact that frogs are the source of lethal arrow poison; but, as frogs are a likely and easily caught source of emergency food, I made some further investigations. These produced the following answers (but as I am reluctant to guarantee accuracy, don't gather frogs except for survival). There are approximately 3,000 species of frog, of which about 100 should be excluded from your menu. These are to be found in Central and South America (though one has hopped to Hawaii). Most of the poisonous ones tend to be small (1–2 inches) and very colourful. Their muscle tissue is black. The poison is in the skin, and it is anyway safest to skin all amphibians and reptiles. Avoid all toads and newts. Lizards, however, will often offer a very real chance of an emergency snack, and they make excellent kebabs. (The handbooks – perhaps a bit optimistically – tell us that lizards can easily be caught with a noose at the end of a pole. I have also read that a lizard can be caught with just a simple noose made of long grass, which is very slowly manoeuvred over its head.)

Although I have little first-hand experience, my reading on the subject has made me believe that a survivor would be immensely helped by the knowledge that **insects** are nutritionally valuable, and that they are nearly always easier than other animals to find and catch. Weight for weight they are much more nutritious than vegetables, and they can be a valuable source of fats, proteins, and other nutrients. Although most survival manuals don't mention insects, their potential usefulness is being increasingly recognized, and there is now even a newsletter on the subject.*

It is only in Europe that insects have been disdained as food; elsewhere they are treasured, whether they are mopani worms in Africa, giant water bugs in Thailand, or leaf-cutter ants (which are sold like popcorn to cinema audiences in Colombia). In his declining days, Emperor Hirohito's favourite dish was cooked wasps with rice.

People have starved to death when edible and nutritious insects were at hand. Don't lose your life through fastidiousness; an astonishing variety of insects are edible. A Victorian booklet, *Why Not Eat Insects?*,† lists hilarious menus, which include slug soup, moths sautéd in butter, and stag beetles on toast. Outlandish snacks could be a godsend in extreme circumstances: the late M. J. Dijkman, an authority on tropical foods, reckoned that he saved his own and fellow prisoners' lives when he introduced cockroaches into their Japanese prison-camp diet. In order to make the cockroaches more palatable, he first ground them to powder. (Cockroaches would be an available snack in most tropical prisons, but because of their habit of running in and out of lavatories, they would probably be carrying dangerous bacteria, and it would be unwise to eat them uncooked. Avoid any insects, such as houseflies, that are likely to settle on anything foul.) Insects can be more than just edible: I have eaten dragon flies (caught by Balinese children, who put the sticky gum from frangipani trees on the end of poles), crickets, and flying ants; they were all delicious.

Edible insects can be found in the widest variety of terrain, including some of the harshest; there are ninety-three scientific papers on the subject of insects as human food in deserts. John

---

Food Insects Newsletter, ed. Gene R. DeFoliart (Department of Entomology, University of Wisconsin)

†Vincent Holt (1885; republished by British Museum, Natural History, 1988, with a new preface by R. I. Vane-Wright)

Wiseman, who is one of the few survival writers to mention insects, writes in his *SAS Survival Handbook* (see Appendix 1), 'Insects are likely to be the survivor's most reliable source of animal food.' He specifically mentions termites, ants, beetles, grasshoppers, locusts, crickets, honeybees, caterpillars, and aquatic insects. The 'witchetty grubs' eaten by Aboriginals are the larvae of beetles, and you might be able to find other beetle grubs by investigating decaying tree stumps, rotten logs, or trees with peeling bark (beware of scorpions, spiders, and snakes). John Wiseman writes that some palms and bamboos are also infested with grubs – 'If you have a knife, cut material away until you find them under the surface.' Beetle grubs are usually pale in colour with three pairs of short legs. Hold the head, and eat the rest.

Nearly all insects that are found in unpolluted fresh water (including the larvae and adults of beetles, bugs, mayflies, stoneflies, and so on) are edible. When entomologists want to collect aquatic insects, they stretch a net across the water, and then agitate the river upstream. This may dislodge from the weeds and stones numerous aquatic insects which drift into their net. Try using a piece of clothing as an emergency net.

The best time for catching most insects is at night or early morning. Some of them are, of course, attracted to lights; moths make a plump snack (take off their wings).

Here are some warnings about eating insects which I have gathered from John Wiseman's manual, an article by R. I. Vane-Wright,* and R. L. Taylor's splendid *Butterflies in My Stomach*.† Don't eat insects that are already dead. If you want to store insects, avoid damp, which can cause a toxic mould. Bright colours are often a warning sign (as they are with tropical fish). Grubs found on the underside of leaves (they are often foul-smelling and slimy to touch) may excrete poisonous fluids. In general, the edible grubs are usually smooth-skinned and one colour – often white or cream. Don't eat grubs that live

* 'Why not eat insects?' (*Bulletin of Entomological Research*, 1991)
† (Woodbridge Press, Santa Barbara, California, 1975)

underground. Squeeze out the insides of caterpillars. Don't eat hairy-skinned caterpillars (or if you must, eat only the squeezed-out innards). Take the armour-like casing off beetles. Remove the wings and legs of large insects, such as locusts, for they may be irritating to your insides or indigestible. Beware of beetles with large jaws. Many ants give fierce stinging bites, and some fire formic acid; they should be cooked for at least six minutes.

Generally, though, *cooking doesn't destroy the poisons in insects*. Even so, if you can, it is best to cook them, because this will destroy any harmful bacteria or parasites. Some insects are extra-delicious when roasted — such as grasshoppers, which can be skewered on the end of a stick or put into the embers of a fire. However, when you need to eat insects to survive, remember that cooking isn't necessary.

R. L. Taylor suggests the following test for poisonous insects, which isn't very different to the test for vegetation (see page 401).

1. Check if the insect irritates the skin.
2. Put a morsel on the inside lower lip; if it is burning, acrid, bitter, or soapy then discard it.
3. If it tastes good, eat a small portion. If you don't vomit or get diarrhoea within the next eight hours, then try some more.

Because insects are high in protein, you should drink plenty of water when you are eating them; if you have little water, cut right down on your consumption of insects, because protein uses up a lot of water in digestion.

Snails, slugs, and worms are very often edible, and the latter are especially nutritious. Avoid land snails with brilliantly col-oured shells. Avoid all sea snails, as some might be very danger-ous. Starve snails for a few days. Slugs are just snails without shells. Worms should be starved for a day, or have their muck squeezed out. Wiseman suggests that they can be sun-dried, ground to a powder, and then added to other food as required.

As far as I can discover, all **fresh-water fish** are edible. Most sea-water fishes are also edible, and luckily the toxic ones, such as the puffer fish, usually look sinister or ugly. If a fish doesn't have scales or the usual shape of a fish, avoid it unless you know for certain it's edible. Some reef fish can be poisonous, and be extra suspicious of those with very bright colours. If fish are toxic, the most poisonous elements may be in the innards and eggs, so discard these as a precaution. A strange fact about sea fish is that a particular species may be safe in one area but poisonous in another; also a species may be safe one month, but poisonous the next. This is because they may have been feeding on other fish which are themselves poisonous. Here is an expert's advice on what to do if you are obliged to eat questionable fish:

It is advisable to cut the fish into thin fillets and soak them in several changes of water (fresh or salt) for at least thirty minutes (do not use the same water for cooking purposes). This will serve to leach out the poison, which is somewhat water-soluble. If a questionable species is cooked by boiling, the water should always be discarded.*

If you are uncertain about the edibility of any insect, fish, or reptile, it is best to cook and eat a small portion, then wait a few hours to see if there are any after-effects. Be extremely suspicious of any numbness, itching, or any type of soreness in your mouth. Even though the flesh of an animal is edible, other parts may not be. For instance, the skins of frogs and toads may be toxic, as may the roe of pike. The liver of a polar bear is toxic owing to an excessively high content of vitamin A, and a shark's liver because of a high content of vitamin D. So to err on the safe side, it may be wisest to gut all mammals, and to gut and skin all reptiles and fish. Besides, in a hot climate, animals must be gutted immediately after they are killed, or the insides go bad and taint the flesh. Whenever possible the flesh should be cooked thoroughly because of possible infestation by parasites.

*Dangerous Marine Animals, Bruce W. Halstead (Cornell Maritime Press, 1959)

Choosing vegetation to eat is far more difficult than choosing animals, and whenever possible you should take local advice. Where this isn't available, and where you are obliged to eat vegetation, you can reduce the dangers by following some basic rules applicable in most hot countries; avoid all fungi, all plants which exude a white sap, all plants which smell strange, and any plants with red leaves, berries, or fruits. The seductive orange fruits of one tree, for instance, are lethal. A taste or smell of almonds or marzipan may also be a warning sign, as it often indicates essence of cyanide. Many people know that young nettle leaves are edible here, but don't transfer this knowledge to the tropics. There is a bush with nettle-like leaves which is extremely poisonous.

Nevertheless, a surprising variety of vegetation is edible – particularly young ferns, young grasses (especially bamboo), tubers, and roots. The latter two usually have to be cooked. If you are obliged to eat any unknown vegetation, always test a small portion under your lip to see if it has a bitter or acidic taste; if so, spit it out and try something else. If it passes these tests, boil and eat a small portion, and if after three hours there are no ill-effects, then you can eat the plant with a little more confidence. Before eating, it is generally better to cook unfamiliar vegetation, because some plants, particularly roots, are only nutritious after being cooked, and cooking sometimes reduces the risk of being poisoned. As with the suspect fish, throw away the cooking water afterwards.

Guns

In the first edition, I didn't mention guns because it never occurred to me that anybody would want to take one. Since then several people, usually about to mount an adventurous expedition, have asked me whether they should be armed.

Whenever possible, avoid taking a gun: it enormously increases your chances of problems with customs officers, frontier officers, and all other types of authority.

As a general rule, a gun will add to the journey's dangers

rather than diminish them. When you are in lawless countryside, its attraction as an object to steal often outweighs its effect as a deterrent. Also, the experience of gun-owning societies has shown that the number of accidents is often higher than the number of murders. For these reasons, one lady I know decided to live alone throughout Kenya's Mau-Mau troubles without a gun's protection. She survived unscathed. (In fact, only thirty-two white civilians were murdered throughout the whole of that notorious emergency.)

Even in more swashbuckling days, many wiser travellers explored without a gun. Walter Harris, who during more than fifty years made perilous journeys among Moroccan tribes, declared, 'I have almost without exception carried no arms, which are often more a source of danger than of security.'* Dr T. L. Pennell of the Afghan frontier wrote:

It is often asked of me whether I carry a revolver or other arms when travelling about among the wild tribes. For a missionary to do so would not only be fatal to his chance of success, but would be a serious and constant danger. It would be impossible for him to be always on his guard; there must be times when, through fatigue or other reasons, he is at the mercy of those among whom he is working. Besides this, there is nothing which an Afghan covets more, or to steal which he is more ready to risk his life, than a firearm; and though he might not otherwise wish harm to the missionary, the possibility of securing a revolver or gun would be too great a temptation, even though he had to shed blood to secure it. My plan was, therefore, to put myself entirely in their hands, and let them see that I was trusting to their sense of honour and to their traditional treatment of a guest for my safety.†

The most likely grounds for taking a gun are when you need to kill animals for fresh food.

In a village

It is not always polite to walk straight into a village. Check local customs with your guide; he may advise you to wait outside until formally invited to enter.

* *Morocco That Was* (Blackwood, 1921)
† *Among the Wild Tribes of the Afghan Frontier* (Seely Service, 1912)

When you are going to spend the night in a village, aim to get there well before nightfall. Apart from the danger of walking in the dark (a fractured ankle can incapacitate you), it is often discourteous to enter a village after dusk.

Travellers often see no reason for changing their normal behaviour when staying in a village, and consider it sufficient to 'be themselves'. This fits in well with modern relaxed attitudes, but travellers should make a greater effort and be extra-sensitive about their conduct. While in unfamiliar society, there are numerous opportunities for causing offence. Many travellers tend to enter taboo areas, dress scruffily when visiting the headman's hut, and, most frequently, cause offence by their bathing habits. In most parts of the world, people are extremely modest; indeed it may be the custom to remain partially dressed while bathing. Too often, travellers have not copied the locals, and sometimes they have even bathed completely naked – which is nearly always considered shocking.

Even though a village may not have obvious sanitation, offence is often caused by visitors who choose any piece of ground as a lavatory. In many parts of the world there is one area designated for men and another for women. It is sometimes best to ask where to go (though, unfortunately, this can lead to personal supervision). In some parts of the world it is the custom for women to go to the lavatory at different times of the day from men. If you take the morning express train from Delhi to Agra, you will see thousands of men doing their morning dump; the women have completed everything before dawn.

Remember that you are receiving hospitality, and should give consideration in return – especially if you are not in the habit of asking total strangers into your own home. In a village there may be no radio, almost certainly no television, and of course no cinema, therefore most villagers expect visitors to bring diversion from everyday life, and provide opportunities for gossip and amusement. This tends to mean that a decent, self-effacing visitor is often less popular than a hearty extrovert.

Sometimes when preparing myself for bed in a village hut, I have been scrutinized by an audience of thirty or forty – usually a phalanx of children crouching in front, women at one side, and the men standing at the back. I usually feel guilty at not providing better entertainment. Some travellers have a wonderful knack of amusing people; they may achieve this without special tricks, or they may be expert at conjuring, juggling, or standing on their heads. Anyone who can sing a few songs achieves instant popularity. Time and again I've been asked for a song, and each time I promise myself that on my return home I will practise some songs for future expeditions. All too often I have resorted to the tune of my old-school song, accompanied by the only lyrics I know, which begin:

The sexual life of a camel is stranger than anyone thinks,
At the height of the mating season it tries to bugger the Sphinx,
But the Sphinx's posterior passage is clogged by the sands of the Nile,
Which accounts for the hump of the camel, and the Sphinx's inscrutable
    smile.

Every traveller, however badly he or she sings, should learn some songs before staying in remote villages.

In Europe we eat at a table and sit on chairs, whereas in the traditional Third World people usually eat and sit on the floor. First-time travellers who have sat on chairs all their lives often need time to get used to this, and men tend to find it more difficult than women. This is not only a problem when you are staying in villages: at a feast in an Afghan merchant's house, and at a ceremony in an Indonesian palace, I have suffered agonies from having to sit cross-legged for several hours.

Presents

While you are staying in a village, the villagers may kill a few chickens, or even a goat for your benefit. Because this could make a very substantial inroad into their food stocks, their generosity shouldn't be taken for granted, and in some way should be repaid. In Chapter 3, I have already mentioned that it is a good idea to carry a wide range of presents.

I must add here that my friend Hilary Bradt, who has led many expeditions in South America, dislikes the practice of giving presents. She says that presents can distort the relationship between the villagers and the donor – that villagers may gradually be seduced into unnecessary consumerism and that they eventually consider gringos only as the bearers of consumer products. She has considerable experience of returning to the same villages, and relates how in some places she has often seen the villagers, who were at first generous, gradually become demanding, and then thieving. Hilary believes that it is best to repay people in a non-material way, such as giving entertainment or teaching children. She does, of course, agree that villagers should be repaid for food and services.

While I agree with many of these views (and certainly think that present-giving should be conducted with greater sensitivity), I still like to travel with a range of presents. Very often I have been handed gifts, and have felt awkward if I have nothing to give back. In some regions where people are poor or unsophisticated, they have – more frequently than you would expect – a tradition of giving presents to the privileged and powerful; in remote areas, foreign travellers are sometimes perceived as being in this category, though one is more likely to be given presents as a token of friendship. For whatever reason, a woman in a poor Indian village suddenly gave me a box of coloured paper-clips; I didn't have anything suitable to give her in return, but I was glad that I was able to give a postcard of Tower Bridge to her five-year-old daughter. Although it didn't measure up to the paper-clips, at least I was able to make a gesture.

There are also occasions when I haven't been given a present, but I want to repay hospitality in a non-financial way; I have never considered that the rendition of my old-school song was quite enough. Finally, there are many areas where there is a strong tradition of exchanging presents; when you aren't able to give one, you may be considered rude.

Most villagers, unless in a very remote area, are within a few days' walk of a market and won't be impressed by cheap trinkets. Take more generous presents for the family that houses and feeds you (often the headman's family), and also take cheaper presents, such as postcards from home, as tokens of friendship. (For ideas on presents, see Chapter 3.)

Both Hilary and I agree that too many travellers lavishly hand out sweets to children. They often indulge in this pointless and patronizing habit wherever they visit. Any travellers who follow in their footsteps are expected to do the same, but there is no good reason why they should; it makes for awkward relationships if all foreigners are considered as nothing more than itinerant sweet dispensers. Instead of feeling obliged to dole out sweets, visitors can amuse the children in many ways, including pulling funny faces, fooling about with a rubber pet mouse, or teaching them to count in English. Should you stay in the house of people with nice children, then it is acceptable to give the children presents, perhaps balloons, pens, or foreign coins.

If you are a photographer, it is often greatly appreciated if you take some photographs of your local acquaintances, and later arrange to have them sent or delivered to the village. Far too many travellers break their promise to do this. This type of present is a very suitable one, especially when you have been taking photographs for your own purposes. And if you have run out of presents when you were staying in the village, it is an excellent way of redeeming yourself and also showing that you haven't forgotten the kindness of your hosts.

POSTSCRIPT

When revisiting Bali after a gap of ten years, I knew there would be a lot of change; but I was thunderstruck at how much the island had altered. Within minutes of leaving the airport I was gazing at a castle-sized Kentucky Fried Chicken. Arriving at the cultural capital, Ubud, I found it altered beyond recognition: formerly it was little more than a delightful sleepy village; now it was filled with tourist boutiques and budget hotels. Highland roads, previously empty, were crammed with diesel-belching lorries; remote mountain footpaths were strewn with bits of plastic. It wasn't just the tourists who had altered Bali; it was prosperity and modern technology.

Economic growth has brought an increasing tendency to universal homogeneity. With the exception of a few Asian states, nearly every nation is adopting Western dress. Local music is being driven out by discotheques and cassettes; a villa in suburban Jakarta increasingly resembles one in suburban Quito; out in the countryside ubiquitous corrugated iron is replacing wooden tiles and thatch.

The traditional environment is also being destroyed: forests and jungles are being devastated; coral reefs are being pillaged; wild game is disappearing except in tame and overcrowded game reserves.

So pack your bags and go on your travels before it is too late. There are still vast tracts of the world which beg to be visited; travel will give you a wealth of experience and pleasure which can be drawn on for the rest of your life – a wealth which no government can ever take away. And if you are inquisitive and enterprising, many unlikely places are interesting; even Bali can still be worth visiting. I have never regretted visiting a single country (though three days in Dubai were enough), and I have rarely met anyone who regretted going on their travels. Our greatest disappointments are nearly always for what we *haven't* done – not for what we have done. And don't let the feeble excuse of work keep you back; remember the Haitian proverb: 'If work is such a good thing, how come the rich haven't grabbed it all for themselves?' Or consider the wisdom of President Reagan, who said, 'They say that work never kills anyone. But why take the risk?'

FURTHER READING

The books in this appendix have been included because they may be of practical value, and therefore I have listed the most recent editions. It will still be worth checking whether there has been a later edition.

I have included some books that have recently gone out of print, because they might either come back into print or be available in your local library.

The books mentioned in the footnotes of previous chapters are listed more as sources for quotes than for practical value; therefore I have given the date of the actual edition from which I have quoted.

Guidebooks to specific areas aren't listed, because it will always be best to get the most up-to-date information about them from the bookshops mentioned in Appendix 3.

You should be aware of the wonderful fact that our splendid public-library system is obliged to order any book you want. Therefore, if local libraries can't obtain a book through the sophisticated inter-library lending system, they will buy it for you.

HEALTH

Travellers' Health: How to Stay Healthy Abroad, ed. Richard Dawood (Oxford University Press, 1992)
This is a helpful and thorough book, especially useful as each section is written by an expert.

The Traveller's Health Guide, Dr Anthony Turner (Roger Lascelles, 1991)
Sensible, clear, and readable.

Expedition Medicine, ed. Bent Juel-Jensen (Expedition

Advisory Centre, Royal Geographical Society, revised edition 1991; tel. 071 581 2057)

A useful book by experienced authors, aimed at the intrepid.

Where There is No Doctor, David Werner (Macmillan, 1980)

Invaluable for anyone settled far from the nearest doctor.

First Aid Manual: The Authorized Manual of St John's Ambulance, St Andrew's Ambulance Association, British Red Cross (Dorling Kindersley, 1993)

GENERAL BOOKS AND OTHERS

The Traveller's Handbook, ed. Sarah Gorman and Caroline Brandenburger (Wexas, distributed by Trade & Travel Publications, 1991)

Each section is written by a specialist, so this book of more than 800 pages is a valuable work of reference. It also has many useful appendices on subjects such as airline head-offices, Kodak laboratories, and departure taxes.

The Independent Good Holiday Guide, Frank Barrett (Headline, 1993)

This includes valuable listings of many types of tour and travel operators. Useful if you want to know which companies specialize in Polish holidays, railway holidays, naturist holidays, natural history holidays, and so on.

Adventure Holidays, Victoria Pybus (Vacation Work, 1992)

Lists more than 400 organizations offering activities from windsurfing, through survival or bird-watching, to mountaineering.

The Backpacker's Handbook, Chris Townsend (Oxford Illustrated Press, 1991)

Excellent detail on preparation for backpacking trips.

The Sahara Handbook, Simon Glenn (Roger Lascelles, 1990)

Apart from the geographical sections, it has useful detail on many aspects of preparation for desert trips. Those who can read French will find even more detail on the Sahara in Le Guide du Sahara (in the Guides Bleus series).

Stay Alive in the Desert, Dr K. E. M. Melville (Roger Lascelles, 1993)

A survival manual by a doctor with a wide experience of the Sahara; it includes sections on driving, health, etc.

Desert Expeditions, Tom Sheppard (Expedition Advisory Centre, Royal Geographical Society, 1988; tel. 071 581 2057)

Seventy-nine pages of useful advice for intrepid desert expeditioners.

World Weather Guide, ed. E. A. Pearce and C. G. Smith (Hutchinson, 1990)

Perhaps not one to buy, unless you are a very regular traveller; but make your library get a copy. It doesn't always give enough detail, but on the whole it is excellent, and usefully covers the whole world.

Nothing Ventured: Disabled People Travel the World, ed. Alison Walsh (Rough Guide series/Penguin 1991)

A very useful and heart-warming book.

The SAS Survival Handbook, John Wiseman (Collins, 1990)

A best-seller, nicely illustrated, and with much intriguing information on subjects from car accidents to shipwreck.

Travel with Children: A Survival Kit for Travel in Asia, Maureen Wheeler (Lonely Planet, 1985)

The author travelled with her two children, and believes that they were an asset. Plenty of sensible advice.

The Tropical Beach Handbook, Nick Hanna (Fourth Estate, 1989)

More useful than you would expect from the title, because it gives details of snorkelling and scuba destinations, with good maps.

World Mapping Today, R. B. Parry (Butterworth, 1987)

Not one to buy, as it is expensive. But useful, as it lists world sources of maps, country by country.

WORKING ABROAD AND VOLUNTARY WORK

Work Your Way around the World, Susan Griffith (Vacation Work, 1991)

413

An invaluable book, which has become even more useful with each edition. This book should be your first choice.

Teaching English Abroad, Susan Griffith (Vacation Work, 1991)

An excellent and thorough book by the same author as Work Your Way around the World.

The Directory of Summer Jobs Abroad, David Woodworth (Vacation Work, 1992)

More than 3,000 vacancies in more than forty different countries, listed at the employers' request, plus practical supplements.

The Directory of Work and Study in Developing Countries, David Leppard (Vacation Work, 1990)

A guide to employment, voluntary work, and academic opportunities, as well as sources of further information.

Best Summer Jobs in Alaska, Josh Groves (Vacation Work, 1993)

Summer Employment Directory of the US, ed. Peterson's Guides (Vacation Work, 1992)

Thousands of jobs listed at the employers' request in the United States and Canada. Includes sections on legal requirements and visas.

Working Holidays (edited and published by the Central Bureau for Educational Visits and Exchanges)

Information on more than 99,000 paid and voluntary seasonal work-opportunities in seventy countries.

A Year Between (edited and published by the Central Bureau for Educational Visits and Exchanges, see below)

A guide for those taking a year off between school and higher education or work; or between higher education and a career.

Jobs in Japan, John Wharton (Vacation Work, 1992)

Mostly about English-teaching jobs, but also practical hints.

A Year Off? A Year On?, Alan Jamieson (CRAC Publications, Hobson's Publishing, Bateman Street, Cambridge CB2 1LZ; tel. 0223 354551)

Provides information about work, summer projects, and voluntary service abroad.

The International Directory of Voluntary Work, David Woodworth (Vacation Work, 1989)

*Details of more than 400 organizations wanting different types of
help, for both the skilled and the unskilled.*

Volunteer Work (edited and published by the Central Bureau
for Educational Visits and Exchanges)
*This lists 100 organizations recruiting volunteers for medium- and
long-term projects in 153 countries, and gives other relevant details.*

Vacation Work and the **Central Bureau for Educational
Visits and Exchanges** have published many of the above books
on working abroad and voluntary work, and they might have
published more by the time you read this. Their books should,
in theory, be available from good bookshops; but if they aren't,
or if you want their catalogues, here are the addresses:

Vacation Work, 9 Park End Street, Oxford OX1 1HJ; tel.
0865 241978

Central Bureau for Educational Visits and Exchanges,
Seymour Mews House, Seymour Mews, London W1H 9PE;
tel. 071 486 5101

TRANSPORT

The Off-Road Four Wheel Drive Book, Jack Jackson
(Haynes, 1988)
*A most useful book by someone who has great experience of every
type of expedition.*

Richard's New Bicycle Book, Richard Ballantine (Pan, 1990)
*This 360-page book is full of good, clear detail. Since the first
edition in 1972, it has sold more than 1 million copies.*

Richard's Mountain Bike Book, Charles Kelly and Nick
Crane (Pan, 1993)
*Approximately 196 pages by two very experienced cyclists, one of
whom played a part in the invention of the mountain bike.*

Bicycle Expeditions, Paul Vickers (Expedition Advisory
Centre, Royal Geographical Society, 1990; tel. 071 581 2057)

WOMEN

Half the Earth, ed. Miranda Davies, Laura Longrigg, Lucinda Montefiore, and Natania Jansz (Pandora/Routledge & Kegan Paul, 1986)

Arranged geographically. Useful reports from women on their experiences in different countries. Includes practical Travel Notes.

Handbook for Women Travellers, Maggie and Gemma Moss (Piatkus, 1991)

Not arranged geographically. Two sisters use their experience of travelling to offer advice to other women.

MAGAZINES, ANNUALS, AND OTHER SOURCES

The ABC Guide to International Travel (World Timetable Centre, Dunstable, Bedfordshire LU5 4HE; tel. 0582 60011)

This quarterly guide (112 pages) can be bought singly, or on subscription. It is very expensive, so is probably best consulted at your local travel agent, if your reference library doesn't have a copy. It is updated regularly and lists all the important travel information (such as visas, health requirements, and currency regulations) for every country in the world.

The ABC International Cruise and Ferry Guide (World Timetable Centre, Dunstable, Bedfordshire LU5 4HE; tel. 0582 60011)

This used to be called the ABC Passenger Shipping Guide, and this new edition wasn't out at the time of going to press. Although much of this publication will be covering cruises, it still might be useful (especially for people who won't fly), as there is very little other information about shipping. There is a chapter on cargo services, and several useful indexes. The guide is expensive, so try your library and travel agent first.

The World Travel Guide, including the ABTA/ANTOR Factfinder (Columbus Press, 5 Luke Street, London EC2 4PX; tel. 071 729 4535, 1992/3)

This reference book of more than 1,000 pages gives the same type of

416

details as the above, with some extra discursive information. Consult it at your library or local travel agent.

Holiday Which? (2 Marylebone Road, London NW1 4DX; tel. 071 486 5544)

A worthwhile magazine, because it publishes the only travel pages (apart from the Independent*) which aren't influenced by free trips. For a fee, Holiday Which? also offers a service which helps you in disputes with travel companies.*

Intermediate Technology Publications publishes a booklet, *Books by Post*, which lists a large number of books (including subjects from butterfly-farming to primary health-care) concerned with appropriate technology and development issues. Write to 103 Southampton Row, London WC1B 4HH; tel. 071 436 9761. There is also a bookshop at this address.

Expedition Advisory Centre of the Royal Geographical Society (1 Kensington Gore, London SW7 2AR; tel. 071 581 2057) publishes a very useful series of books and pamphlets for expeditioners. Some of these have already been mentioned in specialist sections. Because these books aren't in general bookshops, and are only available from the above address, here is the centre's latest complete list:

Expedition Planners' Handbook & Directory 1993–94 (447 pp.)
Bicycle Expeditions, Paul Vickers (42 pp.)
Desert Expeditions, Tom Sheppard (79 pp.)
Expedition Medicine, ed. Bent Juel-Jensen (119 pp.)
Joining an Expedition, ed. Shane Winser (68 pp.)
Tropical Forest Expeditions, Roger Chapman (74 pp.)
Underwater Expeditions, ed. Robert Palmer (136 pp.)

EQUIPMENT

Apologies for the bias towards Britain and London in this appendix and the next one. This is because I have tried to concentrate on areas where I have first-hand information. I decided that a selective list of addresses was better than none at all. Even if you don't live in London, it will sometimes be worth making a trip and getting everything – books, kit, visas, and immunizations – all in one outing.

Nomad (3–4 Wellington Terrace, Turnpike Lane, London N8 0PX; tel. 081 889 7014)
As mentioned in Chapter 3, they have agreed to try to stock as many as possible of the items that I have mentioned in the chapters on equipment and health. Although it is quite a distance from central London (but next door to Turnpike Lane tube station), it may be a useful one-stop destination for your immunizations (which are done only on certain days), medical kit (they can pre-scribe), and other equipment.

YHA Adventure Shop (14 Southampton Street, London WC2E 7HY; tel. 071 836 8541)
Both stock and staff are erratic, but it is one of the largest camping shops in London. Usefully, there is also a mountaineering and sports shop just opposite (see below). There are YHA Adventure Shops in Birmingham, Brighton, Bristol, Cambridge, Cardiff, Leeds, Manchester, Nottingham, Oxford, Reading, Sheffield, and Staines. For further inquiries telephone 0784 458625.

Ellis Brigham (30 Southampton Street, London WC2E 7HE; tel. 071 240 9577)
A visit to this mountaineering and sports shop can be usefully

combined with one to the YHA shop opposite. Ellis Brigham also has branches in Manchester, Liverpool, Chester, Rosedale, Bristol, Snowdonia, Aviemore, and Fort William.

Blacks Camping and Leisure (42–53 Rathbone Place, London W1P 1AN; tel. 071 636 6645)

A large shop, which at present I don't find very useful. They have several branches around the country.

Blacks Camping and Leisure (10 Holborn, London EC1N 2LL; tel. 071 404 5681)

This shop is just worth including because it can be combined with a visit to Snow and Rock round the corner in Gray's Inn Road.

Snow and Rock (150 Holborn, London EC1N 2NS; tel. 071 831 6900)

Although the address is in Holborn, you will find this shop in Gray's Inn Road. As they specialize in equipment for the serious trekker and mountaineer, their staff tend to be knowledgeable, and their equipment tends to be of the best quality, and expensive. They have a branch in Kensington High Street (see below) and also one in Birmingham (14 Priory Queensway, Birmingham B4 6BS; tel. 021 236 8280).

Snow and Rock (188 Kensington High Street, London W8 7RG; tel. 071 937 0872)

A branch of the above. A visit to it can be usefully combined with a look at the two shops below.

YHA Adventure Shop (174 Kensington High Street, London W8 7RG; tel. 071 938 2948)

This shop serves a different niche to the more serious and specialist Snow and Rock. Therefore it is very handy to be able to visit the two together; the shops are very close.

Alpine Sports (215 Kensington High Street, London W8 6BD; tel. 071 938 1911)

Little good stock when I visited, but as it is near to the two shops above, it is worth a look-in.

Cotswold Camping (42 Uxbridge Road, London W12 8ND; tel. 081 743 2976)

A useful shop just near Shepherd's Bush tube station. They also have branches in South Cerney, Reading, Cirencester, Manchester, and Betws-y-Coed. They also sell by mail order.

Mountain Air (907 Fulham Road, London SW6 5HU; tel. 071 731 5415)
In winter the main emphasis is on skiing, but they also stock equipment suitable for walkers and trekkers.

Camping and Outdoor Centre (27 Buckingham Palace Road, London SW1W 0PP; tel. 071 834 6007)
This is owned by the Scout Association, and stocks all the usual basic camping equipment.

The Survival Shop (West Colonnade, Euston Station, London NW1 2DY; tel. 071 388 8353)
Clothes, equipment, and gadgets, some of them a bit gimmicky. They also issue a catalogue (see Mail order, below) and it might be worth studying this before you visit the shop.

Trailfinders Travel Goods (56 Earl's Court Road, London W8 6EJ; tel. 071 937 3895)
A very small kit shop, which is near the two Trailfinder ticket shops (see Flight Advice, below).

Silverman's Government Surplus (2 Harford Street, London E1 4PS; tel. 071 790 0900)
A friend recommends this as the best true army-surplus-style shop in London. It is near Mile End tube station.

Laurence Corner (62–64 Hampstead Road, London NW1 2NU; tel. 071 388 6811)
An army surplus shop.

Captain O. M. Watts (49 Albemarle Street, London W1X 3FE; tel. 071 493 4633)
Concentrates mostly on nautical equipment, but occasionally useful for filling gaps.

The World Service Shop (Bush House, Strand, London WC2B 4PH; tel. 071 257 2576. Mail order tel. 071 257 2575)
They sell mostly language publications, but they probably have the best (though small) selection of short-wave radios in the country, and their staff can give you knowledgeable advice.

EQUIPMENT BY MAIL ORDER

Don't necessarily trust the descriptions in their catalogues, as some companies aren't always rigorous in their testing. I have, for instance, found that candles did not last as long as advertised, that 'filter drinking-straws' broke down on first use, and so on. All the same, these companies may be useful, as they sometimes stock items that can't be found elsewhere.

Survival Aids (Morland, Penrith, Cumbria CA10 3AZ; tel. 09314 444)
They produce a lively and amusing catalogue, with some worthwhile items among the gimmicks. They also have shops in London (see above), Aldershot, Glasgow, Edinburgh, Birmingham, and Bristol.

Safariquip (13a Waterloo Park, Upper Brook Street, Stockport SK1 3BP; tel. 061 429 8700)
It stocks an interesting range, and the owner is especially interested in the problems of water purification.

Field & Trek (3 Wates Way, Brentwood, Essex CM15 9TB; tel. 0277 233122)
This company has competitive prices, and is used by many experienced expeditioners.

MASTA (Keppel Street, London WC1E 7HT; tel. 071 631 4408)
Apart from their Health Briefs (see Chapter 5), they also sell various items of equipment, including mosquito nets and insect repellent.

Homeway Ltd (The White House, Littleton, Winchester, Hants SO22 6QS; tel. 0962 881051)
They sell the excellent kit/medical/cosmetic bags with transparent fronts (see Fig. 2, Chapter 3), and also a few other items of travellers' kit.

International Supplies Ltd (Alpha Close, Garth Road, Morden, Surrey SM4 4LX; tel. 081 337 0161)
Supplies relief agencies, missionaries, and overseas workers with all medical needs, from mosquito nets to packing containers. Their list

also extends to large, and very large items, such as solar-powered lighting units and the biggest water filters. They can organize VAT-free sales.

Clothtec (Expedition suppliers) (92 Par Green, Par, Cornwall PL24 2AG; tel. 0726 813602)
Specialists in mosquito nets and 'jungle sleeping units', including a self-supporting net. They also sell hammocks. They are very happy to give expert advice over the telephone, particularly to first-time expeditioners. Although mainly mail order, customers are welcome to call in.

Oasis (1 High Street, Stoke Ferry, Norfolk PE33 9SF; tel. 0366 501122)
Specialists in mosquito nets, including pre-soaked ones.

Cotswold Camping (42 Uxbridge Road, London W12 8ND; tel. 081 743 2976)
Already mentioned under Equipment.

BICYCLE SHOPS

Saviles Cycle Stores (99 Battersea Rise, London SW11 1HW; tel. 071 228 4279)

F. W. Evans Cycles (77 The Cut, London SE1 8LL; tel. 071 928 4785. Also at 127 Wandsworth High Street, London SW18 4JB; tel. 081 877 1878)

SLEEPING-BAG SERVICING

W. E. Franklin (116–120 Onslow Road, Sheffield S11 7AH; tel. 0742 686161)
Specialist cleaners of sleeping bags.

Rab Carrington Sleeping Bags (32 Edwards Street, Sheffield S3 7GB; tel. 0742 757544)
This company sells high-quality sleeping bags only to the retail trade. However, it is useful to know that they offer the rare service of repairing down sleeping bags.

LUGGAGE

Gallops (16 Old Brompton Road, London SW7 3DL; tel. 071 589 1734)

They mend luggage (quite a rarity).

Selfridges (Oxford Street, London W1A 1AB; tel. 071 629 1234)

Has the largest luggage department in London.

PHOTOGRAPHY

Tecno (358 Kensington High Street, London W14 8NS; tel. 071 602 5311)

They stock cheap film, and I have found these shops quite good. They also have other London branches in Euston Road, Moorgate, Brompton Road and Proctor Street.

Leeds Camera Centre (20–26 Brunswick Centre, Berners Street, London WC1N 1AE; tel. 071 833 1661)

I have found the staff of this shop to be more knowledgeable and helpful than those in any of the other shops dealing with professionals. They also repair cameras and sell film at reasonable prices.

Sendean (105 Oxford Street, London W1R 1TF; tel. 071 439 8418)

They repair cameras for many professionals.

Jessop Photo Centre (67–69 New Oxford Street, London WC1A 1DG; tel. 071 240 6077)

A useful shop, especially for gadgetry not stocked by other camera shops. For large quantities of film, they will negotiate an excellent price. They have other branches around Britain.

David Leung (34 Goodmayes Road, Ilford, Essex IG3 9UN; tel. 081 599 6657)

A reliable friend recommends this shop as one of the cheapest and most knowledgeable places for good cameras and lenses (but not always for small accessories). It is almost opposite Goodmayes station on the line from Liverpool Street through Stratford.

USEFUL ADDRESSES

This list is necessarily selective.

LIBRARIES

Royal Geographical Society (1 Kensington Gore, London SW7 2AR; tel. 071 589 5466)

An excellent library but only members are admitted. Members can take books out on loan, so membership of the RGS may be useful (see Other Organizations, below). The RGS also has an outstanding collection of foreign maps; the map room is open to the public, and photocopying facilities are available.

School of Oriental and African Studies (Thornhaugh Street, Russell Square, London WC1H 0XG; tel. 071 637 2388)

A very large and useful library. Apply for a day ticket.

Canning House (2 Belgrave Square, London SW1X 8PJ; tel. 071 235 2303)

South American specialists. Books may be read in the library, but borrowed only if you are a member of Canning House.

Royal Commonwealth Society Library (18 Northumberland Avenue, London WC2N 5BJ; tel. 071 930 6733)

An excellent and most useful library. It is under some threat, and is skeleton-staffed, so make an appointment. The library may have to move to Cambridge.

Commonwealth Institute Resource Centre (230 Kensington High Street, London W8 6NQ; tel. 071 602 9003)

A good library for research into a Commonwealth country, and it also stocks local newspapers.

BOOK AND MAP SHOPS

London is now very well served for travel bookshops. Most of these shops will also send you books through the mail.

The Travel Bookshop (13 Blenheim Crescent, London W11 2EE; tel. 071 229 5260)
The first of the shops in London specializing in both new and second-hand travel books. Also sells maps. Well worth a visit.

Stanfords (12 Long Acre, London WC2E 9LP; tel. 071 836 1321)
The best map-suppliers in Britain. Also an excellent bookshop, and sells a wide range of guidebooks.

Daunt Books (83 Marylebone High Street, London W1M 4AL; tel. 071 224 2295)
This is a beautiful bookshop, and has the largest stock of travel books in Britain. The shop sells even the most esoteric titles.

The Traveller's Bookshop (25 Cecil Court, London WC2N 4EZ; tel. 071 836 9132)
Smaller than the other travel bookshops, but convenient if you are in the area. They also stock second-hand books.

Intermediate Technology Publications (103 Southampton Row, London WC1B 4HH; tel. 071 436 9761)
This sells a very wide range on intermediate technology, primary health-care, development, and all related subjects. They also issue a catalogue.

Grant & Cutler (55 Great Marlborough Street, London W1V 1DD; tel. 071 734 2012)
They stock the best range of dictionaries and books for learning foreign languages.

The Map Shop (15 High Street, Upton-on-Severn, Worcestershire WR8 0HJ; tel. 0684 593146)
They produce a catalogue, and also useful information sheets about maps for the particular area where you are going. They will also laminate maps for you.

FLIGHT ADVICE

I'm not giving a list of recommendations, because these go out of date so fast (managements are prone to change). But I am giving a short list of companies specializing in cheap flights to long-haul destinations; these will at least give you a benchmark against which to judge the service and prices of other companies.

Trailfinders (194 Kensington High Street, London W8 7RG; tel. 071 938 3939. Also at 46 Earl's Court Road, London W8 6EJ; tel. 071 938 3366)

They are the largest operators selling cheap long-haul seats. They also have a branch in Manchester (tel. 061 839 6969). The shop in Kensington High Street also keeps useful files (which you can read) of articles on long-haul destinations, and sells guidebooks. It also houses an immunization centre.

Quest Worldwide (29 Castle Street, Kingston-upon-Thames, Surrey KT1 1ST; tel. 081 547 3322)

This is a newish, lean and hungry company, so you might get extra attention and a good deal.

Bridge the World (1–3 Ferdinand Street, Camden Town, London NW1 8ES; tel. 071 911 0900)

Travel Bug (597 Cheetham Hill Road, Manchester M8 6EJ; tel. 061 721 4000)

Journey Latin America (14–16 Devonshire Road, Chiswick, London W4 2HD; tel. 081 747 3108)

They specialize in Latin America, and know their subject very well.

Austravel (50 Conduit Street, London W1R 9FB; tel. 071 734 7755)

Specialists in travel to Australia and New Zealand.

Here are two companies that specialize in students and young people, though they also sell plenty of other tickets:

Campus Travel (52 Grosvenor Gardens, London SW1W 0AG; tel. 071 730 8111)

They have thirty offices around Britain, some of them at universities. They also have a special link with Amtrak (the railway system in the US) and Eurorail.

STA (74 Old Brompton Road, London SW7 3LQ; tel. 071 937 9962)
They have several offices around Britain, and more than a hundred worldwide.

I have listed Round the World Ticket specialists in Chapter 4.

IMMUNIZATION CENTRES

Recently many more immunization centres have opened up in small towns, so it is always worth asking your local doctor for details. Here is a list of some London ones, which may also be useful for getting up-to-date advice.

British Airways Immunization Centre, Regent Street (156 Regent Street, London W1R 5TA; tel. 071 439 9584)
Open on Saturdays. Recorded message for opening times and other information.

British Airways Travel Clinic (101 Cheapside, London EC2V 6DT; tel. 071 606 2977)
It may be necessary to make an appointment.

British Airways Immunization Centre, Victoria Station (by the check-in desk on the first floor at Victoria Station; tel. 071 233 6661)
It may be necessary to make an appointment.

British Airways Immunization Centre, Gatwick Airport (North Terminal, on the ground floor; tel. 0293 666255)
This is open twenty-four hours a day, seven days a week. No appointment is necessary.

PPP Travel Clinic (also run by British Airways) (99 New Cavendish Street, London W1M 7FQ; tel. 071 436 0224)
By appointment only and not open on Saturdays. Prices the same as all the other British Airways clinics.

Trailfinders (194 Kensington High Street, London W8 7RG; tel. 071 938 3999)

Thomas Cook (45 Berkeley Street, London W1A 1EB; tel. 071 408 4157)

No need to book during weekdays, but essential on a Saturday.

Hospital for Tropical Diseases Travel Clinic (180–182 Tottenham Court Road, London W1P 9LE; tel. 071 637 9899)

Although run by Islington & Bloomsbury health authority, they still have the same charges as the British Airways Clinics.

VISA SERVICES

Worldwide Visas Ltd (9 Adelaide Street, London WC2 4HZ; tel. 071 379 0419)

Travcour (Postal address: 9 Chester Mews, London SW1X 7AJ. For personal visits: Tempo House, 15 Falcon Road, London SW11 2PJ; tel. 071 223 7662)

Thames Consular Services (363 Chiswick High Road, London W4 4HS; tel. 081 995 2492)

INSURANCE

I wrote a pseudonymous letter to ten different companies, asking searching questions about their small-print clauses. The most speedy and efficient response (and one offering what appeared to be the best policy) came from:

Briggs & Hill (Airedale House, Campbell Street, Keighley, W. Yorks. BD21 3AA; tel. 0535 606121. Fax. 0353 610479)

Contact: Howard Gallagher or Carole Toothill.

You could also try these other specialists:

Whiteley Insurance Consultants (Kingfisher House, Portland Place, Halifax HX1 2JH; tel. 0422 348411. Fax. 0422 330345)

Endsleigh (Cranfield House, 97–107 Southampton Row, London WC1B 4AG; tel. 071 436 4451)

Campbell Irvine Ltd (48 Earl's Court Road, London W8 6EJ; tel. 071 937 9903)

OTHER ORGANIZATIONS

Royal Geographical Society (1 Kensington Gore, London SW7 2AR; tel. 071 581 2057)

Membership will give you access to the library (books can be loaned), to the map room, and to the excellent series of talks. You need to be proposed and seconded by other 'fellows' but this can usually be arranged.

Expedition Advisory Centre (Royal Geographical Society, 1 Kensington Gore, London SW7 2AR; tel. 071 581 2057)

This office, which is run by the Royal Geographical Society and the Young Explorer's Trust, provides information and training for anyone planning an overseas expedition. Their primary focus is expedition research at undergraduate level. Two annual seminars might be of particular interest: 'Planning a Small Expedition' and the 'Independent Travellers Seminar'. They publish and distribute a range of books and pamphlets on expeditions, many of which are listed in Appendix 1.

Globetrotters Club (BCM/Roving, London WC1N 3XX)

The club was founded in 1945 for swapping information about cheap travel. Members are sent a list of each other's addresses, and they often stay in each other's homes. The club arranges slide shows once a month, and sends out a twenty-four-page magazine in which members offer tips and give accounts of their travels.

Women's Corona Society (53 Belgrave Square, London SW1X 8QB; tel. 071 235 1230)

The society offers help, advice, and friendship to women who are going to live temporarily in a country other than their own. They also publish a series of 'Notes for Newcomers' on various countries. The two that I have seen are excellent.

South American Explorers Club (Quito Clubhouse: Apartado

21–431, Eloy Alfaro, Quito, Ecuador; tel. 566–076. Lima Clubhouse: Casilla 3714, Lima 100, Peru; tel. 314–480)

South American Explorers Club is very popular with keen travellers to South America. The two clubhouses have libraries with a mass of very useful trip and expedition reports; they also sell guidebooks, maps, and various bits of expedition equipment. You may even be able to use them for luggage storage. Of the two clubhouses, the Ecuadorian one is probably the most prominent at the moment, partly because of the dangers in parts of Peru. The clubs and their magazine (South American Explorer) *are also most important for informing you which parts of South America are current no-go areas.*

Cyclists Touring Club (Cotterall House, 69 Meadrow, Godalming, Surrey GU7 3HS; tel. 0483 417217)

Britain's largest cycling organization. They can provide advice on legalities, insurance, technical problems, and touring.

British Sub-aqua Club (Telford's Quay, Ellesmere Port, South Wirral, Cheshire L65 4FY; tel. 051 357 1951)

Will tell you where you can get diving instruction, and runs a diving holidays information service.

Earthwatch Europe (Belsyre Court, 57 Woodstock Road, Oxford OX2 6HU; tel. 0865 311600)

A non-profit-making body which matches paying volunteers with scientists who need their help (and money) to study threatened habitats, save endangered species, and document our changing environmental heritage. Since Earthwatch was founded in 1971, it has brought together more than 22,000 volunteers with investigators, and it is currently the third largest private source of funding in the United States for field research. A free information pack is available from them. The prices quoted don't include travel to the site, which also has to be paid for by the volunteer.

VSO (Voluntary Service Overseas) (317 Putney Bridge Road, London SW15 2PN; tel. 081 780 2266)

The largest voluntary organization in the country, taking people between eighteen and seventy. Your commitment must be for at least two years, and you should have a skill that can be passed on to locals.

APPENDIX 3

GAP (Gap House, 44 Queen's Road, Reading, Berks. RG1 4BB; tel. 0734 594914)

Provides school-leavers with overseas work for the year before they go on to higher education. I have heard some very good reports of this institution.

Project Trust (Breacachadh Castle, Isle of Coll, Argyll PA78 6TB; tel. 08793 444)

Helps young people to spend a year between school and university on all types of projects, including work on cattle stations and in children's homes.

Raleigh International, formerly called Operation Raleigh (Alpha Place, London SW3 5SZ; tel. 071 351 7541)

Projects and expeditions for people from seventeen to twenty-five. There is one expedition a year when there is no upper age limit. These are for three to four weeks.

Camp America (37a Queens Gate, London SW7 5HR; tel. 071 589 3223).

It arranges for people from eighteen to thirty-five to work in American summer camps for ten weeks, either looking after children or as general staff. Places are also offered for looking after children in their family homes. Flights, board, and lodging are paid, and you get six weeks of independent travel.

Kibbutz Representatives (1a Accommodation Road, London NW11 8ED; tel. 081 458 9235)

The agency lists schemes for people between eighteen and thirty-two who want to work on a kibbutz (an agricultural collective settlement in Israel). Conditions are likely to be tough, and little or no pocket money is paid. The minimum stay is five weeks.

OVERLANDING COMPANIES

This is a list of companies that specialize in taking groups on long overland trips, mostly in Africa, Asia, and South America.

Apart from mentioning that Guerba is at present highly regarded in the overlanding category, the list below is not necessarily a list of recommendations. Trips with these companies can be

431

booked through any of the agents mentioned (above) under Flight Advice, and they will be able to give you the best up-to-date advice. Don't forget to ask about the seating plans (see Overlanding Groups, in Chapter 1).

Although these companies will run tours of up to twenty-nine weeks, most of them also have much shorter ones as well.

Guerba Expeditions (101 Eden Vale Road, Westbury, Wiltshire BA13 3QX; tel. 0373 826611)

Journey Latin America (16 Devonshire Road, Chiswick, London W4 2HD; tel. 081 747 3108)
They cover only South America, where they run their own trips, but using local transport. Their reputation is at present excellent.

Exodus Expeditions (9 Weir Road, Balham, London SW12 0LT; tel. 081 675 5550)
They are very large, and cover the widest range of countries.

Encounter Overland (267 Old Brompton Road, London SW5 9JA; tel. 071 370 6845)

Dragoman Adventure Travel (Camp Green Farm, Kenton Road, Debenham, Suffolk IP14 6LA; tel. 0728 861133)

Kamuka Expeditions (40 Earl's Court Road, London W8 6EJ; tel. 071 937 8855)

Tracks Africa (12 Abingdon Road, London W8 6AF; tel. 071 937 3028)

HOSTELS

YMCA (640 Forest Road, London E17 3DZ; tel. 081 520 5599)
They publish a World Directory of hostels.

YWCA (52 Cornmarket Street, Oxford OX1 3EJ; tel. 0865 726110)
They also publish a World Directory.

Youth Hostels Association (Guessens Road, Welwyn Garden City, Herts. AL8 6QW; tel 0727 55215)
They issue a Guide to Budget Accommodation. Membership may be necessary for some hostels, and a sheet sleeping bag is often essential.

EMERGENCY TELEPHONE LISTS

THE UK DIRECT SYSTEM

With these telephone numbers you can call straight through free of charge (though in a hotel there may be a small charge for telephone use) to an operator in Britain. You can then either use your British Telecom charge card (see Chapter 8) or ask for a reverse-charge call (more often now called 'call collect') to any number you like. These numbers could be invaluable in all types of emergencies, including the loss of your credit cards; or if you want to save extortionate hotel telephone charges.

This is the most up-to-date list at the time of writing; but as UK Direct is quite a new system, it is worth checking whether any country you will be visiting has been added.

These numbers are not the same as International Direct Dialling numbers (some of which are listed later).

Australia	00 14 881 440	Croatia	99 38 0044
Austria	022 903 044	Cyprus	080 900 44
Bahamas	1 800 389 4444	Czechoslovakia	00 42 00 44 01
Bahrain	8000 44 & Dedicated	Denmark	80 01 04 44
	phones	Dominican	1 800 751 2701
Belgium	078 11 00 44	Republic	
Belize	Dedicated phones	Egypt	Dedicated phones
Bermuda	Dedicated phones	Eire	1 800 55 00 44
Bolivia	0800 0044	Finland	9800 1 0440
Brazil	0008 044	France	19 ★ 00 44 &
Canada	1 800 363 4144		Dedicated phones
Chile	00 ★ 0344	Gabon	000 44
Colombia	980 44 00 57	Gambia	000 44
Costa Rica	167	Germany	0130 80 0044

Ghana	0194	Netherlands	06 (tone) 022 9944
Gibraltar	84 00	New Zealand	0009 44
Guyana	169	Norway	050 11 044
Hawaii	1 800 865 4444	Philippines	105 44
Hong Kong	800 0044	Poland	0 ★ 044 0099 48
Hungary	00 ★ 800 44 011	Portugal	0505 00 44
Iceland	999 044	Saudi Arabia	1 800 20
India	000 44 17 &	Seychelles	044 800
	Dedicated phones	Singapore	800 4400
Indonesia	00 801 44	South Korea	Dedicated phones
Israel	177 44 02727	Spain	900 99 0044
Italy	172 0044	Sweden	020 795 144
Japan	0039 441 &	Switzerland	155 2444
(by the KDD	Dedicated phones	Taiwan	Dedicated phones
system)		Thailand	001 999 44 1066 &
(by the IDC	00 66 55 144		Dedicated phones
system)		Trinidad	Dedicated phones
Kenya	0800 44 & Dedicated	Turkey	99 800 44 1177
	phones	UAE	800 1 0044
Kuwait	800 855	Uruguay	0004 44
Liberia	797 444	USA (AT&T)	1 800 44 55667
Luxembourg	0800 0044	USA (MCI)	1 800 44 42162
Macao	0800 440 &	USA	1 800 80 00008
	Dedicated phones	(SPRINT)	
Malaysia	800 00 44 &	USA (TRT)	None
	Dedicated phones	Venezuela	800 11440
Mexico	791 (Payphones	Zambia	00 888
	only)	Zimbabwe	110 898

★ Wait for a second dialling tone before continuing

Dedicated phones. These are payphones pre-programmed with the UK Direct number. The customer simply has to press the button marked UK Direct and the number is automatically dialled. The telephones are usually sited in areas where there is high tourist traffic: for example, airports and hotels.

EMERGENCY CANCELLATION NUMBERS

Credit card and traveller's cheque companies will give you a local telephone number in case of loss or theft. And in theory you should be able to cancel stolen cheques by going to any outlet that displays their logo. But it may not be practical to find the outlet, and it may be safer to ring home (possibly via UK Direct). All the companies will accept reverse-charge calls. So here is a list of the numbers that are most likely to be important in emergencies.

Remember that if calling direct from abroad, you should omit the initial zero.

To cancel credit cards

Natwest Access & Visa	0532 778899
Barclaycard (International rescue)	081 667 1393
Lloyds Access	0702 362988
Lloyds Visa, cheque card, cashpoint, etc.	0800 585 300
Midland Mastercard and Visa	081 450 3122
Royal Bank of Scotland Access & Visa	0702 351303

To cancel charge cards

American Express	0273 696933
Diners Club	0252 513500

To cancel traveller's cheques

American Express	0273 571600
Thomas Cook	0733 502995
Visa	071 937 8091

CODES FOR DIALLING BRITAIN FROM ABROAD

When dialling the UK area code number, always leave out the initial 0.

★ Wait for a second dialling tone before continuing

Alaska	011 44	Germany	00 44
Anguilla	011 44	Ghana	00 44
Antigua	011 44	Gibraltar	00 44
Argentina	00 44	Greece	00 44
Ascension	01 44	Guam	001 44
Australia	0011 44	Guyana	001 44
Austria	00 44	Hawaii	011 44
Bahamas	011 44	Honduras	00 44
Bahrain	0 44	Hong Kong	001 44
Barbados	011 44	Hungary	00★44
Belgium	00 44	Iceland	90 44
Belize	011 44	India	00 44
Bermuda	011 44	Indonesia	00 44
Botswana	00 44	Iran	00 44
Brazil	00 44	Israel	00 44
Brunei	01 44	Italy	00 44
Bulgaria	00 44	Japan	001 44
Canada	011 44	Jordan	00 44
Caribbean	011 44	Kenya	000 44
Cayman Is.	0 44	Kuwait	00 44
Chile	00★44	Lesotho	00 44
China	002 44	Liberia	00 44
Cyprus	00 44	Luxembourg	00 44
Czechoslovakia	00 44	Macao	00 44
Denmark	009 44	Madagascar	16
Ecuador	01 44	Malawi	101 44
Egypt	00 44	Malta	00 44
Eire	03	Martinique	19★44
Ethiopia	00 44	Mauritius	00 44
Falkland Is.	01 44	Montserrat	0011 44
Fiji	05 44	Namibia	09 44
Finland	990 44	Netherlands	09★44
France	19★44	New Zealand	00 44
Gabon	00★44	Niger	00 44

436

Norway	095 44	Sweden	009 44★
Papua New		Switzerland	00 44
Guinea	05 44	Taiwan	002 44
Poland	00★44	Thailand	001 44
Portugal	00 44	Tonga	00 44
Seychelles	0 44	Turkey	9★9 44
Singapore	005 44	UAE	00 44
South Africa	09 44	Uruguay	00 44
South Korea	001 44	USA	011 44
Spain	07★44	Venezuela	00 44
Sri Lanka	00 44	Virgin Is.	011 44
St Lucia	0 44	Yemen	00 44
Surinam	001 44	Zimbabwe	110★44
Swaziland	00 44		

LANGUAGE SURVIVAL LIST

Hello/Greetings
Goodbye
Sir/Madam
It is often practical and polite to know the equivalents of these words. Consider the use of 'Monsieur' and 'Madame' in French.
British (I am British)
You will always be asked what nationality you are.
Profession (e.g. I am an engineer)
You will always be asked what profession you are.
Wife/husband
You will always be asked whether you are married.
Girls
Boys
You will always be asked how many children you have, and whether they are boys or girls.
Name (My name is . . . What is the name of this? etc.)
Yes
No

Please
Thank you
Sorry
I do not speak (Arabic)
Possible? (Is it possible?)
Words such as 'se puede' in Spanish, or 'mumkin' in Arabic, are useful for many situations, such as when you want to ask, 'Can I leave the car here?' or 'May I enter this temple?'
How much?
Too much
Good
Bad
Large
Small
Very
Where is?
Here
When
Lavatory
(In most countries the word 'toilet' is understood.)
Police
(In most countries the word 'police' is understood.)

Doctor

Hotel

More

Less

Tea

  Or coffee, whichever is your addiction.

Hot

Cold

Water

  Or 'mineral water' if that might be useful.

Today

Tomorrow

Slow

  Useful for 'speak more slow', 'drive more slow', etc.

Fast

I want

I don't want (I no want)

I like (I no like)

CONVERSION TABLES

Some conversions can be calculated in one's head.

To convert from kilometres to miles: divide by 8, then multiply by 5. This is accurate, and works in reverse. Some people find it easier to multiply by 0.6 (0.62 is completely accurate).

To convert (very approximately) from Centigrade to Fahrenheit: double and add 30. This works for any figures above freezing, and can be done in reverse.

To convert more accurately from Centigrade to Fahrenheit: double, subtract 10 per cent, add 32. This works for any figures above freezing, and can be done in reverse.

To convert from centimetres to inches, divide by 10, then multiply by 4. This is accurate to within 1 per cent and can be done in reverse.

It is sometimes useful to know that 5 millilitres approximately fills a teaspoon.

Length			Length		
centimetres	cm or inches	inches	metres	metres or feet	feet
2.54	1	0.39	.3048	1	3.281
5.08	2	0.79	.6096	2	6.562
7.62	3	1.18	.9144	3	9.843
10.16	4	1.58	1.2192	4	13.123
12.70	5	1.97	1.5240	5	16.404
15.24	6	2.36	1.8288	6	19.685
17.78	7	2.76	2.1336	7	22.966
20.32	8	3.15	2.4384	8	26.247
22.86	9	3.54	2.7432	9	29.528
25.40	10	3.90	3.0480	10	32.808
50.80	20	7.90	6.0960	20	65.617
76.20	30	11.80	9.1440	30	98.425
101.60	40	15.80	12.1920	40	131.234
127.00	50	19.70	15.2400	50	164.042

Length

kilo- metres	km or miles	mile
1.61	1	0.62
3.22	2	1.24
4.83	3	1.86
6.44	4	2.49
8.05	5	3.11
9.66	6	3.73
11.27	7	4.35
12.88	8	4.97
14.48	9	5.59
16.09	10	6.21
32.19	20	12.43
48.28	30	18.64
64.37	40	24.86
80.47	50	31.07

Capacity

litres	litres or gallons	gallons
4.55	1	0.22
9.09	2	0.44
13.64	3	0.66
18.18	4	0.88
22.73	5	1.10
27.28	6	1.32
31.82	7	1.54
36.37	8	1.76
40.91	9	1.98
45.46	10	2.20
90.92	20	4.40
136.4	30	6.60
181.8	40	8.80
227.3	50	11.00

Weight

kilo- grammes	kg or pounds	pounds
0.45	1	2.21
0.91	2	4.41
1.36	3	6.61
1.81	4	8.82
2.27	5	11.02
2.72	6	13.23
3.18	7	15.43
3.63	8	17.64
4.08	9	19.84
4.54	10	22.05
9.07	20	44.09
13.61	30	66.14
18.14	40	88.19
22.68	50	110.20

Temperature

Centigrade	°C or °F	°Fahrenheit
−23	−10	14
−18	0	32
−12	10	50
−7	20	68
−1	30	86
4	40	104
10	50	122
16	60	140
21	70	158
27	80	176
32	90	194
38	100	212
66	150	302
93	200	392

A GUIDE TO THE RAINY SEASONS

The Traveller's Handbook (Trade & Travel Publications) have kindly given me permission to reproduce this splendid appendix. With one glance it is possible to get an impression of the wet-weather patterns in any part of the globe. This is useful because rain can be such a disaster for travellers.

Within each region the destinations are listed from north to south, which helps give an overall impression. Of course, these charts aren't a very scientific guide: the places aren't necessarily representative of their country, and not enough are listed to make the charts comprehensive. Furthermore, total rainfall should be taken into account, because the rainiest season in one place may be less wet than the dry season in the other. But when you are at the earliest stage of your planning, a close study of these charts will give you an excellent indication of overall rain patterns.

× indicates the month(s) with the highest average rainfall of the year
△ represents a month having more than $\frac{1}{12}$ of the annual total rainfall
∞ represents a month having less than $\frac{1}{12}$ of the annual total rainfall

	Total annual rainfall (cm)	J	F	M	A	M	J	J	A	S	O	N	D	Latitude
Asia														
Istanbul, Turkey	80.5	△	△	△	8	8	8	8	8	8	△	△	×	41°00′N
Beijing, China	134.1	8	8	8	8	8	△	△	×	×	△	8	8	39°50′N
Seoul, Korea	125.0	8	8	8	8	8	△	×	×	△	8	8	8	37°31′N
Tokyo, Japan	156.5	8	8	×	△	△	△	△	△	8	△	8	8	35°45′N
Tehran, Iran	24.6	×	8	8	8	8	8	8	8	×	8	8	△	35°44′N
Osaka, Japan	133.6	8	8	8	△	8	8	△	△	8	△	8	8	34°40′N
Kabul, Afghanistan	34.0	8	△	△	×	8	8	8	8	△	8	△	△	34°28′N
Beirut, Lebanon	89.7	×	×	8	8	8	8	8	8	8	8	△	×	33°53′N
Damascus, Syria	22.4	×	8	8	△	8	8	8	8	8	8	△	△	33°30′N
Baghdad, Iraq	15.0	△	8	△	8	8	8	8	8	8	8	8	△	33°20′N
Nagasaki, Japan	191.8	8	8	8	8	△	△	8	△	8	8	△	△	32°47′N
Amman, Jordan	27.9	×	8	△	△	8	8	8	8	△	8	△	△	32°00′N
Jerusalem, Israel	53.3	×	8	△	8	8	8	8	8	8	8	△	△	31°47′N
Shanghai, China	113.5	8	8	8	8	△	△	△	△	8	8	△	8	31°15′N
Wuhan, China	125.7	8	8	8	8	8	8	8	8	8	8	8	8	30°32′N
Kuwait City, Kuwait	12.7	△	△	8	8	△	×	×	×	△	8	8	×	29°30′N
Delhi, India	64.0	8	8	8	8	△	△	×	×	8	8	8	8	28°38′N
Kathmandu, Nepal	142.7	8	8	8	8	△	△	×	×	△	8	8	8	27°45′N
Agra, India	68.1	8	8	8	8	△	△	×	×	△	8	8	8	27°17′N
Cherrapunji, India	1,079.8	8	8	△	8	△	×	△	×	△	8	8	8	25°17′N
Taipei, Taiwan	212.9	8	8	8	8	△	×	×	×	△	8	8	8	25°20′N
Karachi, Pakistan	18.3	8	8	8	8	8	△	×	△	△	8	8	8	24°53′N
Riyadh, Saudi Arabia	9.1	8	8	8	△	△	8	8	8	8	8	8	8	24°41′N
Guangzhou, China	164.3	8	8	8	8	△	△	△	△	△	8	△	8	23°10′N
Calcutta, India	160.0	8	8	8	8	△	△	×	△	△	8	8	8	22°36′N
Hong Kong	216.1	8	8	8	8	△	×	×	×	△	8	8	8	22°11′N

	Total annual rainfall (cm)	J	F	M	A	M	J	J	A	S	O	N	D	Latitude
Asia *continued*														
Mandalay, Burma	82.8	∞	∞	∞	∞	×	△	△	△	△	△	∞	∞	22°00'N
Jeddah, Saudi Arabia	8.1	∞	∞	∞	∞	∞	∞	∞	∞	△	∞	×	×	21°29'N
Hanoi, Vietnam	168.1	∞	∞	∞	∞	△	△	△	×	△	∞	∞	∞	21°50'N
Bombay, India	181.4	∞	∞	∞	∞	∞	×	×	△	△	△	∞	∞	18°55'N
Hyderabad, India	75.2	∞	∞	∞	△	△	△	△	△	△	△	∞	∞	17°10'N
Rangoon, Burma	261.6	∞	∞	∞	∞	∞	×	×	×	△	△	∞	∞	16°45'N
Manila, Philippines	208.5	∞	∞	∞	∞	△	△	×	×	×	△	∞	∞	14°40'N
Bangkok, Thailand	139.7	∞	∞	∞	∞	△	△	△	△	△	△	∞	∞	13°45'N
Madras, India	127.0	∞	∞	∞	∞	∞	∞	∞	△	△	×	×	∞	13°80'N
Bangalore, India	329.2	∞	∞	△	∞	∞	∞	∞	△	∞	∞	∞	∞	12°55'N
Aden, Yemen	4.8	△	∞	∞	△	×	×	×	△	×	×	×	∞	12°50'N
Colombo, Sri Lanka	236.5	∞	∞	∞	△	×	∞	∞	∞	∞	×	∞	∞	6°56'N
Sandakan, Malaysia	314.2	×	△	∞	×	∞	∞	∞	∞	∞	△	△	△	5°53'N
Kuala Lumpur, Malaysia	244.1	∞	∞	△	×	△	△	△	∞	△	△	△	∞	3°90'N
Singapore	241.3	×	∞	∞	∞	∞	∞	∞	∞	∞	△	×	×	1°17'N
Djakarta, Indonesia	179.8	×	×	△	∞	△	∞	∞	∞	∞	△	∞	△	6°90'S
Africa														
Algiers, Algeria	76.5	△	△	△	∞	∞	∞	∞	∞	∞	△	×	×	36°42'N
Tangier, Morocco	90.2	△	△	△	△	△	∞	∞	∞	△	△	×	△	35°50'N
Tripoli, Libya	38.9	△	△	△	△	∞	∞	∞	∞	△	△	∞	×	32°49'N
Marrakesh, Morocco	23.9	△	△	×	△	∞	∞	∞	∞	△	△	△	△	31°40'N
Cairo, Egypt	3.6	△	△	△	∞	∞	△	∞	∞	△	∞	∞	△	30°10'N
Timbuctou, Mali	24.4	∞	∞	∞	∞	∞	∞	△	×	△	∞	∞	∞	16°50'N
Khartoum, Sudan	17.0	∞	∞	∞	∞	∞	△	△	×	△	△	∞	∞	15°31'N
Dakar, Senegal	155.4	∞	∞	∞	∞	∞	∞	△	×	△	∞	∞	∞	14°34'N

	Tannual (cm)	J	F	M	A	M	J	J	A	S	O	N	D	
Addis Ababa, Ethiopia	123.7	∞	∞	∞	∞	×	△	∞	×	△	∞	∞	∞	9°20'N
Freetown, Sierra Leone	343.4	∞	∞	∞	∞	△	∞	∞	×	∞	△	∞	∞	8°30'N
Lagos, Nigeria	183.6	∞	∞	∞	∞	×	△	△	∞	△	∞	∞	∞	6°25'N
Cotonou, Benin	132.6	∞	△	∞	∞	×	△	×	∞	×	△	△	∞	6°20'N
Monrovia, Liberia	513.8	∞	∞	△	∞	△	△	×	∞	△	△	△	∞	6°18'N
Accra, Ghana	72.4	∞	∞	△	△	△	△	×	∞	△	△	∞	∞	5°35'N
Mongalla, Sudan	94.5	∞	∞	△	∞	△	△	∞	∞	∞	△	×	∞	5°80'N
Libreville, Gabon	251.0	△	∞	△	△	△	△	∞	△	△	△	∞	△	0°25'N
Entebbe, Uganda	150.6	∞	∞	∞	∞	∞	∞	∞	∞	∞	∞	△	∞	0°30'N
Nairobi, Kenya	95.8	∞	∞	△	△	∞	△	∞	∞	∞	∞	∞	△	1°20'S
Mombasa, Kenya	120.1	∞	△	△	∞	×	∞	∞	∞	∞	∞	×	∞	4°00'S
Kinshasa, Zaire	135.4	△	△	∞	∞	△	∞	∞	∞	∞	∞	×	△	4°20'S
Kananga, Zaire	158.2	△	×	△	∞	△	∞	∞	∞	×	△	∞	×	5°55'S
Lilongwe, Malawi	78.7	×	△	△	∞	∞	∞	∞	∞	∞	∞	∞	△	14°00'S
Lusaka, Zambia	83.3	×	△	△	△	∞	∞	∞	∞	∞	∞	△	△	15°25'S
Harare, Zimbabwe	82.8	×	△	∞	∞	∞	∞	∞	∞	∞	∞	∞	△	17°50'S
Tamatave, Madagascar	325.6	△	△	△	∞	△	∞	∞	△	∞	∞	∞	∞	18°20'S
Beira, Mozambique	152.2	×	×	△	∞	∞	△	∞	∞	∞	∞	△	△	19°50'S
Johannesburg, SA	70.9	△	△	△	∞	△	∞	∞	∞	△	△	△	×	26°10'S
Maputo, Mozambique	75.9	×	△	△	∞	△	∞	∞	∞	∞	∞	△	△	26°35'S
Cape Town, SA	50.8	∞	∞	∞	△	△	△	△	△	△	∞	∞	∞	35°55'S

Sub-Arctic

| Reykjavik, Iceland | 77.2 | △ | ∞ | ∞ | △ | △ | × | ∞ | × | △ | △ | △ | △ | 64°10'N |

Australasia and the Pacific

| Honolulu, HI, USA | 64.3 | × | △ | △ | ∞ | ∞ | ∞ | ∞ | ∞ | ∞ | ∞ | △ | × | 21°25'N |
| Tulagi, Solomon Is. | 313.4 | △ | × | △ | △ | ∞ | ∞ | ∞ | ∞ | ∞ | ∞ | ∞ | △ | 9°24'S |

	Total annual rainfall (cm)	J	F	M	A	M	J	J	A	S	O	N	D	Latitude
Australasia and the Pacific *continued*														
Port Moresby, PNG	101.1	△	×	△	△	○	○	○	○	○	○	○	△	9°24'S
Manihiki, Cook Is.	248.2	×	△	○	○	○	○	○	○	○	△	○	△	10°24'S
Thursday Is., Australia	171.5	×	△	△	○	△	○	○	○	○	○	△	△	10°30'S
Darwin, Australia	149.1	×	△	△	△	○	○	○	○	○	○	△	△	12°20'S
Apia, Western Samoa	285.3	×	△	△	△	○	○	○	○	○	○	△	△	13°50'S
Cairns, Australia	225.3	△	△	×	△	○	○	○	○	○	○	○	△	16°55'S
Tahiti, French Polynesia	162.8	×	×	△	△	○	×	×	△	○	○	△	×	17°45'S
Suva, Fiji	297.4	△	△	△	○	○	×	○	△	△	△	○	△	18°00'S
Perth, Australia	90.7	○	○	○	○	△	△	×	△	○	○	○	○	31°57'S
Sydney, Australia	118.1	○	△	△	△	△	△	△	○	○	○	○	○	33°53'S
Auckland, NZ	124.7	○	○	△	○	△	△	△	○	△	○	△	○	36°52'S
Melbourne, Australia	65.3	○	○	○	△	○	△	△	△	○	○	△	△	41°19'S
Wellington, NZ	120.4	△	○	○	○	△	△	△	○	○	△	○	○	41°19'S
Christchurch, NZ	63.8	△	○	○	○	△	×	×	○	○	○	○	△	43°33'S
Central America														
Monterey, Mexico	58.2	○	○	○	○	○	△	△	△	×	△	○	○	25°40'N
Mazatlan, Mexico	84.8	○	○	○	○	○	○	△	△	×	○	○	○	23°10'N
Havana, Cuba	122.4	○	○	○	○	△	△	△	△	△	×	△	○	23°80'N
Merida, Mexico	92.7	○	○	○	○	△	×	△	△	△	△	△	○	20°50'N
Mexico City, Mexico	74.9	○	○	○	×	△	△	×	△	△	○	○	○	19°20'N
Port-au-Prince, Haiti	135.4	○	○	△	△	△	△	○	△	△	△	○	○	18°40'N
Santo Domingo, Dom. Rep.	141.7	○	○	○	△	△	△	△	△	×	△	△	○	18°30'N
Kingston, Jamaica	80.0	○	○	○	○	○	○	○	△	△	×	△	○	18°00'N
Acapulco, Mexico	154.2	○	○	○	○	△	△	△	△	△	△	△	○	16°51'N
Salina Cruz, Mexico	102.6	○	○	○	○	○	△	△	△	×	○	○	○	16°10'N

	rainfall (cm)	J	F	M	A	M	J	J	A	S	O	N	D	Latitude
Central America *continued*														
Tegucigalpa, Honduras	162.1	●	●	●	●	●	×	×	●	△	△	●	●	14°10'N
San Jose, Costa Rica	179.8	●	●	●	●	△	△	△	△	×	×	●	●	10°00'N
Balboa Heights, Panama	177.0	●	●	●	●	△	△	△	△	△	×	×	●	9°00'N
South America														
Caracas, Venezuela	83.3	●	●	●	●	△	×	×	×	×	×	△	●	10°30'N
Ciudad Bolivar, Venezuela	101.6	△	△	△	●	△	△	△	△	△	●	△	△	8°50'N
Georgetown, Guyana	225.3	●	×	×	△	△	×	×	●	●	×	△	●	6°50'N
Bogota, Colombia	105.9	△	×	×	△	△	●	●	●	●	●	△	●	4°34'N
Quito, Ecuador	112.3	△	×	×	●	●	●	●	●	●	●	●	●	0°15'S
Belem, Brazil	243.8	×	△	×	△	●	●	●	●	●	●	●	●	1°20'S
Guyaquil, Ecuador	97.3	●	●	●	△	△	●	●	△	●	●	△	△	2°15'S
Manaus, Brazil	181.1	△	●	●	△	△	×	×	×	●	●	●	●	3°00'S
Recife, Brazil	161.0	●	●	●	●	●	△	△	●	●	●	△	△	8°00'S
Lima, Peru	4.8	●	●	△	×	●	△	△	●	×	●	●	●	12°00'S
Salvador (Bahia), Brazil	190.0	●	●	●	●	×	●	●	●	●	●	●	●	13°00'S
Cuiaba, Brazil	139.5	△	△	×	●	●	●	●	●	●	△	△	△	15°30'S
Concepcion, Bolivia	114.3	×	△	△	●	●	●	●	●	●	●	×	△	15°50'S
La Paz, Bolivia	57.4	×	△	△	△	●	△	△	△	●	●	△	△	16°20'S
Rio de Janeiro, Brazil	108.2	△	△	△	△	△	●	●	●	●	●	△	×	23°00'S
Sao Paolo, Brazil	142.8	△	△	●	●	●	●	●	●	●	●	△	×	23°40'S
Asuncion, Paraguay	131.6	△	●	●	●	●	●	●	●	●	△	△	×	25°21'S
Tucuman, Argentina	97.0	×	△	△	●	△	×	×	△	●	●	△	△	26°50'S
Santiago, Chile	36.1	●	●	●	△	●	●	●	●	●	●	●	●	33°24'S
Buenos Aires, Argentina	95.0	●	●	△	●	△	△	△	●	●	△	△	×	34°30'S
Montevideo, Uruguay	95.0	●	●	×	×	●	●	●	●	●	●	●	●	34°50'S
Valdivia, Chile	260.1	●	●	●	△	△	×	△	△	●	●	●	●	39°50'S

CHECK-LIST

NO ONE WILL WANT TO TAKE A FRACTION OF THE ITEMS LISTED BELOW, but I have made this a long list just in case it reminds readers of something they might otherwise have left behind. You can use the list by underlining any items you are likely to take, and adding in the blank spaces (at the end of the list) any other items which you regularly find useful. With some diffidence I have put a star against items which are likely to be the most important, especially for those intending to travel simply.

adaptor, travel
address book
air ticket★
alarm clock
batteries (spare)
belt (preferably with
    somewhere to hide
    money)
binoculars
bivouac bag
books★
cagoule (or similar)
camera
  spare battery
  film
  flash
  spare battery for flash
  lens cleaning cloth

spare lens cap
camera manual
spare filter
candles
cash★
cheque guarantee card
cheques or chequebook
clothes, cold-weather
clothes, one respectable
    set of
clothes-line
compass
contact lenses
condoms
contraceptive pills
credit card (e.g. Access)
diary
dictionary

document holder★
  immunization documents★
  security chart★ (with
      traveller's cheque
      numbers, etc.)
  insurance policy★
  driving licence
  international driving licence
  photocopies of air ticket,
      passport title and visa
      pages
  spare passport photographs
  testimonial
door-wedge
earplugs
elastic bands
envelopes, airmail
flip-flops
gaffer tape★
games (cards, backgammon,
    etc.)
glasses, spare pair of
guidebooks
hammock
hat★
heliograph
insecticide or insect powder
insect repellent★
insulation mat
kit/medicine/cosmetic bag
labels, luggage
lavatory paper (or pocket
    tissues)
lighters, disposable
lock (padlock or combination
    lock)

maps★
matches
money-belt
mosquito net
nail/scrubbing brush
neck pillow
notebook
pack-away bag
passport
passport photograph, spare
pillow
plastic bags
plug, universal★
pocket-knife★
presents★
radio, short-wave
safety pins (nappy pins)
sandals
sarong
scarf
sewing kit
shampoo
shaving kit
shirts
shoes
shorts
shoulder bag★
sleeping-bag liner★
snacks, emergency
snorkel
soap
socks
sponge bag (including
    toothbrush, toothpaste,
    etc.)★
string (or para-cord)

student card
sun-cream
sunglasses
sweater★
swimming costume
tampons★
tea-infuser
teaspoon★
tie
tissues, foil-wrapped wet
torch★
  spare torch batteries
  spare torch bulb
towel★

tracksuit/jogging suit
traveller's cheques
trousers/skirt
T-shirts
Tubigrip★
underclothes
visiting cards
washing detergent for clothes
water-flask★
water purification tablets★
water filter
wedding ring
whistle

_____ _____
_____ _____
_____ _____
_____ _____
_____ _____

MEDICAL BAG

antibiotics
antiseptic cream or powder★
aspirin or paracetamol
bandage, crêpe
blister remedy
dental floss
diarrhoea remedy★
dressings
eye ointment
fungal-infection remedy

lip-salve
malaria pills★
malaria remedies,★ if going
  off the beaten track
motion-sickness remedy
oil of cloves
painkillers (stronger than
  aspirin)
plasters★
rehydrating mixture★

sterile kit (needles, etc., for
    Aids and hepatitis B
    avoidance)

Steristrips
tape,★ fabric strapping
vitamin tablets

_____   _____

_____   _____

_____   _____

_____   _____

ARTIFICIAL RESUSCITATION

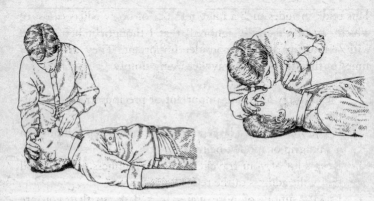

Mouth to mouth resuscitation

External chest compression

Fig. 6.

TWELVE TOP TIPS

This book includes such a huge number of bossy edicts (most of which can be cheerfully ignored) that I thought it best to end with a few tips I really consider important. They are mostly aimed at the independent traveller living simply.

1. Never carry anything important or precious in your shoulder bag.
2. If you must carry a large amount of cash, keep it hidden in a Tubigrip or money-belt.
3. Keep a list of your traveller's cheque numbers separate, and know the address of the refunding agency.
4. Keep a supply of pure water in a flask, so that you are never forced to drink infected water.
5. If you aren't already immune, get immunized against hepatitis A.
6. Take your malaria pills, *and continue taking them for at least four weeks after your return.*
7. Bring an effective insect repellent.
8. Carry a diarrhoea remedy for those difficult times (such as a long bus journey) when you have no access to a lavatory.
9. Ask to see a hotel room before you accept it.
10. Take a torch.
11. Always keep a book and some lavatory paper in your shoulder bag.
12. Learn a few words of the local language.

INDEX

Abbot, S. and Tyrell, M. A.,
    World Wheelchair Traveller,
    285
ABC Guide to International Travel,
    20–21, 93
ABTA, 149, 151
acclimatization, 292–3
    see also altitude; heat
acetaminophen (paracetamol),
    165, 185, 189, 193, 197–8,
    232
acetazolamide, 190
acupressure, 193
adaptor, 93
Adcortyl, 194
address book, 81
aeroplane, 133–4
    ambulance, 22, 24; air pressure,
    133–5, 191, 274; crash, 140–
    43; seat choice, 131–3
    see also airline; airport;
    disputes; flying; insurance;
    luggage; ticket; travel
    company
Afghanistan, 340, 360
Africa, 10, 60, 175, 184, 188, 222,
    243, 252, 260, 286, 287, 292,
    333, 359, 366, 371–2
    East, 121, 160; West, 163, 186,
    208, 342
    see also by country
Aids *see* HIV

air conditioning, 293, 294
air fare *see* ticket
air pass, 148
Air Travel Advisory Bureau,
    146
airline
    Aeroflot, 130; Air India, 130;
    Alitalia, 26; British Airways,
    125; choice of, 11, 130, 141;
    dispute with, 151; KLM,
    131; overbooking by, 125,
    129, 130, 152; promotions,
    144–5; SAS, 148; Swissair,
    140; Virgin, 284
    see also aeroplane; insurance;
    luggage; ticket
airport, 20, 22, 25, 34, 39, 40,
    259
    arrival at, 124, 125–6, 136–7;
    Delhi, 136; Gatwick, 127,
    147; Heathrow, 124, 125, 127,
    130, 147, 284; Kennedy, 130;
    Kinshasa, 344; Schiphol,
    131
    see also crime; luggage;
    exchange rate; officials; tax;
    ticket
Albania, 283
alcohol, 138, 142, 170, 182, 183,
    196, 198, 232, 246
    duty free, 68, 130–31; home
    brew, 340

Aleppo, Syria, 60, 363
Alexander the Great, 172
Allahabad, India, 13, 290
allergy, 196, 232, 237
alligators, 235–7
aloe vera, 172
altitude, 74, 83, 188, 189–92,
    201, 211, 216, 241, 274,
    295
  and flying, 138, 140
altitude sickness see mountain
    sickness
American Express, 26, 38, 39–40,
    331
  Centurion Assistance, 26; mail,
    276–7; MoneyGram, 39;
    refund, 39, 150
  see also credit card
animals
  edible, 401; hazards, 218–49;
    watching, 275–7
  see also by animal; safari
ankles, 138, 185, 239
  sprain, 200
anorak, 117
anoxia, 274
antelopes, 275
ants, 246–7, 398, 399
antibiotics, 156, 176–7, 180, 182,
    194–7, 199, 200, 202–3, 229,
    235
antihistamine, 192, 227, 233
antiques, 281–3
antiseptics, 174, 178, 179, 182,
    192, 202, 229, 246, 379
  wipes, 54, 76, 178, 179,
    192
anti-venom, 232, 233
Argentina, 148
Aristotle, 172
Arret (loperamide), 166, 167

artificial resuscitation see mouth-
    to-mouth resuscitation
Asia, 160, 184, 252, 286, 333, 363
  see also by country
aspirin, 171–2, 185, 189, 197–8,
    232, 237
assassin bugs, 186
Association of British Insurers, 28
asthma, 189
athlete's foot, 173
Ativan (lorazepam), 142
ATOL, 149, 150
Aubrey, John, 360
Augmentin (co-amoxiclax),
    196
Australia, 16, 21, 148, 172, 225,
    227, 231, 233, 235, 270,
    277
Avomine (promethazine), 194

babies see children
baboons, 219
backpack, 92, 102, 103, 104–6,
    380, 384
Backpacker's Handbook, 52
Bactrim (co-trimoxazole), 154,
    182, 195, 196
badges, 67
bags
  packaway, 92; plastic, 92, 94,
    384
bag-snatching, 327–9
balaclava, 119
Bali, 121, 157, 282, 322, 357, 370,
    384, 408
bananas, 167
bandages, 64, 180, 200
  see also dressings; medical kit;
    plasters; Tubigrip
Bandi-i-Amir Lake, Afghanistan,
    359

Bangkok, Thailand, 136, 175, 286, 345

Bangladesh, 370

banks, 30, 33, 34, 35–6, 39–40
Lloyds, 33; National Westminster, 33, 36, 150; Royal Bank of Scotland, 40

Barbados, 172

Barcelona, Spain, 327

bargaining, 42–4, 268

Barley, Nigel, *Innocent Anthropologist*, 289, 371

barracuda, 226–7

bath, 217, 290–91

bath oil, 53

bathing, 405

battery, 51, 68, 79
camera, 48, 54, 298–9, 300–301, 213, 314; torch, 48–51

BBC
External Services, 21, 86–7; language tapes, 349–50; *Wildlife*, 9, 244

bedbugs, 101, 200, 245

bees, 236–8

beggars, 344

belt, 111
see also money belt; trouser belt

benzoic acid, 173

beta-blockers, 142

Betadine (povidone-iodine), 179–80

bicarbonate of soda, 169, 174

bicycling, 261–5, 415, 422

bilharzia, 184–5, 192, 270, 356

bills, checking, 331–2

biltong, 389

bin liners, 11, 92, 106

binoculars, 85, 92–3

bivouac bag, 91, 96–7, 100, 118, 382

black markets, 31, 44–5

blanket, 98, 143

blister, 180, 376, 378–80

blood, 20, 24, 169, 170, 182
group, 175–6; test, 163, 186
see also bowel movements; HIV; urine; vagina

books, 2, 55–7, 102, 411–16
see also bookshops; dictionaries; guidebooks; libraries; phrasebooks

bookshops, 57, 425
see also libraries

boots *see* shoes

Boric acid, 88–9

botfly, 243–4

Botswana, 237, 360

bottle, 69
baby's, 12; leaking, 74, 201
see also water-bottle; thermos

bottle-opener, 64

bottom, 246, 361
burning, 62; itchy, 187; wet, 117

bowel movements, 138–9, 176, 187–8, 291–2, 387, 388
blood in, 169, 170
see also constipation; diarrhoea

Bradt, Hilary, 384, 406

Brazil, 19, 148, 184

breakbone fever *see* dengue fever

breast-feeding, 162

breathlessness, 189, 191

Bremner, Moyra, 74, 228

bribery, 342–3, 392

Briggs and Hill, 23, 26, 428

bromazepam, 142

Brooks, John, 3

Brittany, France, 370

Brown, G. A., *Airline Passenger's Guerrilla Handbook*, 132–3

Brownchurch Ltd, 253
brucellosis, 205
brush, 75
  see also shaving equipment
BT charge card, 278–9
budgeting, 29–30
buffalo, 220–21
bum bag, 64
bumping see airline overbooking
Burgess, Anthony, Language Made
    Plain, 351
Burma, 34, 67, 85
Burton, Sir Richard, 350
butterfly dressing, 181, 182

cagoule, 117–18
calculator, 54, 68
California, US, 225
cameras, 92, 296–320
  cost, 130; instructions, 70;
    insurance, 25–6, 27;
    mending, 63; shops, 424;
    types, 299–302
  see also battery; camera
    equipment; film;
    photography
camera equipment, 48, 51, 54, 55,
    74, 296, 300, 311–15
  lens, 302–4
  see also battery; film
camping, 46, 382–3
  equipment, 48, 51, 101–2
Canadian Air Force, 14
Canaries, the, 231
cancer, skin, 82, 107, 172–3
candiru, 224–5
candle, 79, 186, 228
Canesten (clotrimazole), 174
cannabis, 289
Capilene, 116
car, 1, 250–61

documents, 254–5; equipment,
    255–7; hire, 36, 258–9, 325;
    insurance, 25, 255, 259–6;
    theft, 325, 331
car sickness see motion sickness
car-itis, 261
Caras, Roger, Dangerous to Man,
    226
carbon paper, 40
cards, pack of, 81
carnet de passage, 254–5
Carter, President, 188
Cary, Joyce, Mister Johnson, 371
cash, 24, 26, 31, 34–5, 38, 64, 88,
    327, 332, 334
  bargaining, 43; cash card, 33;
    cash dispenser, 36;
    emergency, 329; presents, 67;
    sending, 40
  see also bank; black markets;
    currency; exchange rate
cat
  domestic, 341; large, 218–20
cataract, eye, 83
catfish, 89, 224, 229
Center for Disease Control,
    Atlanta, US, 156, 161, 163
Chagas disease, 186
Chapman, Roger, Advice for Small
    Expeditions, 380
charge card, 38–9
  Diners Club, 38, 150
  see also American Express; BT
    charge card
check-up, 178, 185, 186, 187, 192
cheese, 78, 390
cheetah, 218
cheque, 38, 39, 102
  see also Eurocheque
Chequepoint, 40
chewing gum, 198

chigger, 244
children, 10–12, 53, 59, 94, 132,
    279, 413
    health, 167, 168, 174, 184, 187,
        193, 194, 198, 215, 230;
        presents for, 406, 407
chilli, 245
chimpanzees, 219
China, 37, 72, 86, 235, 265, 348,
    352, 357, 361, 370
chlorine, 213–15, 216
chlorpheniramine maleate, 197
chocolate, 176, 388
cholera, 155, 156, 169, 186–7, 210,
    211
cigarette, 246
CILT, 350
cinnarizine, 194
ciprofloxacin, 195–6
circadian rhythms, 137, 138–9
CITES, 378
Civil Aviation Authority, 133–4,
    149, 151
Clarke, Dr Charles, 191
climate chart, 13, 20, 442–7
    see also altitude; weather
Climber and Hillwalker, 9
clioquinol, 167
clock, 51, 75
clothes, 47, 52, 107–23, 292
    clean, 365–7; colour of, 120–21;
        desert, 111–12, 113; dirty, 92,
        384; evening, 383–4; flying
        in, 133; mending, 63; prickly
        heat, 174; respectable, 108,
        109–10, 123, 334; sleeping in,
        98
    see also by garment
clothes-line, 75
clotrimazole, 174
cloves, oil of, 198

co-amoxiclax, 196
cockroaches, 88–9, 398
coconut oil, 240
codeine-phosphate, 166, 167, 185,
    192, 198, 232
Codis, 198
coffee, 138–9, 176, 211
cold, 108, 110, 113–19
cold, common, 133–4, 293
Colombia, 148, 250, 290, 321–2
Colombo, Sri Lanka, 339
coma, 191
comb, 67
combination lock see lock
compass, 54, 68
compass points, finding, 393
compensation, 128, 129–30
    see also insurance
condoms, 92, 159, 175, 176–7,
    286
cone shell, 229
conjunctivitis, 198
constipation, 139, 166, 170, 207
    see also bowel movements
consulate, 19, 183, 204, 280
    Consular Dept., 19, 280
contact lenses, 76, 85
contraceptive pill, 167, 189, 190,
    199–200
    see also menstruation
conversion tables, 440–41
cooker, 46, 101
cooking equipment, 46, 101–2
coral, 229
corkscrew, 64
cosmetic bag see kitbag
Costa Rica, 21, 244, 270
co-trimoxazole, 154, 182, 195,
    196
cotton, 99–100, 107–8, 109, 110,
    114

cough, 188, 191, 197, 293
couriers, 148
courtesy *see* etiquette
crafts, 281–3
cramp, 138, 189, 209
Crane, Nick, 264
credit card, 31, 33, 35–8, 102,
    150–51, 258, 260, 278, 326
    Access, 35, 36, 38; cancellation,
    19, 37, 434–5; fraud, 324;
    loss, 326; numbers, 17–19,
    38; *Visa*, 35, 37
Crete, 383
crime, 322–38
    see also credit card; insurance;
    rape; robbery; theft;
    traveller's cheques
crocodiles, 235–6
crotamiton, 242
cryptosporidiosis, 210, 214
Cuba, 15, 34, 87–8, 286
culture shock, 346–74
currency, 19–20, 31, 32–3, 34, 41,
    151
    centavo, 44; dollar, 32, 43–5,
    151; franc, 41; sterling, 24,
    32, 44; voucher, 16
    see also black markets; cash;
    credit card; exchange rate
customs, 131
    dockets, 15
    see also officials; tax
cuts, 178–82, 195
Cuzco, Peru, 46, 189
cyst, 244
    amoebic, 211, 213–14, 215, 216;
    giardia, 214, 215, 216

Daktarin (miconazole), 174
Dalton, Bill, 61
    Indonesia Handbook, 323

Dann's Digest, 145, 146
Dastur, J. F., *Medicinal Plants of
    India*, 207
data-sheet, medical, 196–7
dates, 78, 387
Davey, Jack, 84
day-pack, 107
Dawood, Dr Richard, 193, 246
De Mente, Boye, *Etiquette Guide to
    Japan*, 372
decongestant, 134–5
Deet, 52–3, 239, 248
dehydration, 10, 137, 168, 192,
    198, 216
    see also rehydration; salt; water
Delhi, India, 260
Deng Xiaoping, 348
dengue fever, 164, 169, 185, 238
dental floss, 75, 77, 199
dental kit, 199
dentist, 17, 199
Department of Health, 158
depression, 347
Desert Expeditions, 253
dhobi itch, 109, 173
diagnosis, 19, 203–4
    see also illnesses by name
Diamox (acetazolamide), 190
Diareze (loperamide), 166, 167
diarrhoea, 2, 163, 165–9, 170, 176,
    185, 192, 198, 200, 207, 213,
    214, 340, 400
diary, 38, 66, 281
diazepam, 142
dictionaries, 59–60, 67
diesel, 253–4
diet, 204–6, 208, 387
    see also food
Dijkman, M. J., 398
dimenhydrinate, 194
Dioralyte *see* rehydration mix

diphenoxylate, 166
diploid cell vaccine, 183
Diplomatic Service List, 19, 280
disabled travellers, 283–6
  Holiday Care Service, 285; Paul
    Vander-Molen Trust, 285
disputes
  airline, 151; insurance, 26–8;
    travel company, 151
dizziness, 189
doctor, 19, 24, 171, 173
  tropical, 164, 167, 170, 186, 192
document bag, 7, 39, 70–72, 144
dogs, 236, 377
dolphins, 189
door-wedge, 80
Dramamine, 193
draught, 295
dress, 109
dressings, 180–82, 192, 200
  blister, 380–81; sterile, 182
  see also Elastoplast; plaster
driving, night, 260
driving licence, 21, 70–71, 255
drowning, 270–71, 381–2, 383
drugs
  illegal, 286, 289–90, 340
  see also by generic name
dust, 85, 92, 253–4, 257, 312, 384
dysentery, 2, 164, 168, 192, 195–6
  amoebic, 170, 210; bacillary,
    170, 210
  see also cyst

earplugs, 77–8, 140
ears, 133–5, 195
EC, 22, 131, 149, 161
Ecuador, 346
Egypt, 50, 184, 185, 356
elastic bands, 15, 93–4
Elastoplast, 65, 94, 179, 379

electricity, 21, 53, 93
elephant, 221–2, 275
elephantiasis, 186
Ellen, Mary, Best of Helpful Hints,
  89
embassy, 16, 155, 162, 183, 280
emergency
  antibiotics, 195–6; cash, 34, 38,
    325, 326, 329; heatstroke,
    171; message, 392; passport,
    14, 280; traveller's cheques,
    31
  see also food; insurance; water
encephalitis, Japanese B, 160, 238
English see teaching
Entervioform see clioquinol, 167
envelopes, 71–2
epidemic, 160, 161
epsom salts, 53
Epstein, Jack, Along the Gringo
  Trail, 177
equipment, 46–123
  bicycle, 263–4; car, 255–7;
    check-list, 48–51; selling,
    391; shops, 418–23
  see also camera equipment;
    camping equipment
erythromycin, 182
Ethiopia, 115
etiquette
  eating, 358, 405; linguistic, 362,
    363–4, 369, 371–2, 403–4;
    physical, 360–62
Eurax (crotamiton), 242
Eurocheque, 33
Europe, 175, 231, 255
evaporation, 112, 293–4
Everest Base Camp, 190
exchange rate, 31, 34, 36, 40–42,
  44, 281
exit permit, 20

Expedition Advisory Centre, 417
expeditions, 4, 7, 175–6, 195,
    196–7, 199, 213, 215, 417
  food, 387–8; leadership, 93;
    medical officer, 203; vehicles,
    253
expenses, shared, 2, 3–4
  see also money
eyes
  contact, 364–5, 367; ointment,
    198
  see also contact lenses; glasses;
    sunglasses

falciparum malaria *see* malaria
Falklands War, 194, 349
Falkus, Hugh, *Sea Trout Fishing*,
    381–2
Fansidar, 164
fares *see* ticket
farts, 170, 360
Fasigyn (tinidazole), 195
fear of flying, 140–43
feet, 120, 188, 360–61, 376, 378–
    80
  soles of, 111, 334, 361
  see also athlete's foot; ankles;
    shoes; socks
festivals *see* holidays; Ramadan
fever, 164, 169, 170, 171, 174, 185,
    197
  see also dengue fever; yellow
    fever
Fiji, 147, 361
filariasis, 186, 238, 356
film, 39, 74, 79, 304–9
  X-ray, 128, 308–9
film canister, 24, 79
filter bag, 216
fire, 109, 279–80, 324
firefish, 229

fish
  dried, 391; fresh, 401
fishing, 276, 341, 352
  equipment, 47, 89; spear, 226
fitness, 14, 376
Flagyl (metronidazole), 195, 196
flask *see* water-bottle
fleas, 245
fleece, 116–17
flight advice, 426–7
flip-flops *see* shoes
flippers, 90, 271
Florida, US, 53
flucloxacillin, 195, 196
flukes, 205
flying, 124–53
  see also aeroplane; airline;
    airport; fear of flying;
    insurance; luggage
food, 204–8, 386–91
  adulterated, 339–40; dried,
    388–90, 394; drugged, 325–6;
    emergency, 78–9, 396–402
  see also fruit, dried; snacks
food poisoning, 164
Foreign Office, Travel Advice
    Unit, 17
Forrester, Martyn, *Survival*, 393
fraud *see* credit card; ticket
frisbee, 47, 102
frogs, 397
frontier, 16, 34–5, 41, 329
fruit, dried, 78–9, 387
fungal infection, 109, 120, 173–4,
    192
Fybogel (ispaghula husk), 166–7

gaffer tape, 47, 51, 63, 246, 325
gaffes, 357–66, 404
  see also etiquette;
    misunderstanding

Galapagos, 231
games, 12
  pocket, 81
  see also sports by name
gamma globulin see hepatitis
gas, 326
gazelle, 275
Gellhorn, Martha, *Travels with Myself and Another*, 385–6
Ghana, 188, 270
giardiasis, 170, 210
  see also cyst
ginger, 193
glasses, 85
  see also contact lenses; sunglasses
gnat, 13
Goa, India, 30
Goodyer, Dr Larry, 154
Gore-Tex, 91, 100
Greece, 161
Griffith, Susan, 354, 355
  Teaching English Abroad, 413; *Work Your Way Around the World*, 343, 413
Griffiths, Ken, 320
group travel, 2–4, 7–10, 81
  charter tickets, 145, 146–7
  see also overland groups
Guatemala, 52, 316
Guide for Women, 289
guides, 9, 221, 377, 384–5
  unofficial, 338–9
guidebooks, 6, 61, 264
guinea worm, 188, 210
guns, 402–3
guppy fish, 241

hair, 366
  see also scarf
Haiti, 21, 60, 385

Half the Earth, 338, 416
Halfan, 164
Halstead, Bruce W., *Dangerous Marine Animals*, 401
hammock, 46, 100–101
handkerchief, 102, 182, 294, 359–60
hands, 358–9, 361, 362
harassment of women, 80, 83–4, 85, 136, 333–8
  see also rape
Harding, Gilbert, 136
Harris, Walter, *Morocco That Was*, 403
hashish, 340
hat, 107, 114, 119, 294
hay-fever, 133–5, 197
headache, 165, 185, 189, 190, 191
headphones, 87
  see also battery; radio; Walkman
health, 154–217, 411
  see also drugs by generic name; illnesses by name
'Health Advice for Travellers Anywhere in the World', 22, 161
heat, 292–5, 305, 309
  see also air conditioning; heatstroke; prickly heat; sunburn
heater, portable immersion, 94
heatstroke, 2, 170–71
  see also prickly heat; sunburn
Helias, P.-J., *The House of Pride*, 370
heliograph, 80
hepatitis, 197, 200, 210
  A, 156, 157–8, 176, 212
  B, 17, 158–9, 169, 175, 199, 286

Hewat, Theresa and Jonathan, *Overland and Beyond*, 30, 360
Himalayas, 23, 80, 135, 264
hippies, 104, 290, 322, 365–6
hippopotamus, 220–21
Hirohito, Emperor, 398
hitch-hiking, 265–6, 335
HIV, 17, 22, 92, 155, 156, 157–8, 169, 175–6, 199, 286
holidays, public, 13, 21, 34
Holiday Travel Abroad: A Guide for the Disabled, 285
Holmes, Robert, 317
Holt, Vincent, *Why Not Eat Insects?*, 398
Homer, 208
homosexuality, 286–9
Hong Kong, 305
hookworm, 187, 188, 245, 356
hospitality, 403–7
    see also etiquette
hotel, 6, 21, 43–4, 266–9, 373
    air conditioning, 293; bathroom, 284; booking, 7–8, 136; food, 204; plugs, 76–7; telephone, 278, 331; theft, 324, 331
    see also fire
housedust mite, 189
humidity, 80, 96, 306, 314, 315
Hunter, Robin, *Outdoor Companion*, 79
hyena, 222
hygiene, 290–91, 365–7
    see also food; laundry; soap; water

IATA, 145, 150
ice-cream, 205, 327
immigration, 135–6
    see also officials

immunization, 16, 48, 154, 161
    centres, 155, 427–8; certificate, 15, 16–17; specialist, 162–3
Imodium (loperamide), 166, 167
India, 16, 41, 60, 113, 139, 148, 155, 160, 161, 166, 188, 235, 250, 290, 347
Indonesia, 61, 120, 323, 361
infection, 195–7
    see also antibiotics; fungal infection
insect repellent, 51–54, 165, 202, 238–40, 242, 245, 250
    powder, 88–9, 95
insecticide, 88–9, 95, 239
insects, 12–13, 51, 186, 291, 293
    edible, 397–400
insomnia, 139, 189, 293
insurance, 21–8, 85, 128, 145, 161, 309, 326, 428
    see also bicycling; car; illness; luggage
Insurance Ombudsman Bureau, 28
International Student Card, 146
'International Travel Guide', 35
iodine, 182, 183, 215–16
    see also povidone-iodine
Iran, 206, 281
iron, 199
ISIC, 71
Isogel *see* ispaghula husk
ispaghula husk, 166–7
Israel, 15
Istanbul, Turkey, 41, 60, 326
itinerary, 5–8, 70

jacket, 116–17
    blazer, 109; down, 119
    see also shell garment
Jackson, Jack, 253–4, 256, 388

The Traveller's Handbook, 35, 228, 229, 252, 253, 412; *Off Road Four Wheel Drive*, 252
Japan, 92, 354, 361, 370, 372
jaundice, 163, 196
Java, 121
jeans, 110, 114, 317
jellyfish, 227–8, 270
jet lag, 137–40, 169
jewellery, 109, 226
jigger, 245
jojoba cream, 201
Jordan, Tanis and Martin, *South American River Trips*, 4, 46, 223, 388
Juel-Jensen, Dr Bent, *Expedition Medicine*, 205, 230, 411–12
Juli, Peru, 3

Kashmir, India, 60
Kavanagh, Arthur, 283
Kendal mint-cake, 78
keyring, 65
kidney stone, 216
Kihange River, central Africa, 236
kitbag, 48, 72–3, 76, 105
  see also luggage
Klauber, Dr Laurence L., 234
knife, 64–6, 181, 202
Knox, Robert, *Historical Relation of Ceylon*, 291
Koran, the, 333, 335
Kuching, Malaysia, 13
Kuta Beach, Bali, 322

La Paz, Bolivia, 189
labels, 127, 128–9, 201, 325
lamination, 61
lamp, UV, 230
Lamu, Kenya, 360

Land Rover, 252–3
language, 362, 363–4, 369, 371–2, 403–4
  ignorance, 336, 339; local, 59, 336, 347–51;
  misunderstanding, 368–9;
  survival list, 368–9, 438–9
  see also etiquette; gaffes;
  misunderstanding; teaching
Lapland, 90
Larache, Morocco, 330
Lariam (mefloquine), 164
laundry, 69, 115–16, 359, 383
  soap, 111
lavatory habits, 291–2, 404
lavatory paper, 54, 68–9, 76, 291, 292, 378
laxative, 188
Leach, Ivy, 284
leech, 64, 247–9
leishmaniasis, 245
Lelyveld, Joseph, *Move Your Shadow*, 370
lenses *see* camera equipment
leopard, 218
leptospirosis, 210
Lexotan (bromazepam), 142
Lhasa, Tibet, 189, 190
libraries, 21, 145, 280, 424
Libya, 243
lice, 88, 240
lifejacket, 143
light bulb, 87–8
lighter, cigarette, 80
Linley, Mike, 244
lion, 218–19, 220
lip-salve, 201
litter, 378
Lloyd's of London Advisory Dept., 28
lock, 81, 127, 357

see also suitcase
Lomotil (diphenoxylate), 166
Lonely Planet Update, 136, 327, 330
loperamide, 166, 167
lorazepam, 142
loss adjustor, 26
Lowe-McConnell, Rosemary, 224
Lucan, 234
luggage
flying with, 126–9; insurance, 128; mislaid, 20, 21, 22, 26; shops, 423; unaccompanied, 126
Lundberg, Dr John, 224
Luwegu River, Tanzania, 220

McLeod, Barb, 243
Madagascar, 231
maggots, 65, 243–4
mail, 276–7
see also envelope; post office; postcard
Maillart, Ella, *Forbidden Journey*, 72
Maine, US, 13
malaria, 2, 17, 82, 94, 161–5, 169, 185, 238, 240
falciparum, 164–5, 192
Malay Archipelago, 235
Malaysia, 121, 148
Mali, 15, 323
Malta, 231
Manila, Philippines, 136, 340
manners *see* etiquette
maps, 60–61, 70, 137, 392, 425
marlin spike, 123
Marmite, 241
Marrakesh, Morocco, 284
Masai Mara reserve, Kenya, 219

Mastercard, 35
mat, insulation, 98–9
see also sleeping bag
matches, 79–80
Maxwell, Gavin, 219
mebendazole, 187
medical kit, 65, 192–202
see also articles by name; data-sheet; kitbag
medical officer, 203–4
medicine
fake, 193; individual, 194; village, 202–4
see also data-sheet; diagnosis; drugs by generic name
mefloquine, 164
Melolin *see* dressings
Melville, K. E. M., *Stay Alive in the Desert*, 377
meningitis, meningococcal, 160
menopause, 188–9
menstruation, 77, 188–9, 226, 333
mercurichrome, 182
merthiolate, 182
mess-tin, 101–2
metronidazole, 195, 196
miconazole, 174
Micronesia, 231
Micropore *see* dressings
Middle East, 112, 160
see also by name; Muslim countries
milk, 167, 205–6
Miller, Christian, *Daisy, Daisy*, 262
mini-cabs, 126
see also taxis
minnow gambusia, 241
misinformation, 340–41
misunderstanding, 367–72
see also etiquette; gaffes

mole *see* cancer
Moleskin, 379
money, 29–45
   see also bank; cash; credit card;
      currency; expenses;
      traveller's cheques
money belt, 20, 88, 328
morning sickness, 193
Morocco, 147, 255, 290, 338
mosquito nets, 94–5, 100, 101,
      102, 186, 239, 240, 389
mosquitoes, 161, 164, 165, 185,
      200, 238–42, 243, 244, 247
motion sickness, 193–4
motorcycle, insurance, 23
Mount Kenya, 113
mountain sickness, 189–92
mouth-to-mouth resuscitation,
      227–8, 233, 272–3, 452
mouthwash, 199
Moynihan, Brian, *Tourist Trap*,
      331–2
mugging *see* robbery
Murphy, Dervla, 337–8
Murray, Hallam, 262, 263, 264,
      352
Muslim countries, 13, 120, 333,
      334–5, 338, 359, 365
Myers, Dr George, *Piranha Book*,
      223

nailbrush, 69
Nairobi, Kenya, 175
Nalgene bottle, 69
nappies, 11, 243
nausea, 170, 176, 189
needle, 77, 379
  see also syringe
neem tree, 240
Nepal, 160, 219
New Guinea, 235

New York, US, 137
New Zealand, 231
Niger, 331
Nigeria, 193, 260, 342
night-bag, 103–4
Nile, 235, 283
Nomad shop, 47–8, 58, 73, 103–
      4, 110, 122, 418
nose-blowing, 359–60
notebook, 66
Nothing Ventured, 283–4, 285
nuts, 78, 387
nylon, 120

oedema
   cerebral, 191; high altitude
      pulmonary, 191
officials, 342–4, 364
   customs, 66, 197, 307, 309;
      immigration, 104, 136, 155,
      342–3; police, 27, 66, 290,
      325, 326–7, 336
Okavango Swamps, Botswana,
      230
onions, 206, 388
opium, 290
optician, 85
orang-utan, 189
O'Reilly, Wing Commander,
      134
overland groups, 10, 431–2
   insurance, 22–3
oxygen, 190, 191
ozone layer, 52, 83, 172
   see also UV rays

pac-a-macs, 118
Pacaya volcano, Guatemala, 385
packing, 20, 201–2, 267–8, 384
padlock *see* lock
painkillers, 197–8, 202

Pakistan, 138, 148, 188, 193
Palamau reserve, India, 222
pantyhose *see* tights
papaya, 188, 206–7, 228
paracetamol, 165, 185, 189, 193,
    197–8, 232
parachute cord, 93
paraffin, 101, 244, 245, 246, 247
Paraguay, 223
parasite, 163, 184–5
Paris, France, 331–2
Park, Mungo, 208
parka, 117
passport, 14, 29, 64, 81, 135, 280,
    324, 325, 326, 327, 328
  photograph, 16, 70
  see also photocopy
Patagonia (underwear), 116
Paton, Dr, 379
paw-paw *see* papaya
pen, 67, 392
Penang, Malaysia, 37
Penguin Book of Physical Fitness, 14
penicillin, 195, 196
penknife *see* knife
Pennell, Dr T. L., *Among the Wild
    Tribes of the Afghan Frontier*,
    403
people, 321–45
  photographing, 315–17
permethrin, 53, 89, 95, 239, 246,
    248
Peru, 46, 50, 63, 67
pessaries, 175
petrol, 101, 253–4, 256
Philippines, the, 235, 288
photocopy, 15, 17, 20, 25, 26, 27,
    28, 144, 255
photography, 296–320, 363, 407
  see also camera; camera
    equipment; film

phrasebooks, 59, 67, 350
pickpockets, 327–9
  see also pocket
pills, 74, 202
  diarrhoea, 166; insecticide, 53;
    malaria, 17, 82, 163, 164, 167,
    192, 194
  see also contraceptive; drugs by
    generic name; sleeping pills;
    tranquillizers; vitamins
pillow, 62, 91–2, 143
  neck-pillow, 91
pins, 77
pinworm *see* threadworm
piperazine, 187
piranhas, 223–4
Piranjo, Duke of, *A Cure for
    Serpents*, 358–9
Piriton (chlorpheniramine), 197
Pisa, Italy, 130
placebo, 199
plasters, 54, 94, 178–9, 193, 202
  see also Elastoplast
Plato, 208
plug, universal wash, 76–7
pneumonia, 196
pocket, anti-theft, 111, 328
  see also pickpockets
pole-bed, 101
police *see* officials
polio, 156, 157, 210
polyester, 108, 110
Polynesia, 231
polyp, 134
poncho, 100, 119
porter, 386
Portugal, 10
post office, 22, 161
  poste restante, 276; telephone,
    278
postcard, 54, 67, 71, 277, 407

potassium, 167, 169
  permanganate, 178, 195, 232
pound *see* sterling
povidone-iodine, 179–80
Pratt, Paul, *World Understanding on Two Wheels*, 354
pregnancy, 155, 162, 167, 190, 193, 194, 200, 215
  see also morning sickness
preparations for travel, 1–28
presents, 54, 66–8, 77, 109, 130, 287, 357, 362, 369, 374, 405–7
Preston, Susan, 284
prickly heat, 174–5, 293
primates, 219
promethazine, 194
prophylaxis
  see diarrhoea; malaria; mountain sickness
prostitution, 158, 175, 176, 287, 326, 337
pubic hair, 292–3
public transport, 266, 335
Puritabs, 213–14, 215
pus, 195
pyjamas, 112, 115, 116
  see also underwear

Quallofil-7, 96
Queen, the, 67, 333
quinine, 164–5

rabies, 155, 159–60, 182–4, 222, 236
radio, 86–7
  see also battery; BBC; headphones
rain, 12–13, 100, 383, 384
  clothing for, 113–19; rainy season, 442–7

  see also altitude; climate
Ramadan, 14
rape, 136, 335
rash, 172, 174, 185, 196, 197
razor, 75
Reagan, President, 409
reamer, 64
receipt, 135, 309
  medical, 27; of purchase, 25, 27; ticket, 149, 150
refund *see* traveller's cheques
Rehidrat *see* rehydration mix
rehydration, 137–9, 156, 165, 167–9, 185
  mix, 168–9, 192, 209
  see also dehydration; salt; water
repatriation, 22, 24, 346–7
rhesus monkey, 219
rhinoceros, 221
Richard's Mountain Bike Guide, 264
Richard's New Bicycle Book, 264
riding, 23, 64, 181, 375–6
ringworm, 173
river
  bed, 383; crossing, 380–82
robbery, 136, 329–31, 385
  see also crime
Roosevelt, Theodore, *Through the Brazilian Jungle*, 223
Ross, Sir Ronald, 161
roundworm, 187, 192, 210
Royal Air Force, 91, 134
Royal Commonwealth Society for the Blind, 344
rucksack, 92, 323
  see also backpack; luggage

safari, 93, 185–6, 275–6
Sahara Handbook, 253
salad, 205

salami, 79

salt, 137–8, 168, 169, 207, 209, 391

  tablets, 207, 209

  see also dehydration; rehydration; water

salwar kameez, 355

sand, 271–2

sandals *see* shoes

sandfly, 241, 245

sanitary towel, 77

Sarawak, Malaysia, 333

sarong, 121

SAS, 101, 387

Savlon Dry, 179–80

Savuti, Botswana, 222

scarf, 119, 334–5, 337

Schultz, Harald, 223

scissors, 64–5, 67, 178

scorpions, 94, 229–30

Scrabble, 81

screwdriver, 64

scuba-diving, 23, 274

Sea Bands, 193–4

sea-cow, 189

sea-lion, 225

seasickness, 193–4

sea-snake, 235

sea-urchin, 228–9

security chart, 17–20, 28, 85, 151

sentimentality, 317–18, 356–7

Seoul, Korea, 136

Septrin (co-trimoxazole), 154, 182, 195, 196

sewing-kit, 77

sex, 159, 175, 176–8, 286–9

  see also condoms; contraceptive pill; harassment; HIV; homosexuality; prostitution

shampoo, 69, 73

Shanefield, Irene, 285

sharks, 189, 225–6, 270

shaving equipment, 75–6

shellfish, 205

shell garment, 117–19

shirt, 107–8, 383

  see also T-shirt

shoe laces, 94, 123

shoes, 48, 109, 120, 121–3, 133, 228, 230, 231, 248, 271, 275, 378

  removal of, 359

shops, 46

  carpet, 9; changing money, 44–5; equipment, 418–23, 425; ganga, 290; guide, 339; mailing goods, 277; tourist, 67

shorts, 111–12

shoulder-bag, 54–5, 327–8

  contents of, 67, 68, 179

  see also luggage

sick-bag, 135

sightseeing, 351–3

silica gel, 314–15

silk, 112, 115–16, 119

Silver, Janet, 84

Singapore, 305

Singh, Raghubir, 62

sinus, 63, 134

skirt, 111, 334

ski-stick, 378

sleeping bag, 46, 95–9, 99–101, 245, 324, 422

  liner, 95, 99–100, 101, 382

  see also bivouac bag; mat; survival bag

sleeping pills, 190

sleeping sickness, 185–6

Small Claims Court, 28, 151

smile, 365

Smythies, B. E., 249

snacks, 78–9, 206
  see also food
Snailham, Richard, 230
snakes, 197, 230–35
  see also anti-venom
sneezing, 276
snorkelling, 82, 85, 89–90, 271,
  273–4
snow, 83
soap, 69, 73, 74, 75–6, 174, 178,
  181, 182, 183, 242, 291
  as bait, 89
socks, 120, 211, 239, 248, 379
Socotra Island, 172
solar still, 394–6
Solo, Indonesia, 282
Solomon Islands, 137, 152, 235
South Africa, 15, 148, 220, 235,
  356
South America, 10, 40, 46, 61,
  100, 163, 184, 186, 192, 223,
  290, 292, 323, 366, 406
  see also by country
South American Explorer, 243
South American Handbook, 3, 61,
  254, 264, 321, 325, 343, 363
South East Asia on a Shoestring,
  269
Soviet Union, 189
space-blanket, 90–91
Spartacus Guide for Men, 289
spiders, 247
sponge-bag, 74
sports, 23
  see also by sport
squatting, 14
Sri Lanka, 12, 231, 235
stain-remover, 69, 75
stamps, 277, 331
Starr, June, Dispute and Settlement
  in Rural Turkey, 365

sterilizing tablets, 57
Steristrips, 182
stings, 197, 207, 227–8, 229–30,
  236–8, 242
stingray, 228–9, 270
Stokes, Martin, 365
stonefish, 228, 229
stool see bowel movements
stress, 140, 346–7
string, 93
student travel, 146, 426–7
  card, 71
Stugeron (cinnarizine), 194
Sudan, 86
sugar see rehydration
suit, jogging/shell/track/zoot, 112
suitcase, 102–3, 128–9
  see also luggage
Sulawesi, Indonesia, 93
sulphonamides, 196
sunburn, 12, 171–2, 197, 274, 275
  see also cancer; heatstroke
sun-cream, 82, 171, 173, 274, 275
  see also cancer
Sundarbans, India, 218, 219
sunglasses, 83–5, 107, 335
surgical tape see dressings
Surinam, 224
survival, 392–402
survival bag, 91
sweat, 107, 108, 113–14, 118, 137,
  164, 170, 174, 208–9, 291,
  292, 294, 382
  night, 185
sweater, 55, 116
swelling, 186, 197, 199, 233
swimming, 82, 85, 226–8, 270–72,
  326, 381–2
  see also drowning; scuba-diving;
  snorkelling
swimming costume, 120

Sympatex, 100
Syria, 34
syringe, 24, 155, 159, 175

Taiwan, 15
Taj Mahal, India, 5
TALC, 168
tampon, 77, 189
Tanzania, 68, 121, 356
tape, language, 349–50
tapeworm, 187
tax
    airport, 20; departure, 19–20;
        duty-free, 131; import, 250,
        255; VAT, 131
    see also customs
taxis, 136–7, 265, 266
Taylor, R. L., Butterflies in My
        Stomach, 399, 400
tea, 138–9, 211, 216, 388, 390
teaching, 17, 354–5, 413–15, 430–
        31
tea-infuser, 78
teaspoon, 78, 168, 390
teeth, 196, 199, 210
telephone, 136, 202, 277–9
    cancellation, 19, 435; codes,
        277–8, 435–7; hotel, 331; UK
        Direct, 20, 37, 278–9, 326,
        433–4
temazepam, 142
temperature see climate chart;
        fever
tent, 46, 90, 96, 100, 102, 382
termites, 246
testimonial, 71
testosterone, 292
tetanus, 157, 182
    booster, 229
tetracyclines, 196
Thailand, 21, 248, 290

Thatcher, Mrs, 48, 333
theft, 135, 330
    car, 250, 257, 259; insurance,
        20, 24, 25–6, 27; luggage,
        103, 104, 106
    see also lock; pickpockets;
        pocket; robbery
thermal underwear, 115–16
thermos, 11, 59
Theroux, Paul, Riding the Iron
        Rooster, 352
Thesiger, Wilfred, 115
thirst, 216
Thomsen, Moritz, Living Poor,
        346
threadworm, 187
throat, sore, 196, 198
thrush, 109, 173–4
thyroid, 215
Tiananmen Square massacre, 86,
        348
ticket, 25, 30, 127, 128, 143–53,
        266, 324, 327
    details, 19, 28, 143–4, 327;
        fraud, 149–50; reconfirmed,
        152–3; round-the-world, 147
ticks, 246
tie, 109
tiger, 218, 219
Tiger Balm, 200, 242
tights, 116
time-keeping, 362, 363
tinidazole, 195
tin-opener, 64, 65, 388
tissues, 68–9, 76, 312
    see also antiseptic wipes;
        lavatory paper
tobacco, 240
toothache, 198–9, 200
toothbrush, 73
toothpaste, 73, 242

toothpick, 64

torches, 46, 47, 48–51, 54, 143, 202, 220, 231, 383

tourniquet, 232

tout *see* guide, unofficial

towel, 61–3, 91, 184, 230, 241, 267, 326

Toyota, 253

Townsend, Chris, *Backpacker's Handbook*, 96–7, 98, 105–6

trainers *see* shoes

tranquillizers, 141–2

transfusion, 159, 186
  see also blood

transparency, merits of, 70–74, 308

transport, 250–66, 415
  see also public transport

travel company, 9, 20, 33, 145–8, 426–7, 431–2
  disabled, for, 284–5; overlanding, 432; protection against, 149–51; student, 71

travel-pack, 103

Traveler, 32, 193

Traveller, 317, 337

traveller's cheques, 18, 20, 24, 31–33, 324, 326, 327, 331
  see also cash

Traveller's Handbook, 264

Traveller's Health, 154

treatment, medical, 19, 22, 24
  see also data-sheet; diagnosis; drugs by generic name

trekking, 22, 83, 93, 103, 379, 387, 388
  see also walking

trimethoprim, 196

Trinidad, 13, 329

trouser belt, 34, 88, 339

trousers, 110–11, 120–21, 231, 248, 334, 383

tsetse fly, 185

T-shirt, 108, 274, 317

Tuareg, 111

tuberculosis, 205

Tubigrip, 63–4, 88, 200, 248, 328–9

tumbu fly, 243–4

Tunisia, 255

Turkey, 255, 289, 290, 292, 334, 337, 365

Turner, Dr Anthony, *Travellers' Health Guide*, 165, 411

Turner, Miles, *Paupers' Paris*, 363–4

tweezers, 64–5, 181, 229, 230, 244, 246

typhoid, 155, 156, 159, 185, 196, 205, 210

Ubud, Bali, 282, 408

Uganda, 288

UK Direct *see* telephone

ulcers, 178, 207
  mouth, 194, 198

underwear, 109, 112, 115–16, 187, 359

United States, 21, 25, 32, 148, 159, 175, 231, 236, 247, 257, 277–8

Upper Volta, 333

urine, 176, 216, 228, 242
  blood, 185, 196

UV rays, 82–5, 90, 311
  see also ozone layer

vaccine *see* immunization

vacuum pump, 234–5

vagina, bleeding, 248

Valium (diazepam), 142

Vane-Wright, R. I., 399

Vaseline, 244, 379

Vaughan, J. D., *Manners and Customs of the Chinese*, 361
vegetarian, 204–5
vegetation, edible, 402
vehicle registration certificate, 255
venereal disease, 176–8
Venice, Italy, 68
Vermox (mebendazole), 187
Vickers, Paul, *Bicycle Expeditions*, 264
Videne (iodine), 182, 183, 215–16
video camera, 300–302
vinegar, 227
visa, 14, 15–16, 20
  services, 16, 428
visiting cards, 72
vitamins, 199, 202, 241, 401
Volkswagen, 251, 252
voluntary work, 353–4, 413–15, 430–31
vomiting, 168–9, 170, 233, 272, 273, 400

waist pouch *see* bum bag
walking, 14, 140, 375–8, 391
walking-stick, 377–8, 381
Walkman, 12, 130
warble fly *see* botfly
Warrell, Professor David, 154
Warsaw Convention, 21
washing, 290–92
  see also food; laundry; sand; soap
wash-kit, 104, 315
  see also soap
wasps, 237
watch, 68, 69, 81–2, 330
water, 137, 209–17
  boiling, 211–12; carrying, 391–

2; emergency, 393–6; filtration, 211, 212–13; sterilizing, 211, 213–16; storing, 217; while walking, 376–7
  see also evaporation; dehydration; rehydration
water-bag, 259
  see also filter bag
water-bottle, 46, 57–9, 210–211, 212, 294
watercress, 205
watermelon, 206
water-skiing, 23
Waugh, Evelyn, *Labels*, 268
WD40, 66, 256
weather, 12–13
  see also altitude; climate; cold; rain; wind; *World Weather Guide*
wedding ring, 85, 336
weever fish, 229
Werner, David, *Where There is No Doctor*, 170, 178, 187, 203, 412
wheelchair, 284, 286
Wheeler, Maureen, *Travel with Children*, 11, 413
whipworm, 187
whistle, 80
Whitfield's ointment (benzoic acid), 173
Wilson, Dr Jane, 154
wind, 12, 114, 117
windsurfing, 23, 82, 85, 122, 274–5
wiring money *see* banks
Wiseman, John, *SAS Survival Handbook*, 396, 398, 399, 400, 413
witch hazel, 172

wolves, 222
women, 265–6, 416
   see also harassment; menstrual
      problems; pregnancy; rape
Women's Corona Society,
   429
wool, 115, 116
work abroad, 17, 24, 353–5, 413–
   15
World Health Organization, 156,
   188
World Travel Guide, 21
World Weather Guide, 13, 413
worms, 187–8, 192

X-rays see film

Yaffé, Maurice, Taking the Fear
   out of Flying, 142
yellow fever, 155, 156, 238
Yemen, 265
YIEE, 71
YMCA, 267, 432
yoghurt, 205–6
Youth Hostels, 267
Yugoslavia, 251–62
Yukon, US, 53
YWCA, 267, 432

Zaire, 44
Zimbabwe, 236
zinc oxide tape see dressings
zip, 70, 97–8, 117, 118, 328